Modeling, Simulation and Optimization
Tolerance and Optimal Control

Edited by
Dr. Sc. Shkelzen Cakaj

Modeling, Simulation and Optimization – Tolerance and Optimal Control

Edited by Dr. Sc. Shkelzen Cakaj

Republished by InTech

Janeza Trdine 9, 51000 Rijeka, Croatia

Technical Editor Zeljko Debeljuh

Cover Designer Dino Smrekar

Additional hard copies can be obtained from orders@intechopen.com

Modeling, Simulation and Optimization – Tolerance and Optimal Control,
Edited by Dr. Sc. Shkelzen Cakaj
p. cm.
ISBN 978-953-307-056-8

For EU product safety concerns:
IN TECH d.o.o., Prolaz Marije Krucifikse Kozulić 3, 51000 Rijeka, Croatia,
info@intechopen.com or visit our website at intechopen.com.

Meet the editor

Dr. Shkelzen Cakaj has received his BSc and MSc degrees from Prishtina University in Kosovo. Since 2003 is cooperating with Technical University in Vienna, where he has prepared his Master Thesis. He was awarded a PhD in area of satellite communications from Zagreb University, in January 2008. Later on, in 2009, as Fulbright scholar, he continued his post doctorate research at NOAA (National Oceanic and Atmospheric Administration) at Maryland, USA. He is the author of 60 papers published in worldwide conferences and journals; mostly IEEE and also engaged as a reviewer. His area of interest is the satellite ground station performance. He is lecturing satellite systems at Polytechnic University of Tirana, Albania. On 2016 he was awarded as Albanian ICT Researcher of the Year 2015.

Preface

Multidisciplinary interaction between human activities and nature has deeply influenced human life and technical culture related to the implementation of new processes, and the further application of products and services stemming from such processes. Processes can be performed effectively only if these are correctly identified, modeled and simulated, and therefore suitably controlled.

Process monitoring, from parametric representation, recognition, fault detection and diagnosis, to optimal control is very complex and includes multivariate parametric and statistical analysis. Proper tolerance in parametric representation ensures that the process output behavior may be accurately predicted and optimally controlled.

Parametric representation of shapes, mechanical components modeling with 3D visualization techniques using object oriented programming, the well known golden ratio application on vertical and horizontal displacement investigations of the ground surface, spatial modeling and simulating of dynamic continuous fluid flow process, simulation model for waste-water treatment, an interaction of tilt and illumination conditions at flight simulation and errors in taxiing performance, plant layout optimal plot plan, atmospheric modeling for weather prediction, a stochastic search method that explores the solutions for hill climbing process, cellular automata simulations, thyristor switching characteristics simulation, and simulation framework toward bandwidth quantization and measurement, are all topics with appropriate results from different research backgrounds focused on tolerance analysis and optimal control provided in this book.

Input data of most above mentioned problems, either as parameters or sequences are often affected by uncertainty. This uncertainty and the randomness are considered by tolerance analysis by examining the impact on output variations and accurate control.

Monte Carlo simulation method for statistical tolerance analysis, Markov processes for generating input sequences, FIFO (first-in-first-out) queuing nodes approximating the behavior of real network, Voronoi data structures for representing geometrical and topological information, partial differential equations describing dynamic continuous processes, Laplace and Hankel transformations, are a few mathematical tools and structures applied to derive scientific results presented in each particular chapter.

Finally, I enjoyed reading these impressive chapters which do provide new scientific research hints, each one within its specific field of study. I wish all authors successful scientific research leading towards a better future of nature and people worldwide.

Editor:

Dr. Sc. Shkelzen Cakaj

Post and Telecommunication of Kosovo
Satellite Communications Lecturer at Prishtina University, Kosovo
Fulbright Postdoctoral Researcher
Shkelzen.cakaj@fulbrightmail.org

Contents

Web Technologies for Modelling and Visualization in Mechanical Engineering

Mihai Dupac and Claudiu-Ionuţ Popîrlan
University of Craiova
Romania

1. Introduction

Modeling and visualization techniques are indispensable tools for the understanding of mechanical systems, mechanism generation and visualization being a challenging subject in order to interpret the data and to have a better understanding of system dynamics.

The importance of shape modeling in computational vision, CAD/CAM or virtual prototyping has been recognized for a long time. The idea of function-based approach to shape modeling is that complex geometric shapes can be produced from a "small formula" rather than thousands of polygons. Parametric, implicit or explicit functions and their combinations may be used to define the shapes.

Parametric representations of shapes have been discussed in (Metaxas, 1996), and are very appropriate selections when handling complex shapes in three dimensional dimensions. Implicit surfaces remain difficult to visualize and manipulate interactively because they require root-finding to locate the surface (Sarti & Tubaro, 2001). A standard method for visualizing and interacting with implicit surfaces can be found in (Lorensen & Cline, 1987). Other standard methods for visualizing implicit surfaces are ray-tracing (Levoy, 1990) and volume rendering (Drebin et al., 1988). Implicit surfaces have also been visualized using dynamic particle systems (Witkin & Heckbert, 1994).

The idea of the hybrid function-based approach (Liu & Sourin, 2006a; Liu & Sourin, 2006b) is to use different mathematical functions to modeling shapes. Based on this approach, the Function-based Extension Virtual Reality was proposed in (Liu & Sourin, 2005a). Following this, Liu and Sourin (Liu & Sourin, 2005b) extended FVRML to defining time dependent objects by analytical formulas as well as with a scripting language. A similar approach for shapes modeling applied to mechanical components generation and visualization was discussed in (Dupac, 2007). Liu and Sourin (Liu & Sourin, 2006b) proposed a function-based extension of Extensible 3D (X3D). The extension allows the use of analytical functions to define geometry, color, 3D texture and operations on 3D shapes, or time-dependent metamorphosis. Chen *et al.* (Chen et al., 2004) uses 3D representations to visualize a web structure. The authors results pertains to geographical systems and provides information on maps. Cartwright *et al. (*Cartwright et. al., 2005) presents a project to developing an open system architecture and Web-based shape modeling using HyperFun, a high-level programming language for specifying implicit surfaces and objects. Another approach for

shape modeling was proposed in (Fayolle et. al., 2005), where a web-based system implementation for modeling shapes using real distance functions have been used.
Some general aspects of the WEB technology that may have important effects on modelling, simulation and visualization and the role of Java and Web technologies for modelling and simulation, and suggested approaches and applications are discussed.
For the modeling and visualization in mechanical engineering a variety of mechanical components will be discussed, together with their fundamental concepts and description. Mechanical components such as screws, rolling bearings, sliding bearings, gears, mechanical springs, and flexible belts will be presented.
The web-base approach presented here is intended for mechanism components modeling and visualization using object oriented programming (Java) (Eckel, 2006). A Java Applet which used an XML (Extensible Markup Language) format to specifying shapes for Java objects is developed. The web-application component is responsible for serving up the object data to the Applet for rendering and to handle server-side processing of actions triggered by the user. Different parametric, implicit or combination between implicit and parametric functions, have been used for the modeling of the mechanical components shapes. Shapes such as gears, springs, chains and corkscrews have been generated on the XML file format and viewed as Java objects on the graphical interface. Sophisticated shapes have been generated without increasing the application size, and with a very good computational time. It was demonstrated that simple mathematical functions represent useful tools for shape modeling and visualization.

2. Actual WEB Technologies

2.1 Introduction

The emergence of the World-Wide Web (WWW) has produced a new computing environment. This has motivated researchers in many disciplines to re-evaluate their approaches and techniques in light of the new facilities provided and the new frontiers allowed by the new WWW technology. Web-based simulation is one such new concept that has evolved in the new web era and that has attracted the interest of many researchers and practitioners in the computer simulation field. The appearance of the network-oriented programming language, Java, and of distributed object technologies like the Common Object Request Broker Architecture (CORBA) has had major effects on the state of simulation practice. These technologies have the potential to significantly alter the way we think of, develop, and apply simulation as a problem solving technique and a decision support tool. In this way, modeling and visualization software for the fields of mechanical engineering, chemistry, biology etc. helps to connect high school learners with the kinds of real scholarly inquiry practiced daily by professional scientists. Custom software for scaffolding inquiry learning helps the teams develop classroom lesson topics and connect distributed communities of learners. Scientists want to conduct hands on analysis in an attempt to gain a better understanding of output data. The size of applications poses a significant problem for accessibility and analysis. The solution is to develop the web-based applications where scientists can download the data and are able to create custom visualizations over the web directly from surface data.
Simulation modeling methodology deals with the creation of models and the use and maintenance of these models. Over the fast five decades simulation modeling support has

evolved from the advent era to the era of simulation programming languages to the era of simulation support environments to the modern era (Page, 1998; Fishwick, 1998). The advent era began with the inception of digital computers and is marked by early theories of model representation and execution. Later on, simulation programming languages like Simula, Simscript and GPSS started to appear. The research done during the development of these languages has led to both refining the underlying simulation concepts and defining new conceptual frameworks or world views. The third era was marked by the interest in integrated simulation environments where the focus is on the broader life cycle of a simulation study. Also, a great interest emerged during this era in interoperability of heterogeneous simulators. Currently, most activities are focused on the simulation environments and languages, with some emphasis on simulation methodology development and parallel execution of simulations in academia.
The combination of WWW and Java offers a set of unique capabilities for computing (Chun et. al., 1998). The World Wide Web provides important infrastructure for scientific and engineering computation. The distributed computing hardware of the Web has remarkable potential compute performance times that of the largest supercomputer.

2.2 Web Support for Modelling and Visualization

Web technology has the potential to significantly alter the ways in which simulation models are developed, documented, and analyzed. The web represents a new way for both publishing and delivering multimedia information to the world. Web technologies that could be leveraged in a simulation support role are numerous. For example, the Hypertext Markup Language (HTML) provides both document formatting and direct linkage to other documents. This capability can significantly improve the information acquisition and presentation process for model developers. Moreover, the power of hypermedia available on the web can also influence the way models are developed and used. The forms capability of HTML provides a simple mechanism to construct a graphical user interface that could be used in web-based simulation modeling environments. The WWW can also act as a software delivery mechanism and distributed computation engine. Recent efforts like CORBA are enhancing the mechanisms through which a user can invoke and utilize services resident on remote machines. Java also enables safe and efficient execution of service software on the client machine.
Three approaches for web-based can be identified in the literature (Whitman et. al., 1998). Server-hosted simulation allows existing simulation tools to be hosted on a web server and accessed by clients via normal HTML pages. This approach has the advantage of using a familiar tool and enables the reuse of existing models. The disadvantage is that the communication power provided by animation in these tools is not visible over the web. Client-side simulation allows simulation tools to use an applets-based approach that minimizes the learning curve, but on the expense of power and flexibility. The performance of this type of simulation is also limited by the client machine capabilities. Java is an example of programming languages that may be used to develop simulation applications that may be executed on the client machine. Several Java based simulation packages and languages have been developed. For example, Simjava (McNab & Howell, 1996) uses a basic discrete event simulation engine and extends this with Java's graphical user interface features. JSIM is a Java-based simulation and animation environment based on both the process interaction and event scheduling approaches to simulation. It includes a graphical

designer that allows for graphical model construction on the web (Nair et. al., 1996). Silk (Healy & Kilgore, 1997) is a process-based multithreaded simulation language built in Java. Hybrid client/server simulation attempts to combine the advantages of server hosted and client executed simulations. The approach relies on hosting the simulation engine on the server and using Java for visualization of the animation to provide a dynamic view on the client machine. Numerous relationships between the web and modelling are evident. A review of the current literature suggests several areas of potential impact of the web on modelling. Modelling and simulation research methodology, for example, can be affected by the ability to rapidly disseminate models, results and publications on the web. Remote execution of legacy simulations from a web browser through HTML forms and CGI scripts is another area most commonly associated with the term web-based simulation. This also includes the development of mobile-code simulations using applets that run on client machines. Distributed simulation is an area that includes activities that deal with the use of the WWW and new distributed computing standards and techniques (e.g. CORBA, Java RMI and HLA) to provide an infrastructure to support distributed simulation execution. Finally, the nature of the WWW enables the production of hypermedia documents containing text, images, audio, video, and simulation.

2.3 Web Technolgies Description

The **LAMP Technologies (Linux, Apache, MY-SQL, Peal/PHP/Python)** is refers to a solution stack of software, usually free and open source software, used to run dynamic Web sites or servers. The original expansion is as follows: Linux - an operating system; Apache, for Web server; MySQL, for database management system; Perl, Python, and PHP, for the programming language. The combination of these technologies is used primarily to define a web server infrastructure, define a programming paradigm of developing software, and establish a software distribution package for any application. The most commonly used Operating System for this purpose is Linux - it's Open Source too, and it's based on Unix which was and is an operating systems designed from the ground up for a multiuser environment and for providing all the facilities a computer geek could possibly need to do his job well, with security and without limitations at the Operating System level. Where job of Apache's is to handle requests, interpret it, and provide responses. In order for it to access the basic facilities on the server computer, it makes operating system calls on that computer. In order for Apache to be able to run your (server side) application, it needs to be told how that's to be done - it needs to be programmed. Open Source languages such as Perl, PHP and Python are used to do programming for applications. The MySQL database has become the "de facto" standard for many Linux - Apache - Perl / PHP / Python web applications making up the acronym LAMP. By combining these tools you can rapidly develop and deliver applications. Each of these tools is the best in its class and a wealth of information is available for the beginner. Because LAMP is easy to get started with yet capable of delivering enterprise scale applications the LAMP software model just might be the way to go for your next, or your first application.

Advantages of LAMP:

- Seamless integration with Linux, Apache and MySQL to ensure the highest levels of availability for websites running on LAMP.
- Full 32bit and 64bit support for Xeon, Itanium and Opteron-based systems Runs on enterprise Linux distributions from Red Hat and SuSE.

- Supports Active/Active and Active/Standby LAMP Configurations of up to 32 nodes.
- Data can reside on shared SCSI, Fiber Channel, Network Attached Storage devices or on replicated volumes.
- Automated availability monitoring, failover recovery, and failback of all LAMP application and IT-infrastructure resources.
- Intuitive JAVA-based web interface provides at-a-glance LAMP status and simple administration.
- Easily adapted to sites running Oracle, DB2, and PostgreSQL .

Many web-based application uses LAMP (Linux, Apache, MySQL, PHP) and Java technology for web middle-ware and on the back-end compute side relies on specialized programs to fetch data from the archive, visualize, composite, annotate and make it available to client browser.

Technologies on the client side:

1. Active X Controls: Developed by Microsoft these are only fully functional on the Internet Explorer web browser. This eliminates them from being cross platform, and thus eliminates them from being a webmasters number one technology choice for the future. Disabling Active X Controls on the Internet Explorer web browser is something many people do for security, as the platform has been used by many for unethical and harmful things.
2. Java Applets: are programs that are written in the Java Language. They are self contained and are supported on cross platform web browsers. While not all browsers work with Java Applets, many do. These can be included in web pages in almost the same way images can.
3. DHTML and Client-Side Scripting: DHTML, JavaScript, and VBScript. They all have in common the fact that all the code is transmitted with the original webpage and the web browser translates the code and creates pages that are much more dynamic than static html pages. VBScript is only supported by Internet Explorer. That again makes for a bad choice for the web designer wanting to create cross platform web pages.

Of all the client side options available JavaScript has proved to be the most popular and most widely used.

Technologies on the server side:

1. CGI: This stands for Common Gateway Interface. It wasn't all that long ago that the only dynamic solution for webmasters was CGI. Almost every web server in use today supports CGI in one form or another. The most widely used CGI language is Perl. Python, C, and C++ can also be used as CGI programming languages, but are not nearly as popular as Perl. The biggest disadvantage to CGI for the server side is in it's lack of scalability.
2. ASP: Another of Microsoft's attempt's to "improve" things. ASP is a proprietary scripting language. Performance is best on Microsoft's own servers of course, and the lack of widespread COM support has reduced the number of webmasters willing to bet the farm on another one of Microsoft's silver bullets.
3. Java Server Pages and Java Servlets: Server side JavaScript is Netscapes answer to Microsoft's ASP technology. Since this technology is supported almost exclusively on the Netscape Enterprise Sever, the likelyhood that this will ever become a serious contender in the battle for the webmaster's attention is highly unlikely.

4. PHP: PHP is the most popular scripting language for developing dynamic web based applications. Originally developed by Rasmus Lerdorf as a way of gathering web form data without using CGI it has quickly grown and gathered a large collection of modules and features. The beauty of PHP is that it is easy to get started with yet it is capable of extremely robust and complicated applications. As an embedded scripting language PHP code is simply inserted into an html document and when the page is delivered the PHP code is parsed and replaced with the output of the embedded PHP commands. PHP is easier to learn and generally faster than PERL based CGI. However, quite unlike ASP, PHP is totally platform independent and there are versions for most operating systems and servers.

Servlet technology has become the leading web development technology in the recent years due to its safety, portability, efficiency and elegance in design. The servlets are specialized in browsing the web (web documents and various databases) for data mining, information extraction and meaningful presentation inside the web browser. More important, their power is in online analysis, filtering and structuring of the retrieved information. The servlets are object-oriented and therefore highly modular and multifunctional. We are currently investigating their efficiency for classification and meaningful representation of various aspects of web documents, including modelling and visualization.

BEA WebLogic Server contains Java 2 Platform, Enterprise Edition (J2EE) technologies. J2EE is the standard platform for developing multitier enterprise applications based on the Java programming language. The technologies that make up J2EE were developed collaboratively by Sun Microsystems and other software vendors, including BEA Systems. J2EE applications are based on standardized, modular components. WebLogic Server provides a complete set of services for those components and handles many details of application behavior automatically, without requiring programming. WebLogic Server consolidates Extensible Markup Language (XML) technologies applicable to WebLogic Server and XML applications based on WebLogic Server. A simplified version of the Standard Generalized Markup Language (SGML) markup language, XML describes the content and structure of data in a document and is an industry standard for delivering content on the Internet. Typically, XML is used as the data exchange format between J2EE applications and client applications, or between components of a J2EE application. The WebLogic Server XML subsystem supports the use of standard parsers, the WebLogic FastParser, XSLT transformers, and DTDs and XML schemas to process and convert XML files. WebLogic Server is an application server: a platform for developing and deploying multitier distributed enterprise applications. WebLogic Server centralizes application services such as Web server functionality, business components, and access to backend enterprise systems. It uses technologies such as caching and connection pooling to improve resource use and application performance. WebLogic Server also provides enterprise-level security and powerful administration facilities. WebLogic Server operates in the middle tier of a multitier (or *n*-tier) architecture. The software components of a multitier architecture consist of three tiers:

1. The *client tier* contains programs executed by users, including Web browsers and network-capable application programs. These programs can be written in virtually any programming language.
2. The *middle tier* contains WebLogic Server and other servers that are addressed directly by clients, such as existing Web servers or proxy servers.

3. The *backend tier* contains enterprise resources, such as database systems, mainframe and legacy applications, and packaged enterprise resource planning (ERP) applications.

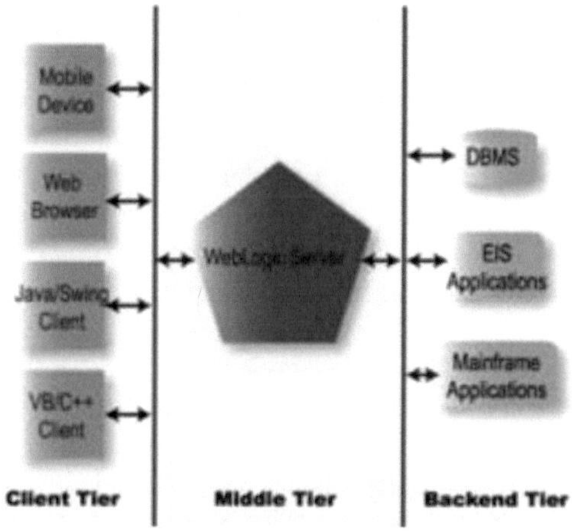

Fig. 1. The Three Tiers of the WebLogic Server Architecture

Client applications access WebLogic Server directly (Fig. 1), or through another Web server or proxy server. WebLogic Server generally connects with backend services on behalf of clients. However, clients may directly access backend services using a multitier JDBC driver. WebLogic Server has complete Web server functionality, so a Web browser can request pages from WebLogic Server using the Web's standard HTTP protocol. WebLogic Server servlets and JavaServer Pages (JSPs) produce the dynamic, personalized Web pages required for advanced e-commerce Web applications. Client programs written in Java may include highly interactive graphical user interfaces built with Java Swing classes. They can also access WebLogic Server services using standard J2EE APIs. All these services are also available to Web browser clients by deploying servlets and JSP pages in WebLogic Server. CORBA-enabled client programs written in Visual Basic, C++, Java, and other programming languages can execute WebLogic Server Enterprise JavaBeans and RMI (Remote Method Invocation) classes using WebLogic RMI-IIOP. Client applications written in any language with support for the HTTP protocol can access any WebLogic Server service through a servlet. The middle tier includes WebLogic Server and other Web servers, firewalls, and proxy servers that mediate traffic between clients and WebLogic Server. Applications based on a multitier architecture require reliability, scalability, and high performance in the middle tier. The application server you select for the middle tier is, therefore, critical to the success of your system. The WebLogic Server cluster option allows you to distribute client requests and back-end services among multiple cooperating WebLogic Servers. Programs in the client tier access the cluster as if it were a single WebLogic Server. As the workload increases, you can add WebLogic Servers to the cluster to share the work. The cluster uses a selectable load-balancing algorithm to choose a WebLogic Server in the cluster that is capable of handling the request. When a request fails, another WebLogic Server that provides the requested service can take over. Failover is transparent whenever possible, which minimizes the amount of code that must be written to recover from failures. For example, servlet session state can be replicated on a secondary WebLogic Server so that if the WebLogic Server that is handling a request fails, the client's session can resume

uninterrupted on the secondary server. WebLogic EJB, JMS, JDBC, and RMI services are all implemented with clustering capabilities.
The backend tier contains services that are accessible to clients only through WebLogic Server. Applications in the backend tier tend to be the most valuable and mission-critical enterprise resources. WebLogic Server protects them by restricting direct access by end users. With technologies such as connection pools and caching, WebLogic Server uses back-end resources efficiently and improves application response. Backend services include databases, enterprise resource planning (ERP) systems, mainframe applications, legacy enterprise applications, and transaction monitors. Existing enterprise applications can be integrated into the backend tier using the Java Connector Architecture (JCA) specification from Sun Microsystems. WebLogic Server makes it easy to add a Web interface to an integrated backend application. A database management system is the most common backend service, required by nearly all WebLogic Server applications. WebLogic EJB and WebLogic JMS typically store persistent data in a database in the backend tier. A JDBC connection pool, defined in WebLogic Server, opens a predefined number of database connections. Once opened, database connections are shared by all WebLogic Server applications that need database access. The expensive overhead associated with establishing a connection is incurred only once for each connection in the pool, instead of once per client request. WebLogic Server monitors database connections, refreshing them as needed and ensuring reliable database services for applications.

3. A Basic Mechanical Components Description

3.1 Screws

A screw may be defined as a shaft with a helical groove formed on its surface. Screws are used to translate torque into linear force, to hold objects together or to move loads. A screw is part of a large category of threaded fastener, with the fasteners classified also as fixed, locking and threaded. Fixed fasteners category include rivets, welds, brazing, and solders, while locking fasteners include pins, keys, springs and washers.

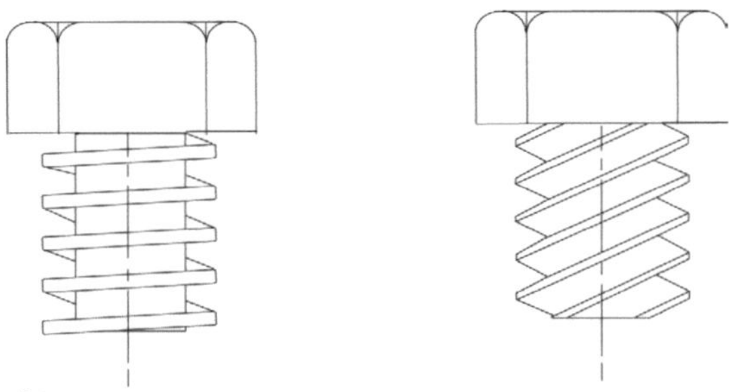

Fig. 2. Two Examples of Screws

A **screw thread** may be thought as a helical structure, an inclined plane wrapped around the internal or external surface of a cylinder/cone. If the surface is a cylinder one have a straight thread, if the surface is a cone one have a taper thread. A screw is used to convert between linear movement and rotational movement, and so, the pitch of the screw (the distance between corresponding points on adjacent thread forms having uniform spacing) is chosen in a way to prevent the screw to slip. By convention (both, Unified-inch series, or ISO-metric International Standards Organization), all threads are considered to be right-hand.

3.2 Rolling Bearings

A rolling bearing may be defined as a connector which carries round elements (balls, rollers, or needles) between two parts (usually a fixed part and a moving part), parts that moves/rotates relative to one another. In the relative motion of the two parts, the round elements rolls/slides with a very little rolling/sliding resistance, based on a very low friction (very small contact area). To further minimize the sliding resistence, contacting surfaces are separated by a liquid (usually oil or gas) or a film, or materials (bronze allows) with a very low coefficient of friction are used.
The important parts of rolling bearings are the outer and the inner ring, the rolling element and the retainer (separator). The main advantages of rolling bearings are: durability in time, easy replacement in case of failure, accuracy for a long time period, ability to operate at very low friction levels, and good trade-off between cost, size and weight.

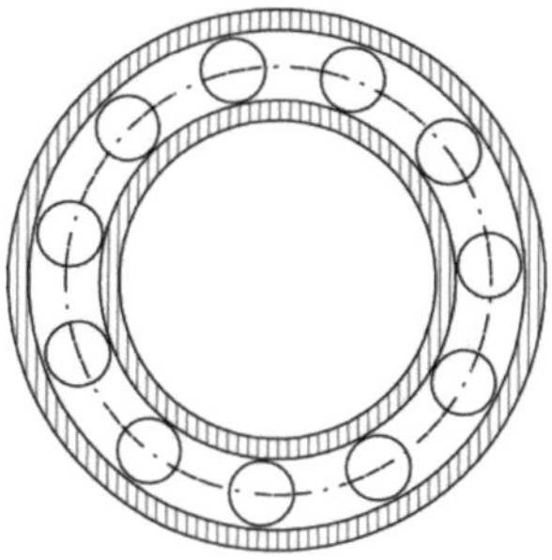

Fig. 3. Side View of a Rolling Bearing

Rolling bearings can be classified by the:
1. rolling element shape: ball bearings (use spheres instead of cylinders), roller bearings (use cylinders of slightly greater length than diameter), needle bearings (use very long and thin cylinders);
2. direction of the principal force: radial bearings, thrust bearings (used to support axial loads, such as vertical shafts), radial-thrust bearings, or thrust-radial bearings;
3. the number rolling bearing rows: rolling bearings with one row, with two rows.

3.3 Gears

A gear may be defined as a toothed element within a transmission device that transmit rotary motion (force) to another device. A gear allows force to be transferred/transmitted (at different speeds, torques, or in a different direction) without slippage with a transmission efficiency as high as 98 percent. The most important feature for a gear is the meshing possibility with another gear (usually of unequal diameter), in order to produce a different rotational speed and torque of the second gear. The constant angular velocity ratios condition, i.e., the angular velocity ratio (between a 30-tooth and a 90-tooth gear) to be 3, represents the gear-tooth geometry main requirement.

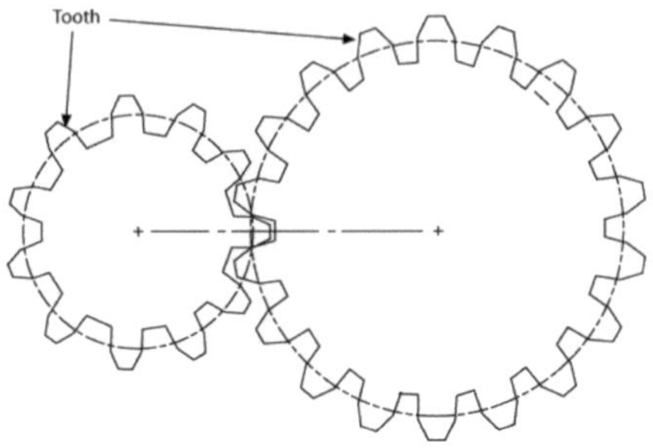

Fig. 4. Two Classical Gears

The main difference between internal and external gears is where the teeth are formed (on the inner or on the outer surface), an internal gear form the teeth on the inner surface (of a cylinder or cone), while an external gear form the teeth on the outer surface (of a cylinder or cone).

Gears can be classified as:

- Spur gears - (the most common type of gear) have a general form of a cylinder or disk with the teeth parallel to the shaft, are used to transfer motion between parallel shafts.
- Helical gears – have the leading edge set at an angle (non-parallel with the axis of rotation), allowing a smoothly and quietly motion, and the possibility of using non-parallel shafts.
- Double helical gears (herringbone gears) – has a general form as a two helical gears mirror image.
- Bevel gears – are conically shaped gears. The bevels are called miter gears if they have an equal numbers of teeth and the shaft axes at 90 degrees.
- Crown gear (contrate gear) - are a particular bevel gear with the teeth at right angles to the plane of the wheel.
- Hypoid gears (usually designed to operate with shafts at 90 degrees) - are spiral bevel gears with a not intersecting shaft axes and with a conical pitch surface.
- Worm gear - is a species of helical gear that resembles a screw, with his helix angle usually close to 90 degrees and a long body in the axial direction.

3.4 Mechanical Springs

A spring is a mechanical element used to store mechanical energy and to exert forces or torques. Springs are usually made out of metal (annealed steel hardened after fabrication, plain carbon steels, alloy steels, or corrosion-resisting steels), and for small loads or minimum mass, by plastics or composite materials. Depending on the requirements, almost any material having the right combination of elasticity and rigidity may be used to construct a mechanical spring. A spring rate (stiffness) is defined as the change in the force, divided by the change in spring deflection. The inverse of spring rate is the compliance.

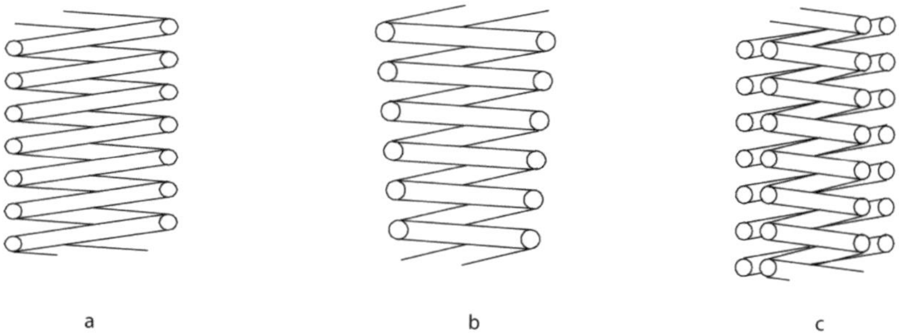

Fig. 5. Three Types of Mechanical Springs: a – simple, b – conical, c – double

Depending on load springs may be classified as: Tension/Extension spring, Compression spring, Torsional spring. Depending on material spring can be classified as: Wire/Coil spring, Flat spring. The most common types of spring are:

- Cantilever spring - a spring which is fixed only at one end.
- Coil spring (helical spring) - a helical spring around a cylinder or a cone. These are in turn of two types: Compression springs (designed to become shorter when loaded), and tension springs (designed to become longer when loaded and for maintaining the torsional stress in the wire).
- Hairspring (balance spring) - a type of spiral torsion spring
- Leaf spring - a flat springy sheet (can be simple cantilever or semi elliptic leaf)
- V-spring - antique type of springs

3.5 Flexible Belts

A Belt may be defined as a looped strip of flexible material (usually fabric or rubber). The most important feature of a belt is the efficiently to transmit power as a source of motion. A flexible belt mechanically link two or more rotating shafts such as pulleys or conveyors. In such systems the belt can drive the pulleys in the same or in an opposite direction. In the design of belts and band brakes the slippage of flexible cables, belts, and ropes over sheaves and drums represents a very important aspect.

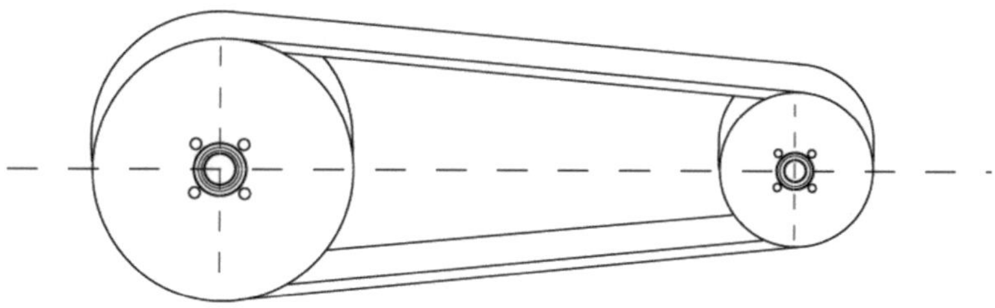

Fig. 6. A Classical Belt

3.2 Chains

A chain may be defined a series of connected links usually made of metal.
Chains are made in two styles:

- designed with torus shaped links for lifting or pulling
- designed with links made to mesh with the teeth of a machine for transferring power

Specific uses for chain include:

- Bicycle chain - to transfers power from the pedals to the drive-wheel
- Chain pumps - type of water pump
- Chainsaw - portable mechanical, motorized saw
- Roller chain - type of chain used for transmission of mechanical power in industrial or/and agricultural machinery
- Snow chains - used to improve traction in snow
- High-tensile chain - used for towing or securing loads.
- Anchor chain cable - as used by ships and boats

4. A Web Application Structure for Shape Modeling and Visualization

For the design of the mechanism components, a web-base approach for shape modeling and visualization using object oriented programming (Java) is proposed. A Java Applet which use an XML format to specify 3D implicit or parametric surfaces for Java objects is used. The Java objects are defined using implicit or parametric functions, or their combinations. The Java objects used in the Applet and defined on the graphic interface (Java 3D view support) allow the user to rotate, scale and translate the associated shapes (mechanism components) on screen. In order to create a more complex mechanical component shape, a mating process in which two or more shapes are combined is used. The mating process, that allows a great degree of interactivity, is described in detail in the next section. In the mating process, the shapes viewed as Java objects are stored in predefined objects classes. The predefined classes are based on the classical object oriented programming (OOP) and use the "inheritance" and "part off" concepts in the mating process. The "inheritance" concept allows a new created object to take over (or inherit) attributes and behavior of the pre-existing classes. The "part off" concept creates a new object using parts of the pre-existing classes. The objects not yet included on a pre-existing classes, are stored in new classes and referred as pickable objects. The web application consist of two components, an Applet concordant to the standard Java Application Programming Interfaces (API) and a server/web-application written against the most recent version of the SDK and J2EE API's, and running in a common web application server (in this case a Tomcat web server was used). The web application is responsible for sending the Java objects to the Applet (Popîrlan & Popîrlan, 2007; Baumann, 2000) for rendering and handling server side processing (events) of actions triggered by user clicks.
The Java Applet allows to send a user-initiated action that contains the default orientation (matrix transform) of the object in the viewer. The interface between the client and the server is occurring via Hypertext Transfer Protocol (HTTP) to minimize the impact of the firewall between the Applet and the server. The Java 3D view support is used in the interface to incorporate head tracking directly, thus providing the users with the illusion that they actually exist inside a virtual world.

Using the standard Java 3D view support we constructed and manipulated Java 3D objects inside a Web application to make visible shapes within the virtual world. The Web application structure that include the related components is described below and can be visualized in Fig. 7.

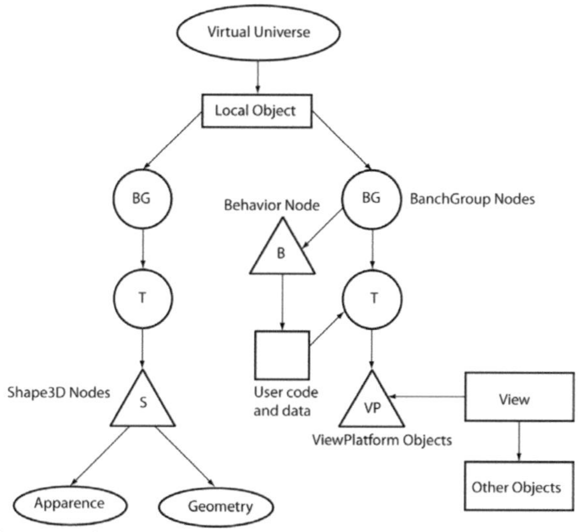

Fig. 7. The WEB Application Structure

The roles of the view-related components are as follows:

- The *Virtual Universe* represents the domain where the mathematical functions are defined in a XML format.
- The *View- Platform* (VP) represents the drawing surface (included in the graphical interface) for the Java objects.
- The *ViewPlatform*'s parents as shown in Fig. 7 specify its location, orientation, and scale within the virtual universe.
- The *View* component represents the main view Java object.
- The *Local Objects* component represents the 3D version of the AbstractWindowing Toolkit (AWT) Canvas object, i.e., a window in which Java 3D draws images. It contains a reference to a Shape3D object (described below) and information of the Shape3D's size and location.
- The *Shape3D Nodes* (S) component represents an Java object that result from the defined mathematical function and contains information describing the display properties. By using the Java 3D view support the Java objects are placed on the display as separate components, preventing the duplication of screen information within every *Local Object.*
- The *BrancheGroup Nodes* (BG) component represents an Java object that contains information describing the physical world, mainly the associated six-degrees-of freedom screen and scale (view capabilities).
- The *Transition* (T) component represents the Java object state from implementation to visualization.
- The *User Code and Data* component represents the XML file format used for function representation. The *Other Objects* component represents the final shape representation.
- The viewer of Applet is capable of rendering objects in the XML file format. XML format is used to define the mathematical functions and support predefined tags.

4.1 The Web Application Components Implementation

Regarding the implementation of the application components which are used by the user to generate shapes, the next classes representing the basic structure of the Java Applet and described below have been used. It is to be mentioned one more time, that the Applet has the role to take the representation of mathematical functions from XML format and to transform them to Java objects, which allows the user to mate and to generate a final shape. The class structure of the Java Applet is as follow:

- *MainApplet*: The Applet class which parses the <param> tags and creates a ShapePanel object.
- *ShapePanel*: This is the class that actually corresponds to the panel included in the MainApplet class, panel that display the shapes. The ShapePanel contains a thin horizontal ControlPanel (main menu of the user) at the top, and a large ShapeCanvas underneath it. The ShapePanel object also serves as the main controller for the Applet.
- *ControlPanel*: The thin horizontal panel at the top of the ShapePanel containing the control widgets.
- *ShapeCanvas*: The drawing area of the generated shapes.
- *KeyCommandHandler*: The object which translates keystroke events into actions. This could probably be just a part of the ShapePanel class, but it's defined as a different class object for modularity sake.
- *Drag3D, Drag3DOrbit, Drag3DRotate, Drag3DScale, Drag3DTranslate, DragConstants*: These class objects handle mouse dragging events in order to translate, rotate, and scale the generated shapes in the ShapeCanvas window.
- *ShapeMatrix3D*: This class defines the coordinates of the new generated shapes viewed as Java Objects.
- *Camera3D*: This class incorporates the implicit and parametric mathematical functions used to generate the shapes.

4.2 The Shape Generation Process

Defining shapes using mathematical functions is the most straightforward method of function-based shape modeling. Some shapes can easily be defined with implicit and explicit formulas, while others can be defined better by using a parametric representation. Besides these methods, there are many other ways to define shapes. For example, skeleton modeling and blending functions (Blinn, 1982) describe how two primitives can be merged into one shape. In addition to defining geometry, functions can also be used to create sophisticated colors and textures. Parametric functions for mapping texture images, or simple texture mapping, is a common approach implemented in many software and hardware systems (Peachey, 1985; Wyvill et al., 1987). Distortion of shape geometries (Lewis, 1989) can also be done by other techniques used for coloring shapes.

Implicit surfaces are well-suited for simulating physically based deformations (Terzopoulos & Metaxas, 1991) and for objects modeling (Turk & O'Brien, 1999). Like parametric representation, implicit representation codes the shape information in a higher dimensional space. The coding process is referred as embedding, which requires decoding to obtain the object shape. The embedding in higher dimensional space makes it possible to model topologically complex shapes as ones with simple's topology. The implicitly defined objects are objects described by an implicit function. Implicit functions define an implicit surface or shape. The implicit representation of a curve has the form $F(x, y) = 0$. An implicit function F representing a shape is a continuous scalar-valued function over the domain R^3, where $F=F(x, y, z)$ and x, y, z, are Cartesian coordinates, i.e. the dependent variable is not isolated on one side of the equation. The implicit surface of such a function is the locus of points at which the function takes the zero value, i.e., $F(p)=0$, where $p = x,y,z$, *i.e.*, the equation is satisfied by the all points in the surface. The function equals to zero for the points located on the surface of a shape. An implicit surface is a set of points p such that $F(p) = 0$, where F is a trivariate function (i.e., $p \in R^3$). In many cases, F partitions space into an inside and outside

$$F(p) = \begin{cases} < 0 \text{ if } p \text{ is on the interior of the object} \\ = 0 \text{ if } p \text{ is on the boundary of the object} \\ > 0 \text{ if } p \text{ is on the exterior of the object} \end{cases}$$

This ability to enclose volumes and the ability to represent blends of volumes endow implicit surfaces with inherent advantages in geometric surface design.
An explicit shape representation describes the points that belong to the object explicitly which makes it the most intuitive of representations. The most simple explicit functions are defined as $g = f(x)$, and for this case represents an explicit representation of a curve. An explicit representation is not a general representation, since for each x value, only a single y value is computed by the function. Explicit more general function are defined as $g=f(x,y,z)=0$, where x, y, z are Cartesian coordinates, i.e., the dependent variable are written explicitly in terms of the independent variable(s). The function equals to zero for the points located on the surface of a shape, and so the explicit surface is as an image of the function defined on a domain of a plane. Positive values indicate points inside the shape and negative values are for the points outside the shape. In short, explicit surface representations are well suited for graphics purposes but less suited for fitting and automated modeling. The reverse can be said for implicit surface representations.
Parametric shape generation and visualization is very popular in computer graphics mainly because of their easy mathematical manipulation and simple evaluation. Using parametric representation, the shape information is transpose into variables by creating mapping functions. The types of information have to be kept when using the parametric representation, are the co-ordinates and topological information which relate the geometric shapes to each other. For defining geometry of shapes (surfaces and solid objects) with parametric functions, one can use the following form,

$$x = f_1(u,v,w), \quad y = f_2(u,v,w), \quad z = f_3(u,v,w) \tag{1}$$

where x, y and z are the Cartesian coordinates of the points, and u, v and w are the parametric coordinates. For modeling surfaces, parametric functions with two parameters are used. Solid objects are defined using parametric functions with three parameters and operations, such as union, intersection, complement, etc., operations that add flexibility in creating complex shapes. Parametric functions may also define color values.

In the graphical user interface (Shape3D class), a three dimensional shape (a final mechanism component) is generated using combinations between the defined shapes created using implicit, and/or parametric functions. The mating process between the shapes is shown in Fig. 8 and Fig. 9, and is relatively similar with the one described by Liu and Sourin (Liu & Sourin, 2006a). Mating is the process by which two or more shapes are combined to create a new complex shape.

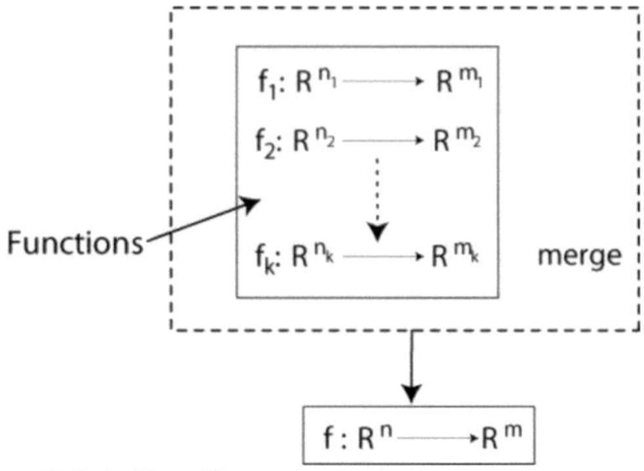

Fig. 8. Function-based Shape Modeling Representation

The obtained final shape is a combination of the defined functions f_i, where each of these functions represents the shapes geometry generated using implicit and/or parametric functions. Using the mating process complex shapes (from an initial pool of basic shapes) are created using a predetermined set of rules that are a priori defined and programmed. Once the new object (the final shape) as illustrated in Fig. 8 is created, it is added to the library.

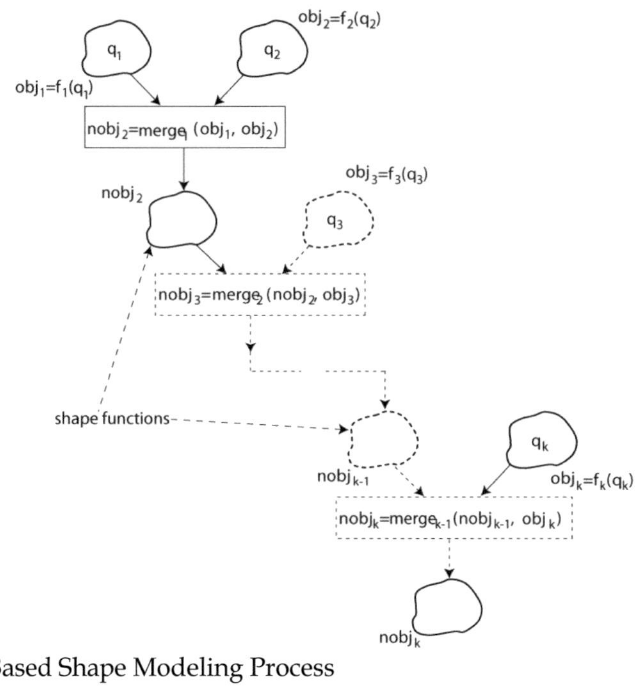

Fig. 9. Function-Based Shape Modeling Process

The functions $\mathbf{nobj}_i$, where i = 2, 3, . . . , k shown in Fig. 9 represent the ith generated shape geometry as a combination of implicit and/or parametric functions (the mth generated shape $\mathbf{nobj}_m$ is obtained from $\mathbf{nobj}_{m-1}$ and $\mathbf{obj}_m$). The functions $\mathbf{obj}_i$ where i = 1, 2, 3, . . . , k are simple basic shapes used to obtain the final shape. It is to be mentioned that one of the advantages of the model is the simplicity and easiness of developing the final geometry by combining several basic shapes.

5. Results

The results from the web-base approach for shape modeling and visualization using object oriented programming (Java) is presented. The Java Applet specify the parametric surfaces viewed as Java objects, allowing the user to rotate, scale and translate the objects on the screen. The visualization of different mechanism components has been tested using different mathematical functions and has proven to produce viable shapes. The important criteria of the application have been considered the easy implementation, functionality and a good running time. A very good computational time has been obtained per each mechanical component generation. Sophisticated shapes have been generated without increasing the file size, as it happens when polygon models based on a complicated meshing process are used. The Web graphical interface of the application is used to represent the shapes, shown as 3D surfaces. The Web graphical interface provide various interactive features, containing a toolbar, a panel describing the properties of the 3D shapes, and a small window for the final shape representation, as shown in Fig. 10.

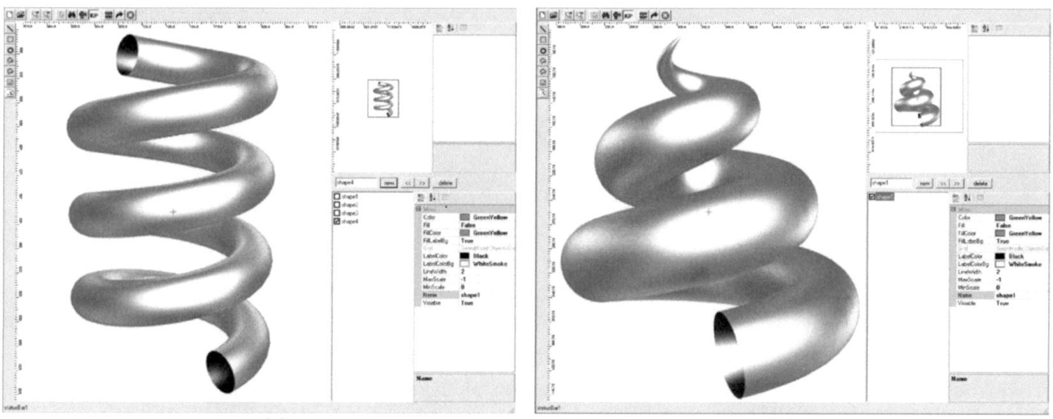

(a) (b)

Fig. 10. (a) Spring Surface, (b) Corkscrew Surface

In the graphical interface different mechanical component have been generated and visualized. A spring surface, shown in Fig. 10 (a), was generated using the next parametric function

$$f(u,v)=\begin{cases} a\cos(u)+\left(\cos(u)\cos(v)+\dfrac{b\sin(u)\sin(v)}{\sqrt{a^2+b^2}}\right) \\ a\sin(u)+\left(\sin(u)\cos(v)-\dfrac{b\cos(u)\sin(v)}{\sqrt{a^2+b^2}}\right)\cos(u) \\ bu+\dfrac{r\sin(v)}{\sqrt{a^2+b^2}} \end{cases}, \quad (2)$$

where a, $b \in R$, and u, $v \in [0, 2\pi]$.

Two types of seashell surfaces have been generated using two different kinds of parametric functions given by

$$f(u,v)=\begin{cases} 2\left(1-e^{\frac{u}{2k\pi}}\right)\cos(u)\cos^2\left(\dfrac{v}{2}\right) \\ 2\left(-1+e^{\frac{u}{2k\pi}}\right)\sin(u)\cos^2\left(\dfrac{v}{2}\right) \\ 1-e^{\frac{u}{2k\pi}}-\sin(u)+e^{\frac{u}{2k\pi}}\sin(v) \end{cases}, \quad (3)$$

and

$$f(u,v)=\begin{cases} \left[\left(1-\dfrac{v}{2\pi}\right)(1+\cos(u)+c)\right]\cos(nv) \\ \left[\left(1-\dfrac{v}{2\pi}\right)(1+\cos(u)+c)\right]\sin(nv) \\ \dfrac{bv}{2\pi}+a\sin(u)\left(1-\dfrac{v}{2\pi}\right) \end{cases}, \quad (4)$$

where $k \in N$ and u, $v \in 2\ [0, 2\pi]$. The visualization of the seashell surface given by Eq.(3) is shown in Fig. 10 (b). The mating process has been illustrated using a seashell type surface generated by a parametric function, a cylinder and a handle (ellipsoidal type shape).

Two operations have been applied for the mating of the previous defined parts, and the new resulting shape after each mating have been visualized inside the Web graphical interface.

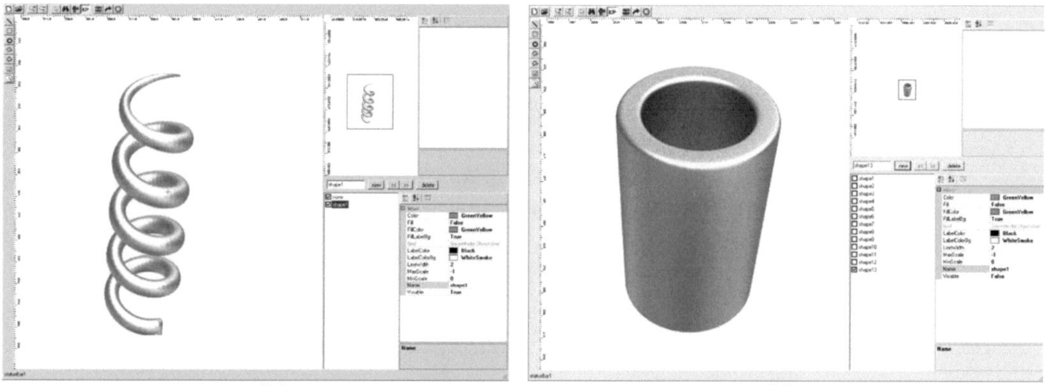

(a) (b)

Fig. 11. (a) Seashell Surface, (b) Corkscrew Cylinder

More specifically the seashell type surface shown in Fig. 11 (a) is mate with the cylinder shown in Fig. 11 (b) to obtain the shape in Fig. 12 (a).

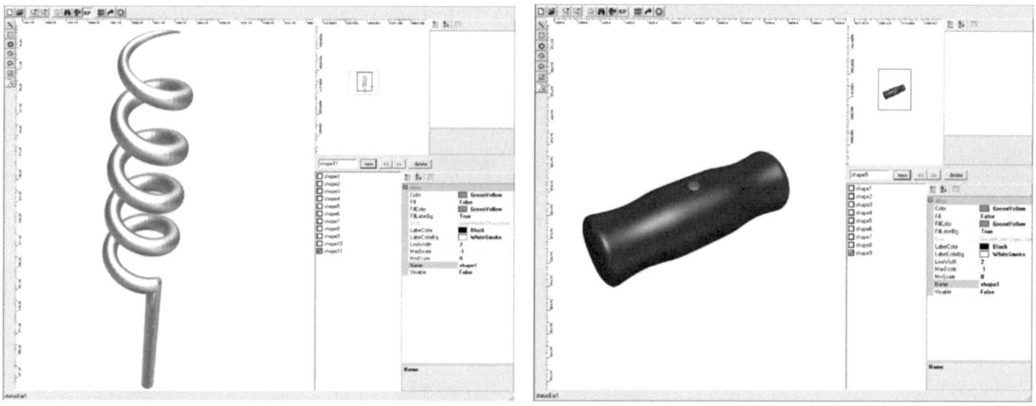

(a) (b)

Fig. 12. (a) First Corkscrew Mating Process, (b) Corkscrew Handle

The resulting shape shown in Fig. 12 (a) is mate with handle previewed in Fig. 12(b) to obtain the final shape as shown in Fig. 13.
Another example is a chain generation that was accomplished using the next two parametric functions

$$f_k(u,v) = \begin{cases} kn_0 + [n_2 + \cos(v)]\sin(u) \\ n_1 + [n_2 + \cos(v)]\cos(u) \\ n_1 + \sin(v) \end{cases}, \quad (5)$$

and

$$f_s(u,v)=\begin{cases} sn_0+[n_2+\cos(v)]\sin(u) \\ n_1+\sin(v) \\ n_1+[n_2+\cos(v)]\cos(u) \end{cases}, \quad (6)$$

where u, $v \in [0, 2\pi]$, $k = 1, 3, 5, \ldots, 2n + 1$, $s = 2, 4, 6, \ldots, 2n$, and $n \in N$. The chain in Fig. 14 (a) was obtained using Eq.(5) and the parameters $n_0 = n_1 = 4$ and $n_2 = 3$.

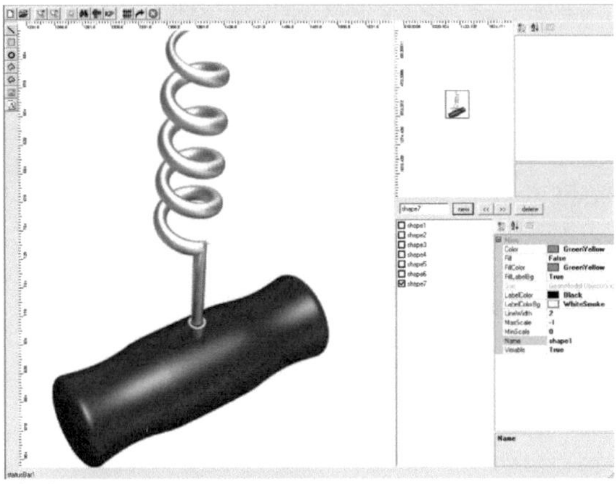

Fig. 13. Corkscrew Final Shape

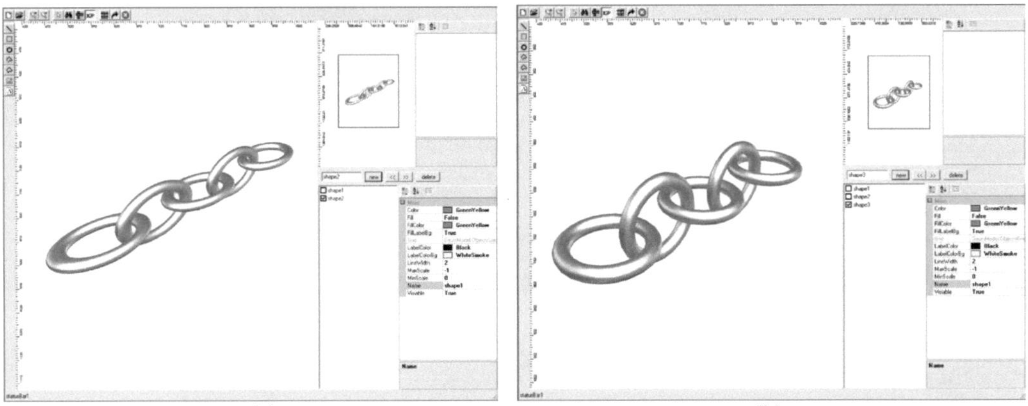

(a) (b)

Fig. 14. (a) A Chain Obtained Using Eq.(5), (b) A Chain Obtained Using Eq.(6)

The chain in Fig. 14 (b) was obtained using Eq.(6) and the parameters $n_0 \neq n_1$, $n_0 = 6$, $n_1 = 4$ and $n_2 = 3$. It is to observe that a link of the chain shown in Fig. 14 (a) has a elliptical shape beside the link of the chain shown in Fig. 14 (b) that have a circular shape.

Two types of gears have been obtained using the mating process previously mentioned. The 3D visualization of two types of gears, a classical type and a conical one, are shown in Fig. 15 (a) and Fig. 15(b).

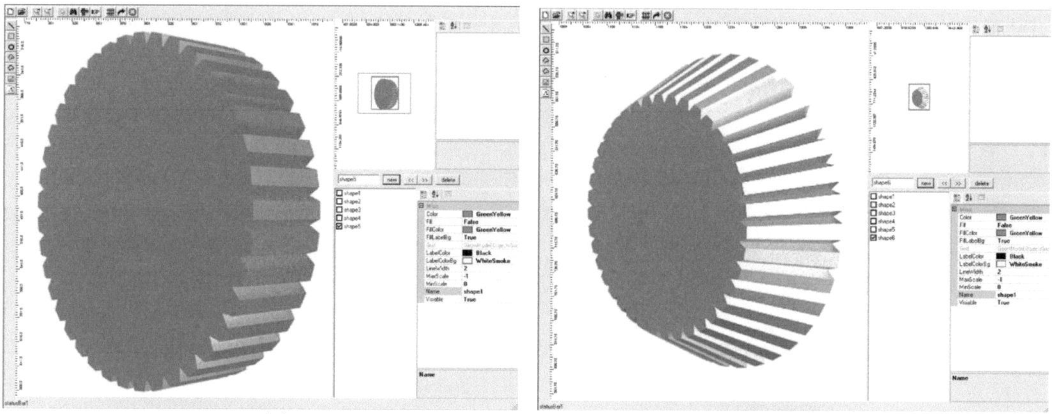

(a) (b)

Fig. 15. (a) A Classical Gear Type, (b) A Conical Gear

The gears have been obtained mating a cylinder and a frustum of a cone with the gear tooth surface. In order to generate the gears tooth geometry the following Fourier series (a very useful tool for generating periodic functions as a sum of sinusoidal components)

$$F(x) = \alpha_0 + \left[\sum_{n=1}^{\infty} \left(\alpha_n \cos\left(\frac{2n\pi x}{k} \right) + \beta_n \sin\left(\frac{2n\pi x}{k} \right) \right) \right], \quad (7)$$

has been used to approximate the trapezoidal shape. The 3D trapezoidal geometry was obtained using $\alpha_n = -n\frac{\pi}{3}$ and $\beta_n = n\pi$, with the function F extended in the z direction to obtain the gear tooth surface.

A classical cylinder is shown in Fig. 16 (a), a connector is shown Fig. 16 (b), and a curved cylinder is shown in Fig. 17 (a).

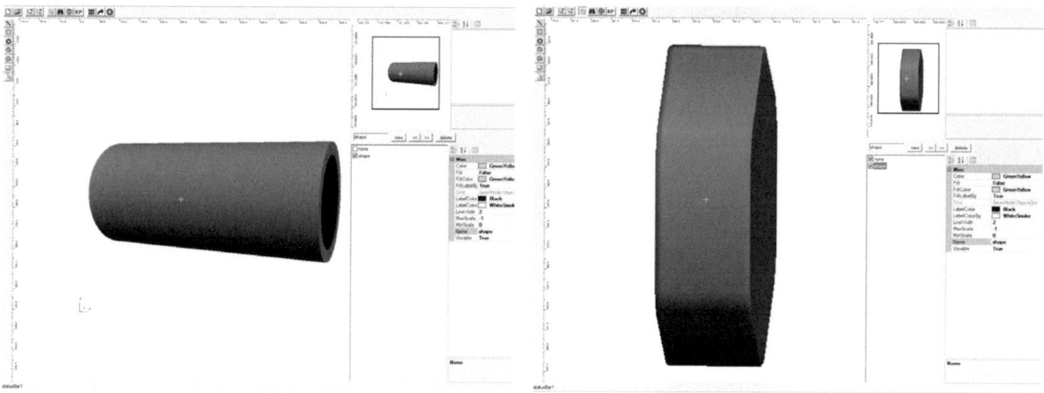

(a) (b)

Fig. 16. (a) A Classical Cylinder, (b) A Connector

The resulting shape shown in Fig. 17 (b) is the mate obtained using the shapes shown in Fig. 16 (a), Fig. 16 (b) and Fig. 16 (c).

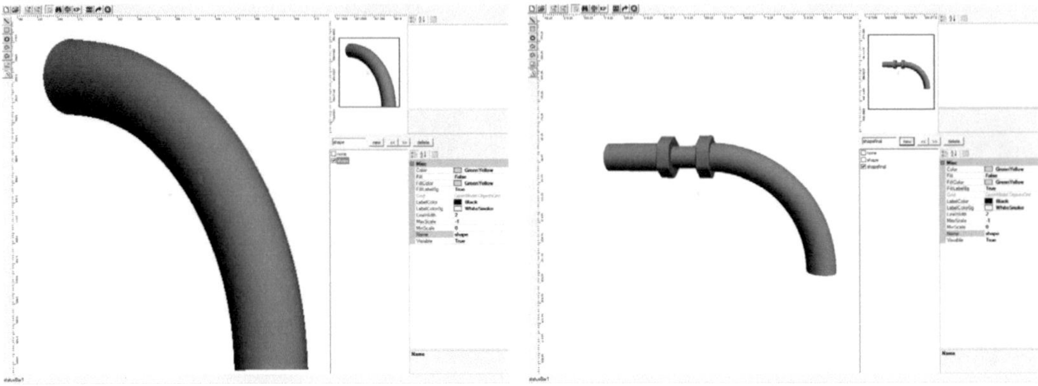

(a) (b)

Fig. 17. (a) A Curved Cylinder, (b) Obtained Final Shape

6. Conclusions

In this work a web-base approach for mechanism components modeling and visualization using object oriented programming (Java) is proposed. A Java Applet which use an XML format for specifying 3D shapes (Java objects) was developed. Parametric, implicit or combination between implicit and parametric functions defined on the graphic interface and viewed as Java objects, have been used to generate the mechanical components shapes. Different mechanism components such as gears, springs, chains, and corkscrews, have been generated and visualized. Simple geometry as well as the combination of the 3D shapes (using a mating process) is provided. It was demonstrated that simple mathematical functions represent useful tools for shape modeling and visualization, with no increase of the application size and with a very good computational time. To learn, understand and dissect a complex mechanical system in order to perform analysis and design a 3D visualization of the mechanical components is essential. Furthermore the presented models do not indicate the limit in shape (mechanism components) generation.

7. References

Metaxas, D. (1996). *Physics-Based Deformable Models*, Kluwer Academic Publishers

Sarti, A. & Tubaro, S. (2001). Multiresolution Implicit Object Modeling, *Proceedings of the Vision Modeling and Visualization*, pp. 129-141

Lorensen, W. & Cline H. E. (1987). Marching Cubes: A High Resolution 3-D Surface Construction Algorithm. *Computer Graphics (SIGGRAPH 87)*, Vol. 21, No. 4, pp. 163-169

Levoy M. (1990). Efficient Ray-Tracing of Volume Data, *ACM Transactions on Graphics*, Vol. 9, No. 3, pp. 245-261

Drebin, R. A.; Carpenter, L. & Hanrahan P. (1988). Volume Rendering, *Computer Graphics Proceedings (SIGGRAPH 88)*, pp. 65-74

Witkin A. & Heckbert P. (1994). Using Particles to Sample and Control Implicit Surfaces, *Computer Graphics Proceedings (SIGGRAPH 94)*, pp. 269-277

Liu, Q. & Sourin A. (2006). Function-based shape modeling extension of the Virtual Reality Modelling Language. *Computers & Graphics*, Vol. 30, No. 4, pp. 629-645

Liu Q. & Sourin A. (2006). Function-based Shape Modeling and Visualization in X3D, *Proceedings of the eleventh international conference on 3D web technology*, pp. 131-141.

Liu, Q. & Sourin A. (2005). Function-based representation of complex geometry and appearance, *Proc. Of the Tenth. Int. Conf. on 3D Web Technology- Web3D '05*, pp. 123-134, Bangor, United Kingdom, March 29 - April 01, 2005, ACM Press, New York, NY

Liu, Q. & Sourin A. (2005). Function-defined Shape Metamorphoses in VRML, *Proc of the 3-rd Int. Conf. on Computer Graphics and Interactive Techniques - GRAPHITE '05*, pp. 339-346, Dunedin, New Zealand, November 29 - December 2, 2005, ACM Press, New York, NY

Dupac M. (2007). Mechanism Components Generation and Visualization Using Mathematical Functions, *ASME Journal of ECT* (accepted for publication)

Chen J.; Sun L.; Zaane O. R. & Goebel R. (2004). Visualizing and Discovering Web Navigational Patterns, *ACM International Conference Proceeding Series, Proceedings of the 7th International Workshop on the Web and Databases: colocated with ACM SIGMOD/ PODS*, pp. 13-18

Cartwright R.; Adzhiev V.; Pasko A.; Goto Y. & Kunii T. L. (2005). Web-based Shape Modeling with HyperFun, *Computer Graphics and Applications, IEEE*, pp. 60-69

Fayolle P.-A.; Schmitt B.; Goto Y. & Pasko A. (2005). Web-based Constructive Shape Modeling Using Real Distance Functions, *IEICE TRANS. INF. & SYST., E88D*(5), pp. 828-835

Eckel B. (2006). *Thinking in Java*, Prentice Hall (4-th Edition)

Blinn, J. F. (1982). A generalization of algebraic surface drawing, *ACM Trans. Graph.*, Vol. 1, No. 3, pp. 235-256

Peachey D. R. (1985). Solid texturing of complex surfaces, *Proceedings of the 12th annual conference on Computer graphics and interactive techniques*, ACM Press, pp. 279-286

Wyvill G.; Wyvill B. & McPheeters C. (1987). Solid texturing of soft objects, In: *CG International 87 on Computer graphics*, pp. 129-141, Springer-Verlag, New York, Inc.

Lewis, J. P. (1989). Algorithms for solid noise synthesis, *Proceedings of the 16-th annual conference on Computer graphics and interactive techniques*, ACM Press, pp. 263-270

Terzopoulos, D. & Metaxas D. (1991). Dynamic 3D models with local and global deformations: Deformable superquadrics, *IEEE Transactions on Pattern Analysis and Machine Intelligence*, Vol. 13, pp. 703-714

Turk G., & O'Brien J. F. (1999). Shape transformation using variational implicit functions, *SIGGRAPH Proceedings of Computer Graphics*, Vol. 33, pp. 335-342.

Popîrlan C. I. & Popîrlan C. (2007). Mobile Agents communication for knowledge representation, *Proceedings of the 11-th World Multiconference on Systemics, Cybernetics and Informatics (WMSCI 2007)*, pp. 92-96, July 8-11, Orlando, USA

Baumann J. (2000). Mobile Agents: Control Algorithms, In: *Lecture Notes in Computer Science*, Springer

Chun E. Y.; Chen H. & Lee I. (1998). Web-Based Simulation Experiments, *Proceedings of the 1998 Winter Simulation Conference*, pp. 1649-1654

Fishwick P. A. (1998). Issues with Web-Publishable Digital Objects, *Proceedings of the 1998 International Conference on Web-Based Modeling and Simulation*

Healy K. J. & Kilgore R. A. (1997). Silk: A java-based process simulation language, *Proceedings of the1997 Winter Simulation Conference*, pp. 475-482

McNab R. & Howell F. W. (1996). Using Java for Discrete Event Simulation, *Proceedings of the Twelfth UK Computer and Telecommunications Performance Engineering Workshop*, pp. 219-228, University of Edinburgh, UK

Nair R. S.; Miller J. A. & Zhang Z. (1996). Java-Based Query Driven Simulation Environment, *Proceedings of the 1996 Winter Simulation Conference*, pp. 786- 793

Page E. H. (1998). The Rise of Web-Based Simulation: Implications for the High Level Architecture, *Proceedings of the 1998 Winter Simulation Conference*, pp. 1663- 1667

Whitman L.; Huff B. & Palaniswamy S. (1998). Commercial Simulation Over the Web, *Proceedings of the 1998 Winter Simulation Conference*, pp. 335-339

Juvinall, R.C. & Marshek, K.M. (2001). *Fundamentals of Machine Component Design*, John Wiley & Sons

Shigley, J.E. & Mischke, C.R. (2001). *Mechanical Engineering Design*, McGraw Hill

Marghitu D.B. (2005). *Kinematics Chains and Machine Components Design*, Elsevier

Marghitu D.B. (2001). *Mechanical Engineer's Handbook*, Academic Press

Parmley, R. O. (2005). *Machine Devices and Components Illustrated Sourcebook*, McGrow-Hill

Suryaji, R. & Weinmann Bhonsle K. J. (1999). *Mathematical Modeling for Design of Machine Components*, TK Integrated, Prentice Hall

Golden Ratio in the Point Sink Induced Consolidation Settlement of a Poroelastic Half Space

Feng-Tsai Lin[1] and John C.-C. Lu[2]
[1]*Department of Naval Architecture, National Kaohsiung Marine University*
[2]*Department of Civil Engineering & Engineering Informatics, Chung Hua University*
Taiwan

1. Introduction

The golden ratio ϕ has been well known in mathematics, science, biology, art, architecture, nature and beyond (Sen & Agarwal, 2008), which is the irrational algebraic number $\left(1+\sqrt{5}\right)/2 \approx 1.618033989$. It's interesting to find that the golden ratio exists in the point sink induced consolidation settlement of a homogeneous isotropic poroelastic half space. Examples of the golden ratio in engineering include the study of shear flow in porous half space (Puri & Jordan, 2006) and classical mechanics of coupled-oscillator problem (Moorman & Goff, 2007).

Land subsidence due to groundwater withdrawal is a well-known phenomenon (Poland, 1984). The pore water pressure is reduced in the withdrawal region when an aquifer pumps groundwater. It leads to increase in effective stress between the soil particles and subsidence of ground surface.

The three-dimensional consolidation theory presented by Biot (1941, 1955) is generally regarded as the fundamental theory for modeling land subsidence. Based on Biot's theory, Booker and Carter (1986*a*, 1986*b*, 1987*a*, 1987*b*), Kanok-Nukulchai and Chau (1990), Tarn and Lu (1991) presented solutions of subsidence by a point sink embedded in saturated elastic half space at a constant rate. In the studies of Booker and Carter (1986*a*, 1986*b*, 1987*a*, 1987*b*), the flow properties are considered as isotropic or cross-anisotropic whereas the elastic properties of the soil are treated as isotropic with pervious half space boundary. Tarn and Lu (1991) found that groundwater withdrawal from an impervious half space induces a larger amount of consolidation settlement than from a pervious one. Chen (2002, 2005) presented analytical solutions for the steady-state response of displacements and stresses in a half space subjected to a point sink. Lu and Lin (2006) displayed transient ground surface displacement produced by a point heat source/sink through analog quantities between poroelasticity and thermoelasticity. Hou *et al.* (2005) found that pumping induced ground horizontal velocities range from 31 to 54 mm/yr towards azimuths 247° to 273° in the Pingtung Plain of Taiwan. Their results show that ground horizontal displacement occurred

when pumping from an aquifer. Nevertheless, the consolidation settlement due to pumping were not thoroughly discussed in the above theoretical studies.
The aquifer is modeled as an isotropic saturated pervious elastic half space in this analytical research. Using Laplace and Hankel integral transform techniques, the transient horizontal and vertical displacements of the ground surface due to a point sink are obtained. The study also focused on the distributions of excess pore water pressure of the half space on the consolidation history. Results are illustrated and compared to display the time dependent consolidation settlement due to pumping.

2. The Golden Ratio

The golden ratio ϕ can be derived from a geometrical line segment in extreme and mean ratio as shown in Fiqure 1, where the ratio of the full length 1 to the length of x is equal to the ratio of section part x to shorter section $1-x$:

$$\frac{1}{x}=\frac{x}{1-x}. \tag{1}$$

Assuming, $x=1/\phi$, hence, ϕ satisfies

$$\phi^2-\phi-1=0. \tag{2}$$

The golden ratio is the positive root of Eq. (2):

$$\phi=\frac{1+\sqrt{5}}{2}. \tag{3}$$

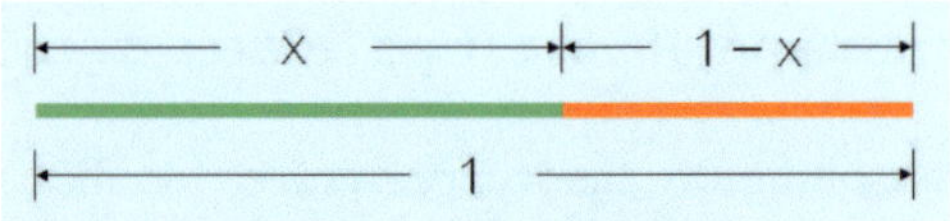

Fig. 1. Dividing the unit interval according to the golden ratio

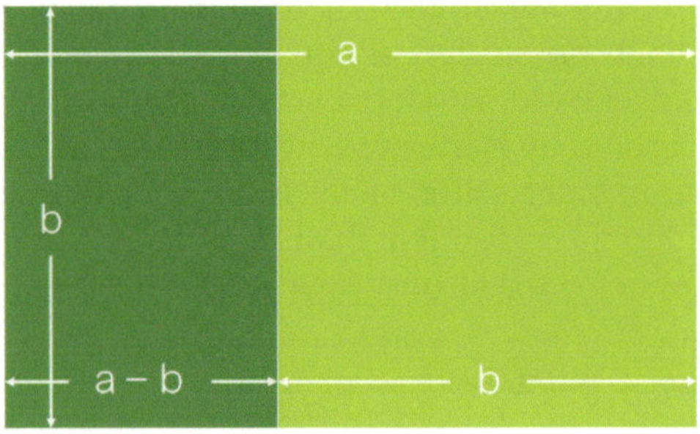

Fig. 2. The golden rectangle

Ratio of two successive numbers of Fibonacci series	Value
1/1	1.0000000000
2/1	2.0000000000
3/2	1.5000000000
5/3	1.6666666667
8/5	1.6000000000
13/8	1.6250000000
21/13	1.6153846154
34/21	1.6190476190
55/34	1.6176470588
89/55	1.6181818182
144/89	1.6179775281
233/144	1.6180555556

Table 1. The ratio of two successive numbers of Fibonacci series approaches golden ratio ϕ

Figure 2 displayed another geometric description of golden ratio through the golden rectangle. Giving a rectangle with sides' ratio a : b, the removing of square section leaves the remaining rectangle with the same ratio as original rectangle, i.e.,

$$\frac{b}{a-b}=\frac{a}{b}. \tag{4}$$

Thus, this solution is the golden ratio ϕ :

$$\phi=\frac{a}{b}=\frac{1+\sqrt{5}}{2}. \tag{5}$$

The golden ratio is a remarkable number that arises in various areas of mathematics, natures and arts. There are many interesting mathematical properties of ϕ . For example, ϕ can be expressed as a continuous fraction with the single number 1 (Livio, 2002):

$$\phi=1+\cfrac{1}{1+\cfrac{1}{1+\cfrac{1}{1+\cfrac{1}{1+\cdots}}}}. \tag{6}$$

Also, the golden ratio ϕ can be expressed as a continuous square root of the number 1:

$$\phi=\sqrt{1+\sqrt{1+\sqrt{1+\sqrt{1+\cdots}}}}\ . \tag{7}$$

However, the most interesting is that ϕ is within Fibonacci series (Livio, 2002; Dunlap, 1997). The Fibonacci series is a set of numbers that begins with two 1s and each term therefore is the sum of the prior two terms, i.e., 1, 1, 2, 3, 5, 8, 13, 21, 34, 55, 89, 144, 233, $\cdots$. The relationship between two successive numbers of Fibonacci series tends to approach ϕ as shown in Table 1.

Based on Biot's (1941, 1955) three-dimensional consolidation theory of porous media, this study modeled the saturated aquifer as a homogeneous isotropic poroelastic half space. Closed-form solutions of the transient and long-term consolidation deformations and excess pore water pressures due to a point sink are presented in this paper. It's interesting to find that the golden ratio ϕ appears in the point sink induced maximum ground surface horizontal displacement and corresponding settlement of a poroelastic half space.

3. Mathematical Models

3.1 Basic Equations

Figure 3 presents a point sink buried in a saturated porous elastic aquifer at a depth h . The aquifer is considered as a homogeneous isotropic porous medium with a vertical axis of symmetry. Assuming the model is decoupled, i.e., the flow field is independent from the displacement field. Considering a point sink of constant strength Q located at point $(0,h)$, the basic governing equations of the elastic saturated aquifer for linear axially symmetric deformation can be expressed in terms of displacements u_i and excess pore water pressure p in the cylindrical coordinates (r,θ,z) as follows (Lu & Lin, 2006, 2008):

$$G\nabla^2 u_r + \frac{G}{1-2\nu}\frac{\partial \varepsilon}{\partial r} - G\frac{u_r}{r^2} - \frac{\partial p}{\partial r} = 0\,, \tag{8a}$$

$$G\nabla^2 u_z + \frac{G}{1-2\nu}\frac{\partial \varepsilon}{\partial z} - \frac{\partial p}{\partial z} = 0\,, \tag{8b}$$

$$-\frac{k}{\gamma_w}\nabla^2 p + n\beta\frac{\partial p}{\partial t} + \frac{Q}{2\pi r}\delta(r)\delta(z-h)u(t) = 0\,, \tag{8c}$$

where $\nabla^2 = \partial^2/\partial r^2 + 1/r\,\partial/\partial r + \partial^2/\partial z^2$ is the Laplacian operator. The excess pore fluid pressure p is positive for compression. The displacements u_r and u_z are in the radial and axial directions, and $\varepsilon = \partial u_r/\partial r + u_r/r + \partial u_z/\partial z$ is the volume strain of the porous medium. The quantities ν , G , k , n , γ_w and β denote the saturated aquifer's Poisson's ratio, shear modulus, aquifer permeability, porosity, pore water unit weight and compressibility, respectively. The functions $\delta(x)$ and $u(t)$ are Dirac delta and Heaviside unit step function, respectively.

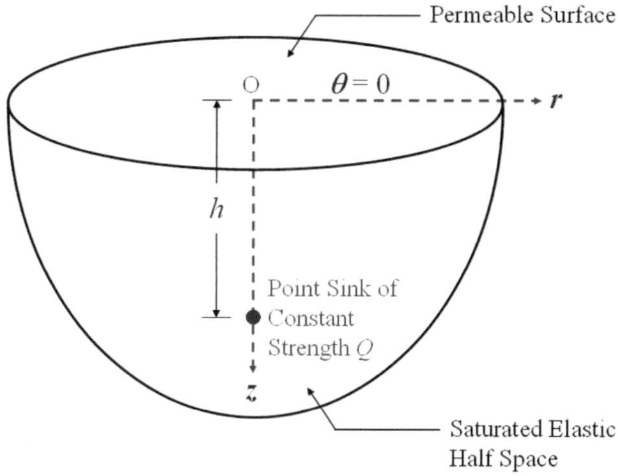

Fig. 3. Point sink induced land subsidence model

3.2 Boundary Conditions

The saturated aquifer is considered as a homogeneous isotropic half space and the constitutive behavior of the aquifer can be express by the total stress components $\tau_{ij} = \frac{2G\nu}{1-2\nu}\varepsilon\delta_{ij} + 2G\varepsilon_{ij} - p\delta_{ij}$, where $\varepsilon_{rr} = \frac{\partial u_r}{\partial r}$, $\varepsilon_{\theta\theta} = \frac{u_r}{r}$, $\varepsilon_{zz} = \frac{\partial u_z}{\partial z}$, respectively; and δ_{ij} is the Kronecker delta. In this paper, the half space surface, $z = 0$, is considered as a traction-free pervious boundary for time $t \geq 0$. From the constitutive relationships shown above, the mechanical boundary conditions at $z = 0$ are expressed in terms of u_r and u_z by

$$\frac{2G\nu}{1-2\nu}\left[\frac{\partial u_r(r,0,t)}{\partial r} + \frac{u_r(r,0,t)}{r}\right] + \frac{2G(1-\nu)}{1-2\nu}\frac{\partial u_z(r,0,t)}{\partial z} = 0, \tag{9a}$$

$$G\left[\frac{\partial u_r(r,0,t)}{\partial z} + \frac{\partial u_z(r,0,t)}{\partial r}\right] = 0. \tag{9b}$$

An additional condition is provided by considering the half space as pervious and the mathematical statement of the flow condition at the boundary $z = 0$ is given by

$$p(r,0,t) = 0. \tag{9c}$$

The boundary conditions at $z \to \infty$ due to the effect of the point sink vanish when $t \geq 0$.

3.3 Initial Conditions

Assuming no initial changes in displacements and seepage of the aquifer, the initial conditions of the mathematical model at time $t = 0$ are

$$u_r(r,z,0) = 0,\ u_z(r,z,0) = 0, \text{ and } p(r,z,0) = 0. \tag{10}$$

4. Analytic Solutions

4.1 Laplace and Hankel Transforms Solutions

The governing partial differential equations (8a)-(8c) are reduced to ordinary differential equations by performing Laplace and Hankel transforms (Sneddon, 1951) with respect to the time variable t and the radial coordinate r :

$$\left(\frac{d^2}{dz^2}-2\eta\xi^2\right)\tilde{u}_r-(2\eta-1)\xi\frac{d\tilde{u}_z}{dz}+\frac{1}{G}\xi\tilde{p}=0\,, \tag{11a}$$

$$(2\eta-1)\xi\frac{d\tilde{u}_r}{dz}+\left(2\eta\frac{d^2}{dz^2}-\xi^2\right)\tilde{u}_z-\frac{1}{G}\frac{d\tilde{p}}{dz}=0\,, \tag{11b}$$

$$-\frac{k}{\gamma_w}\left(\frac{d^2}{dz^2}-\xi^2\right)\tilde{p}+n\beta s\tilde{p}+\frac{Q}{2\pi s}\delta(z-h)=0\,, \tag{11c}$$

where ξ and s are Hankel and Laplace transform parameters. The parameter $\eta=(1-\nu)/(1-2\nu)$ and the symbols $\tilde{u}_r$, $\tilde{u}_z$, $\tilde{p}$ are defined as

$$\tilde{u}_r(z;\xi,s)=\int_0^\infty rL\{u_r(r,z,t)\}J_1(\xi r)dr\,, \tag{12a}$$

$$\tilde{u}_z(z;\xi,s)=\int_0^\infty rL\{u_z(r,z,t)\}J_0(\xi r)dr\,, \tag{12b}$$

$$\tilde{p}(z;\xi,s)=\int_0^\infty rL\{p(r,z,t)\}J_0(\xi r)dr\,, \tag{12c}$$

in which $J_\nu(x)$ represents the first kind of Bessel function of order ν . The Laplace transforms in equations (12a)-(12c) with respect to u_r, u_z and p are denoted by

$$L\{u_r(r,z,t)\}=\int_0^\infty u_r(r,z,t)exp(-st)dt\,, \tag{13a}$$

$$L\{u_z(r,z,t)\}=\int_0^\infty u_z(r,z,t)exp(-st)dt\,, \tag{13b}$$

$$L\{p(r,z,t)\}=\int_0^\infty p(r,z,t)exp(-st)dt\,. \tag{13c}$$

The general solutions of equations (11a)-(11c) are obtained as

$$\tilde{u}_r(z;\xi,s)=C_1exp(\xi z)+C_2z\,exp(\xi z)+C_3exp(-\xi z)+C_4z\,exp(-\xi z)$$
$$+C_5exp\left(\sqrt{\xi^2+\frac{s}{c}}z\right)+C_6exp\left(-\sqrt{\xi^2+\frac{s}{c}}z\right)$$

$$+\frac{Q\gamma_w}{8\pi\eta Gk}\left[-\frac{c}{s^2}exp\left(-\xi|z-h|\right)+\frac{c}{s^2}\frac{\xi}{\sqrt{\xi^2+\frac{s}{c}}}exp\left(-\sqrt{\xi^2+\frac{s}{c}}|z-h|\right)\right], \tag{14a}$$

$$\tilde{u}_z(z;\xi,s)=\left(-C_1+\frac{2\eta+1}{2\eta-1}\frac{1}{\xi}C_2\right)exp(\xi z)-C_2 z\,exp(\xi z)+\left(C_3+\frac{2\eta+1}{2\eta-1}\frac{1}{\xi}C_4\right)exp(-\xi z)+C_4 z\,exp(-\xi z)$$

$$-\frac{1}{\xi}\sqrt{\xi^2+\frac{s}{c}}C_5\,exp\left(\sqrt{\xi^2+\frac{s}{c}}z\right)+\frac{1}{\xi}\sqrt{\xi^2+\frac{s}{c}}C_6\,exp\left(-\sqrt{\xi^2+\frac{s}{c}}z\right)$$

$$\mp\frac{Q\gamma_w}{8\pi\eta Gk}\left[\frac{c}{s^2}exp\left(-\xi|z-h|\right)-\frac{c}{s^2}exp\left(-\sqrt{\xi^2+\frac{s}{c}}|z-h|\right)\right], \tag{14b}$$

$$\tilde{p}(z;\xi,s)=-2\eta G\frac{1}{\xi}\frac{s}{c}C_5\,exp\left(\sqrt{\xi^2+\frac{s}{c}}z\right)-2\eta G\frac{1}{\xi}\frac{s}{c}C_6\,exp\left(-\sqrt{\xi^2+\frac{s}{c}}z\right)$$

$$-\frac{Q\gamma_w}{4\pi k}\frac{1}{s}\frac{1}{\sqrt{\xi^2+\frac{s}{c}}}exp\left(-\sqrt{\xi^2+\frac{s}{c}}|z-h|\right), \tag{14c}$$

where the parameter $c=k/n\beta\gamma_w$ and $C_i\,(i=1,2,\cdots,6)$ are functions of the transformed variables ξ and s which are determined from the transformed boundary conditions. The upper and lower signs in Eq. (14b) are for the conditions of $(z-h)\geq 0$ and $(z-h)<0$, respectively.

4.2 Transformed Boundary Conditions

Taking Hankel and Laplace transforms for Eqs. (9a)-(9c), the mechanical and flow boundary conditions at $z=0$ of the transformed domains are derived as follows:

$$\eta\frac{d\tilde{u}_z(0;\xi,s)}{dz}+(\eta-1)\xi\tilde{u}_r(0;\xi,s)=0,\quad \frac{d\tilde{u}_r(0;\xi,s)}{dz}-\xi\tilde{u}_z(0;\xi,s)=0,\ \text{and}\ \tilde{p}(0;\xi,s)=0, \tag{15}$$

where $\tilde{u}_r$, $\tilde{u}_z$ and $\tilde{p}$ follow the definitions in Eqs. (12a)-(12c).

The constants $C_i\,(i=1,2,\cdots,6)$ of the general solutions are determined by the transformed half space boundary conditions at $z=0$ and $z\to\infty$. Finally, the desired quantities u_r, u_z and p are obtained by applying appropriate inverse Hankel and Laplace transformations (Erdelyi, *et al.*, 1954).

4.3 Expressions for Ground Surface Displacements

The focus of the study is on horizontal and vertical displacements of the ground surface, $z=0$, due to a point sink. The transformed ground surface displacements are derived from Eqs. (14a)-(14b) with the help of transformed boundary conditions and they are obtained as follows:

$$\tilde{u}_r(0;\xi,s) = \frac{Q\gamma_w}{2\pi(2\eta-1)Gk}\left[-\frac{c}{s^2}exp(-\xi h) + \frac{c}{s^2}exp\left(-\sqrt{\xi^2+\frac{s}{c}}h\right)\right], \tag{16a}$$

$$\tilde{u}_z(0;\xi,s) = \frac{Q\gamma_w}{2\pi(2\eta-1)Gk}\left[\frac{c}{s^2}exp(-\xi h) - \frac{c}{s^2}exp\left(-\sqrt{\xi^2+\frac{s}{c}}h\right)\right]. \tag{16b}$$

Applying the Hankel inversion formulae lead to the following displacements:

$$u_r(r,z,t) = \int_0^\infty \xi L^{-1}\{\tilde{u}_r(z;\xi,s)\} J_1(\xi r)d\xi, \tag{17a}$$

$$u_z(r,z,t) = \int_0^\infty \xi L^{-1}\{\tilde{u}_z(z;\xi,s)\} J_0(\xi r)d\xi, \tag{17b}$$

in which the Laplace inversions are defined as

$$L^{-1}\{\tilde{u}_r(z;\xi,s)\} = \frac{1}{2\pi i}\int_{\alpha-i\infty}^{\alpha+i\infty} \tilde{u}_r(z;\xi,s)exp(st)ds, \tag{18a}$$

$$L^{-1}\{\tilde{u}_z(z;\xi,s)\} = \frac{1}{2\pi i}\int_{\alpha-i\infty}^{\alpha+i\infty} \tilde{u}_z(z;\xi,s)exp(st)ds. \tag{18b}$$

Using Eqs. (17a)-(17b) and (18a)-(18b), the transient horizontal displacement $u_r(r,0,t)$ and vertical settlement $u_z(r,0,t)$ of the pervious ground surface due to a point sink are obtained as follows:

$$u_r(r,0,t) = \frac{Q\gamma_w}{2(2\eta-1)\pi Gk}\left\{-\frac{ctr}{(h^2+r^2)^{3/2}} + \int_0^{ct}\frac{(ct-\tau)hr}{16\tau^3}exp\left(-\frac{r^2+2h^2}{8\tau}\right)\left[I_0\left(\frac{r^2}{8\tau}\right) - I_1\left(\frac{r^2}{8\tau}\right)\right]d\tau\right\}, \tag{19a}$$

$$u_z(r,0,t) = \frac{Q\gamma_w}{2(2\eta-1)\pi Gk}\left\{\frac{cth}{(h^2+r^2)^{3/2}}erf\left(\frac{\sqrt{h^2+r^2}}{2\sqrt{ct}}\right) - \frac{h}{h^2+r^2}\sqrt{\frac{ct}{\pi}}exp\left(-\frac{h^2+r^2}{4ct}\right) + \frac{h}{2\sqrt{h^2+r^2}}erfc\left(\frac{\sqrt{h^2+r^2}}{2\sqrt{ct}}\right)\right\}, \tag{19b}$$

where $erf(x)$ and $erfc(x)$ are error function and complementary error function, respectively; and $I_\nu(x)$ is known as the modified Bessel function of the first kind of order ν. The long-term ground surface horizontal and vertical displacements are obtained when $t \to \infty$:

$$u_r(r,0,\infty) = -\frac{Q\gamma_w}{4(2\eta-1)\pi Gk}\frac{hr}{\sqrt{h^2+r^2}(\sqrt{h^2+r^2}+h)}, \tag{20a}$$

$$u_z(r,0,\infty) = \frac{Q\gamma_w}{4(2\eta-1)\pi Gk}\frac{h}{\sqrt{h^2+r^2}}. \tag{20b}$$

The maximum long-term ground surface horizontal displacement $u_{r\max}$ and settlement $u_{z\max}$ of the half space due to a point sink are derived from Eqs. (20a) and (20b) by letting $r = \sqrt{\phi}h \approx 1.272h$ and $r = 0$, respectively:

$$u_{r\max} = u_r\left(\sqrt{\phi}h,0,\infty\right) = -\frac{Q\gamma_w}{4(2\eta-1)\pi Gk}\frac{1}{\phi^{2.5}} \approx -\frac{0.3003Q\gamma_w}{4(2\eta-1)\pi Gk}, \tag{21a}$$

$$u_{z\max} = u_z(0,0,\infty) = \frac{Q\gamma_w}{4(2\eta-1)\pi Gk}, \tag{21b}$$

in which $\phi = \left(1+\sqrt{5}\right)/2 \approx 1.618$ is known as the golden ratio (Livio, 2002; Dunlap, 1997). The value $r = \sqrt{\phi}h$ is derived when $du_r(r,0,\infty)/dr$ is equal to zero, i.e.,

$$\frac{du_r(r,0,\infty)}{dr} = -\frac{Q\gamma_w}{4(2\eta-1)\pi Gk}\frac{h\sqrt{h^2+r^2}\left(h^2-r^2\right)+h^4}{\left(h^2+r^2\right)^{1.5}\left(\sqrt{h^2+r^2}+h\right)^2} = 0. \tag{22}$$

This leads to solutions of $r = \pm\sqrt{(1+\sqrt{5})/2}h$ and $r = \pm\sqrt{(1-\sqrt{5})/2}h$, however only $r = \sqrt{(1+\sqrt{5})/2}h$ is realistic for $r \in [0,\infty)$.

It's interesting to find that the golden ratio ϕ not only appears in the point sink induced maximum ground surface horizontal displacement but also on the corresponding settlement by letting $r = \sqrt{\phi}h$ in Eq. (20b). Hence, we have:

$$u_z\left(\sqrt{\phi}h,0,\infty\right) = \frac{Q\gamma_w}{4(2\eta-1)\pi Gk}\frac{1}{\sqrt{1+\phi}} = u_{z\max}\frac{1}{\phi} \approx 0.618u_{z\max}. \tag{23}$$

This shows that the ground surface settlement at $r = \sqrt{\phi}h$, where the maximum ground surface horizontal displacement $u_{r\max}$ occurred, is around 61.8% of the maximum ground surface settlement $u_{z\max}$.

All of the displacement figures are normalized to the maximum ground surface settlement $u_{z\max}$. Besides, the Eqs. (21a)-(21b) show that the maximum long-term horizontal displacement and settlement are not directly dependent on the pumping depth h.

4.4 Expression for Excess Pore Water Pressure

The study also addressed the excess pore water pressure of the porous elastic half space due to a point sink. The transformed excess pore water pressure is obtained from Eq. (14c) with the help of transformed flow boundary conditions, and it can be expressed as following:

$$\tilde{p}(z;\xi,s)=\frac{Q\gamma_w}{4\pi k}\left\{\frac{1}{s}\frac{1}{\sqrt{\xi^2+\frac{s}{c}}}exp\left[-\sqrt{\xi^2+\frac{s}{c}}(z+h)\right]-\frac{1}{s}\frac{1}{\sqrt{\xi^2+\frac{s}{c}}}exp\left[-\sqrt{\xi^2+\frac{s}{c}}|z-h|\right]\right\}. \tag{24}$$

The Hankel inversion formula is applied as:

$$p(r,z,t)=\int_0^{\infty}\xi L^{-1}\{\tilde{p}(z;\xi,s)\}J_0(\xi r)d\xi, \tag{25}$$

where the Laplace inversion is defined as

$$L^{-1}\{\tilde{p}(z;\xi,s)\}=\frac{1}{2\pi i}\int_{\alpha-i\infty}^{\alpha+i\infty}\tilde{p}(z;\xi,s)exp(st)ds. \tag{26}$$

The transient excess pore water pressure $p(r,z,t)$ of the saturated pervious half space due to a point sink is obtained as following:

$$p(r,z,t)=\frac{Q\gamma_w}{4\pi k}\left\{\frac{1}{\sqrt{r^2+(z+h)^2}}erfc\left[\frac{\sqrt{r^2+(z+h)^2}}{2\sqrt{ct}}\right]-\frac{1}{\sqrt{r^2+(z-h)^2}}erfc\left[\frac{\sqrt{r^2+(z-h)^2}}{2\sqrt{ct}}\right]\right\}. \tag{27}$$

The long-term excess pore water pressure is derived when $t\to\infty$. It leads to

$$p(r,z,\infty)=\frac{Q\gamma_w}{4\pi k}\left[\frac{1}{\sqrt{r^2+(z+h)^2}}-\frac{1}{\sqrt{r^2+(z-h)^2}}\right]. \tag{28}$$

5. Numerical Results

5.1 Normalized Numerical Consolidation Results

The particular interest is the settlement of stratum at each stage of the consolidation process. The average consolidation ratio U is defined as following:

$$U=\frac{\text{Settlement at time } t}{\text{Settlement at end of compression}}. \tag{29}$$

The average consolidation ratio U of the saturated pervious half space can be derived as below:

$$U = \frac{2ct}{h^2 + r^2} erf\left(\frac{\sqrt{h^2 + r^2}}{2\sqrt{ct}}\right) - \frac{2}{\sqrt{h^2 + r^2}}\sqrt{\frac{ct}{\pi}} exp\left(-\frac{h^2 + r^2}{4ct}\right) + erfc\left(\frac{\sqrt{h^2 + r^2}}{2\sqrt{ct}}\right). \tag{30}$$

Figure 4 shows the average consolidation ratio U at $r/h = 0$, 1, 2, 5, and 10 for the saturated pervious half space. The figure shows that U initially decreases rapidly, and then the rate of settlement reduces. As U approaches 100% asymptotically, the theoretical consolidation is never achieved. The trend revealed in this model agrees with previous models by Sivaram and Swamee (1977) that U initially decreases rapidly, and then the rate of settlement slows down.

The profiles of normalized vertical and horizontal displacements at the ground surface $z = 0$ for different dimensionless time factor $\sqrt{ct/h^2}$ are shown in Figures 5 and 6, respectively. The ground surface reveals significant horizontal displacement. For example, Fig. 6 shows that the maximum surface horizontal displacement is around 30% of the maximum ground settlement at $r/h \approx 1.272$, which can also be found from the ratio of Eqs. (21a) and (21b).

From equations (27) and (28), the profiles of normalized excess pore water pressure $p(r,z,t)/[Q\gamma_w/4\pi kh]$ of the pervious half space at four different dimensionless time factors $\sqrt{ct/h^2}$ = 1, 2, 3, and ∞ are illustrated in Fig. 7(a)-(d), respectively. The changes in excess pore water pressure have negative value $p(r,z,t)$ which is caused by suction of groundwater withdrawal. Besides, the larger magnitude of subsidence is due to a wider region influenced by the pumping.

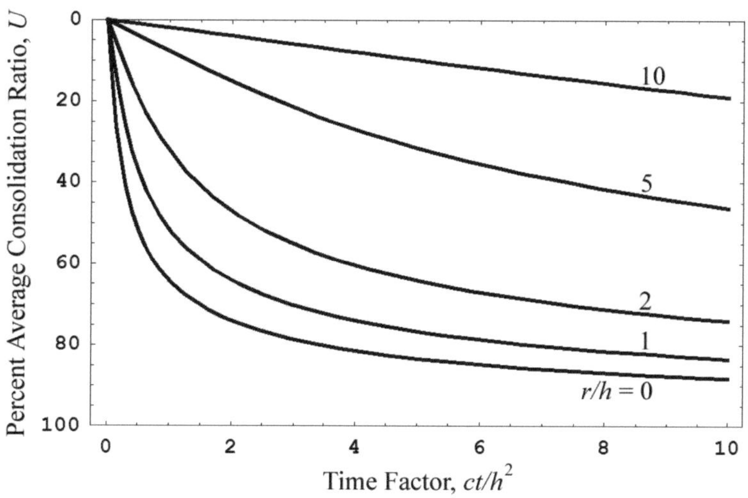

Fig. 4. Average consolidation ratio U for saturated pervious half space

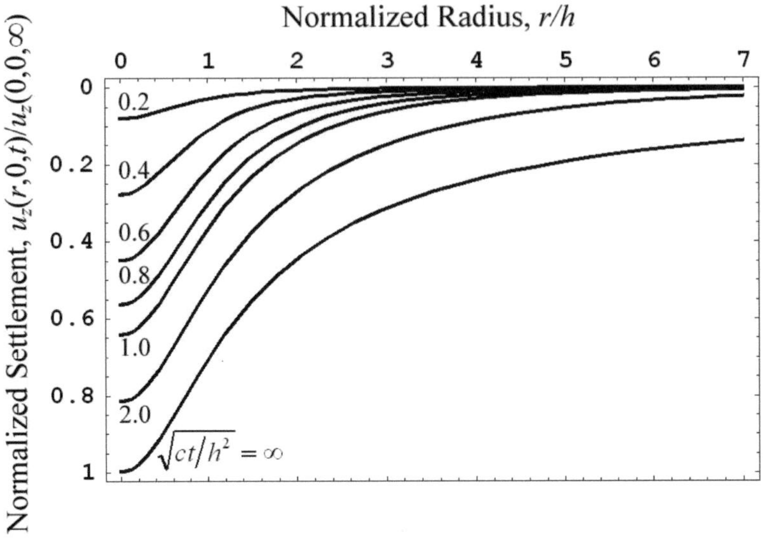

Fig. 5. Normalized vertical displacement profile at the ground surface $z = 0$ for saturated pervious half space

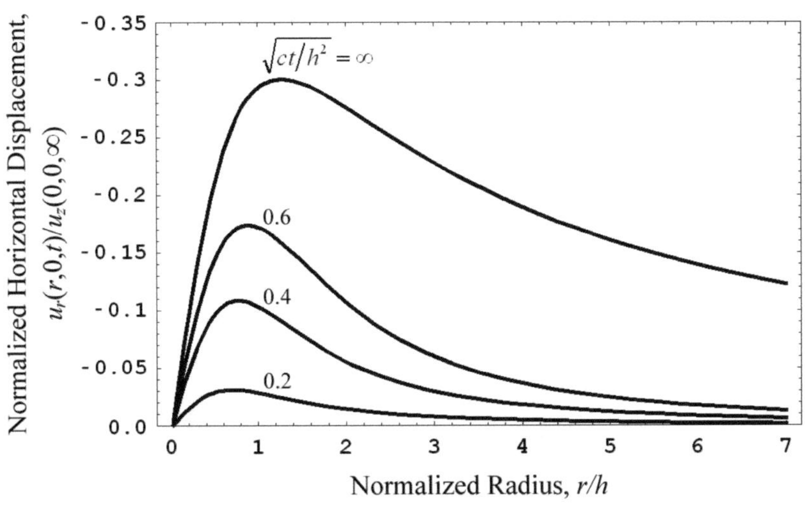

Fig. 6. Normalized horizontal displacement profile at the ground surface $z = 0$ for saturated pervious half space

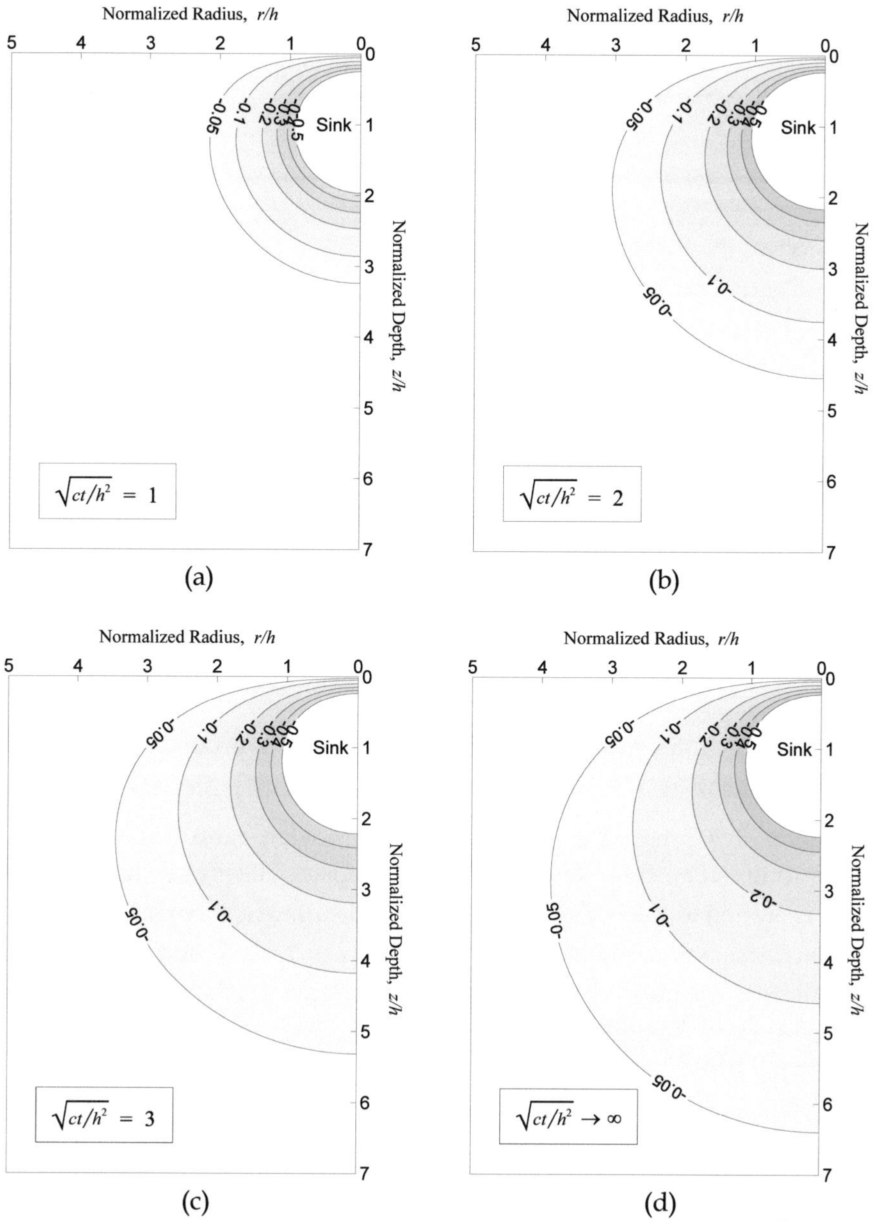

Fig. 7. Distribution of normalized excess pore water pressure $p(r,z,t)/[Q\gamma_w/4\pi kh]$ for saturated pervious half space

5.2 Practical Example

The typical values for the elastic coefficients and permeability used in the practical example of the saturated medium dense sand are listed in Table 2.

If the groundwater withdrawal can be regarded as a point sink and the pumping rate of constant strength $Q = 30\ l/s = 3\times10^{-2}\ m^3/s$, then it can have a long-term maximum horizontal displacement and settlement at the ground surface of $1.42\ cm$ and $4.68\ cm$, respectively. It is noticed from Eqs. (21a) and (21b) that the magnitude of long-term ground surface horizontal displacement and settlement are not directly dependent on the pumping depth h of the point sink.

Parameter	Symbol	Value	Units
Shear modulus	G	20×10^{6}	N/m^{2}
Poisson's ratio	ν	0.3	–
Permeability	k	1×10^{-5}	m/s
Unit weight of groundwater	γ_{w}	9,810	N/m^{3}

Table 2. Typical values of the elastic properties and the permeability of a saturated medium dense sand

6. Conclusions

Closed-form solutions of the transient consolidation due to pumping from pervious saturated elastic half space were obtained by using Laplace and Hankel transformations. The study investigated the vertical and horizontal displacements of the ground surface. It also addressed the excess pore water pressure of the porous elastic half space due to a point sink. The results show:

1. The maximum ground surface horizontal displacement is around 30% of the maximum surface settlement at $r/h \approx \sqrt{\phi} = 1.272$, where $\phi = \left(1+\sqrt{5}\right)/2 \approx 1.618$ is known as the golden ratio. It's interesting to find that the golden ratio ϕ also appears in the corresponding settlement of the poroelastic half space. The ground surface settlement at $r = \sqrt{\phi}h$ is around 61.8% of the maximum ground surface settlement.
2. From the average consolidation ratio U at $r/h = 0$, 1, 2, 5, and 10, it shows that U initially decreases rapidly, and then the rate of settlement reduces.
3. The magnitude of long-term maximum ground surface horizontal displacement and settlement are independent on the pumping depth h of the point sink.

7. Acknowledgements

This work is supported by the National Kaohsiung Marine University, the National Science Council of Republic of China through grant NSC97-2815-C-216-003-E, and also by the Chung Hua University under grant CHU97-2815-C-216-003-E.

8. References

Biot, M.A. (1941). General Theory of Three-dimensional Consolidation, *Journal of Applied Physics*, Vol. 12, No. 2, pp. 155-164.

Biot, M.A. (1955). Theory of Elasticity and Consolidation for a Porous Anisotropic Solid, *Journal of Applied Physics*, Vol. 26, No. 2, pp. 182-185.

Booker, J.R. & Carter, J.P. (1986*a*). Analysis of a Point Sink Embedded in a Porous Elastic Half Space, *International Journal for Numerical and Analytical Methods in Geomechanics*, Vol. 10, No. 2, pp. 137-150.

Booker, J.R. & Carter, J.P. (1986*b*). Long Term Subsidence Due to Fluid Extraction from a Saturated, Anisotropic, Elastic Soil Mass, *Quarterly Journal of Mechanics and Applied Mathematics*, Vol. 39, No. 1, pp. 85-97.

Booker, J.R. & Carter, J.P. (1987*a*). Elastic Consolidation Around a Point Sink Embedded in a Half-space with Anisotropic Permeability, *International Journal for Numerical and Analytical Methods in Geomechanics*, Vol. 11, No. 1, pp. 61-77.

Booker, J.R. & Carter, J.P. (1987*b*). Withdrawal of a Compressible Pore Fluid from a Point Sink in an Isotropic Elastic Half Space with Anisotropic Permeability, *International Journal of Solids and Structures*, Vol. 23, No. 3, pp. 369-385.

Chen, G.J. (2002). Analysis of Pumping in Multilayered and Poroelastic Half Space, *Computers and Geotechnics*, Vol. 30, No. 1, pp. 1-26.

Chen, G.J. (2005). Steady-state Solutions of Multilayered and Cross-anisotropic Poroelastic Half-space Due to a Point Sink, *International Journal of Geomechanics*, Vol. 5, No. 1, pp. 45-57.

Dunlap, R.A. (1997). *The Golden Ratio and Fibonacci Numbers*, World Scientific Publishing, Singapore, River Edge, N.J.

Erdelyi, A.; Magnus, W., Oberhettinger, F. & Tricomi, F.G. (1954). *Tables of Integral Transforms*, McGraw-Hill, New York.

Hou, C.-S.; Hu, J.-C., Shen, L.-C., Wang, J.-S., Chen, C.-L., Lai, T.-C., Huang, C., Yang, Y.-R., Chen, R.-F., Chen, Y.-G. & Angelier, J. (2005). Estimation of Subsidence Using GPS Measurements, and Related Hazard: the Pingtung Plain, Southwestern Taiwan, *Comptes Rendus Geoscience*, Vol. 337, No. 13, pp. 1184-1193.

Kanok-Nukulchai, W. & Chau, K.T. (1990). Point Sink Fundamental Solutions for Subsidence Prediction, *Journal of Engineering Mechanics*, Vol. 116, No. 5, pp. 1176-1182.

Livio, M. (2002). *The Golden Ratio: The Story of Phi, the World's Most Astonishing Number*, Broadway Books, New York.

Lu, J. C.-C. & Lin, F.-T. (2006). The Transient Ground Surface Displacements Due to a Point Sink/Heat Source in an Elastic Half-space, *Geotechnical Special Publication No. 148, ASCE*, pp. 210-218.

Lu, J. C.-C. & Lin, F.-T. (2008). Modelling of Consolidation Settlement Subjected to a Point Sink in an Isotropic Porous Elastic Half Space, *Proceedings of the 17th IASTED International Conference on Applied Simulation and Modelling*, Corfu, Greece, pp. 141-146.

Moorman, C.M. & Goff, J.E. (2007). Golden Ratio in a Coupled-oscillator Problem, *European Journal of Physics*, Vol. 28, pp. 897-902.

Poland, J.F. (1984). *Guidebook to Studies of Land Subsidence Due to Ground-water Withdrawal*, Unesco, Paris, France, 305 p.

Puri, P. & Jordan, P.M. (2006). On the Steady Shear Flow of a Dipolar Fluid in a Porous Half-Space, *International Journal of Engineering Science*, Vol. 44, pp. 227-240.

Sen, S.K. & Agarwal, R.P. (2008). Golden Ratio in Science, as Random Sequence Source, its Computation and Beyond, *Computers and Mathematics with Applications*, Vol. 56, pp. 469-498.

Sivaram, B. & Swamee, P.K. (1977). A Computational Method for Consolidation Coefficient, *Soils and Foundations*, Vol. 17, No. 2, pp. 48-52.
Sneddon, I.N. (1951). *Fourier Transforms*, McGraw-Hill, New York, pp. 48-70.
Tarn, J.-Q. & Lu, C.-C. (1991). Analysis of Subsidence Due to a Point Sink in an Anisotropic Porous Elastic Half Space, *International Journal for Numerical and Analytical Methods in Geomechanics*, Vol. 15, No. 8, pp. 573-592.

9. Notation of Symbols

c	Parameter, $c = k/n\beta\gamma_w$ (m^2/s)
$erf(x)/erfc(x)$	Error function/complementary error function (Dimensionless)
G	Shear modulus of the isotropic porous aquifer (Pa)
h	Pumping depth (m)
$I_\nu(x)$	Modified Bessel function of the first kind of order ν (Dimensionless)
$J_\nu(x)$	First kind of the Bessel function of order ν (Dimensionless)
k	Permeability of the isotropic porous aquifer (m/s)
n	Porosity of the porous aquifer (Dimensionless)
p	Excess pore fluid pressure (Pa)
$\tilde{p}$	Hankel and Laplace transforms of p, Eq. (12c)
Q	Pumping rate (m^3/s)
(r,θ,z)	Cylindrical coordinates system (m, $radian$, m)
s	Laplace transform parameter (s^{-1})
t	Time (s)
$u(t)$	Heaviside unit step function (Dimensionless)
u_r/u_z	Radial/axial displacement of the porous aquifer (m)
$u_{r\max}/u_{z\max}$	Maximum ground surface horizontal/vertical displacement of the porous aquifer (m)
$\tilde{u}_r/\tilde{u}_z$	Hankel and Laplace transforms of u_r/u_z, Eqs. (12a)-(12b)
β	Compressibility of groundwater (Pa^{-1})
γ_w	Unit weight of groundwater (N/m^3)
$\delta(x)$	Dirac delta function (m^{-1})
δ_{ij}	Kronecker delta (Dimensionless)
ε	Volume strain of the porous aquifer (Dimensionless)
ε_{ij}	Strain components of the porous aquifer (Dimensionless)
η	Parameter, $\eta = (1-\nu)/(1-2\nu)$ (Dimensionless)
ν	Poisson's ratio of the isotropic porous aquifer (Dimensionless)
ξ	Hankel transform parameter (m^{-1})
τ_{ij}	Total stress components of the porous aquifer (Pa)
ϕ	Golden ratio, $\phi = 1.618$ (Dimensionless)

3

Voronoi diagram: An adaptive spatial tessellation for processes simulation

Leila Hashemi Beni, Mir Abolfazl Mostafavi, Jacynthe Pouliot
Laval University
Canada

1. Introduction

Modelling and simulation of spatial processes is increasingly used for a wide variety of applications including water resources protection and management, meteorological prevision and forest fire monitoring. As an example, an accurate spatial modelling of a hydrological system can assist hydrologists to answer questions such as: "where does ground water come from?", "how does it travel through a complex geological system?" and "how is water pollution behaviour in an aquifer?" It also allows users and decision-makers to better understand, analyze and predict the groundwater behaviour.
In this chapter, we briefly present an overview of spatial modelling and simulating of a dynamic continuous process such as a fluid flow. Most of the research in this area is based on the numerical modelling and approximation of the dynamic behaviour of a fluid flow. Dynamic continuous process is typically described by a set of partial differential equations (PDE) and their numerical solution is carried out using a spatial tessellation that covers the domain of interest. An efficient solution of the PDE requires methods that are adaptive in both space and time. The existing numerical methods are applied in either a static manner from the Eulerian point of view, where the equations are solved using a fixed tessellation during a simulation process, or in a dynamic manner from the Lagrangian point of view, where the tessellation moves. Some methods are also based on the mixed Eulerian-Lagrangian point of view. However, our literature review reveals that, unfortunately, these methods are unable to efficiently handle the spatial-dynamic behaviour of phenomenon. Therefore, in this chapter, we investigate spatial tessellation based on Voronoi diagram (VD) and its dual Delaunay tessellation (DT) which is good candidate to deal with dynamics behaviour of fluid flow. Voronoi diagram is a topological data structure that discretizes the dynamic phenomenon to a tessellation adaptive in space and time.

2. Numerical modelling methods

In computational fluid dynamics, there are two fundamental approaches to simulate fluid flow: Eulerian and Lagrangian flow formulations (Price, 2005). The former is based on a fixed tessellation while the latter uses a moving tessellation. Eulerian methods offer the advantage of a fixed tessellation that is easier to generate, and they can efficiently handle dispersion dominated transport problems. Eulerian methods are therefore used for a majority of numerical modelling of fluids flow. However, in these methods, the time step size and the tessellation size have to be selected to ensure realistic solutions and avoid overshoot and undershoot of concentrations. However, since a uniformly fine tessellation is computationally costly, these methods are generally not well suited to handle of moving concentration fronts and advection-dominated and tracking problems.

Lagrangian methods model the processes by tracking the changing location, shape and values of particles over space and provide an accurate and efficient solution to advection-dominated problems with steep concentration gradients. For Lagrangian methods, the tessellation movement softens the solution behaviour in time, such that larger time steps can be taken compared to a fixed spatial tessellation (Whitehurst, 1995). However, the connectivity between tessellation elements remains unchanged during simulation, which may cause difficulties such as tessellation tangling and deformation that become especially acute in non-uniform media with multiple sources and complex boundary conditions (Neuman 1984)]. In addition, due to the relative nodal motion, the tessellation used for Lagrangian methods becomes distorted over time and complete re-tessellating is frequently required (Malcevic, 2002).

Development of mixed Eulerian-Lagrangian methods has led to the class of arbitrary Lagrangian-Eulerian (ALE) codes (Whitehurst, 1995). These codes reduce tessellation distortion by continuous "remapping" or "reconnecting" of the mesh. Tessellation remapping can be regarded as an Eulerian process, because mass is transported across tessellation cell boundaries. The principle of continual remapping led to the Free- Lagrange method. The difference between the Free-Lagrange and the classical Lagrange methods is that the latter attempt to maintain the initial tessellation connectivity during simulation. The Free-Lagrange method allows updating the tessellation connectivity as part of the problem to be solved. Simulation of free-surface flow and variable-density flow and transport are two examples that are well-suited for dynamic modelling. For example, for a hydrogeological system, the free surface or water table is an imaginary surface below ground where the absolute groundwater pressure is atmospheric. The water table moves and dynamic modelling could be used to track its temporal and spatial evolution by using a moving tessellation that conforms to the motion of the free surface. One complexity of using a moving tessellation is to maintain the tessellation alignment with stratigraphic layers or with geological formations having different hydraulic properties. The tessellation alignment can be maintained by continuously updating physical parameters, such as hydraulic conductivity, porosity, storage coefficient, as the tessellation moves.

Density-variable flow and transport is another application well-suited for a moving tessellation. A classical example is given by salt-rock formations, where groundwater may become very rich in salt. Zegeling et al. (1992) applied a moving tessellation to simulate 1D brine transport in porous media. They used a dynamic Lagrangian approach to track the sharp fresh-salt water interface and state that, when high concentrations prevail, fixed tessellation methods are inefficient. Moving tessellations have not been efficiently used in 3D since three-dimensionality adds several complexities for simulations. To minimize the problems, the Lagrangian algorithm presented by Knupp (1996) only moves the upper part of the tessellation and movement is restricted to the vertical direction to avoid tessellation deformation.

To solve the tessellation deformation problem and also to avoid the problems involving fixed time-step methods, we propose a new 3D Free-Lagrangian method based on dynamic 3D Voronoi diagram. Voronoi diagram (VD) and its dual, Delaunay triangulation (DT), have been shown to provide an adequate discretization of the space for fluid flow simulation, ensuring that physically realistic results are obtained. The next section describes the Voronoi and Delaunay tessellation with a brief review of their definitions, structures and relevant spatial properties in the context of spatial modelling and simulation of continuous processes.

3. Voronoi and Delaunay tessellation

Fluid flow is continuous and it is practically impossible to measure it anywhere and anytime. Therefore, this continuous phenomenon must be represented using a set of observations in given locations and time which are usually a set of unconnected points. Each point is defined by its position in 2D or 3D space and its attribute at a given time. Voronoi tessellation for this finite set of points is a division of the simulation space based on nearest neighbor rule where every location in the space is assigned to the closet member in the point set. Formally, let S be a set of points in the *d*-dimensional Euclidean space, the Voronoi tessellation of S associates to each point $p \in S$ a Voronoi cell (element) $V(p)$ such that (Okabe et al. 2000, Edelsbrunner 2001):

$$V(p) = \left\{x \in R^d \| x - p\| \leq \|x - q\|, \forall q \in S\right\} \quad (1)$$

where $\|x - p\|$ denotes the Euclidean distance between points x, p. Therefore, a Voronoi element is defined as the set of points $x \in R^d$ that are at least as close to p as to any other point in S. Therefore, a Voronoi tessellation of S is the collection of all Voronoi elements (Okabe et al. 2000):

$$v = \{\mathrm{V(p)}, \ldots, \mathrm{V(q)}\} \quad (2)$$

Voronoi tessellation v covers the domain of interest due to the fact that each point $x \in R^d$ has at least one nearest point in S and it, thus, lies in at least one Voronoi cell.

Fig. 1 shows an example of a Voronoi tessellation in 2D and 3D which is a polygonal subdivision of a space consisting of vertices, edges, polygonal faces and cells.

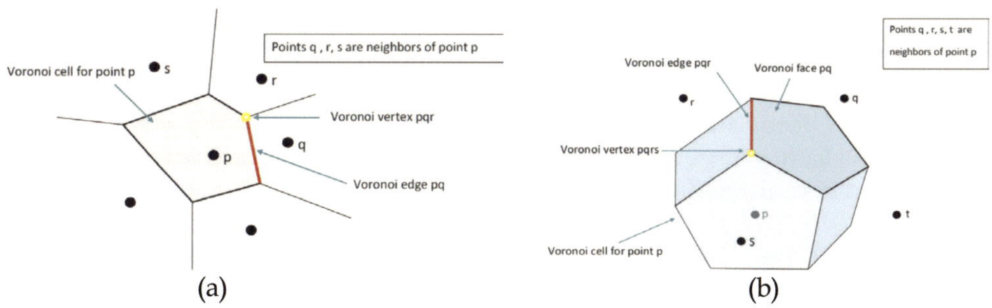

Fig. 1. An example of a Voronoi tessellation a) in 2D, b) in 3D and its components

A Delaunay tessellation $DT(S)$ is a collection of d-dimensional simplexes where a simplex is the convex hull of a set of (d + 1) points and no point in S is inside the circum-ball of any other simplex in $DT(S)$ (okabe et. al 2000, Edelsbrunner 2001). A simplex is the convex hull of a set of (d + 1) points. For example, a 0D simplex is a point, a 1D simplex is a line segment, a 2D simplex is a triangle, and a 3D simplex is a tetrahedron (fig. 2).

(a) (b) (c) (d)

Fig. 2. Simplex in a) 0D, b) 1D, c) 2D and d) 3D

$DT(S)$ is unique, if S is a set of points in general position. This means no (d + 1) points are on the same hyperplane and no (d + 2) points are on the same ball. Therefore, a 2D Delaunay tessellation or *Delaunay triangulation* is a non-overlapping triangular subdivision of the space where each triangle has an empty circumcircle. The triangulation is unique, if no three (or more) points are collinear and no four (or more) points are on the same circumcircle. Similarity, a 3D Delaunay tessellation or Delaunay tetrahedralization is a non-overlapping tetrahedral subdivision of the space where each tetrahedron has an empty circumsphere. The tetrahedralization is unique, if no four (or more) points are coplanar and no five (or more) points are on the same circumsphere. Fig. 3 illustrates a 2D Delaunay triangulation and its components such as vertices, edges, triangles (elements).

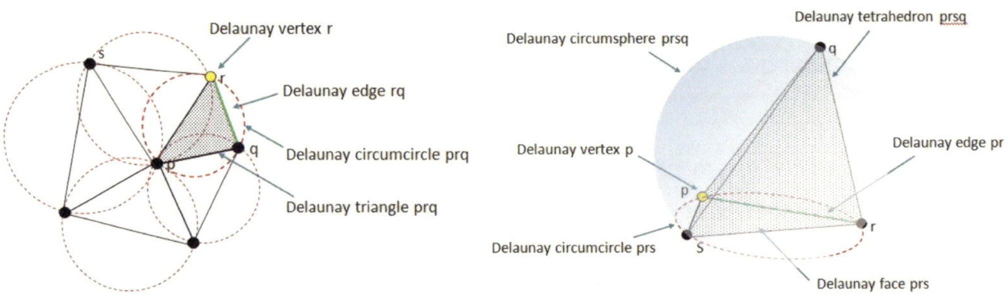

(a) (b)

Fig. 3. Delaunay tessellation a) in 2D and b) in 3D space and its components

3.1 Properties of Voronoi and Delaunay tessellations

Voronoi and Delaunay tessellations have several interesting properties that make them attractive for numerical simulation methods:

Duality between DT and VD: There is a connection between the Delaunay and the Voronoi tessellations called duality. The duality means that VD and DT are closely related graphs. The duality between VD and DT is based on some specific correspondences between geometric elements of the two data structures. This allows extracting the Voronoi tessellation from the Delaunay tessellation and vice versa. For a set of S points in a d-dimensional space, Delaunay tessellation can be obtained by joining all of pairs of points in

S whose Voronoi cells share a common (d-1) Voronoi facet. In addition, a k-dimensional face of d-dimensional Voronoi tessellation corresponds to a (d − k) dimensional face in the Delaunay tessellation.
In 2D, each Delaunay triangle corresponds to a Voronoi vertex (fig. 4a), each Delaunay edge corresponds to a Voronoi edge (fig. 4b), and a Delaunay vertex corresponds to a Voronoi cell (fig. 4c) and vice versa.

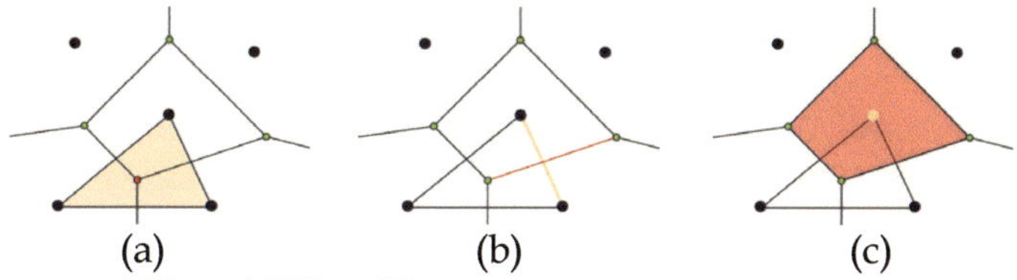

Fig. 4. Duality between VD and DT in 2D

Similarity, in a 3D space, each Delaunay tetrahedron corresponds to a Voronoi vertex (fig. 5a), each Delaunay triangular face becomes an edge (fig. 5b), a Delaunay edge corresponds to a Voronoi face (fig. 5c), and finally, each Delaunay vertex corresponds Voronoi polyhedron (fig. 5d) and vice versa.

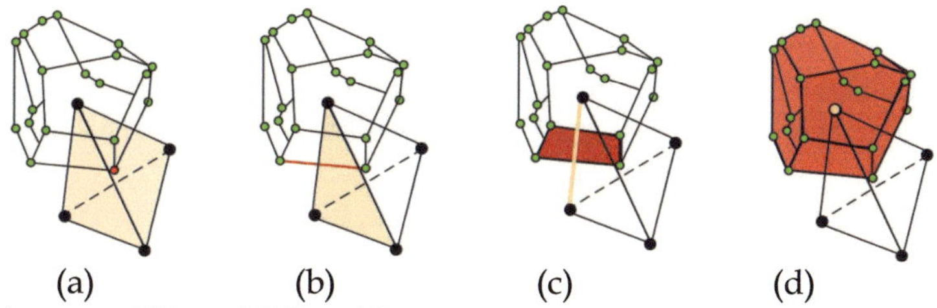

Fig. 5. Duality between VD and DT in 3D

It is technically easier to tessellate a simulation domain using tetrahedra than arbitrary polyhedral (VD) where each tetrahedron has a constant number of vertices and adjacent elements (Icking et al. 2003). Therefore, using the duality between two data structures, the Voronoi tessellation can be easily obtained by connecting the circumsphere centers from the Delaunay tetrahedra. This property is very important in the simulation of fluid flow where the representation of the continuous phenomenon from the discrete samples (point objects) is required. Therefore, DT can adequately represent the discrete samples and their relationship while, VD can be used for representing the variation of the fluid properties across this data i.e. numerical integrating of PDEs.

Maximum-Minimum angle: Another interesting property of Delaunay tessellation in 2D is that it maximizes the minimum angle among all triangulations of a given set of points (Lawson 1977). This property is important, because it implies that Delaunay triangulation tends to avoid skinny triangles. This is useful for many applications where triangles are used for the purposes of interpolation of flow values. However, this property is valid in only 2D space and it does not generalize to three dimensions where tetrahedra with four almost coplanar vertices can be found. These tetrahedra are usually referred to as slivers and have a very small volume (almost zero).

Empty sphere: A sphere circumscribing any simplex in the Delaunay tessellation does not contain any other points in S in its interior. For example, for 3D simplex *pqrs* in fig. 3b, there is an empty circumsphere passing through three points p, q,r and s. The center of this sphere is a vertex of the Voronoi tessellation between these points, because this vertex is equidistant from each of these sites and there is no other closer point. This property offers a more adequate discretization among all arbitrary triangular tessellation of the space. In addition, it is frequently used to choose the best place to insert new points within the poor quality elements in refinement methods (please see Shewchuk, 1997).

Nearest-neighbor property: If point q is the nearest-neighbor of point p in S, their associated Voronoi cells are adjacent cells in the tessellation and share a face (Boissonnat and Yvinec 1998). Since, according to the empty sphere criterion, the circle having these two points as its diameter cannot contain any other points. This property satisfies an important requirement in numerical simulation of a fluid flow: the connectivity between the tessellation elements (topology). Because, in the numerical modeling methods, motion equations (PDEs) are solved using a given tessellation elements and their neighbors. Therefore, the relationship between the elements of the tessellation (topological information) must be defined. Based on the nearest-neighbor property the adjacency relationship between tessellation elements (topological relations) is readily defined among the Voronoi cells.

Local optimality: As mentioned previously, a Delaunay tessellation means a collection of d-dimensional simplexes which subdivide the convex hull of S in such a way that the union of all the simplexes covers the convex hull and every (d-1)-facet of the simplexes is locally Delaunay. For example in 2D, a triangulation is Delaunay if and only if its edges are locally Delaunay i.e. there is an empty circle passing through the endpoints of each edge (empty circle property). Therefore, local editing of all of non-Delaunay (d-1)-facet (edges in 2D and faces in 3D) in a tessellation (local optimality) results in a Delaunay tessellation (global optimality) (Devillers 2002). Based on this interesting property, some local topological operations, *bistellar flips*, were developed (Joe 1991, Shewchuk 2005). These operations modify the configuration of adjacent elements to satisfy the Delaunay criterion (i.e. empty circumcircle test in 2D or circumsphere test in 3D). For example, in 2D, a *flip22* convert two neighboring triangles *pqr* and *rtp* to two triangles *pqt* and *qrt* by changing the diagonal of quadrilateral formed by four points p , q , r , t (fig. 6).

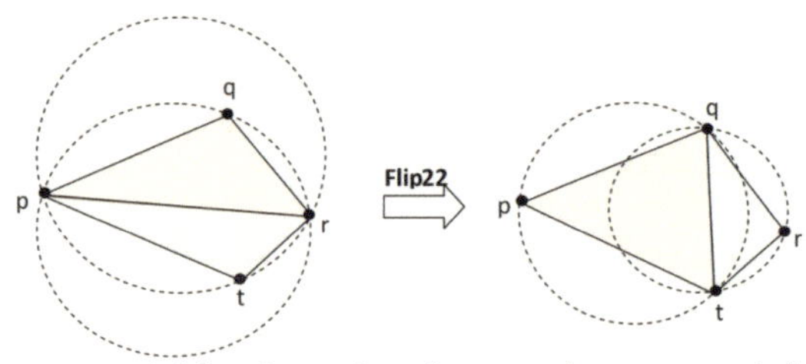

Fig. 6. A flip22 converts two neighboring triangles to other two neighboring triangles

Flip14, flip41, flip32, flip23 are examples of local topological operations in 3D (Shewchuk 1997). As fig. 7a illustrates, a *flip14* replaces tetrahedron *pqrt* with four tetrahedra *pqst, qrst, srpt, pqrs* by connecting the point s to the vertices of the tetrahedron (*p,q,r,t*) and a *flip 41* converts inverse problem. The *flip41* and *flip14* have the effect of inserting or deleting a new point (*s*) in a tetrahedron, respectively (Shewchuk 1997). A *flip23* or face-to-edge flip operator converts two neighboring tetrahedra (tetrahedra *pqrs, qprt* in fig. 7b) to three tetrahedra (tetrahedra *pqts, ptrs, rqts*) and a *flip32* or edge-to-face *flip* operator converts three neighboring tetrahedra to two with respect to the Delaunay criterion.

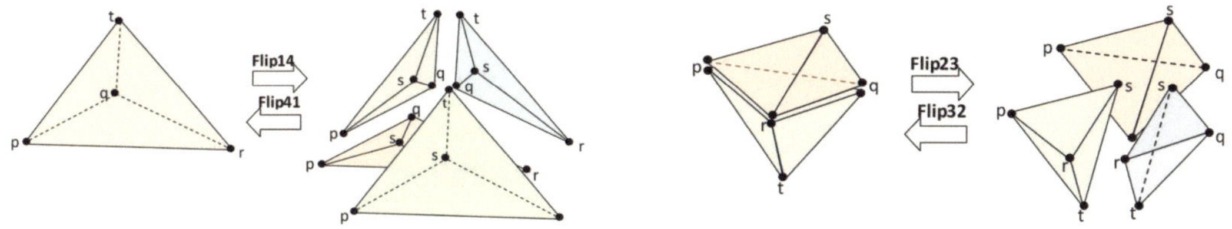

(a) (b)

Fig. 7. a) Flip14 and flip41, b) flip 23 and flip 32

The duality between VD and DT, clear definition of spatial relations between tessellation elements, the adaptability of these geometrical data structures for the representation of complex phenomena, and finally their dynamic and interactive properties make them very interesting for the simulaion and representation of fluid flow. Voronoi diagram (VD) and Delaunay tessellation thorough theses useful properties provide an adequate discretization of the space for both Eulerian and Lagrangian fluid flow simulation approaches, ensuring that physically realistic results are obtained from the numerical integration of the PDE.

4. Eulerian methods and Voronoi tessellation

A tessellationbased on a dynamic Voronoi diagram is an interesting alternative for Eulerian methods. Voronoi cells can be defined by points with an arbitrary distribution, creating tessellationelements of different sizes and shapes which can adapt to complex geometries. For instant, for regions with either high rates of flow or discontinuities, the Voronoi diagram can provide a fine resolution mesh. Each cell can have an arbitrary number of neighbors which their connectivity with the given cell is clearly defined and can be explicitly retrieved if needed. In addition, dynamic Voronoi diagram offers the local editing and manipulating possibility of the tessellationwhich is usually necessary for the refining of the tessellationwithout having to rebuild the whole mesh. Regarding these properties, several research works used VD and DT as underlying tessellationin fluid flow simulation. Hale (2002) applied DT and VD to reservoir simulations using 3D seismic images and demonstrated the potential of both DT and VD for flow simulation during all steps of seismic interpretation, fault framework building, and reservoir modeling. Lardin (1999) and Blessent et al. (2008) applied this data structure to groundwater simulation in 3D space and showed that VDs are well-adapted to the Control Volume Finite Element (CVFE) method. The CVFE methods are based on the principle of mass conservation. Thus, a volume of influence is assigned to each point or element and equations are defined to describe the interaction of the element with its neighbors. This interaction is expressed by mass balance, which states that the difference between inflow and outflow in each element must be equal to the variation in fluid stored in the same volume (Therrien et al. 2006). Fig.8 shows the examples of Voronoi elements in 2D and 3D.

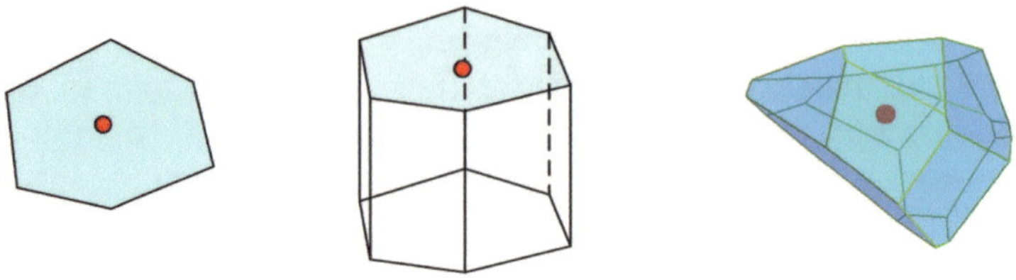
(a) (b) (c)

Fig. 8. Examples of Voronoi elements in 2D (a) and 3D (b),(c).

5. Free-Lagrangian methods and Voronoi tessellation

A Lagrangian method are often the most efficient way to simulate a fluid flow, as the tessellationmoves and conforms to the complexity of geometries (Price, 2005). However, a main problem of these methods is related to determining the optimal time interval. For example, a large time-step causes problems such as overshoots and undetected collisions and, as a result, we may observe some abnormal behavior in the simulation results. For a small time-step, an extensive computation effort will be required to check for changes at time when none occurred. Another problem with Free-Lagrangian methods lies on maintaining and processing of the connectivity relations between tessellationelements at each time. To solve these problems, a kinetic data structure can be helpful which is based on the fact that "variation in space with time may be modeled not by snap-shots of the whole map at regular time intervals, but by local updates of spatial model at the time when they happen (event)" (Gold 1993). In a fluid flow simulation, these events can be the changes either on the field value or on the spatial relationship of the points which refer to as trajectory event and topological event respectively (Roos, 1997; Gavrilova and Rokne, 2003). Trajectory events are related to the physical problem description and defined by the governing equations (PDEs), while topological events can properly be detected and updated by a kinetic Voronoi and Delaunay data structures as explained in follows.

Point movement may change the adjacency relationships of the point and its neighbors. Then, this displacement changes the configuration of the triangle/tetrahedra having the moving point as one of their vertexes. In a DT, a topological event occurs when a point (p) moves in or out of the circle/sphere of a triangle/tetrahedron. Therefore, to find the topological event of a moving point, only the spatial information of the triangles/tetrahedra having the moving point as one of their vertexes and their neighbors are used and the remaining triangles/tetrahedra in the tessellation do not need to be tested. This can be computed using well-known predicted test (Guibas and Stolfi, 1985) to preserve the Delaunay empty circumcircle/circumsphere criterion. Since in a kinetic data structure, the position of points are time dependent, then, the value of the determinant will be time dependent as well. However, the cost of generating, computing and updating the predicate function is very expensive, especially when dealing with simultaneous moving of the points on complex trajectories as seen in a physical system. For example, a quadratic trajectory of a point in a 3D space results in a degree eight predicate function. As described in Guibas and Russel (2004), the computational cost can be reduced by minimizing the degree of the predicate function. To minimize the degree of the function, we assume that only one point is allowed to move at a time on a linear trajectory. Therefore, one row of the predicate determinant must be allowed to vary linearly. Equation 1 shows the predicted function for a moving point in 3D Delaunay triangulation. According to this equation, a topological event for point p occurs when p moves in or moves out of the circumsphere of the tetrahedron, i.e. the value of the predicate function is 0.

$$\begin{vmatrix} p_x(t) & p_y(t) & p_z(t) & p_x^2(t)+p_y^2(t)+p_z^2(t) & 1 \\ a_x & a_y & a_z & a_x^2+a_y^2+a_z^2 & 1 \\ b_x & b_y & b_z & b_x^2+b_y^2+b_z^2 & 1 \\ c_x & c_y & c_z & c_x^2+c_y^2+c_z^2 & 1 \\ d_x & d_y & d_z & d_x^2+d_y^2+d_z^2 & 1 \end{vmatrix} = 0 \quad (4)$$

Mostafavi and Gold (2003) have implemented a similar algorithm on the plan that minimizes the number of triangles which must be tested to detect the closest topological event of a moving point using a simple geometrical test. To do so, the algorithm computes the intersection between the trajectory of moving point p (a line segment) and some of the neighboring circumcircles cut the trajectory between the origin and the destination of the moving point. In fact, the triangles that the orthogonal projection of their circumcenter on the trajectory of p are behind the point p, with respect to the moving direction, are not considered. Then, every topological event which is the distance required for the moving point to cut the first circle on its trajectory is computed. Ledoux (2006) extended this algorithm to 3D for managing one moving point in 3D tessellation. However, there is a large number of moving points and topological events in a deforming kinetic spatial tessellation which must be managed in order to preserve the validity of the 3D tessellation. The sequence of the management of these events has an important impact on the simulation results.

The topological events of all the moving points in the tessellation can be managed simultaneously using a priority queue data structure, where the moving points are organized with respect to their priority. This priority is defined based on the value of the simulation time ($t_{simulation}$) for each moving point. The simulation time is the total time that takes for each point to reach from its origin to its new location on the trajectory. Therefore, first, all the topological events of the moving points are computed. Next, the time taken for each point to reach its closest topological event t_{event} is obtained. This time depends on the velocity (v) of the moving point and the distance (d) between its current position and the location of its next closest topological event on its trajectory. We define the local time (t_{local}) as the time that it takes for each point to move from its origin to its current position. The relation between these times is:

$$t_{simulation} = t_{local} + t_{event} \quad (5)$$

To facilitate the management of the topological events, we used a priority queues data structure by organizing the moving points based on the increasing value of $t_{simulation}$. Therefore, the first member of the queue which has the smallest simulation time is processed first i.e. the moving point is moved to its new location and a local update is carried out for in the tessellation for the moving point and its neighbors.

Following the topological changes in the tessellation, we need to update the physical parameters of the affected points. In a fluid flow simulation, the governing equation that defines the nature of the dynamic fluid, allows to compute the new physical parameters, such as the velocity, for each moving point and its neighbors. This means that is updated after each topological event for the points involved in this operation. As a result, the priorities of some of the moving points may change. This occurs because, when a point moves, the related circumcircle/circumspheres and event times of the neighboring points change. The above process is reiterated until the end of the simulation process.

6. Conclusions

In this chapter we discussed simulation of a dynamic process , a fluid flow in particular, that is a difficult task for the exsisting data structures which are 2D and static. A Voronoi data structure, as an alternative, can generate a tessellationthat accurately represents the geometrical, topological information of a fluid flow as well as its dynamic behavior in both static and dynamic manner. In the static or Eulerian methods, the structure assigns a volume of influence to each point and flow is assumed to be a transfer of fluid between these elements. Therefore, the change of fluid flow for each element is difference between inflow and outflow in it at a series of snapshots. In the dynamic or Lagrangian methods, data structure assigns a fixed mass of the fluid to each point. Therefore, tessellationmoves as fluid flow progress. The kinetic Voronoi diagram is also very well-adapted to free-Lagrangian tessellationas it can properly update the topology, connectivity, and physical parameters of the tessellationelements when they change.
This chapter is a part of an ongoing research work that proposes a kinetic data structure for the simulation of 3D dynamic contionus process in spatial context. In the research work, different issues regarding the development, implementation and application of such a data structure for the 3D simulation of fluid flow in hydrodynamics using Voronoi diagram have been studied.

Acknowledgments

The authors would like to acknowledge funding from NSERC and the GEOIDE Network under the GeoTopo3D project.

7. References

Blessent, D.; Hashemi, L.; Therrien, R. (2008). 3D modeling for hyrogeological simulations in fractured geological media, In: *Proceeding of Int. Conference on Modelling and Simulation.*

Boissonnat, J.D.; Yvinec, M. (1998). Algorithmic Geometry, *Cambridge University Press,* New York, NY.

Devillers, O., (2002). The Delaunay hierarchy, *International Journal of Foundations of Computer Science,* 13(2), pp. 163–180.

Edelsbrunner, H. (2001). Geometry and topology for mesh generation, *Cambridge University Press,* Cambridge, 190 pp.

Gold, C.M., and Condal, A.R. (1995). A spatial data structure integrating GIS and simulation in a marine environment, *Marine Geodesy,* 18, pp. 213–228.

Gold, C.M. (1993). An outline of an event-driven spatial data structure for managing time varying maps, *In: Proceeding: Canadian conference on GIS*, pp.880-888.

Guibas, LJ., and Russel, D. (2004). An empirical comparison of techniques for updating Delaunay triangulations, *Symposium on Computational Geometry*, pp.170-179.

Guibas, L.J., Stolfi, J. (1985). Primitives for the manipulation of general subdivisions and the computation of Voronoi diagrams, *ACM Transactions on Graphics*, 4, 74–123.

Hale, D. (2002). Atomic meshes: from seismic imaging to reservoir simulation, *In: Proceedings of the 8th European Conference on the Mathematics of Oil Recovery.*

Hashemi, L., and Mostafavi, M.A. (2008). A kinetic spatial data structure in support of a 3D Free Lagrangian hydrodynamics algorithm, *In: Proceeding of Int. Conference on Applied Modeling and Simulation.*

Icking, C.; Klein, R.; Köllner, P.; Ma, L. (2003). Java applets for the dynamic visualization of Voronoi diagrams, in: *Lecture Notes in Computer Science*, pp. 191 - 205.

Joe, B. (1991). Construction of three-dimensional Delaunay triangulations using local transformations, *Computer Aided Geometric Design*, 8(2), pp. 123-142.

Knupp, P.(1996). A moving mesh algorithm for 3D regional groundwater flow with water table and seepage face, *International Journal for Numerical Methods in Fluids* 19(2), pp. 83-95.

Lawson, C.L.(1977), Software for C1 Surface Interpolation, in: Rive, J. (Ed.) *Mathematical Software III*, Academic Press, New York, pp. 161-194.

Ledoux, H. (2006). Modelling Three-dimensional Fields in Geosciences with the Voronoi Diagram and its Dual, *Ph.D. thesis*, University of Glamorgan.

Malcevic, O. G. (2002). Dynamic-mesh finite element method for Lagrangian computational fluid dynamics, *Advances in Water Resources* 38, pp. 965-982.

Mostafavi, M.A. (2002). Development of a global dynamic data structure, *PhD thesis*, university of Laval, Canada.

Mostafavi, M.A., and Gold, C. M. (2004). A Global Spatial Data Structure for Marine Simulation, *Intl J Geographical Information Science*, 18, pp. 211-227.

Neuman, S.P., (1984). Adaptive Eulerian-Lagrangian finite element method for advection-dispersion, International Journal for Numerical Methods in Engineering, 20, pp. 321-337.

Okabe, A.; Boots, B.; Sugihara, K. and Chiu, S.N. (2000). Spatial tessellations: concepts and applications of Voronoi Diagrams, *John Wiley & Sons*, Chichester, West Sussex, England.

Price, J.F., (2005). Lagrangian and Eulerian representations of fluid flow: Part I, kinematics and the equations of Motion.

Roos, T. (1997). New upper bounds on Voronoi diagrams of moving points, *Nordic J Computing*, 4, pp. 167-171.

Shewchuk, R. (1997). Delaunay refinement mesh generation, PhD Thesis, Carnegie Mellon University.

Shewchuk, R. (2005). Star splaying: an algorithm for repairing Delaunay triangulation and convexhulls, In: *Proceeding of the Twenty-First Annual ACM symposium on Computational Geometry*, ACM Press New York, pp.237-246.

Therrien, R.; McLaren, R.G.; Sudicky, E.A.; Panday, S.M. (2006). HydroSphere: A three-dimensional numerical model describing fully-integrated subsurface and surface Flow and solute Transport, *User's manual.*

Whitehurst, R. (1995). A Free-lagrangian method for gas dynamics, *Mon. Not. R. Astron. Soc. 277*, pp. 655-680.

Zegeling, A.; Verwer, J.G. and Eijkeren, J.C.H. (1992). Application of a moving grid method to a class of 1D brine transport problems in porous media, *International Journal for Numerical Methods in Fluids*, 15, pp. 175-191.

FUZZY MODEL BASED FAULT DETECTION IN WASTE-WATER TREATMENT PLANT

Skrjanc I.
Faculty of Electrical Engineering
University of Ljubljana
Tržaška 25, 1000 Ljubljana
SLOVENIA
Tel.: +38614768311, Fax: +38614264631
Email: igor.skrjanc@fe.uni-lj.si

Abstract: In this paper monitoring and sensor fault detection of waste-water treatment benchmark is discussed. The monitoring is based on the fuzzy model of the plant which is obtained by the use of Gustafson-Kessel fuzzy clustering algorithm. The main idea in the case of process monitoring by the use of fuzzy modeling is to cope with the non-linearity which is inherent for the plants of this type. We are comparing the fuzzy model response of the normal operation regime with the current behavior. The data which are treated here are obtained by the simulation model of the waste-water treatment plant and also the sensor faults are simulated. The signals which have to be measured in the case of the monitoring are the following: influent ammonia concentration, dissolved oxygen concentration in the first aerobic reactor tank, temperature, dissolved oxygen concentration and the ammonia concentration in the second aerobic reactor. The results of the plant monitoring and fault detection based on fuzzy model are shown and discussed.

Key-Words: fuzzy clustering, fuzzy modelling, waste-water treatment plant, process monitoring, fault detection

1. Introduction

Process monitoring including fault detection and diagnosis based on multivariate statistical process control has been rapidly developed in recent years. Model based techniques, expert systems and pattern recognition have been widely used for fault detection Chen and Liao (2002). The appearance of a range of new sensors and data gathering equipments has enabled data to be collected with greater frequency from most chemical processes. Many statistical techniques for extracting process information from massive data and interpreting them have been developed in various field Johnson and Wichern (1992); Daszykowski et al. (2003). We are dealing with sensor faults detection in the simulated waste-water treatment benchmark Vrečko (2001; 2002); Hvala (2002). These types of plants are due to their nature subjected to daily, weekly and seasonal variation because of the temperature change, rain and varying process load. The theoretical modeling is in the case of waste-water treatment plant is a really demanding task with questionable results. Therefore, the methods of data mining are adopted for statistical proces monitoring. The process of waste-water treatment is highly nonlinear and needs to be treated in a nonlinear way. In our case we have applied a fuzzy clustering algorithm to preprocess the data. The false alarms due to the nonlinear behavior of the plant are avoided (if compared to the linear methods of detection which are generally used) by the use of fuzzy model which enables universal approximation of nonlinearities.

1.1 Fuzzy model based on Gustafson-Kessel clustering

In this section the methods and algorithms applied to the analysis of the data will be presented. The Gustafson-Kessel fuzzy clustering algorithm will be explained and the Takagi-Sugeno fuzzy model for waste-water treatment plant will be constructed and identified. The use of Gustafson-Kessel clustering algorithm introduce the possibility of defining the clusters of different shape, which is the true in the case of the data from waste-water treatment plant.

1.1.1 Gustafson-Kessel fuzzy clustering

The input data matrix is then given as

$$X \in \mathbb{R}^{n \times p} \tag{1}$$

The input data vector in the time instant k is defined as

$$x_k = \left[x_{k1}, \ldots, x_{kp}\right], \; x_k \in \mathbb{R}^p \tag{2}$$

The set of n observations is denoted as

$$X = \{x_k \mid k = 1,2,\ldots,n\} \tag{3}$$

and is represented as $n \times p$ matrix:

$$X = \begin{bmatrix} x_{11} & x_{12} & \cdots & x_{1p} \\ x_{21} & x_{22} & \cdots & x_{2p} \\ \vdots & \vdots & \vdots & \vdots \\ x_{n1} & x_{n2} & \cdots & x_{np} \end{bmatrix} \tag{4}$$

The main objective of clustering is to partition the data set X into c subsets, which are called clusters. The fuzzy partition of the set X is a family of fuzzy subsets $\{A_i \mid 1 \le i \le c\}$. The fuzzy subsets are defined by their membership functions, which are implicitly defined in the fuzzy partition matrix $U = [\mu_{ik}] \in \mathbb{R}^{c \times n}$. The i-th row of matrix U contains values of the membership function of the i-th fuzzy subset A_i of data set X. The partition matrix satisfies the following conditions: the membership degrees are real numbers from the interval $\mu_{ik} \in [0,1]$, $1 \le i \le c$, $1 \le k \le n$; the total membership of each s_k in all the clusters equals one $\sum_{i=1}^{c} \mu_{ik} = 1$, $1 \le k \le n$; none of the fuzzy clusters is empty nor it contains all the data $0 < \sum_{k=1}^{n} \mu_{ik} < n$, $1 \le i \le c$. This means that the fuzzy partition matrix U belongs to the fuzzy partition set which is defined as:

$$M = \{U \in \mathbb{R}^{c \times n} \mid \mu_{ik} \in [0,1], \forall i,k; \sum_{i=1}^{c} \mu_{ik} = 1, \forall k; 0 < \sum_{k=1}^{n} \mu_{ik} < n, \forall i\}. \tag{5}$$

In our application the fuzzy partition matrix is obtained by applying the fuzzy c-means algorithm based on the Mahalanobis distance norm. The algorithm is based on the minimization of the fuzzy c-means functional adjoined by the constraints from Eq. 5 given as:

$$J(X,U,V,\lambda) = \sum_{i=1}^{c}\sum_{k=1}^{n} \mu_{ik}^{m} d_{ik}^{2} + \lambda \sum_{i=1}^{c}\sum_{k=1}^{n} (\mu_{ik} - 1), \tag{6}$$

where U is the fuzzy partition matrix of X, the vector of cluster prototypes (centers)

$$V = [v_1, v_2, \ldots, v_c], \; v_i \in \mathbb{R}^p \tag{7}$$

which have to be determined, and

$$d_{ik}^{2} = (x_k - v_i)^T A_i (x_k - v_i)$$

is the inner-product distance norm, where

$$A_i = (\rho_i det(C_i))^{1/p} C_i^{-1}$$

where $\rho_i = 1, i = 1, ..., c$ and p is equal to the number of measured variables and where C_i is the fuzzy covariance matrix of the ith cluster defined by

$$C_i = \frac{\sum_{k=1}^{n} \mu_{ik}^{m} (x_k - v_i)(x_k - v_i)^T}{\sum_{k=1}^{n} \mu_{ik}^{m}}$$

This allows the detection of hyper-ellipsoidal clusters in the distribution of the data. If the data are distribution along the nonlinear hyper-surface, the algorithm will find the clusters that are local linear approximations of this hyper-surface. The cluster overlapping is defined by the parameter $m \in [1, \infty)$.

The number of clusters is defined by using the cluster validity measure or by iterative merging or insertion of the clusters. The overlapping factor or the fuzziness parameter m influences the fuzziness of the resulting partition; from the hard ($m = 1$) to the partition which is completely fuzzy ($m \to \infty$). In our approach the standard value $m = 2$ is used.

1.1.2 Gustafson-Kessel algorithm

For the given data set X, for the given number of clusters c, which can be defined iteratively, the chosen weighting exponent $m > 1$ and which is around 2 for our measured signals and the algorithm termination tolerance $\epsilon_{end} > 0$ and is defined as 0.001 the algorithm will be the following:

- **initialization**

  Initialization of fuzzy partition matrix: $U \in M$ (randomly). Initialization of epoch: $r = 0$.

- **repeat**

  $$r = r + 1$$

  computation of the cluster centers:

  $$v_i^{(r)} = \frac{\sum_{k=1}^{n} \left(\mu_{ik}^{(r)}\right)^m x_k}{\sum_{k=1}^{n} \left(\mu_{ik}^{(r)}\right)^m}, \; 1 \le i \le c. \tag{8}$$

computation of the cluster covariance matrices and inner-product distance norm :

$$C_i = \frac{\sum_{k=1}^{n} \mu_{ik}^{m} (x_k - v_i)(x_k - v_i)^T}{\sum_{k=1}^{n} \mu_{ik}^{m}}, \tag{9}$$

$$A_i = (\rho_i det(C_i))^{1/p} C_i^{-1}, 1 \leq i \leq c \tag{10}$$

computation of the distance from the cluster centers

$$d_{ik}^2 = \left(x_k - v_i^{(r)}\right)^T A_i \left(x_k - v_i^{(r)}\right), 1 \leq i \leq c, 1 \leq k \leq n \tag{11}$$

update of the partition matrix:

$$if\ d_{ik} > 0,\ \mu_{ik}^{(r)} = \frac{1}{\sum_{j=1}^{c} \left(\frac{d_{ik}}{d_{jk}}\right)^{\frac{2}{m-1}}} \tag{12}$$

- **until** $||U^{(r)} - U^{(r-1)}|| < \epsilon_{end}$

1.1.3 The fuzzy model in TS form

The fuzzy model, in Takagi-Sugeno (TS) form, approximates the nonlinear system by smoothly interpolating affine local models. Each local model contributes to the global model in a fuzzy subset of the space characterized by a membership function. We assume a set of input vectors

$$X = [x_1, x_2, \ldots, x_n]^T \tag{13}$$

and a set of corresponding outputs which is defined as

$$Y = [y_1, y_2, \ldots, y_n]^T \tag{14}$$

A typical fuzzy model is given in the form of rules

$$R_i : if\ x_k\ is\ A_i\ then\ \hat{y}_k = \phi_i(x_k),\ i = 1, \ldots, c \tag{15}$$

The vector x_k denotes the input or variables in premise, and the variable $\hat{y}_k$ is the output of the model at time instant k. The premise vector x_k is connected to one of the fuzzy sets $(A_1, \ldots, A_c)$ and each fuzzy set A_i $(i = 1, \ldots, c)$ is associated with a real-valued function $\mu_{A_i}(x_k)$ or $\mu_{ik} : \mathbb{R} \rightarrow [0, 1]$, that produces the membership grade of the variable x_k with respect to the fuzzy set A_i. The functions $\phi_i(\cdot)$ can be arbitrary smooth functions in general, although linear or affine functions are normally used.

The model output in Eq. (15) is now described in closed form as follows:

$$\hat{y}_k = \frac{\sum_{i=1}^{c} \mu_{ik} \phi_i(x_k)}{\sum_{i=1}^{c} \mu_{ik}} \tag{16}$$

To simplify Eq. (16), a partition of unity is considered where the functions $\beta_i(x_k)$, defined by

$$\beta_i(x_k) = \frac{\mu_{ik}}{\sum_{i=1}^{c} \mu_{ik}},\ i = 1, \ldots, c \tag{17}$$

give information about the fulfilment of the respective fuzzy rule in the normalized form. It is obvious that $\sum_{i=1}^{c} \beta_i(x_k) = 1$ irrespective of x_k as long as the denominator of $\beta_i(x_k)$ is not equal to zero (this can be easily prevented by stretching the membership functions over the whole potential area of x_k). Combining Eqs. (16) and (17) we arrive at the following equation:

$$\hat{y}_k = \sum_{i=1}^{c} \beta_i(x_k)\phi_i(x_k),\ k = 1,\ldots,n \tag{18}$$

Very often, the output value is defined as a linear combination of consequence states

$$\phi_i(x_k) = x_k\theta_i, \quad i = 1,\ldots,c,$$

$$\theta_i^T = \left[\theta_{i1},\ldots,\theta_{i(p+q)}\right] \tag{19}$$

The vector of fuzzified input variables at time instant k is written as

$$\psi_k = \left[\beta_1(x_k)x_k,\ldots,\beta_c(x_k)x_k\right],\ k = 1,\ldots,n \tag{20}$$

and then the fuzzified data matrix follows as:

$$\Psi^T = \left[\psi_1^T,\psi_2^T,\ldots,\psi_n^T\right] \tag{21}$$

If the matrix of the coefficients for the whole set of rules is written as

$$\Theta^T = \left[\theta_1^T,\ldots,\theta_c^T\right] \tag{22}$$

then Eq. (18) can be rewritten in the matrix form

$$\hat{y}_k = \psi_k\Theta \tag{23}$$

and the compact form which describes the relation from the whole set of data becomes

$$\hat{Y} = \Psi\Theta \tag{24}$$

where $\hat{Y}$ stands for the vector of model outputs $\hat{y}_k$ where $k = 1,\ldots,n$

$$\hat{Y} = \left[\hat{y}_1,\hat{y}_2,\ldots,\hat{y}_n\right]^T \tag{25}$$

The fuzzy model in the form given in Eq. (23) is referred to as the affine Takagi-Sugeno model and can be used to approximate any arbitrary function with any desired degree of accuracy Kosko (1994); Ying (1997); Wang and Mendel (1992). The generality can be proven with the Stone-Weierstrass theorem Goldberg (1976) which suggest that any continuous function can be approximated by a fuzzy basis function expansion Lin (1997).

1.1.4 Estimation of fuzzy model parameters

The estimation of the fuzzy model parameters will be done using the least square error approach. The measurements satisfy the nonlinear equation of the system

$$y_i = g(x_i), \quad i = 1, \ldots, n \tag{26}$$

According to the Stone-Weierstrass theorem , for any given real continuous function g on a compact set $U^c \subset \mathbb{R}^p$ and arbitrary $\delta > 0$, there exist a fuzzy system f such that

$$\max_{x_i \in X} |f(x_i) - g(x_i)| < \delta, \quad \forall i \tag{27}$$

This implies the approximation of any given real continuous function with a fuzzy function from class $\mathcal{F}^p$ defined in Eq. (23). However, it has to be pointed out that lower values of δ imply higher values of c that satisfy Eq. (27). In the case of the approximation, the error between the measured values and the fuzzy function outputs can be defined as

$$e_i = y_i - f(x_i) = y_i - \hat{y}_i, \; i = 1, ..., n \tag{28}$$

where y_i stands for the measured output and $\hat{y}_k$ for the model output at time instant k. To estimate the optimal parameters of the proposed fuzzy function (Θ) the minimization of the sum of square errors over the whole input set of data is performed as

$$E = \sum_{i=1}^{n} e_i^2 = (Y - \hat{Y})^T (Y - \hat{Y}) == (Y - \Psi\Theta)^T (Y - \Psi\Theta) \tag{29}$$

The parameter Θ is obtained as $\frac{\partial E}{\partial \Theta} = 0$ and becomes

$$\Theta = \left(\Psi^T \Psi\right)^{-1} \Psi^T Y$$

The idea of an approximation can be interpreted as the most representative fuzzy function to describe the domain of outputs Y as a function of inputs X. This problem can also be viewed as a problem of data reduction, which often appears in identification problems with large data sets.

2. Biological waste-water treatment process

Waste-water treatment plants are large nonlinear systems subject to large perturbations in flow and load, together with uncertainties concerning the composition of the incoming waste-water. The simulation benchmark has been developed to provide an unbiased system for comparing various strategies without reference to a particular facility. It consists of five sequentially connected reactors along with a 10-layer secondary settling tank. The plant layout, model equations and control strategy are described in detail on the www page (http://www.ensic.u-nancy.fr/costwwtp). In our approach the layout was formed where the waste-water is purified in the mechanical phase and after this phase the moving bed bio-film reactor is used. Schematic representation of simulation benchmark is shown in Fig. 1. The detection of sensor faults was applied to the simulation model where the following measurements were used to calculate the fuzzy clusters and fuzzy model: influent ammonia concentration in the inflow Q_{in} defined as $C_{NH4N_{in}}$, dissolved oxygen concentration in the first aerobic reactor tank $C_{O_2}^1$, dissolved oxygen concentration in the second aerobic reactor tank $C_{O_2}^2$ and

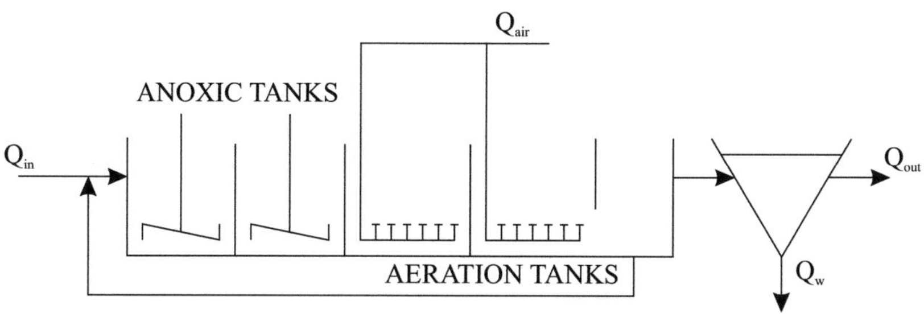

Fig. 1. Schematic representation of simulation benchmark.

the ammonia concentration in the second aerobic reactor tank $C_{NH4N_{out}}$. The fuzzy model was build to model the relation between the ammonia concentration in the second aerobic reactor tank and the other measured variables:

$$C_{NH4N_{out}}(k) = \mathcal{G}\left(C_{NH4N_{in}}(k), C_{O_2}^1(k), C_{O_2}^2(k)\right) \quad (30)$$

where $\mathcal{G}$ stands for nonlinear relation between measured variables. First 15000 measurements (sampling time $T_s = 120s$) were used to find the fuzzy clusters and to estimate the fuzzy model parameters. At the measurement 17000 the slowly increasing sensor fault occur, which is than at time 18000 eliminated. This means that sensor to measure the ammonia concentration in the second aerobic reactor tank $C_{NH4N_{out}}$ is faulty. The signal with exponentially increasing value was added to the nominal signal. The whole set of measurements is shown in Fig. 2. The

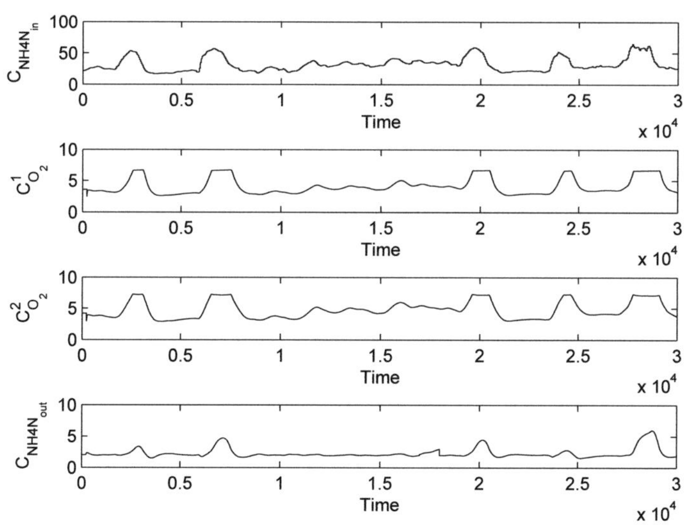

Fig. 2. The whole set of measurements. The influent ammonia concentration $C_{NH4N_{in}}$, dissolved oxygen concentration in the first aerobic reactor tank $C_{O_2}^1$, dissolved oxygen concentration in the second aerobic reactor tank $C_{O_2}^2$ and the ammonia concentration in the second aerobic reactor tank $C_{NH4N_{out}}$.

fuzzy model is obtained on the set of first 15000 samples. The fuzzy model output $\hat{C}_{NH4N_{out}}$ and the process output $C_{NH4N_{out}}$ are shown in Fig. 3. The fault detection index is defined as:

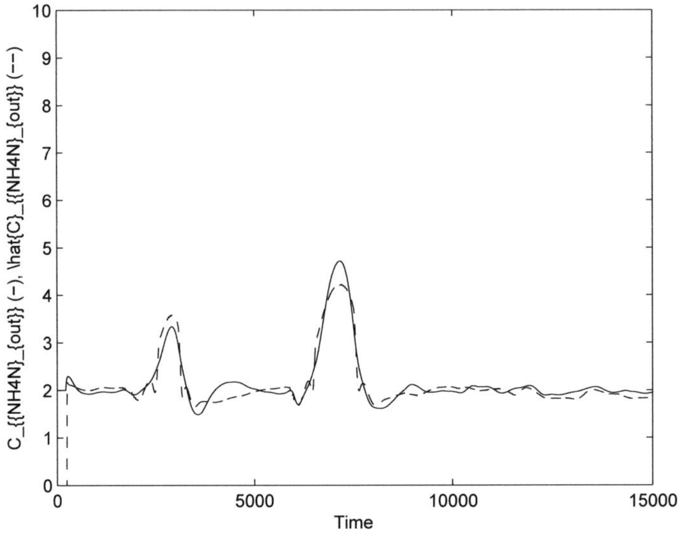

Fig. 3. The verification of fuzzy model where the fuzzy model output $\hat{C}_{NH4N_{out}}$ and the process output $C_{NH4N_{out}}$ are shown.

$$f = \left(\frac{C_{NH4N_{out}} - \hat{C}_{NH4N_{out}}}{\hat{C}_{NH4N_{out}}} \right)^2 \tag{31}$$

The fault tolerance index is defined as relative degree of maximal value of fault detection index in the identification or learning phase $f_{tol} = \gamma \max f$ where in our case $\gamma = 1.5$. This means that the fault detection index becomes ($f_{tol} = 0.15$). The fault which occur at the sample 17000 is detected at the sample 17556. The detection is delayed, but this is usual when the faults are slowly increasing.

3. Conclusion

In this paper the monitoring and detection of sensor faults in waste-water treatment benchmark is discussed. It is realized by the use of fuzzy model which is obtained by the use of Gustafson-Kessel fuzzy clustering algorithm. The detection of sensor fault was applied to the simulation model where the following measurements were used to calculate the fuzzy model: influent ammonia concentration, dissolved oxygen concentration in the first aerobic reactor tank, temperature, dissolved oxygen concentration and the ammonia concentration in the second aerobic reactor. The sensor fault on the sensor of the ammonia concentration in the second aerobic reactor has been detected without false alarms and with small time-delay because of the fault nature.

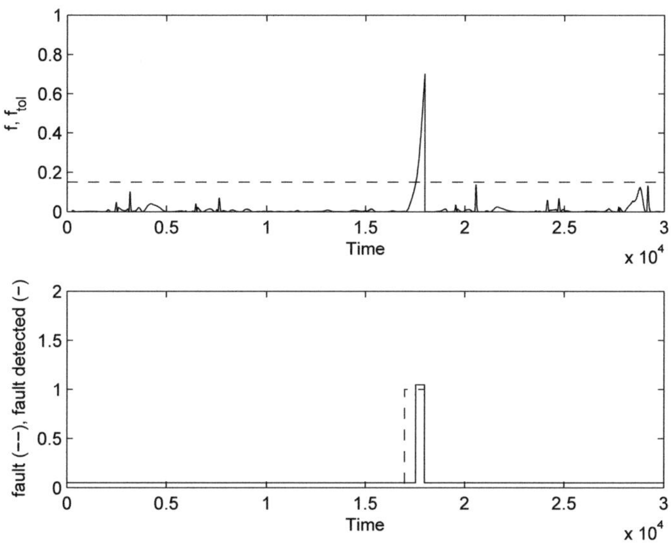

Fig. 4. The fault detection index, the fault tolerance index *f* and the actual and detected fault

4. References

Chen, J., Liao, C. M., "Dynamic process fault monitoring based on neural network and PCA". *Jour. of Process Control*, vol. 12, pp. 277-289, 2002.

Johnson, R. A., Wichern, D. W., *Applied Multivariate Statistical Analysis*, Prentice-Hall, New Jersey, 1992.

Daszykowski, M., Walczak, B., Massart, D. L., "Projection methods in chemistry". *Chemometrics and Intelligent Laboratory Systems*, vol. 65, pp. 97-112, 2003.

Kosko, B., "Fuzzy Systems as Universal Approximators", *IEEE Transactions on Computers*, vol. 43, no. 11, pp. 1329-1333, 1994.

Ying, H. GC., "Necessary conditions for some typical fuzzy systems as universal approximators", *Automatica*, vol. 33, pp. 1333-1338, 1997.

Wang, L.-X., Mendel, J. M., "Fuzzy basis functions, universal approximation, and orthogonal least-squares learning", *IEEE Trans. Neural Networks*, vol. 3, no. 5, pp. 807-814, 1992.

Goldberg, R. R., *Methods of Real Analysis*, John Wiley and Sons, 1976.

Lin, C-H., "Siso nonlinear system identification using a fuzzy-neural hybrid system", *Int. Jour. of Neural Systems*, vol. 8, no. 3, pp. 325-337, 1997.

Vrečko, D., Hvala, N., Kocijan, J., Zec, M. "System analysis for optimal control of a wastewater treatment benchmark". *Water sci. technol.*, vol. 43, pp. 199-206, 2001.

Vrečko, D., Hvala, N., Kocijan, J., "Wastewater treatment benchmark : What can be achieved with simple control?". *Water sci. technol.*, vol. 45, pp. 127-134, 2002.

Hvala, N., Vrečko, D., Burica, O., Stražar, M., Levstek, M., "Simulation study supporting wastewater treatment plant upgrading". *Water sci. technol.*, vol. 46, pp. 325-332, 2002.

5

An experimental parameter estimation approach for an on-line fault diagnosis system

C. Angeli
Department of Mathematics and Computer Science
Technological Education Institute of Piraeus
Konstantinoupoleos 38, N. Smirni
GR-171 21 Athens, Greece

1. Introduction

Electro-hydraulic systems are extensively used in applications of the automation technology from robotics and aerospace to heavy industrial systems and are becoming more complex in design and function. On-line diagnostic approaches for these systems have been considerably interesting for modern production technology as they play a significant role in maintenace of automation processes.

Modelling information involved in a diagnostic method is considered as a quite effective diagnostic technique and many approaches have been published for the automated industrial processes over the last years such as (Frank 1996, Gertler 1998, Zhou and Bennett 1998, Chen and Patton 1999, Patton, Frank and Clark 2000, Kinnaert 2003, Angeli 2008). Models that run in parallel to the dynamical industrial processes require parameter estimation methods that could respond effectively to time restriction situations.

Various parameter estimation methods have been applied for fault detection in dynamic systems including the use of system models linearized about operating points (Reza and Blakenship 1996), nonlinear parameter estimation (Marschner and Fischer 1997), least-square methods (Hjelmstad and Banan 1995), methods using observers (Drakunov, Law and Victor 2007) , Kalman filters (Chow et al 2007), expert systems (Isermann and Freyermuth 1991), neural networks (Raol and Madhuranath 1996), qualitative reasoning (Zhuang and Frank 1998) and genetic algorithms (Zhou, Cheng and Ju 2002).

For the most of these methods the need for highly accurate estimates of the parameters require high computational load and memory requirements that reduces the capability of the method (Chen 1995) for on-line estimation of the parameters and as consequence makes them less suitable for on-line systems. Additional difficulties are presented from the noise in the system or the noise by the measurements where most of the methods proposed for parameter estimation in non linear systems cannot be applied (Fouladirad and Nikiforov 2006, Tutkun 2009). On the other hand linearised models have difficulties in representing a wide range of operating conditions.

This Chapter describes a parameter estimation scheme which overcomes some of these difficulties. The method is particularly suitable for on-line fault diagnosis because of the low memory and computational load requirements and its capability to operate in parallel to dynamic industrial process for on-line fault diagnosis. For the development of the parameter estimation method the DASYLab data acquisition and control software was used. The proposed method is used for the estimation of parameter values that include uncertainty while other parameter values were estimated from analytical considerations. The developed mathematical model was incorporated in an on-line expert system that diagnoses real time faults in hydraulic systems.

2. The actual system and the variables of the system

A hydraulic system consists of various hydraulic elements connected with pipes and a hydraulic medium.

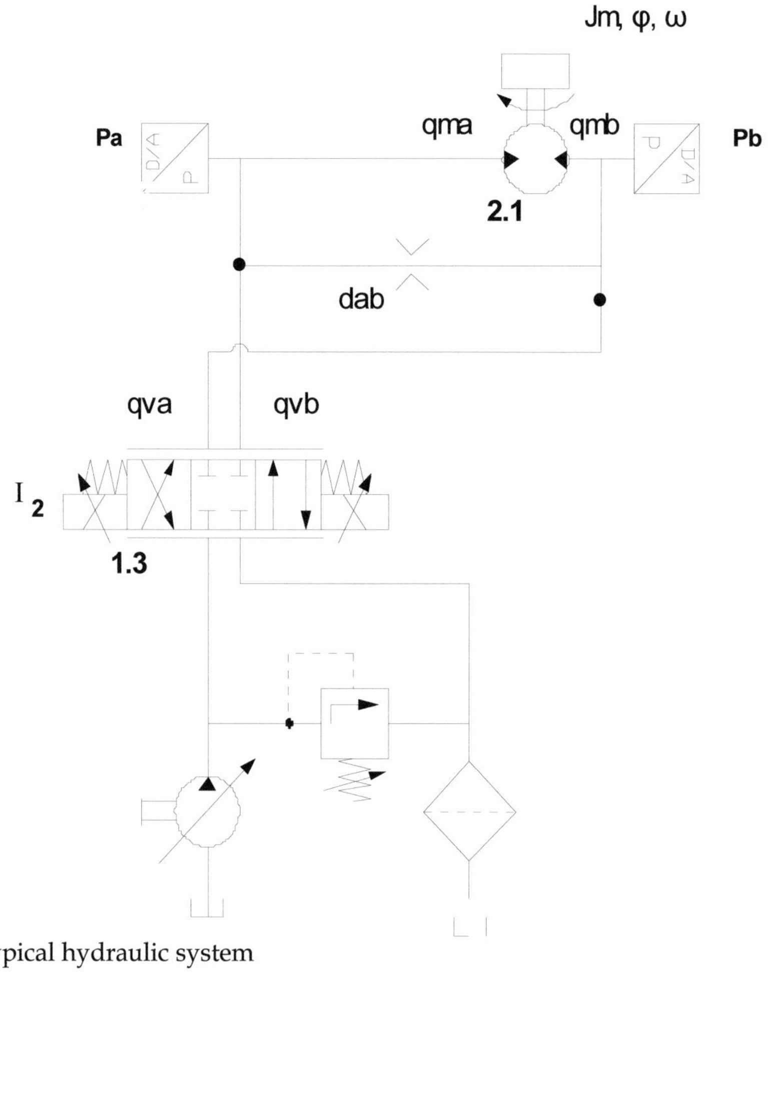

Fig. 1. A typical hydraulic system

A typical hydraulic system, Fig. 1, consists, besides the power unit, mainly of a proportional 4-way valve (1.3) and a hydraulic motor (2.1) with an attached rotating mass J_m. Assuming that the working pressure is constant, the variables of the system are following: The pressure at the port A of the hydraulic motor p_a, the pressure at the port B of the hydraulic motor p_b, the rotation angle of the motor shaft ϕ, the angular velocity ω, the flows q_{va} and q_{vb} through the A and B ports of the proportional 4-way valve, the flows q_{ma} and q_{mb} through the ports A and B of the hydraulic motor, the input current to the proportional valve I_2 or the corresponding voltage to the amplifier of the proportional valve U_2.

3. Operation of the system

The task of the actual system is to drive a hydraulic motor through a cyclical routine, which requires a high speed for a short time, and then return to a low speed.

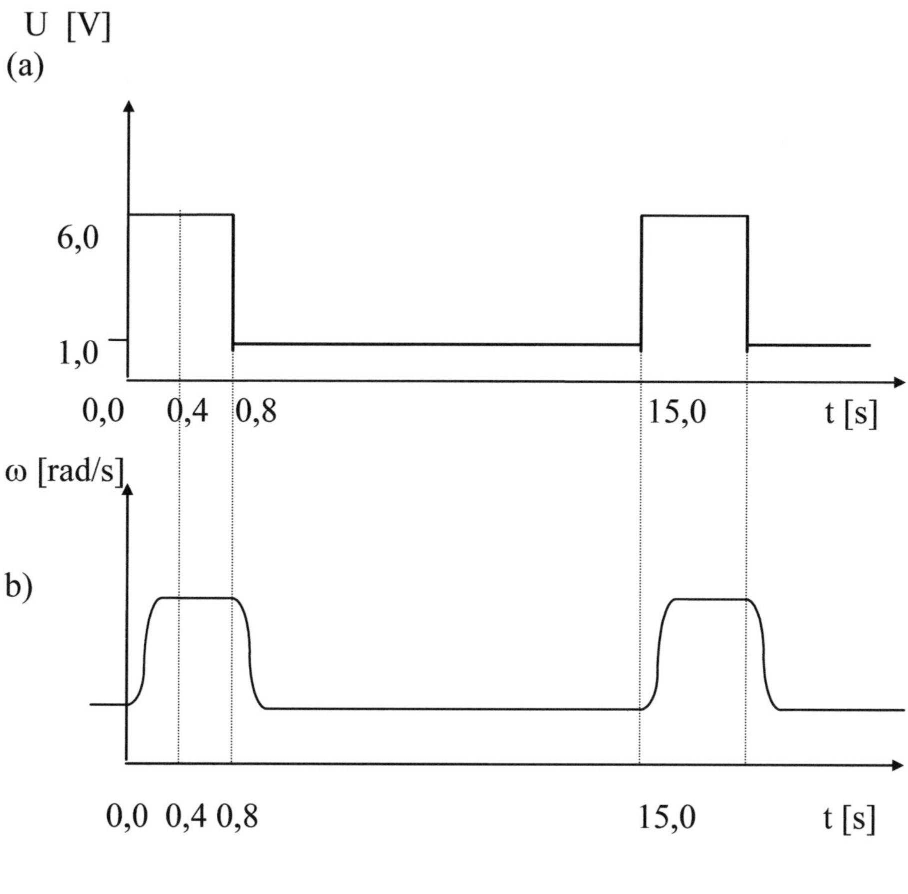

Fig. 2. Operation cycle of the system: (a) U - pulse; (b) Response of the hydraulic motor

To achieve this a typical input voltage is applied to the system as shown in Fig. 2. The speed of the hydraulic motor is proportional to the flow coming from the proportional 4-way valve and the displacement volume of the hydraulic motor. The flow is proportional to the input voltage to the amplifier of the proportional 4-way valve. The proportional 4-way valve is controlled by a periodically changed voltage value U. Fig. 2 shows the pulse waveform of the signal U to the amplifier of the proportional 4-way valve and the form of the corresponding waveform of the speed ω of the hydraulic motor.
On the normal operation the hydraulic motor takes approximately 0,4 s to change the speed from a low value corresponding to U=1 V to a high value corresponding to U=6 V. Any fault that occurs in the system can affect both the dynamic and the steady state of the system. Thus if data are taken over a period 0 to 0,4 s after having applied the change of voltage U both the dynamic and the steady condition should be determinable. In this work the positive response of the curve is used for the fault detection.

4. Estimation of the Uncertain Parameters

The simulation results depend on the values of the parameters. The model parameters are: the oil elasticity E, the volumetric efficiency η_v, the nominal flow of the proportional 4-way valve Q_{nv}, the nominal voltage signal to the amplifier of the proportional 4-way valve U_{nv}, the hydraulic motor displacement V_m , the oil volume in the pipes V_l , the moment of inertia J_m , the friction torque M_r, the system pressure p_0, the initial value of the command voltage to the amplifier of the proportional 4-way valve and the initial value of the rotation angle φ.
The parameter p_0 is the constant system pressure. The command value U_2 depends on the operating conditions. The parameters V_m , V_l and J_m are clearly determinable values depending on measurable physical characteristics of the system. The parameter U_{nv} is operation limit defined by the manufacturer. The parameters η_v and Q_{nv} are derivable from the manufacturer's data and their values are individually tested in the laboratory.
The parameters M_r (friction torque) and E (oil elasticity) are not easily determined from analytical considerations. For the determination of the value of these uncertain parameters the simulation for a set of values was performed, and the simulation results were compared with the corresponding measurements. The optimal values for M_r and E are the values that minimize the difference between the measurements of the actual system and the model. These values are estimated using the integral squared error (ISE) method. The determination of M_r is performed in relation to the commonly used range of values for the parameter E (oil elasticity including air) in order to determine more precisely the optimal value for both parameters. This process is extensively presented in following Sections 4.2 and 4.3.

4.1 The DASYLab software

As already mentioned, for the development of the proposed parameter estimation method the DASYLab software was used. The DASYLab (Data Acquisition SYstem Laboratory) is graphical programming software that takes advantage of the features and the graphical interface provided by Microsoft Windows. This software provides an "intuitive" operating environment, which offers data analysis functions, a high signal processing speed, an effective graphical display of results and data presentation possibilities. A measuring task can be set up directly on the screen by selecting and connecting modular elements which can then be freely arranged.

Among the module functions provided are A/D and D/A converters, digital I/O, mathematical functions from fundamental arithmetic to integral and differential calculus, statistics, digital filters of several types, logical connectors like AND, OR, NOR etc., counters, chart recorders, I/O files, digital displays, bar graphs, analogue meters and more.

With DASYLab it is possible to achieve high signal input/output rates using the full power of the PC. Special buffers with large, selectable, memory address ranges enable continuous data transfer from the data acquisition device through to the software. It obtains real-time logging at a rate of up to 800 kHz and real-time on-screen signal display at a rate of up to 70 kHz.

The worksheet displayed on the screen can be edited at any time. New modules can be developed and added, others can be moved to a different position or deleted. Dialogue boxes prompt for all the necessary parameters to be set for the experiment. By using the "Black Box" module it is possible to combine elements of the worksheet that are repeatedly required in the experiments, integrate them into a Black Box module and insert them into worksheets as ready-to-use units. The consequences of this are a saving of time and the simplification of the worksheets.

The maximum worksheet size is 2000 by 2000 pixels, and a worksheet can contain up to 256 modules. For most modules up to 16 inputs and/or outputs can be configured.

The acquired data and process results can also be saved to files so that they can be retrieved for further processing at a later time. Using DDE (Dynamic Data Exchange), data can be transferred directly to other Windows applications supporting the DDE protocol or applications with DDE capabilities may be used to start DASYLab and control it while running an experiment.

A worksheet can be created on the screen by selecting and connecting in a suitable way stored modules that represent a specific action. The modules are connected by data channels so that data can be transferred between them. The worksheet graphically displays on the screen the complete experiment setup or measurement procedure including all necessary modules and data channels.

A module represents a functional element in the experiment setup. The function symbolised by the modules comprises all the operations required for an experiment e.g. data acquisition (by a data acquisition board), signal generation (simulated by a software generator), data analysis, evaluation and processing (mathematics, statistics, control trigger and other functions), presentation on screen (display instruments) or export for documentation purposes (printer, metafile).

In the worksheet, modules are represented as complete symbols. These symbols display each module's name and the input and output channels that have been selected for it. A data channel is the connection between the output of a module and the input to another module. Data are transferred between the respective modules via these connections.

Modules are organised in module groups. A module group is made up of a number of modules providing similar functions. The available module groups are: input/output, trigger functions, mathematics, statistics, signal analysis, control, display, files, data reduction, special, and black box.

The overall data processing performance as well as the response time of the individual functions is determined by the experimental setup. In addition, the settings for the sampling rate, the block size, the analogue and digital outputs and the size of the driver buffer can be regulated by the experimental setup.

4.2 Derivation of the Integral Squared Error (ISE)

The estimation of the parameter value M_r is performed by measuring the integral squared error (ISE) between the measured and calculated signals over a period of time and looking for the minimum value of the ISE according to the following relations:

$$I_a = \int_0^{tend} (p_{am} - p_{as})^2 \cdot dt = F_a(M_r) \rightarrow \min$$

$$I_b = \int_0^{tend} (p_{bm} - p_{bs})^2 \cdot dt = F_b(M_r) \rightarrow \min$$

In principle, an optimum value for the friction M_r would exist if both integrals were at a minimum for this value.

The integral squared error is measured using the signal analysis capabilities of the DASYLab software by combining two DASYLab "experiments". The first “experiment”, Fig. 3, performs the control of the hydraulic system and the measurements under various operating conditions and updates the operational parameter values of the input files to the simulation program. In the second “experiment”, Fig. 4, the results from measurements and simulation are compared and processed. Between the two "experiments" the simulation program runs using the corresponding input data files with the updated parameter values. This method reduces the experimentation time considerably and allows us to perform experiments with a large variety of parameter sets.

The worksheet of Fig. 3 consists of three groups of modules. The module group A is responsible for the starting of the hydraulic system. The module group B is responsible for the control of the command voltage U_2. The module group C is responsible for the data measurement and storing for further processing by the second “experiment” (Fig.4).

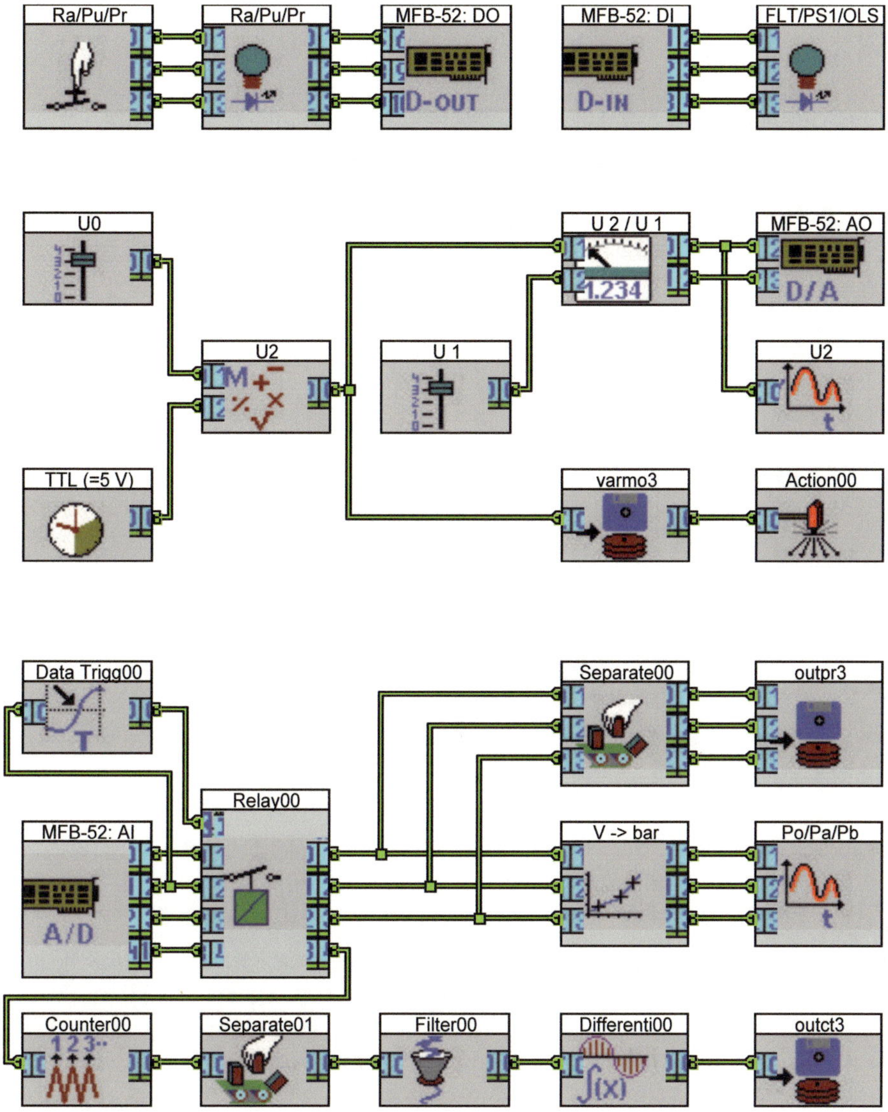

Fig. 3. Worksheet for experiment control and measurements

In the "experiment" of Fig. 3. the output from model (outmo3) and the output from measurements (oupr3) are compared. After this comparison of measured and calculated data, the integral squared error between them is derived using suitably formulated mathematical and statistical DASYLab modules.

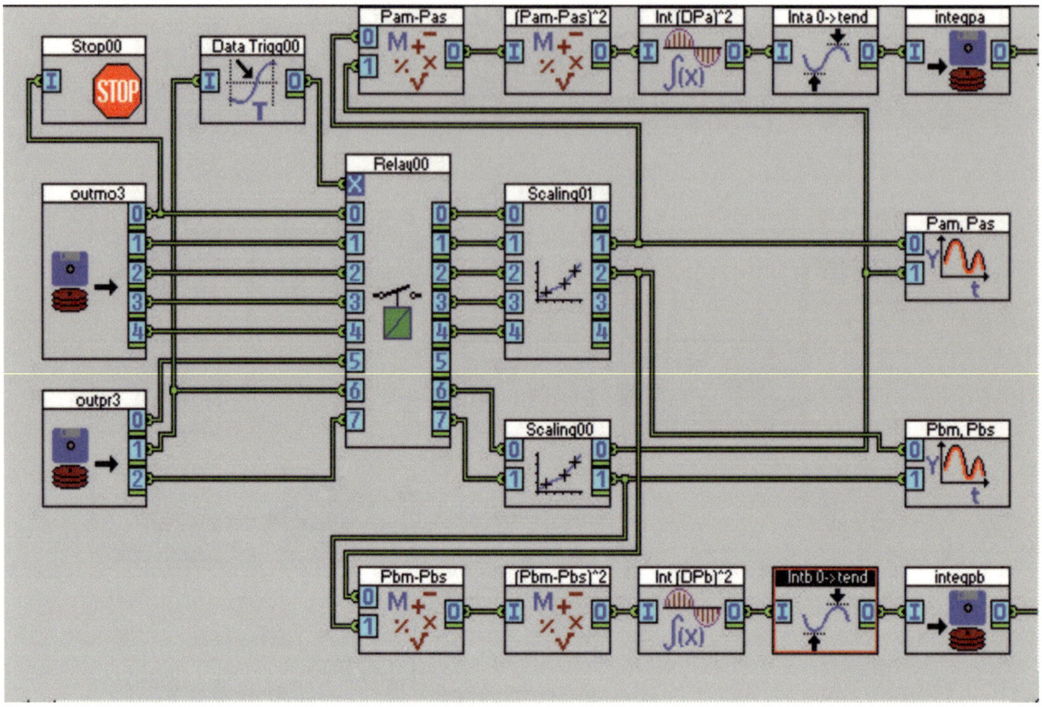

Fig. 4. Comparison of measured and calculated data and derivation of the integral squared error (ISE)

In this "experiment" the arithmetic module "Pam-Pas" calculates the difference between calculated and measured pressure p_a over the time period t = 0 to 0,4 s. The arithmetic module "(Pam-Pas)^2" calculates the square of the pressure difference.

The module " Int(DPa)^2" calculates the integral of (Pam-Pas)^2. The module "Inta0->tend" calculates the value of this integral in the time period t = 0 to tend (0,4 s). The result is the integral squared error over the observed period of time and is written to the file "integpa.asc", represented by the module "integpa". This procedure is performed for a set of values near the expected value of the friction torque M_r and the result is appended to the data of the file "integpa.asc".

The processing of pressure p_b is performed in a similar way with the corresponding modules "Pbm-Pbs", "(Pbm-Pbs)^2", "Int(DPb)^2", "Int b 0 ->tend" and "integpb".

The files "integpa.asc" and "integpb.asc" together with the file "rm.asc", that contains the set of the M_r values, are processed by the "experiment" illustrated in Fig. 5, Section 4.3 for the estimation of the optimal parameter values.

4.3 Estimation of the optimal parameter values

The integral squared difference for the pressures p_a and p_b is the basis for the estimation of the best M_r value. In the DASYLab "experiment" of Fig. 5 the files "integpa" and "integpb" are graphically represented in relation to the M_r values and are processed for the determination of the optimal M_r value.

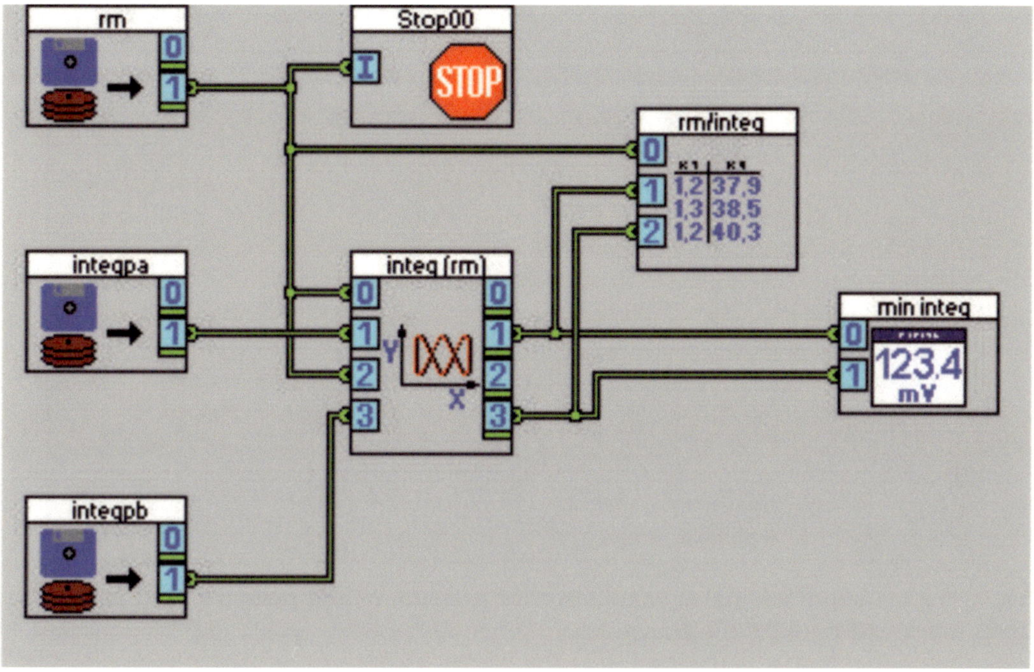

Fig. 5. Determination of the minimum integral squared error for pressures p_a and p_b

The module "integ(rm)" displays the integral squared error values for pressure p_a and p_b from the files "integpa" and "integpb" for various M_r values. The module "rm/integ" displays these values in a list form. The module "min integ" is a digital meter module that displays the minimum value between the integral squared error values of the list.

In order to estimate an accurate value for the parameter E this procedure was performed for oil elasticity values of $0{,}90 \cdot 10^9$, of $1{,}00 \cdot 10^9$ and $1{,}10 \cdot 10^9$ N/m^2 in the simulation, because these values lie near to the commonly used value for hydraulic mineral oil of 10^9 N/m^2.

The DASYLab "experiment" of Fig. 5 was performed for the pressures p_a and p_b with p_0 = 50 bar, U_2 = 6 V and oil elasticity values E = $0{,}90 \cdot 10^9$. N/m^2, E = $1{,}00 \cdot 10^9$ N/m^2 and E = $1{,}10 \cdot 10^9$ N/m^2 . The results of the minimum integral squared error are plotted in Fig. 6.

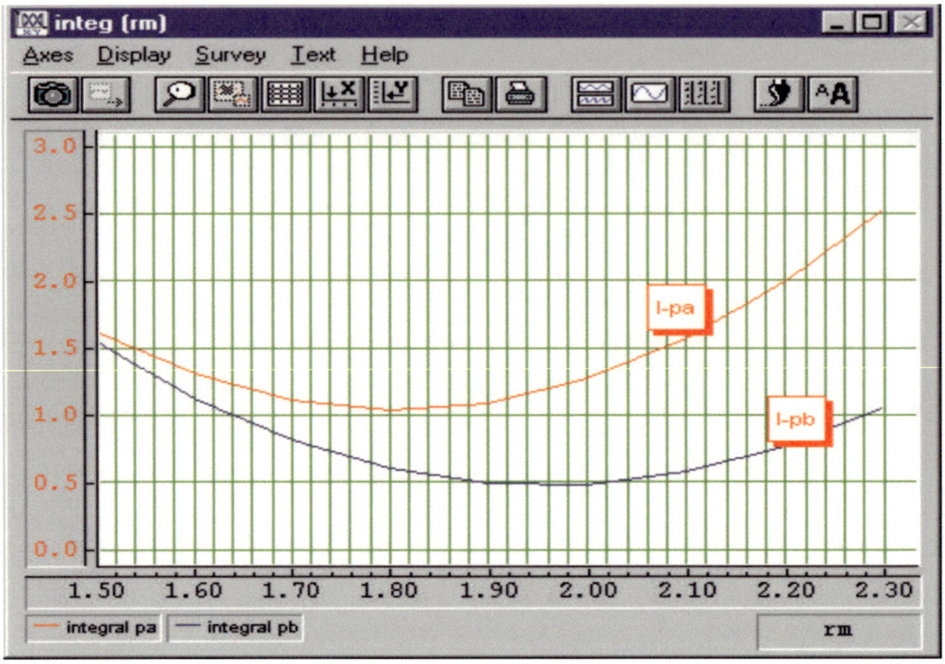

Fig. 6. The minimum integral squared error for pressure p_a and pressure p_b by p_0 = 50 bar, U_2 = 1 to 6 V and E = 0,90· 10^9 N/m²

In this Figure it is seen that the value M_r=1,8 minimises the difference between measured and calculated pressure p_a and the value M_r = 2,0 minimises the difference for the pressure p_b. Therefore the average value of 1,9 N · m is taken for M_r.

The value 1,00 . 10^9 N/m² for the oil elasticity parameter E is also the most accurate, because for a slightly lower and a slightly higher E value the minimum values of the Integral Squared Errors of the pressure differences are higher than for E = 1,00 . 10^9 N/m².

In order to test the performance of the model with the above estimated parameter values and to illustrate the changes of the pressure differences in relation to the operating parameters, the "experiment" of Figure 3 was used. The maximum differences of pressures p_a and p_b between measurement and simulation were calculated from the modules "Pam-Pas" and "Pbm-Pbs" for various command voltage values U_2 and various M_r values.

For comparison reasons the experimental results are summarised in Table 1, where the maximum pressure differences for the transient condition in relation to the command voltage values U_2 (5, 6 and 7 V) and the M_r values 1,70, 1,90 and 2,10 N.m are shown.

In this table, it can be observed that the maximum pressure differences from simulation and measurements are minimised for the estimated M_r value (= 1,9 N.m) while for other M_r values near to the estimated M_r value the differences increase.

Another observation is that all pressure difference values for the estimated M_r value 1,9 N.m are below the threshold which will be selected later as the criterion for the occurrence of a fault by the fault diagnosis process.

Deviation of Pa & Pb						
U2 [V]	1 to 5		1 to 6		1 to 7	
Mr [N.m]	DPa	DPb	DPa	DPb	DPa	DPb
1,70	3,3	2,8	3,1	2,6	3,2	2,7
1,90	3,1	2,6	2,9	2,4	3,0	2,5
2,10	3,4	2,9	3,2	2,7	3,3	2,8

Table 1. Experimental results of the pressure differences by various Mr values

5. Results of the Approach

The experimental work shows that the most accurate value for M_r is 1,9 N·m and the most accurate value for the oil elasticity E is 1,00 .10^9 N/m^2. From the experimental results it was observed that the deviation between the pressure curves from measurement and simulation was always lower than the threshold that will be defined for the occurrence of a fault in the fault detection process.

The behaviour of model and system using the estimated parameter values is illustrated in the diagrams of Fig. 7 where data from the simulation and from the data acquisition process are plotted on the same diagram. In these diagrams the high degree of approximation of the corresponding curves for the pressure p_a can be observed. Similar response for the pressure p_b and the angular velocity ω were observed.

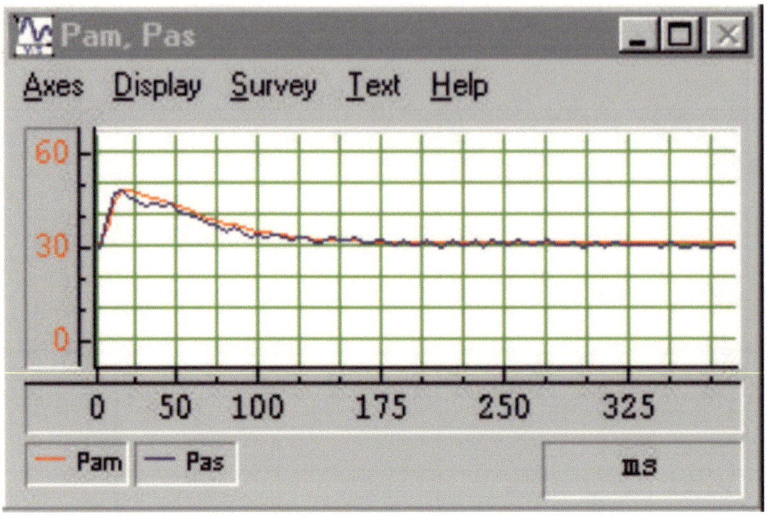

Fig. 7. Response of model and system regarding the pressure p_a by p_0 = 50 bar, U_2 = 1 to 6 V, E = 1,00 . 10^9 N/m^2, M_r = 1,9 N . m

6. Accuracy of the Diagnostic Results of the System

The effects of changes in parameter values on the simulation results were examined in order to test the performance of the system.

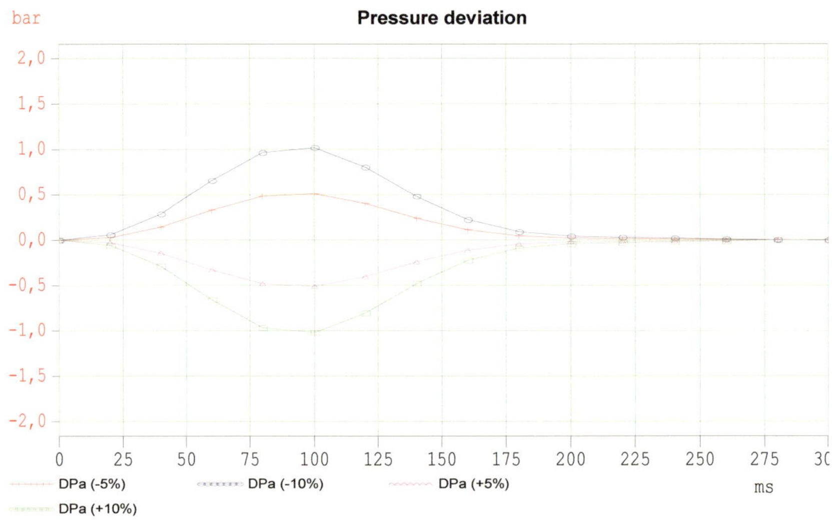

Fig. 8. Influence of a variation of ± 5 %, and ± 10% of the parameter J_m on pressure p_a.

The parameters, as the friction torque Mr, the moment of inertia Jm and the oil elasticity E were varied. For a variation of ± 5 %, ± 10 % and ± 20 % of these parameters the variation of the simulation results was observed and studied. As example, for the oil elasticity E the deviations of the simulation results for the above parameter changes are shown in Fig. 8. The maximum deviations are approximately 0,5 bar for a variation of ± 5 % and 1 bar for a variation of ± 10 %. These variations are acceptable for these systems and, in case, the specific should not affect the effectiveness of the fault detection. Observations indicated a similar effect for changes of the other parameters as well as on the pressure p_b.

7. Conclusion

Parameter estimation methods for real-time fault detection in dynamical systems are related to the effectiveness of the total diagnostic system. In this Chapter, a parameter estimation approach that uses low computational load and memory requirements has been presented which is also able to respond effectively to time restriction situations. The method has been applied to a dynamic drive and control system and has the capability to estimate on-line parameter values as well as to operate in parallel to the final real-time fault detection system. For the development of the parameter estimation method the capabilities of the DASYLab data acquisition and control software were used.

The final model, used by the fault detection system, is able to simulate quite precisely the actual behaviour of the physical system and can respond to the requirements of on-line performance. The experimental results provide evidence of the consistency degree between the behaviour of model and the system that makes the parameter estimation method particularly suitable for on-line fault diagnosis systems.

8. References

Angeli, C. (2008). On-line Expert Systems for Fault Diagnosis in Technical Processes. *Expert Systems.* Vol. 25, No2, pp. 115-132.

Chen, H.W. (1995). Modelling and Identification of Parallel Nonlinear Systems: Structural Classification and Parameter Estimation Methods. *Proceedings IEEE,* 83, pp. 39-45.

Chen, J. & R. Patton (1999). *Robust Model Based Fault Diagnosis for Dynamic Systems,* Kluwer Academic Publishers.

Chow, S.-M.; Ferrer, E. & Nesselroade, J. (2007). An Unscented Kalman Filter Approach to the Estimation of Nonlinear Dynamical Systems Models, *Multivariate Behavioral Reseach,*Vol. 42, No. 2, pp. 283-321.

Drakunov, S.; Law, V. & Victor, J. (2007). Parameter Estimation Using Sliding Mode Observers: Application to the Monod Kinetic Model," *Chemical Product and Process Modeling*: Vol. 2 : Iss. 3, Article 21.

Fouladirad, M.; & Nikiforov, I. (2006). On line change detection with nuisance parameters, *In Proceedings 6th IFAC Safeprocess,* Beijing, China, pp. 258-263.

Frank, P.M. (1996). Analytical and qualitative model-based fault diagnosis: A survey and some new results. *European Journal of control,* Vol. 2, pp 6-28.

Gertler, J. (1998). *Fault Detection and Diagnosis in Engineering Systems,* New York, Marcel Dekker.

Hjelmstad, K.; & Banan, M. (1995). Time-domain parameter estimation algorithm for structures. I: Computational Aspects. *Journal of Engineering Mechanics,* 121, pp. 424-430.

Isermann, R.; & Freyermuth, B. (1991). Process Fault Diagnosis Based on Process Model Knowledge-Part I: Principles for Fault Diagnosis with Parameter Estimation. *Transaction of the ASME*, 113, pp. 620-626.

Kinnaert, M. (2003). Fault Diagnosis based on Analytical Models for Linear and Nonlinear Systems- A tutorial, In Proceedings *IFAC* Safeprocess 03, Washington, U.S.A. pp. 37- 51.

Marschner, U.; & Fischer, W. (1997). Local parameter estimation performed by tailor-made microsystems. *In Proceedings IFAC Safeprocess*, Kingston Upon Hull, UK, pp. 295-300.

Patton, R.; Frank, P. & Clark, R. (2000). Issues in Fault Diagnosis For Dynamic Systems, Springer-Verlag.

Raol, J.R.; & Madhuranath, H. (1996). Neural network architectures for parameter estimation of dynamicalsystems, , *In IEEE Proceedings on Control Theory and Applications* - Volume 143, Issue 4, pp. 387 - 394.

Reza, G.; & Blakenship, G.(1996). Adaptive control of nonlinear systems via approximate linearization. *IEEE Transactions on Automatic Control*, 41, pp. 618-625.

Tutkun N. (2009), Parameter Estimation in Mathematical Models using the Real Coded Genetic Algorithms "Expert System with Applications", Vol. 36, Issue 2, pp. 3342-3345.

Zhou, J.; & Bennett, S. (1998), Dynamic System Fault Diagnosis Based on Neural Network Modelling, *In Proccedings of IFAC Safeprocess*, Kingston Upon Hull, UK, 26-28 August 1997, pp. 55-60.

Zhou, X.; Cheng, H. & Ju, P. (2002). The third-order induction motor parameter estimation using an adaptive genetic algorithm. *Proccedings of the 4th World Congress on Intelligent Control and Automation*. Volume 2, pp. 1480 - 1484.

Zhuang, Z.; & Frank, P. (1998). Fault Detection and Isolation with Qualitative Models. *In Proccedings of IFAC Safeprocess,* Kingston Upon Hull, UK, 26-28 August 1997, pp. 663-668.

6

Simulated Day and Night Effects on Perceived Motion in an Aircraft Taxiing Simulator

Daniel C. Zikovitz, Keith K. Niall, Laurence R. Harris and Michael Jenkin
CAE-Professional Services, Ottawa, Canada [1]
Defence Research & Development Canada Toronto [2]
York University, Toronto, Canada [3,4]
dzikovitz@cae.com, keith.niall@drdc-rddc.gc.ca, harris@yorku.ca, jenkin@cse.yorku.ca

Abstract. Flight simulation often depends on both visual simulation and movement by a motion base. The present study asks if tilt is equivalently perceived as linear translation, and if so, whether other information such as simulated day or night conditions may affect accuracy. We examine the perception of self-motion in non-pilots during passive simulated airplane taxiing along a straight runway. Providing physical motion cueing by a motion platform, simulation scenarios were presented at a constant physical or visual acceleration of either 0.4 m/s^2 or 1.6 m/s^2 (simulated using tilt). Nine subjects indicated the moment when they perceived that they had travelled through distances between 10 to 90 m under either day or night-time display conditions. Their estimates were made either with or without tilt (to simulate linear acceleration). We present results as a ratio of response distance (response distance) to stimulus distance (stimulus distance). Subjects' motion estimates under tilt conditions do not significantly differ from under vision-only conditions. We found an interaction of tilt and illumination conditions, particularly for targets greater than 30 m. The ratio of response distance to stimulus distance significantly increases in the dark (1.1 vs. 0.85), at higher accelerations (1.01 for 1.6 m/s^2 vs. 0.95 for 0.4 m/s^2) and, during daytime illumination, in the presence of a physical-motion cue (0.92 vs. 0.78).
Conditions affecting the magnitude of perceived self-motion include:

- illumination
- magnitude of the simulated acceleration
- presence of physical tilt during daytime illumination

This study shows that passive humans can be expected to make significant, predictable errors in judging taxiing distances under specific simulation conditions. Questions for further research include:

- if similar effects occur in pilots as in non-pilots
- if such effects also occur in real taxiing scenarios

The results obtained here may help to counter perceptual errors, as the results become part of the knowledge on which appropriate cueing schemes can be based.

1. Introduction

Although aircraft taxiing initially appears the least demanding and least dangerous part of air travel, it requires the pilot to use sensory cues in judging the aircraft's motion, unlike flight, which predominantly uses instruments and computer control. Pilot misperception of self-motion during taxiing has led to an increasing number of runway incursions since 2000, as reported by Transport Canada [1]. Small errors in position judgment during aircraft taxiing can lead to accidents. Fotos' [3] report of the following accident in Aviation Week & Space Technology, is illustrative: "On 3 December 1990; Northwest DC9-14; Detroit, MI: a DC9 was taxiing in fog and strayed onto an active runway where it was hit by a departing Northwest 727. One of the four crew members and seven of the 40 passengers were killed." As shown by this example, misperceptions of self-motion can prove fatal.

Sensory input such as vision, the vestibular apparatus and other proprioceptive information transduce self-motion information in providing an estimate of self-motion. How do humans integrate these cues in perceiving their self-motion? Which cues are critical to the accurate perception of self-motion? We examine these issues in the domain of passive aircraft taxiing. A better understanding of the factors that affect the perception of self-motion while taxiing provides the opportunity for more effective pilot training and the development of measures for countering errors in self-motion perception.

What factors affect pilots' judgements of their travel on the ground? We begin with a simple case: do taxiing subjects accurately perceive how far they have travelled in a straight line along the ground? In maximizing flight-simulation training accuracy, the pilot's self-motion perception in the simulator should match the self-motion perception in the vehicle being simulated as closely as possible. Many current vehicle simulators incorporate visual systems displaying detailed scenes over a wide field of view. Visual stimulation should work well for simulations of constant velocity and simulations below vestibular threshold because the vestibular system is normally inactive under these conditions. However, many vehicle operations involve acceleration, e.g., abrupt changes in direction, altitude or air speed, with accompanying simulation of acceleration; providing this input to the pilot may be important for training. Although these issues are important in simulating motion, low accelerations and extreme distances to objects in the visual field reduce the effectiveness of most sensory cues to motion perception during steady flight. This cueing is most important during ground manoeuvres (e.g., taxiing), with nearby objects and short accelerations providing significant sensory cues to motion as in other ground vehicle simulation, see Vos et al. [4].

Flight simulation with accompanying physical-motion cues is not necessarily perceived as veridical, as shown by Groen and Hosman [5] and Harris et al. [2]. Typical motion-based simulators have a short physical throw distance; sustaining linear acceleration is impossible. Motion simulators attempting to achieve the same perceptual effect as the physical motion of an aircraft must use other methods. One common approach to achieve this simulation is to use the physical tilt of the simulator to simulate linear acceleration. According to Einstein's Equivalence Principle [6], inertial accelerations during translation are physically indistinguishable from gravitational accelerations from tilt. When a component of gravity parallels the otolith macula, distinguishing this component from a comparable linear acceleration due to motion becomes impossible. The equivalence can be exploited by tilting a person, activating the otoliths and simulating linear acceleration. Although a static tilt can simulate forward acceleration, the tilting process also stimulates the semicircular canals. To avoid the sensation of tilting and have the resulting motion perceived as linear motion, the rate of tilt applied should be below the canal's detection threshold, reported as 0.5°/s2 by Benson et al. [7].

The present study investigates the perceived magnitude of self-motion as forward motion is simulated during taxiing. This simulation was effected by tilting subjects at a rate below the threshold level of the semicircular canals and by determining the effectiveness of this tilting technique and the resulting angular displacement on night-time and daytime simulations. One goal of this work is to determine the relative weighting of visual and physical motion provided in motion-based simulators. A further goal is to lay the groundwork for the development of training techniques for, and countermeasures to, perceptual inaccuracies that can lead to disastrous errors while taxiing. The hypothesis is that tilt significantly increases the perceived magnitude of self-motion perception, while additional factors such as changing from day to night and changing the simulated acceleration level (i.e., changing the angle of tilt) may reduce the effects of tilt.

2. Methods

Subjects

Twelve healthy male volunteers from the ages of 18 to 32 years were recruited from York University. Subjects had normal or corrected-to-normal vision. None of the subjects had pilot training or reported a history of vestibular dysfunction. Subjects were told to signal the operator if they experienced any symptoms of simulator sickness, but no subject asked to stop the experiment for any reason. Subjects read and signed York University and DRDC consent forms and were paid for their participation at standard subject rates. The York University Ethics Committee and DRDC Toronto Human Research Ethics Committee approved the experimental protocols.

Apparatus

As shown Figure 1, a Jet Ranger® helicopter cockpit mounted on a MotionBase Max Cue, electrically-driven motion platform was used. Translational movement of up to 0.47 m and rotational movement of up to 45° yaw and 34° pitch could be achieved with the platform, although this study only pitched subjects 9.4°, producing a constant acceleration of 1.6 m/s^2 and 2.3°, simulating 0.4 m/s^2 movement. A joystick with a response button was located in the cockpit. An emergency button for subjects to stop the experiment was also located in the cockpit. This button was not used by any of the subjects.

Fig. 1. Front and side views of the simulator used in this study.

Subjects wore a head-tracked Virtual Research V8 stereo head-mounted display (HMD) in binocular mode driven by a Silicon Graphics Inc. (SGI) ® computer. The HMD provided a 60° diagonal field of view at an optical distance of 7 m. Providing 6° of freedom, user head-tracking was provided by an Ascension laserBIRD 2TM head-tracker (accurate within 0.77 mm), updating the visual display based on the subject's head position.

Visual simulation

Even though the Jet Ranger® cab was used, the simulator was configured to create a visual simulation of the view seen from the cockpit of a HerculesTM aircraft. A crude representation of the instrument panel was displayed below the simulated window; subjects viewed a 780-m-long runway of 54-m width through the window. Subjects could explore the cabin visually and look out of any of the forward- and side-facing windows, illustrated in Figures 2 and 3, before the trial began. A white cross with a horizontal red line running perpendicular to the fore-aft line was shown on the floor of the simulated aircraft. Subjects were instructed to notice this line because it was their reference for distance judgment. Subjects were, however, instructed not to move their heads during the trials.

The visual display simulated either night-time conditions with low illumination or daytime conditions with higher illumination. The daytime condition visual display was bright, with textured grass on either side of the runway. Simulated down the middle of the runway were 36-m-long hashmarks with a 24-m gap between them (see Figure 2). The night-time-condition visual displayed runway lights at the side of the runway 120 m apart and lights down the middle of the runway positioned not more than 15 m apart (see Figure 3). To signal target distances, two 1.8-m (six-foot) tall men were shown holding a red-and-white striped ribbon across the runway at specified target distances. The target, the ribbon and the men were illuminated for night-time scenes.

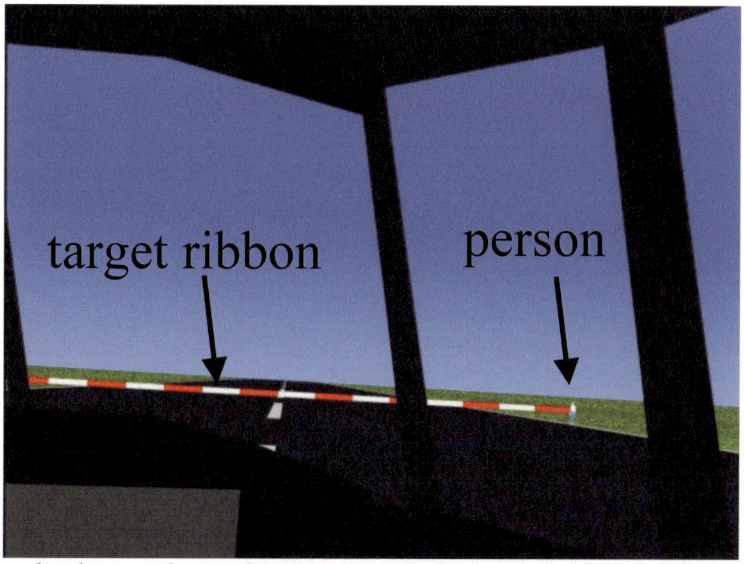

Fig. 2. Daytime display condition showing two six-foot men holding a striped-ribbon target across the runway.

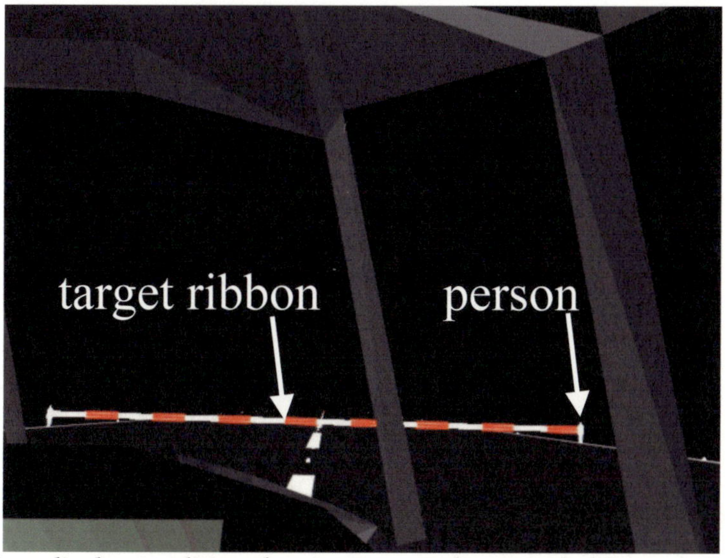

Fig. 3. Night-time display condition showing two six-foot men holding a striped-ribbon target across the runway.

Tilt profile

Tilting the simulator cockpit generated non-visual cues. Subjects' heads were not restrained; subjects were instructed to hold their head steady so their head and thus the HMD had about the same tilt as the platform. The HMD was equipped with a tracking system attached to the cockpit; the movements of the cockpit had no effect on the visual display. The tilt angle selected simulated acceleration expressed as sine (θ) g (with g being the universal gravitational constant). Introducing tilts at maximum acceleration of 0.5°/s² avoided signals from the subject's semicircular canals. Figure 4 shows a sample tilt profile. Figure 5 shows how tilt simulated linear acceleration.

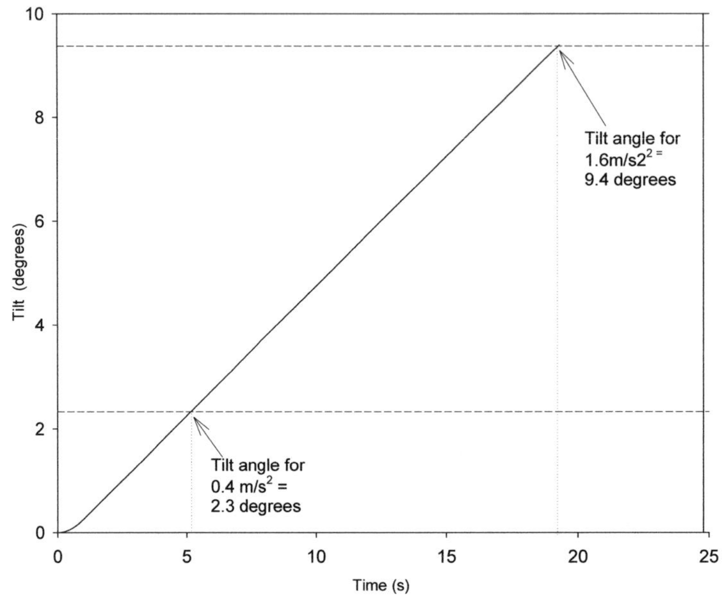

Fig. 4. The motion profile of the tilt used in this experiment.

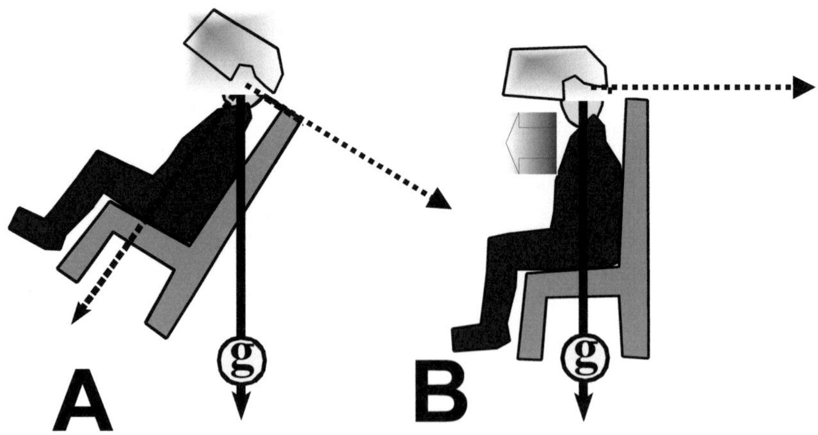

Fig. 5. An illustration of how tilt simulated linear acceleration.

During the first second of movement the platform moved through the first quarter of a degree at $\theta = 1/2\ \alpha\ t^2$ where α is 0.5°/s². Following the first second the platform continued tilting at $\omega{*}t + \theta{*}t = 1$ where ω is 0.5°/s until the intended tilt was reached. This tilt was held until the subject pressed the button, at which time the platform returned to its starting orientation.

When the subject was tilted as shown in Figure 5A, gravity separated into two vectors, one lying in the horizontal plane of the head and the other aligning with the body axis. As shown in Figure 5B, the direction of the horizontal-plane component was the same as the acceleration caused by a horizontal acceleration. Subjects viewed a virtual-reality display throughout the tilt.

Procedure

Prior to strapping into the cockpit, subjects were told they would be judging their simulated motion in a flight simulator by pressing a button indicating when they perceived they had moved through a specified target distance. During the experiment subjects pressed a button mounted on the control stick; they were then presented with either the daytime or nighttime runway on the visual display. The constant sound of an idling Hercules aircraft, playing over loudspeakers, masked the sounds from tilting the platform. Subjects pressed the button again when ready to start the trial. A target then appeared at some distance along the runway depicting two simulated six-foot men holding a striped ribbon at a height of 1.8 m across the runway, as seen in Figures 2 and 3. Subjects were instructed to move their head, obtaining parallax information to help in determining the distance to the target. Subjects were also instructed to check the position of the reference line on the floor of the cockpit. They were to align this reference line with the position of the target. When ready, subjects pressed the button again and held their heads steady while the target (along with the men) disappeared; the simulated plane began moving down the simulated runway at a constant acceleration using either visual cues (via the HMD) or a combination of visual- and physical-motion cues. For conditions with an associated platform tilt, the tilt was introduced as the visual simulation of motion began. Subjects indicated when the aircraft had moved in the simulated environment to a position where the reference line on the floor of the cockpit was over the point marked by the ribbon by pressing the button one more time. Afterwards the screen went blank, and the platform returned slowly (0.5°/s, avoiding activating the canals) to its initial orientation. For non-tilt conditions, a blank period of the same duration it would take the platform to return to its initial orientation was used. Subjects indicated they were ready for a new trial by pressing the button once again.

Conditions

Targets were shown at 9 distances: 10, 20, 30, 40, 50, 60, 70, 80 and 90 m for each condition. The tilt condition had three levels; no tilt and tilt at either 2.3° or 9.4°, corresponding to 0.4 m/s² and 1.6 m/s². (See Figure 4 for the tilt profile.) The acceleration condition had two levels, constant acceleration of either 0.4 m/s² or 1.6 m/s²; this was accompanied by a tilt or by no tilt. The visual condition had two levels, day and night. Table 1 shows the full set of experimental conditions. The experiment was a 2 x 2 x 2, complete within subjects design with each subject receiving 72 different trials in one of two random orders (counterbalanced).

ACCELERATION CONDITION	VISUAL CONDITION	TILT CONDITION	PRESENTED DISTANCES FOR EACH CONDITION (IN METERS)
0.4 m/s^2	Day	2.3°	10, 20, 30, 40, 50, 60, 70, 80, 90
0.4 m/s^2	Day	0°	10, 20, 30, 40, 50, 60, 70, 80, 90
0.4 m/s^2	Night	2.3°	10, 20, 30, 40, 50, 60, 70, 80, 90
0.4 m/s^2	Night	0°	10, 20, 30, 40, 50, 60, 70, 80, 90
1.6 m/s^2	Day	9.4°	10, 20, 30, 40, 50, 60, 70, 80, 90
1.6 m/s^2	Day	0°	10, 20, 30, 40, 50, 60, 70, 80, 90
1.6 m/s^2	Night	9.4°	10, 20, 30, 40, 50, 60, 70, 80, 90
1.6 m/s^2	Night	0°	10, 20, 30, 40, 50, 60, 70, 80, 90

Table 1. Experimental conditions of study.

Simulator sickness questionnaire

Using the simulator sickness questionnaire (SSQ) of Kennedy et al. [8], we assessed comfort levels and unwanted side effects associated with combining visual and real movement cues. Subjects completed this questionnaire before and after the experiment. A copy of this questionnaire is included as Annex A.

Data analysis

The distance where each subject pressed the button, called the response distance. We call the ratio of the stimulus to response distance the perceptual gain, see Harris et al. [2]. Obtaining a perceptual gain of unity occurs when a subject presses the button at the exact position of the target on the runway. Pressing the button before reaching the target corresponds to a perceptual gain greater than one. Reliable comparisons between different conditions were possible because the matching task used here incorporated the same target distances. Reducing the data to a set of perceptual gains for each subject and each condition, a total of 864 judgements were collected from 12 subjects.

Response distance was regressed on stimulus distance for the six conditions (tilt vs. no tilt, day vs. night, low acceleration vs. high acceleration). The mean r^2 for each subject's slope is shown in Figure 6. Subjects with a mean r^2 not meeting or exceeding a value of 0.70 were removed from further analysis. Figure 7B shows the distribution between the accepted data compared with the distribution of the rejected data. Three subjects (B.K., P.J. and A.G.) did not meet this criterion and their data were discarded from further analysis.

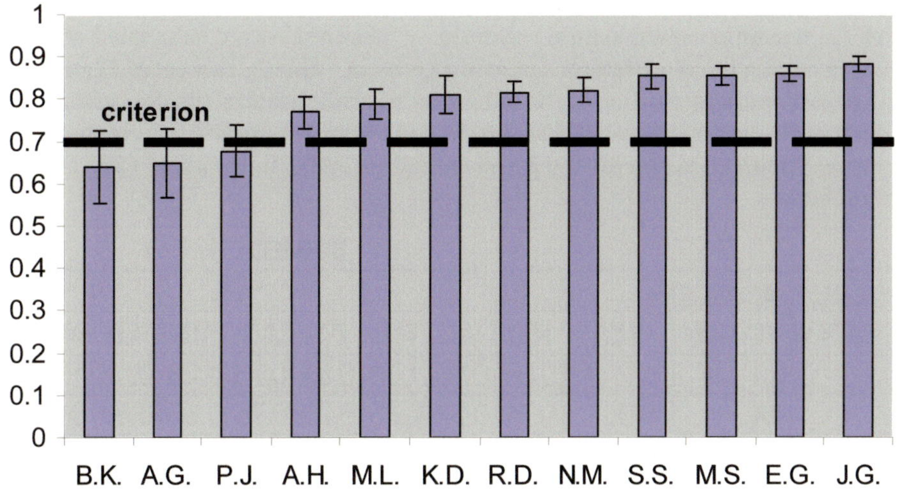

Fig. 6. A graphic illustration of mean r^2 values for all twelve subjects.

Perceptual gain is defined as the slope of stimulus to response distance, as seen in Figure 7A. Perceptual gain is defined as the reciprocal of the slope (dashed line). Figure 7B compares the distribution of rejected response data (i.e. subjects with average r^2 less than 0.70) with the distribution of accepted data.

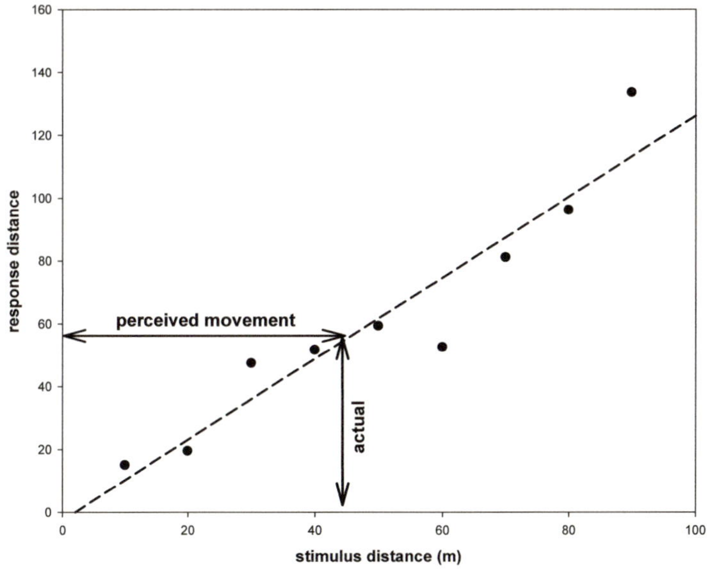

Fig. 7. A graphic example of perceptual gain. Perceptual gain is defined as the slope of stimulus to response where a gain greater than unity (1) indicates an overestimates of one's motion.

Results

A total of 72 perceptual gains (slope : stimulus / response) were calculated from the nine subjects who passed the r^2 criterion. These are given in Table 2. This set of 72 responses was collapsed across various parameters to allow us to make statements concerning the influence of each of the various parameters. A repeated measures analysis of variance (ANOVA) was performed on the data set for the physical motion (tilt), illumination (day vs. night) and acceleration factors.

			SUBJECT								
VISUAL CONDITION	ACCELERATION	TILT	K.D.	M.L.	R.D.	E.S.	J.G.	M.S.	A.H.	N.M.	S.S.
Day	0.4	tilt	0.66	0.55	1.10	0.83	0.75	1.28	0.55	1.01	0.61
Day	0.4	no tilt	0.74	0.52	0.83	0.70	0.75	1.05	0.59	0.99	0.73
Day	1.6	tilt	0.90	1.08	1.31	0.85	0.96	1.20	0.71	1.50	0.64
Day	1.6	no tilt	0.68	0.62	1.03	0.72	0.66	1.11	0.67	1.16	0.51
Night	0.4	tilt	1.05	0.98	1.10	1.14	1.01	1.27	0.69	1.70	0.56
Night	0.4	no tilt	0.92	1.05	1.18	1.30	0.84	1.21	1.22	1.97	0.77
Night	1.6	tilt	1.30	0.94	1.23	1.27	1.27	1.11	0.61	1.70	0.64
Night	1.6	no tilt	0.88	0.76	1.11	1.24	0.92	1.59	1.10	1.50	0.81

Table 2. Summary of perceptual gains for each subject under each condition.

As Figure 8 illustrates, when tilt was applied the p response was 1.00 with a standard error (SE) of ±0.05. When no tilt was applied the p response was 0.96 ±0.05 SE. In daylight conditions, no tilt produced a lower perceptual gain response (0.96 ±0.05 SE) than tilt (1.00 ±0.05 SE), but in night-time conditions tilt had no effect, $\underline{F}\,(1,8) = 5.47$, $\underline{p} < .05$, Tukey-Kramer, $\underline{p} < .05$. There was no significant main effect of tilt, $\underline{F}\,(1,8) = 0.86$, $\underline{p} > 0.5$ or other significant interactions with tilt.

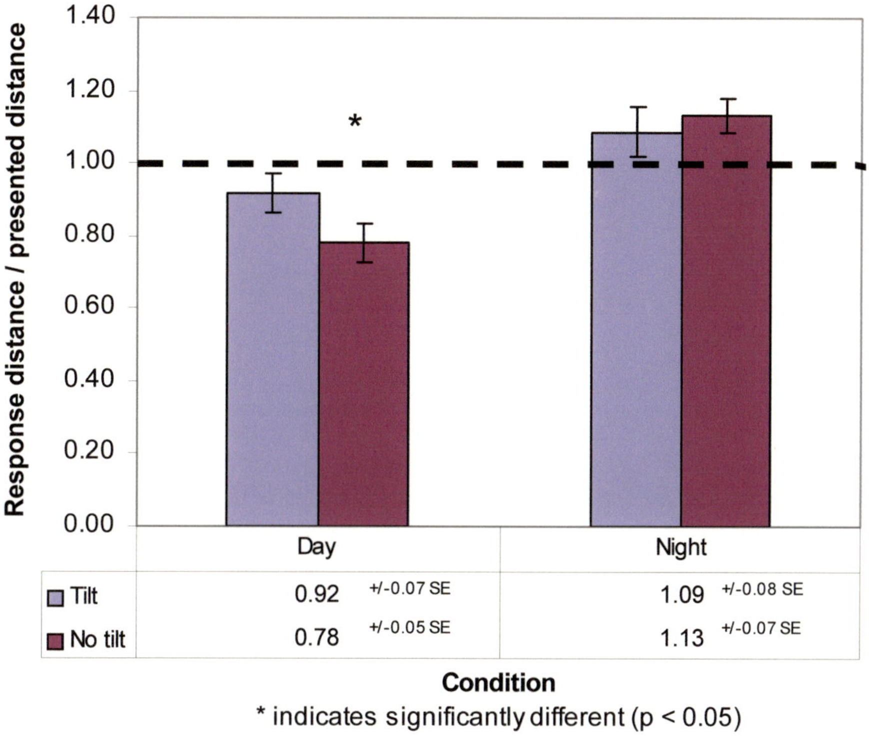

Fig. 8. A graphic summary of perceptual gains obtained in tilt and no-tilt conditions.

To determine any influence of target distance, the log ratio of the difference between response distance and stimulus distance was computed for each target distance (see Figure 9). A Hotelling-t-test was conducted to determine whether these ratios were different from zero.

This Hotelling test accounts for the many t-tests performed on the same data set. Statistically, log ratios of daytime conditions were different from zero for both 0.4 m/s^2 ($t(81) = 4.20$, $p < .01$) and 1.6 m/s^2 ($t(81) = 8.59$, $p < .01$). However, night-time conditions were not statistically different from zero except for targets from 10 to 20 m for the 1.6 m/s^2 condition ($t(18) = 3.60$, $p < .001$). For night-time conditions the log ratios were statistically different from zero for all targets with a 0.4 m/s^2 profile ($t(81) = 0.41$, NS) and for targets from 30 to 90 m with an 1.6 m/s^2 profile ($t(63) = 1.77$, NS). The difference between the daytime and night-time curves differed significantly for targets above 30 m ($t(63) = 3.55$, $p < .05$).

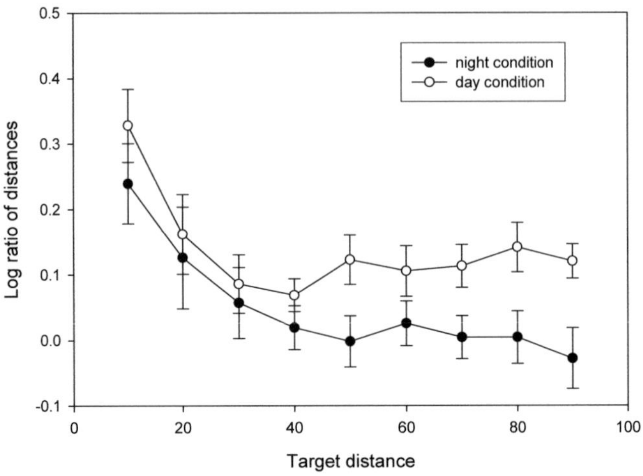

Fig. 9. An illustration of the log ratios of distance estimates with SE bars shown as a function of target distance.

Illumination had a significant effect (1.11 night-time vs. 0.85 daytime, $\underline{F}$ (1,8) = 45.19, $\underline{p}$ < 0.01). Unlike the interaction of illumination and tilt, interaction between illumination and acceleration ($\underline{F}$ (1,8) = 1.64, $\underline{p}$> .05) was insignificant.

Mean perceptual gain responses for the low acceleration (0.4 m/s^2) were 0.95 ±0.06, while the high acceleration (1.6 m/s^2) produced a mean perceptual gain response of 1.01 ±0.05; these differed significantly ($\underline{F}$ (1,8) = 13.62, $\underline{p}$ < 0.01).

Simulator sickness

Figure 10 compares SSQ scores (see Annex A for weighted calculation methodology) for each subject before and after the experiments. No significant change was found between pre-simulation and post-simulation scores for any of the three sub-scores (nausea, oculomotor and disorientation) measured. The average values both before (5.0) and after (12.4) were well below the minimal discomfort level of 50 suggested by Kennedy et al. [8].

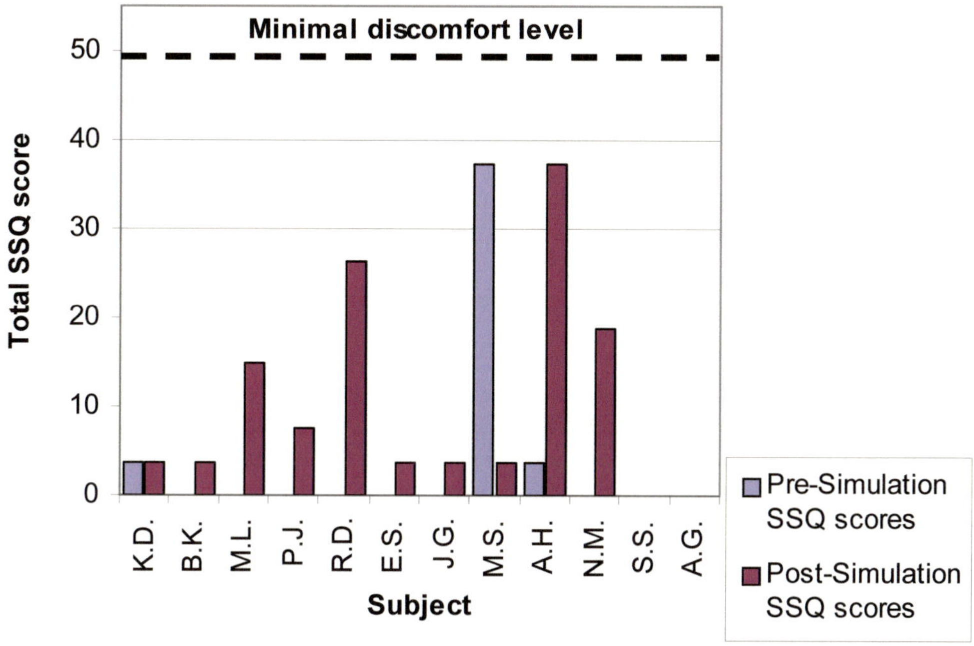

Fig. 10. A graphic summary of pre- and post-motion SSQ scores. Dashed line indicates minimal discomfort level. A response of zero is represented by a missing bar.

Discussion and conclusion

This study has examined a continuum of sensation from full visual to full physical motion stimuli. From fully illuminated day-like conditions to dimly light night-like visual conditions to complete darkness with only physical motion to simulate the movement of the subject, the experiments presented here offer some interesting results. Simulating day or night conditions affects perceived distance travelled differently during passive translation in a taxiing simulator. Subjects estimate that they have moved further under simulated night-time conditions. Reducing illumination to night-time lighting conditions may reduce the influence of visual cues; that is, they increase dependence on non-visual cues. When visual cues are absent, non-visual cues are heavily weighted by the nervous system. Harris et al. [2] showed that with no light at all, passive physical self-motion was perceived as considerably greater than actual motion (up to three times the perceived visual distance).

Contrast may have played a significant factor in determining the results during night-like simulated conditions. The high contracts of runway lights contrasting starkly with a dim background create high contrast patterns during night simulations. In Snowden et al. [9], observers underestimated their speed when moving in driving simulations under fog conditions. These results are compatible with Thompson's [10] results, which indicated that low contrast induces lower judgments of visual motion. In the study presented here, subjects overestimate their motion, indicating their perception is perhaps dominated by physical motion cues.

By tilting at low rates of rotation, gravity stimulates the otolith's utricular macula without activating the canal system. The otolithic stimulation is in the direction of, and at a magnitude compatible with, the simultaneous visually-simulated movement. The present study compares conditions with and without tilt to visual motion alone as a control, finding perceptual gain responses closer to 1 when tilt was added. Harris et al. [2] found overestimates (response distance 1/3 of the stimulus distance) of self-motion in the presence of linear motion only, or with visually-simulated hallway movement (response distance of ½ of stimulus distance). Perhaps the disparity between Harris et al. [2] and the current findings is due to the simulated translation using tilt rather than the real translation (using a sled) experienced by the Harris et al. [2] subjects. Therefore, although tilt is not physically distinguishable from linear acceleration, perceptually tilt does not match the real amplitude of linear translation.

Although there is no overall effect of tilt on motion in the present study, there is an interaction between simulated illumination and tilt. Under night-time conditions, perceptual gain was higher (1.02 night vs. 0.92 day), as might be expected if the nervous system more readily relies on physical motion. Oddly enough, perceptual gain responses are higher without tilt (1.13 no tilt vs. 1.09) under night conditions; this may be reflective of the speeding up of the perception of self-motion as found by both Snowden et al. [9] and Thompson [10]. During simulated day conditions the perceptual gain is relatively low (0.78); however, accuracy improves substantially (from 0.78 to 0.92) with simultaneous tilt. Therefore, tilt may increase accuracy irrespective of simulated illumination.

The consequences of the tilt-illumination interaction may provide insight into the somatogravic illusion. The somatogravic illusion (illusion of pitch caused by forward acceleration) occurs under night-time flight conditions; see Gillingham and Wolfe [11]. The same overestimation of tilt, and therefore self-motion, occurs under night-time simulation conditions in the current study.

While considering these results, one must also consider the general mismatch between the visual and physical motions of the simulator. Due to limitations of flight simulators, visual motion normally begins before the platform has reached its maximum tilt angle. The low rate of tilt used in these experiments means in certain conditions (shorter-range targets, higher-target accelerations and various combinations) the visual simulated self-motion is not initially matched with enough tilt to be perceived as veridical. However, apparently this mismatch does not hinder performance (average perceptual gain responses were close to 1) and because linear vection has been known to delay onset from 8 to 15 s, it is doubtful the mismatch between vision and physical motion created any misperception, see Berthoz et al. [12].

Pilots taxiing along runways need to know be reasonably accurate at determining their current position relative to other objects as well as the taxiway. Under good lighting conditions, in modern airports, this localization is usually very accurate. When airport systems are faulty or absent, the task of localization falls on the pilot. How well can a taxiing pilot discern positions and distances on the runway?

This experiment suggests users under passive simulation conditions judge their motion differently during night-time and daytime scenarios. Applying the results to pilots who are in active control of real aircraft, we expect errors in taxiing performance. Specifically, if pilots perceive they have travelled further at night than they have, they will tend to stop short. If simulator manufacturers continue using equal amounts of tilt and visual motion for both day and night conditions, errors of self-motion during training may occur, carrying over into real-world taxiing performance. Training pilots to overestimate their motion with a night-time display may transfer this overestimation into real-world taxing performance, leading pilots to stop short or turn too early. Similarly, underestimating self-motion during daytime viewing may result in the aircraft colliding with other vehicles, equipment or buildings.

To correct these errors, research is required to establish the correct tilt-to-vision ratio (tilt-gain) for both night-time and daytime viewing conditions, as they would be in the field. Simulator training can match field training once the correct tilt-gain is established. Until simulation training matches field training, participants should be trained to rely on their instruments (odometer) to judge their self-motion; although, it is more advantageous to have pilots looking up and using out-the-window information during such manoeuvres. These conclusions are based on the assumption that this artificial means of simulating translation through tilt does not correspond to the perception of self-motion during real translations of the observer.

The high perceptual gains found during night-time taxiing are consistent with earlier results; those results indicate an overestimation of motion as the quality or availability of visual cues are reduced, see Harris et al. [2]. Before tackling the problem of tilt-gain, simulation designers must consider the level of illumination available; simulating forward acceleration with pitch is less effective for simulated night conditions than for simulated day conditions. One new approach may be to implement a different strategy incorporating level of illumination as a parameter.

Simulator designers should consider how the results found here (maximum perceptual gain of 1.1) differ from those found in the literature for real linear translation. For example, Harris et al. [2] found perceptual gains of approximately 2.07 when physical motion accompanied visual motion. Simulations using tilt, while producing near veridical gains, may need to add a tilt-gain (greater pitch angle than visual motion requires) when accurately simulating real-world perceptions of motion. Groen and Hosman [5] found that subjects set tilt-gain to 0.6 (roughly equivalent to what we would call a perceptual gain of 1.4), indicating they perceived a tilt-gain of 1 to be too high. The Groen and Hosman [5] study used higher acceleration values (3.34 m/s^2) compared with the values used here (maximum 1.4 m/s^2), & different rate of tilt, possibly accounting for the difference in perceptual gain. The most veridical simulation matches perceptual values found in simulation studies with those found in real linear-translation studies. A study is needed to determine the correct ratio of tilt-gain and tilt-rate (the rate at which the tilt occurs) to visual motion. This study highlights that this ratio likely depends on the amount of illumination in the visual display.

New questions are raised by the presented results. Do these results extend to well-trained pilots? Do these results extend beyond simulation to taxiing in an aircraft? Do the results extend to situations where the operator actively controls the aircraft or simulator? A trade-off between tilt and acceleration is used to simulate forward motion in the design of contemporary flight simulators. This trade-off is not an isolated phenomenon or the representation of a closed system; perceiving distance travelled is affected by other factors. Importantly, this perception is affected by illumination level, i.e., whether a day scene or a night scene is depicted.

References

Transport Canada (2003). Transportation in Canada, annual report: TP 13198E, Minister of Public Works and Government Services, Canada. pp. 1-106.

Harris, L. R., Jenkin, M., and Zikovitz, D. C. (2000). Visual and non-visual cues in the perception of linear self-motion. *Experimental Brain Research,* 135(1), 12–21.

Fotos, C. P. (1990). Northwest 727, DC-9 crash. *Aviation Week & Space Technology,* December 10, 1990, 133 (24), p 33, Washington.

Vos, A.P. de, Hoekstra, W., and Pieterse, M.T.J. (1998). The effect of acceleration. The effect of acceleration cueing on braking behaviour in a driving simulator. Report tm-98-a066 TNO-Human Factors, Soesterberg, the Netherlands. pp. 1-21.

Groen, E. and Hosman, R. (2001). Evaluation of perceived motion during a simulated takeoff. *Journal of Aircraft,* 38, 600–606.

Einstein, A. (1922). The meaning of relativity: Princeton, NJ: Princeton University.

Benson, A. J., Hutt, E. C., and Brown, S. F. (1989). Thresholds for the perception of whole body angular movement about a vertical axis. *Aviation, Space, and Environmental Medicine,* 60, 205–213.

Kennedy, R., Lane, N., Berbaum, K., and Lilienthal, M. (1993). Simulator sickness questionnaire: an enhanced method for quantifying simulator sickness. *International Journal of Aviation Psychology,* 3(3), 203–220.

Snowden, R., Stimpson, N., and Ruddle, R. (1998). Speed perception fogs up as visibility drops. *Nature,* 450, 392.

Thompson, P. (1982). Perceived rate of movement depends on contrast. *Vision Research,* 22, 377–380.

Gillingham, K.K. and Wolfe, J.W. (1985). Spatial orientation in flight. In Dehart R.L., ed. *Fundamentals of aerospace medicine,* pp. 299–381. Philadelphia: Lea and Febiger.

Berthoz, A., Pavard, B., and Young, L. R. (1975). Perception of linear horizontal self-motion induced by peripheral vision (linear vection). Basic characteristic and visual-vestibular interactions. *Exp. Brain Res.,* 23, 471–489.

Annex A: The simulator sickness questionnaire

The SSQ from Kennedy et al., [8] is a self-report form consisting of 17 symptoms the participant rates on a four-point scale. Quantifying the symptoms and their strength if present, the SSQ is based on three components: nausea, oculomotor problems and disorientation. Combining these scores produces a total SSQ score. Participants report the degree to which they experience each of the symptoms as 0 for none, 1 for slight, 2 for moderate and 3 for severe. For each component, the column's reported value is multiplied by the weight for that column and then summed down the columns. The total SSQ score is obtained by adding the scale scores across the three columns and multiplying by 3.74. Weighted scale scores for individual columns are calculated by multiplying the nausea subscale score by 9.54, the oculomotor subscale by 7.58 and the disorientation subscale by 13.92.

Please Circle or X out Appropriate Level

Symptom		Component		
		Nausea	Oculomotor	Disorientation
General Discomfort		0 1 2 3	0 1 2 3	0 1 2 3
Fatigue		0 1 2 3	0 1 2 3	0 1 2 3
Headache		0 1 2 3	0 1 2 3	0 1 2 3
Eyestrain		0 1 2 3	0 1 2 3	0 1 2 3
Difficulty Focusing		0 1 2 3	0 1 2 3	0 1 2 3
Increased Salivation		0 1 2 3	0 1 2 3	0 1 2 3
Sweating		0 1 2 3	0 1 2 3	0 1 2 3
Nausea		0 1 2 3	0 1 2 3	0 1 2 3
Difficulty Concentrating		0 1 2 3	0 1 2 3	0 1 2 3
Fullness of Head		0 1 2 3	0 1 2 3	0 1 2 3
Blurred Vision		0 1 2 3	0 1 2 3	0 1 2 3
Dizzy (eyes open)		0 1 2 3	0 1 2 3	0 1 2 3
Dizzy (eyes closed)		0 1 2 3	0 1 2 3	0 1 2 3
Vertigo		0 1 2 3	0 1 2 3	0 1 2 3
Stomach Awareness		0 1 2 3	0 1 2 3	0 1 2 3
Burping		0 1 2 3	0 1 2 3	0 1 2 3

Rating	Code
None	0
Slight	1
Moderate	2
Severe	3

R.S. Kennedy, N.E. Lane, K.S. Berbaum, and M.G. Lilienthal.

Table 3. Simulated sickness questionnaire: An enhanced method for quantifying simulator sickness.

7

A New Trend in Designing Plant Layouts for the Process Industry

Richart Vazquez-Roman and M. Sam Mannan
Instituto Tecnológico de Celaya & Texas A&M University
Mexico & USA

1. Introduction

Process safety might be considered as the most important area to improve several aspects in the process industry design. Ways of dealing with hazards include means to either control them or totally remove them. Both control and removal ways can be applied during the design stage to produce inherently safer designs. There exist several practical examples where issues related to inherently safer designs have been explored (Kletz, 1984). Seven basic principles of inherently safer design have been identified from many application cases: intensification, substitution, attenuation, simplicity, operability, fail-safe design and second chance design, see for instance (Mannan, 2005). Indeed, the plant layout has been identified as a prominent feature for the second chance design, which means that it represents a second line of defence to guard against initial hazards or failures since the process has been already designed at this stage (Mannan, 2005).

Aids for the synthesis of inherently safer design are not well developed but some work has been done in process designs to conform into this principle. It is considered here that one way to avoid hazards is through safer designs that can be obtained for the process industry by appropriate plant layout designs. Plant siting and plant layout are considered as the last opportunity to enhance inherent safety during the design stage. The plant siting addresses finding a location for a plant as a part of a collection of plants and this task normally concerns with the safety for pupil surrounding the plants. The plant layout addresses the arrangement of units and equipment of each plant and it normally concerns with the safety for pupil inhabiting the plant (CCPS, 2003). In this work, the philosophy underlying the conceptual plant layout is considered applicable to virtually all aspects of siting. Plant layout is the term adopted in this work for both siting and plant layout where inherently safer designs should be the prime aim.

The plant layout problem includes thus accommodation not only of the process facilities but also of other facilities such as offices, parking lots, buildings, warehouses, storage tanks, utility areas, etc. It introduces a number of forms in which the results of any risk may be presented. A preliminary hazard screening will provide information to determine if the site provides adequate separation distances from neighbouring areas or among the process units. Experience has produced guidelines for facility siting and layout that can be used to estimate these distances (CCPS, 2003). However, there remains an inherent tendency to overdesign and any resulting preliminary plot area is never appropriately sized. A good model is required to estimate the risk related to eventually produce the optimal plot plan. A good plant layout will logically indicate a greater degree of inherent safety.

It has been indicated that 15-70% of total operational costs depends on the layout (Tompkins et al., 1996), and piping costs can be as high as 80% of the purchased equipment cost (Peters et al., 2003). It is also considered that a number of accidents can be reduced with an optimal process layout. Thus, the objective function must include sustainability factors to keep space for future expansions, environmental concerns, reliability, efficiency and safety in plant operations, land area and operating costs (Mecklenburgh, 1985).

Earlier plant layouts were based on common sense rules such as following the order in the process and separating adjacent units by sufficient distances to allow maintenance operations (Mecklenburgh, 1973; Moore, 1962). This procedure is not practical for optimization purposes and becomes particularly difficult to accommodate a large number of process units (Armour and Buffa, 1963). The complete problem is often partitioned to generate modules which are easier to solve in a sequence (Newell, 1973). This approach was improved through graph theory (Abdinnour-Helm and Hadley, 2000; Goetschalckx, 1992; Huang et al., 2007; Watson and Giffin, 1997) and fuzzy logic techniques (Evans et al., 1987).

The difficulty of solving the layout problem via programming techniques has been demonstrated in the arrangement of departments with certain traffic intensity which is a strongly NP-hard problem (Amaral, 2006). However, several efficient and systematic strategies have been developed to solve particularities of the layout problem. Several algorithms to solve the facility layout problem have been formulated as a quadratic assignment problem (QAP) (Koopmans and Beckmann, 1957; Pardalos et al., 1994; Sahni and Gonzalez, 1976). The QAP formulation is equivalent to the linear assignment with additional constraints (Christofides et al., 1980). Several QAP models were evolved into mixed integer programming (Montreuil, 1990; Rosenblatt, 1979; Urban, 1987). Another formulation was developed for facilities having fixed orientation and rectangular shape where the big-M method was applied to improve the numerical calculation (Heragu and Kusiak, 1991). Other MILP formulations solved different particularities of the layout problem through ad hoc methods or commercial packages (Barbosa-Póvoa et al., 2001; Barbosa-Póvoa et al., 2002; Guirardello and Swaney, 2005; Papageorgiou and Rotstein, 1998; Westerlund et al., 2007; Xie and Sahinidis, 2008). The layout of process units has been also formulated as a mixed-integer non-linear program (MINLP); however, the MINLP is converted to a MILP to ensure a numerical solution (Jayakumar and Reklaitis, 1996). A substantial improvement to the big-M formulation for the layout problem has been obtained with the convex-hull approach (Sherali et al., 2003). Stochastic techniques have shown their capability to produce practical solutions for the plant layout problem. Genetic algorithms are able to solve optimization problems containing non-differentiable objective functions thought the global optimum is not guaranteed (Castell et al., 1998; Martens, 2004; Mavridou and Pardalos, 1997; Wu et al., 2007). In addition, simulated annealing has been applied in the layout of manufacturing systems (Balakrishnan et al., 2003; McKendall and Shang, 2006).

The models to solve the layout problems cited above did not directly include safety issues. A new trend in designing plant layouts for the process industry consists of extending the layout formulations with safety issues. Though some MILP models have been proposed to reduce financial costs (Papageorgiou and Rotstein, 1998; Patsiatzis et al., 2004; Patsiatzis and Papageorgiou, 2002), modelling safety issues unavoidably end up in MINLP models. Inspired by the Flixborough and Bophal accidents, the first paper on designing the plant layout incorporated financial risk and protection devices cost to the classical piping and land costs in the objective function (Penteado and Ciric, 1996). The Mary Kay O'Connor Process Safety Center started a research to optimize the layout when some of the process units may release toxic gases. The following sections refer to the results of this research.

2. Overall Problem Statement

This work focuses at solving the layout when toxic release might occur in any process unit. The overall process layout consists on accommodating each process unit in a given land. The task can be divided in three parts: a) some units are grouped to remain as closed as possible among them with access for maintenance and fire-fighter actions to form facilities, b) all new facilities must be accommodated within a land where other facilities may exist and c) the pipe routing problem must be included in the two previous parts and it depends on the interconnectivity. Since toxic releases affects pupil and not to process units, it is convenient to describe the layout in terms of facilities where the control room becomes the most important facility to allocate. Furthermore, facilities typically have rectangular shapes. For the sake of simplicity, facilities and the available land are then considered to have rectangular shapes. Thus, the overall problem is established as follow:

Given:

- A set of already existing facilities $i \in I$;
- A set of new facilities for siting $s \in S$;
- A set of release types $r \in R$;
- A subset $ri(i,r)$ of existing facilities $i \in I$ having a particular release $r \in R$, and displacement values, dx_{ri} and dy_{ri} to identify the exact releasing point with respect to the center of the releasing *i*-facility;
- A subset $rs(s,r)$ of existing facilities $s \in S$ having a particular release $r \in R$, and displacement values, dx_{sr} and dy_{sr} to identify the exact releasing point with respect to the center of the releasing j-facility;
- The facilities interconnectivity for both types existing and new facilities;
- Length and depth of each new facility for siting, Lx_s and Ly_s;
- Length and depth of each existing facility, Lx_i and Ly_i, as well as their center point, (x_i, y_i);
- Maximum length, Lx and depth, Ly, of available land;
- Size of the street, *st*;

Determine

- Each new facility center position (x_i, y_i);
- The occupied area out of the total land;
- The final cost associated with the optimal layout;

Two approaches have been developed to solve the above problem. The dispersion of the toxic is important to calculate concentration and then the fatal effect for any toxic release scenario. Hence the wind effect is an important factor in this kind of scenarios. Since the wind behaves as a random variable for practical purposes, the first approach is referred as the stochastic approach where the wind speed, wind direction, and other factors are dealt through probabilistic models. In a second approach, the wind effect is modeled based on the worst scenario and this approach is referred to as the deterministic one. Both stochastic and deterministic approaches have different equations to evaluate the risk. However, they also have common constraints which are given in the following section.

3. Common Constraints

The common constraints are classified as land constraints, non-overlapping constraints and risk-related equations. In addition, the objective function contains also similar terms which are also presented below.

3.1 Land Constraints

Any new facility must be accomodated inside the available land having a street around it. The street size must be sufficient to facilitate the firefighting and emergency responses. Since it is considered that new facilities and the available land are described by rectangles, the center point for any new facility must satisfy:

$$\frac{Lx_s}{2} + st \le x_s \le Lx - \left(\frac{Lx_s}{2} + st\right) \tag{1}$$

$$\frac{Ly_s}{2} + st \le y_s \le Ly - \left(\frac{Ly_s}{2} + st\right) \tag{2}$$

For the sake of simplicity, the East direction is represented by the direction *(0,0)* to *(∞,0)* and the North by the direction *(0,0)* to *(0,∞)*.

3.2 Non-overlapping Constraints

Simple common sense indicates that two facilities cannot occupy the same space, i.e. they must not overlap. A new facility *s* could be accommodated anywhere around another facility *k* provided there is sufficient separation to build a street between them, Fig. 1. These possibilities must be reproduced in a model without duplication or overlapping to avoid numerical difficulties in the optimization procedure. The following disjunction identifies four sections with respect to the facility k: left side, right side, north and south. It should be observed that the north-south is initially grouped but it is later disaggregated:

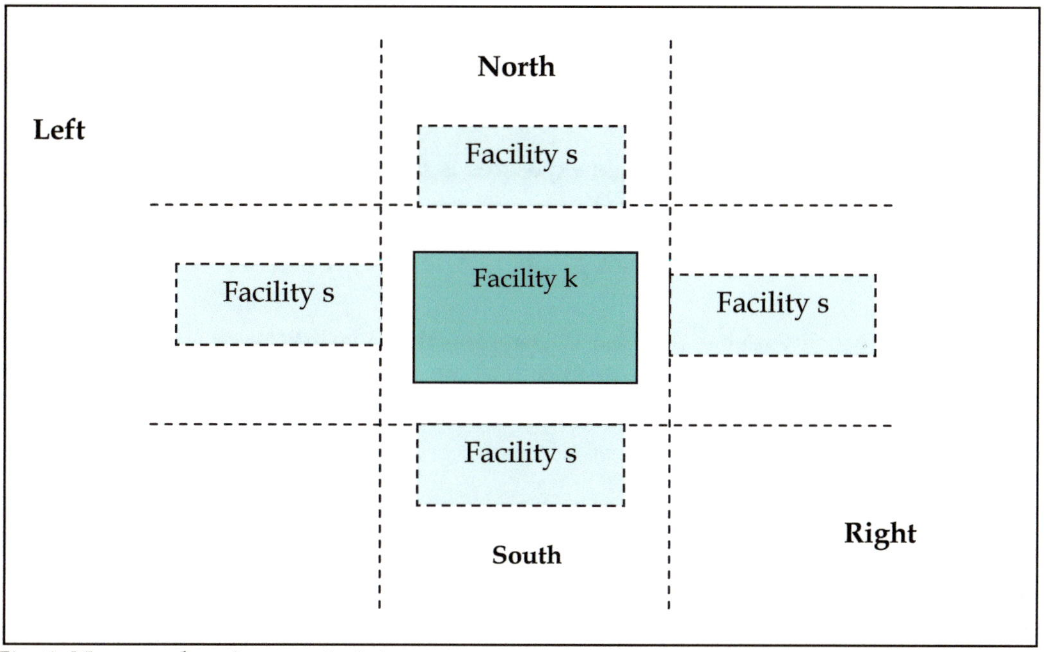

Fig. 1. Non-overlapping constraint

$$\begin{bmatrix} "L" \\ x_s \le x_k - D_{sk}^{\min,x} \end{bmatrix} \vee \begin{bmatrix} "R" \\ x_s \ge x_k + D_{sk}^{\min,x} \end{bmatrix} \vee \begin{bmatrix} "N","S" \\ x_s \ge x_k - D_{sk}^{\min,x} \\ x_s \le x_k + D_{sk}^{\min,x} \\ \begin{bmatrix} "N" \\ y_s \ge y_k + D_{sk}^{\min,y} \end{bmatrix} \vee \begin{bmatrix} "S" \\ y_s \le y_k - D_{sk}^{\min,y} \end{bmatrix} \end{bmatrix} \quad (3)$$

where,

$$D_{sk}^{\min,x} = \frac{Lx_s + Lx_k}{2} + st \quad (4)$$

$$D_{sk}^{\min,y} = \frac{Ly_s + Ly_k}{2} + st \quad (5)$$

and st is the street size and facility s refers to a facility to accommodate and facility k can be either a new or an already installed facility.

Since commercial optimization codes do not accept disjunctive formulations, equation (3) is reformulated as a MINLP. There are three methods to achieve this transformation: direct use of binary variables for each disyunction, the big-M and the convex hull (Grossmann, 2002). The straighforward method of binaryzation generates new bilinear terms which are source of numerical difficulties (McCormick, 1982) whereas the main drawback of the big-M formulation is that a bad selection yields poor relaxation (Grossmann, 2002). Thus the convex hull has been prefered in this conversion procedure (Vázquez-Román et al., 2009).

3.3 Risk-related Equations

The reponse vs. dose curves for single exposures is typically represented with the probit function as a straight-line (Finney, 1971):

$$\Pr = k_0 + k_1 \ln V \tag{6}$$

where *Pr* is the probit variable, the dose *V* represents the causative factor, being the product of concentration and exposure time for toxic releases, and k_0 and k_1 are best-fitting values reported for several substances in several sources. The probit variable is related to the probability of death, *P*, by:

$$P = \frac{1}{\sqrt{2\pi}} \int_{-\infty}^{\Pr-5} e^{-u^2/2} du \tag{7}$$

The probit relationship transforms the typical sigmoid shape of the normal response versus dose curve into a straight line.

3.4 The objective function

The piping cost, C_{piping}, is one of the important cost factors in the layout problem. It can be estimated by multiplying the separation distance, d_{ij}, by the cost of the pipe, C_p:

$$C_{piping} = \sum_{(i,j)} C_P d_{ij} \tag{8}$$

In principle, the distance should include the equivalent distance because of all accesories such as elbows in changes of direction. For the sake of simplicity, the Manhatan and Euclidian distances have been used. The latter is prefered in this work because the derivative can be easily produced:

$$d_{ij}^2 = (x_i - x_j)^2 + (y_i - y_j)^2 \tag{9}$$

where d_{ij} is the separation Euclidian distance between facility i with coordinates (x_i, y_i) and facility *j* with coordinates (x_j, y_j).

The land cost, C_{land}, represents the cost because of the area occupied by the overall layout. To easy this calculation, the process layout starts always in the origin *(0,0)* and the area is considered as the minimum rectangle that includes all facilities:

$$C_{land} = c_l A_x A_y \tag{10}$$

where c_l is the land cost per m2, and A_x and A_y are the lengths in the x and y directions which can be calculated from:

$$\begin{aligned} A_x &= \max(x_s + Lx_s / 2) \\ A_y &= \max(y_s + Ly_s / 2) \end{aligned} \tag{11}$$

Unfortunately the above formulation represents a non-convex function and it is not accepted in all optimization codes. Since the land cost and hence the area is minimized, a more convenient form can be used as follows:

$$\begin{aligned} A_x &\geq x_s + Lx_s / 2 \\ A_y &\geq y_s + Ly_s / 2 \end{aligned} \tag{12}$$

where s runs for all facilities. Next section describes the model developed where the stochastic effect of the wind is considered.

4. Stochastic Approach

Wind represents the main random factor in this stochastic approach developed to optimize the plant layout (Vázquez-Román et al., 2008; 2009). The main affected receptors in a given release scenario are those situsted in direction of the wind but there is also a reduced effect on adjacent sectors. The occurrence of winds at any location are normally represented in the wind rose plot where speed, directions and frequency are indicated. In addition, atmosphere stability is also required in this approach. This information is estimated from other meteorological variables such as altitude, total cloud cover, and ceiling height. A procedure to incorporate meteorological data from several databases in the wind effect analysis is fiven elsewhere (Lee et al., 2009). Fig. 2 shows the wind rose and the cummulative probability versus wind direction for Corpus Christi obtained with this procedure.

A credible release scenario must be proposed to define the expected amount of toxic released material. The credible scenario depends on the size of pipes and process conditions (Crowl and Louvar, 2002). Once the stochastic behavior of wind direction, wind speed and atmospheric stability is charaterised with cummulative probability curves and the release scenario is defined, a Monte Carlo simulation is applied where values for these stochastic variables are randomly selected. For this set of selected values, an appropriate model for the gas dispersion is used to estimate the concentration at all directions and several separation distances.

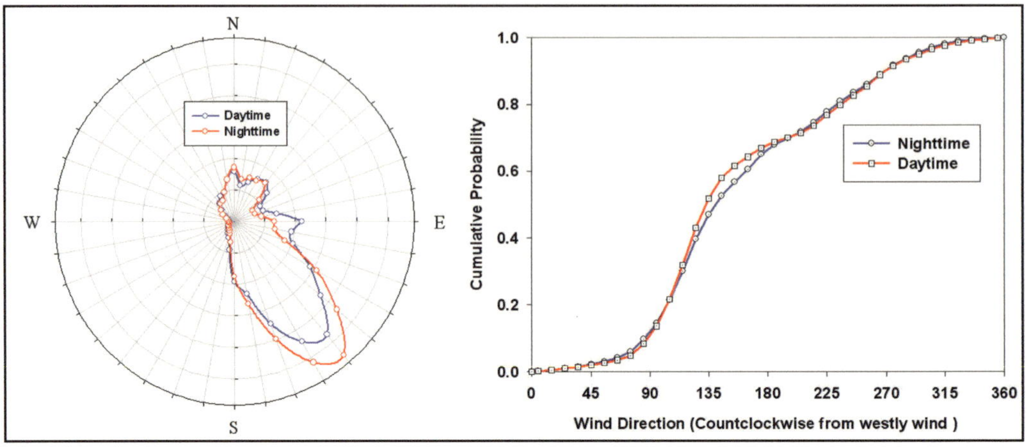

Fig. 2. Wind direction distribution in Corpus Christi

Ad hoc models can be developed to estimate concentrations of the toxic material in selected points. In addition, there exits several methods for different release scenarios such as liquid, dense gas or light gas (CCPS, 1996). The selected points must cover all possibilities in the available land so that the maximum separation between the first point and the last one in a given direction depends on the available land size. It is suggested to have intermediate neighbour points as close as possible without compromising the calculation time. A similar number of points must be used in each of several directions to get the concentration of the toxic gas at all possible directions. Thus the 360° are divided by direction-sectors to have a practical number of estimations. The Monte Carlo generates as many concentration values at each point as Monte Carlo runs and this number should be as large as practically possible. The concentration values can then be easily converted in risk of death values through the probit function. An exponential decay is assumed so that the probability of death at each α-direction, P_{D_α}, is represented by the equation:

$$P_{D_\alpha} = a_\alpha e^{-b_\alpha d_{r,\alpha}} \tag{13}$$

where $d_{r,\alpha}$ refers to the distante from the release point in the α-direction to the point where the probability is estimated and a_α and b_α are fitted parameters.

For the sake of simplicity, it is suggested that the number of direction-sectors be a multiple of four. Thus each sector can be described by the initial and final angle of the sector and the following dinjunction is used to identify the sector in wich an i-facility is being accommodated with respect to the s-facility that may release a toxic gas:

$$\bigvee_{i\in ri}\begin{bmatrix} \text{"}\alpha-\text{interval"} \\ s_{\alpha}^{\Delta y}(y_s - y_i) \geq 0 \\ s_{\alpha}^{\Delta x}(x_s - x_i) \geq 0 \\ s_{\alpha}^{\Delta x}(y_s - y_i) \leq s_{\alpha}^{\Delta x} m_{\alpha}(x_s - x_i) \\ s_{\alpha}^{\Delta x}(y_s - y_i) \geq s_{\alpha}^{\Delta x} m_{\alpha-1}(x_s - x_i) \end{bmatrix} \tag{14}$$

where m is the slope calculated by

$$m_{\alpha} = \left(\tan\left(\frac{2\alpha\pi}{n} \right) \right) \tag{15}$$

being n the number of direction-sectors whereas $s_{\alpha}^{\Delta x}$ and $s_{\alpha}^{\Delta y}$ are convenient vectors with either positive or negative ones to determine in which quadrant the facility i is positioned respect to facility s. $s_{\alpha}^{\Delta x}$ contain positive ones in the elements referring to the first and fourth quadrants but negative ones in thouss referring to the second and third quadrants. $s_{\alpha}^{\Delta y}$ has positive ones in elements referring to the first and second quadrants and negative ones otherwise. The above disjunction is also converted to a MINLP via the convex hull technique.

The following risk term is incorporated into the objective function:

$$C_{risk} = c_{pp} t_l \sum_{s} \sum_{ri(i,r)} f_{i,r} P_{i,r,s} \tag{16}$$

where c_{pp} is the compensation cost per fatality, t_l is the expected life of the plant, $f_{i,r}$ is the frequency of the type of release r in facility i and $P_{D_{i,r,s}i}$ is the probability of death in the facility s because of release type k in facility i.

5. Deterministic Approach

It is often suggested that a better risk assessment for safety in chemical process plants should be based on what is called the worst scenario (Leggett, 2004). A more recent study (Díaz-Ovalle et al., 2009) ratifies that the worst scenario in a toxic release scenario correspond to that one where the wind remains in calm under stable atmospheric condition. Unfortunately, most of current models simplify the convective-diffusive dispersion equation to produce practical equations but these models tend to misbehave when the wind speed tends to zero. Models for both passive and dense dispersion phenomena produce higher concentrations when the wind speed is lower. An accepted value to be used for the wind speed in calm is 1.5 m/sec. Since the wind in calm can occur at any direction, then the risk becomes symmetric and contours having the same risk level have circular shape.

A deterministic model based on the worst scenario is given in (Diaz-Ovalle et al., 2008). A threshold limit value (TLV) can be used to avoid exposures that may produce adverse effects to pupil. It is suggested that the concentration must not exceed the ceiling value, i.e. TLV-C, see for instance (Crowl and Louvar, 2002). Thus, the equation added to the general layout model described above consists in constraining the distance so that the calculated concentration cannot be superior to the TLV-C value. Otherwise and better than TLV, there are emergency responses planning guideline (ERPG) values that can be used with the same purpose in the layout determination. The objective function in the deterministic approach only contains the land and piping cost terms. The following section contains an analysis of the results obtained with both the stochastic and the deterministic approaches.

6. Discussion of Results and Future Research

The numerical difficulty of solving the layout problem even without toxic release has been clearly identified in (Vázquez-Román et al., 2009). An example considers two new facilities and the control room to be installed in a given land where there exist two installed facilities. While applying several optimization methods and using different initializations, three optima results were found. It should then be clear than increasing the number of units may produce more local optima and the question would remain about what is the best layout. The global optimum for this case was obtained through a global optimizer in *GAMS* (Brooke et al., 1998), but the time required to achieve the solution is too high and this time became unpractical when the number of facilities was increased.

To test the stochastic approach, a chlorine release was considered to occur in one of the installed facilities. All information required for the stochastic approach is provided in (Vázquez-Román et al., 2009). In this case two optimum layouts were detected with different GAMS solvers, Fig. 3. Though the global optimum was clearly identified, it was observed that it produced a small value in the cost associated to the financial risk whereas this cost became negligible in the other local optimum. Hence the question is again about what solution should be better to use. Another disadvantage of the stochastic approach is the time required to get the parameters of the exponential decay function for the probability of death. In principle, a high number of simulations should be used in the Monte Carlo procedure. The number of calculations could be reduced by reducing the number of direction-sectors but again a large number would produce more representative results. These results have been ratified with other examples in (Vázquez-Román et al., 2008).

Solving the layout with the deterministic approach tends to produce more conservative layouts (Diaz-Ovalle et al., 2008). However, when the toxic material is too toxic this approach may produce layouts occupying a large area. This was the case for the example used in (Vázquez-Román et al., 2009). This approach has the advantage that no extra calculation is required to incorporate the wind effect since calm conditions and hence symmetric effect is assumed. Thus the deterministic approach tends to enforce prevention, mitigation and removal of hazards to reduce the required land. This is typically achieved by inserting devices so that the final layout becomes more expensive than the one produced with the stochastic approach. This approach is justified by the fact that several severe accidents have occurred when calm conditions prevailed.

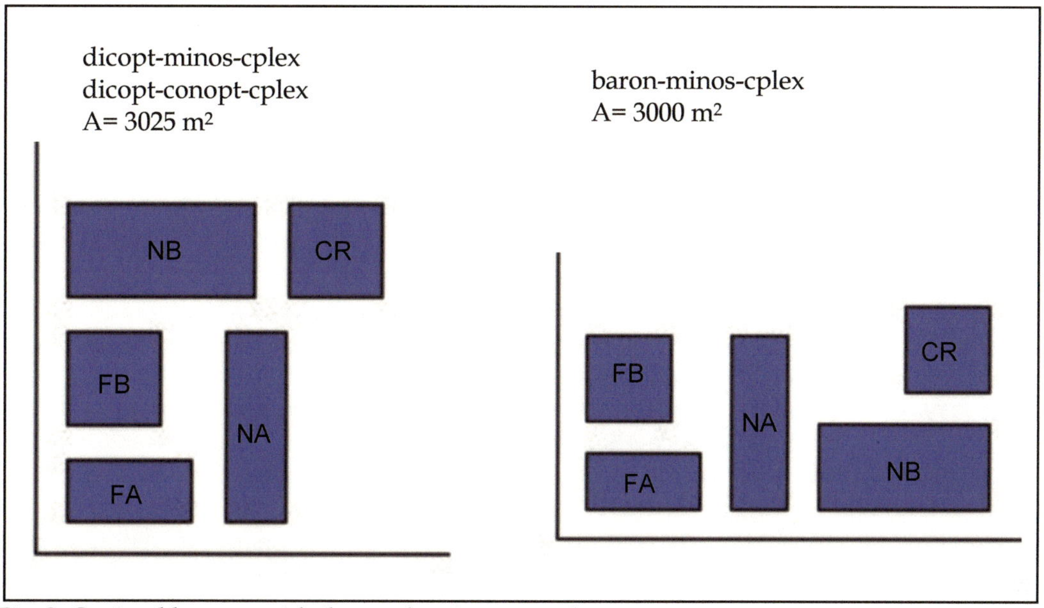

Fig. 3. Optimal layouts with the stochastic approach

The two approaches are in effect an application of the principle of inherently safer design. In fact, an inherently safer design is easier to achieve during the plant layout design. However, more research is required to ensure convergence to the global optimum. We are considering the possibility of convexifying the equations so that any local optimization solver could achieve the global irrespectively of the initialization. Also, we are developing 3D-CFD programs to evaluate particular layouts such as each local optimum to detect if streams can form and potentially increase the risk of a given layout. Finally, other properties such as corrosiveness, flammability and explosibility; operating conditions such as pressure and temperature; reaction conditions such as phase, rate, heat release, yield and side reactions; and effluents and wastes must be incorporated in solving the layout problem.

7. Acknowledgements

The contribution to this research by Jin-Han Lee, Seungho Jun and Chistian Diaz-Ovalle as well as the support by TAMU-CONACyT and DGEST is deeply acknowledged.

8. References

Abdinnour-Helm, S., and Hadley, S. W. (2000). Tabu search based heuristics for multi-floor facility layout. *International Journal of Production Research*, 38, 365-383.

Amaral, A. R. S. (2006). On the exact solution of a facility layout problem. *European Journal of Operational Research*, 173, 508-518.

Armour, G. C., and Buffa, E. (1963). A heuristic algorithm and simulation approach to relative location of facilities. *Management Science*, 9, 294-309.

Balakrishnan, J., Cheng, C. H., and Wong, K. F. (2003). FACOPT: a user friendly FACility layout OPTimization system. *Computers & Operations Research*, 30(11), 1625-1641.

Barbosa-Póvoa, A. P., Mateus, R., and Novais, A. Q. (2001). Optimal two-dimensional layout of industrial facilities. *International Journal of Production Research*, 39(12), 2567-2593.

Barbosa-Póvoa, A. P., Mateus, R., and Novais, A. Q. (2002). Optimal design and layout of industrial facilities: An application to multipurpose batch plants. *Industrial and Engineering Chemistry Research*, 41(15), 3610-3620.

Brooke, A., Kendrick, D., Meeraus, A., and Raman, R. (1998). *GAMS- a user guide*. Washington, DC, USA: GAMS Development Corporation.

Castell, C. M. L., Lakshmanan, R., Skilling, J. M., and Bañares-Alcántara, R. (1998). Optimisation of process plant layout using genetic algorithms. *Computers & Chemical Engineering*, 22(1), S993-S996.

CCPS (1996). *Guidelines for evaluating process plant building for external explosions and fires*. Center for Chemical Process Safety, AIChE.

CCPS (2003). *Guidelines for facility siting and layout*. Center for Chemical Process Safety, AIChE.

Christofides, N., Mingozzi, A., and Toth, P. (1980). Contributions to the quadratic assignment problem. *European Journal of Operational Research*, 4(4), 243-247.

Crowl, D. A., and Louvar, J. F. (2002). *Chemical process safety, fundamentals with applications*. New Jersey, Prentice Hall International Series in the Physical and Chemical Engineering Sciences.

Diaz-Ovalle, C. O., Jung, S., Vázquez-Román, R., and Mannan, M. S. (2008). An approach to solve the facility layout problem based on the worst scenario. In: *11th Annual Symposium, Mary Kay O'Connor Process Safety Center*, College Station, Tx, October 28-29, pp 28-39, ISBN: 978-0-615-25170-7.

Díaz-Ovalle, C. O., Vázquez-Román, R., and Mannan, S. (2009). Determinación de los factores del peor escenario en la emisión de gases tóxicos (Determination of the factors for the worst scenario in gas toxic release). *Información Tecnológica*, 20 (1), 3-10.

Evans, G. W., Wilhelm, M. R., and Karwowski, W. (1987). A layout design heuristic employing the theory of fuzzy sets. *International Journal of Production Research*, 25(10), 1431-1450.

Finney, D. J. (1971). *Probit analysis*. Third Edition, Cambridge University Press.

Goetschalckx, M. (1992). An interactive layout heuristic based on hexagonal adjacency graphs. *European Journal of Operational Research*, 63(2), 304-321.

Grossmann, I. E. (2002). Review of nonlinear mixed-integer and disjunctive programming techniques. *Optimization and Engineering*, 3, 227-252.

Guirardello, R., and Swaney, E. (2005). Optimization of process plant layout with pipe routing. *Computers & Chemical Engineering*, 30(1), 99-114.

Heragu, S. S., and Kusiak, A. (1991). Efficient models for the facility layout problem. *European Journal of Operational Research*, 53(1), 1-13.

Huang, X., Lai, W., Sajeev, A. S. M., and Gao, J. (2007). A new algorithm for removing node overlapping in graph visualization. *Information Sciences*, 177(14), 2821-2844.

Jayakumar, S., and Reklaitis, G. V. (1996). Chemical plant layout via graph partitioning-II. Multiple levels. *Computers & Chemical Engineering*, 20(5), 563-578.

Kletz, T. (1984). *Cheaper, safer plants*. IChemE.

Koopmans, T. C., and Beckmann, M. (1957). Assignment Problems and the Location of Economic Activities. *Econometrica*, 25(1), 53-76.

Lee, J.-H., Vázquez-Román, R., Jung, S., and Mannan, M. S. (2009). An Approach to Incorporate Long-term Meteorological Data in Dispersion Analysis to Estimate Directional Risk. *Atmospheric Environment*, On review.

Leggett, D. J. (2004). Process safety in the future - A view from the chemistry. *Process Safety Progress*, 23(2), 163-169.

Mannan, S. (2005). *Lees' Loss prevention in the process industries: Hazard identification, assessment and control*. USA, Elsevier Butterworth-Heinemann.

Martens, J. (2004). Two genetic algorithms to solve a layout problem in the fashion industry. *European Journal of Operational Research*, 154(1), 304-322.

Mavridou, T. D., and Pardalos, P. M. (1997). Simulated Annealing and Genetic Algorithms for the Facility Layout Problem: A Survey *Computational Optimization and Applications*, 7(1), 111-126.

McCormick, G. P. (1982). *Nonlinear programming, theory, algorithms and applications*. Wiley.

McKendall, A. R. J., and Shang, J. (2006). Hybrid ant systems for the dynamic facility layout problem. *Computers & Operations Research*, 33(3), 790-803.

Mecklenburgh, J. C. (1973). *Plant layout: a guide to the layout of process plant and sites*. New York, Wiley.

Mecklenburgh, J. C. (1985). *Process plant layout*. John Wiley & Sons, New York.

Montreuil, B. (1990). A modeling framework for integrating layout design and flow network design. In: *Proceedings of the Material Handling Research Colloquium*, 43-58, Hebron, KY, MaterialHandling Institute.

Moore, J. M. (1962). *Plant layout and design*. New York, Macmillan.

Newell, R. G. (1973). *Algorithms for the design of chemical plant layout and pipe routing*. Ph.D. thesis, London. U.K., Imperial College.

Papageorgiou, L. G., and Rotstein, G. E. (1998). Continous-domain mathematical models for optimal process plant layout. *Industrial and Engineering Chemistry Research*, 37(9), 3631-3639.

Pardalos, P. M., Rentl, F., and Wolkowicz, H. (1994). The quadratic assignment problem: A survey and recent developments. In: *Quadratic assignment and related problems*. P. M. Pardalos and H. Wolkowicz (eds.), 1-42, DIMACS Series on Discrete Mathematics and Theoretical Computer Science, American Mathematical Society.

Patsiatzis, D. I., Knight, G., and Papageorgiou, L. G. (2004). An MILP approach to safe process plant layout. *Trans IChemE Part A: Chemical Engineering and Design*, 82(A5), 579-586.

Patsiatzis, D. I., and Papageorgiou, L. G. (2002). Optimal multi-floor process plant layout. *Computers & Chemical Engineering*, 26(4-5), 575-583.

Penteado, F. D., and Ciric, A. R. (1996). An MINLP approach for safe process plant layout. *Industrial and Engineering Chemistry Research*, 35(4), 1354-1361.

Peters, M. S., Timmerhaus, K. D., and West, R. E. (2003). *Plant design and economics for chemical engineers*. New York, McGraw Hill.

Rosenblatt, M. J. (1979). The facilities layout problem: a multi-goal approach. *International Journal of Production Research*, 17 (4), 323-332.

Sahni, S., and Gonzalez, T. (1976). P-Complete Approximation Problems *Journal of the Association for Computing Machinery*, 23(3), 555 - 565.

Sherali, H. D., Fraticelli, B. M. P., and Meller, R. D. (2003). Enhanced model formulations for optimal facility layout. *Operations Research*, 51, 629-644.

Tompkins, J. A., White, J. A., Bozer, Y. A., Frazelle, E. H., Tanchoco, J. M. A., and Treviño, J. (1996). *Facility planning*. New York, John Wiley & Sons, Inc.

Urban, T. L. (1987). A multiple criteria model for the facilities layout problem. *International Journal of Production Research*, 25 (12), 1805-1812.

Vázquez-Román, R., Lee, J.-H., Jung, S., and Mannan, M. S. (2008). Designing plant layouts with toxic releases based on wind statistics. In: *IASTED International Conference on Modelling and Simulation*, paper 620-018, May 26-28, Quebec, Canada.

Vázquez-Román, R., Lee, J.-H., Jung, S., and Mannan, M. S. (2009). Optimal facility layout under toxic release in existing plants. *Computers & Chemical Engineering*, on revision by the editor.

Watson, K. H., and Giffin, J. W. (1997). The Vertex Splitting Algorithm for facilities layout. *International Journal of Production Research*, 35 (9), 2477-2492.

Westerlund, J., Papageorgiou, L. G., and Westerlund, T. (2007). A MILP Model for N-dimensional allocation. *Computers & Chemical Engineering*, 2007.2002.2006.

Wu, X., Chu, C.-H., Wang, Y., and Yan, W. (2007). A genetic algorithm for cellular manufacturing design and layout. *European Journal of Operational Research*, 181(1), 156-167.

Xie, W., and Sahinidis, N. V. (2008). A branch-and-bound algorithm for the continuous facility layout problem. *Computers & Chemical Engineering*, 32(4-5), 1016-1028.

The Elliptic Solvers in the Canadian Limited Area Forecasting Model GEM-LAM

Abdessamad Qaddouri and Vivian Lee
Atmospheric Science and Technology Directorate, Environment Canada
Canada

1. Introduction

The Global and Limited area versions of the Canadian global Environmental (GEM) model (Coté et al.,1998), currently used for operational numerical weather prediction (NWP) at Canadian Meteorological centre (CMC) employ an implicit time discretization on the spatial grids of tensors product. This gives rise to a separable 3D elliptic boundary value (EBV) problem that must be solved at each model time step. This EBV problem is also found in the implicit formulation of the high order diffusion equation which is used in GEM. Most models in operational NWP apply this selective diffusion in order to eliminate high wave-number noise due (for example) to numerical discretization. The solution of the EBV is in general, at the heart of most models used for NWP. It is currently solved in the limited area version (GEM-LAM) by applying either a direct or an iterative method.
As in the global GEM model (Qaddouri et al., 1999), the direct method in GEM-LAM model is implemented with either fast or slow Fourier transforms. Because of the nature of the boundary conditions in GEM-LAM, discrete cosine transforms (DCTs) are use instead of discrete Fourier transforms (DFTs). In the case of the slow transform, which involves a full matrix multiplication and this will be referred as MXMA, the cost per grid point increases linearly with the number of grid points along the transform direction and if this number divides properly, the fast Fourier transforms (FFT) can be used. It is important to find ways to optimize this slow transform as it dominates the cost of the solver and, it does represent a significant fraction of the total cost of the model time step. The iterative method is implemented in GEM-LAM to reduce the cost of the slow transform in the elliptic solver and it is based on a preconditioned Generalized Minimal REsidual (GMRES) algorithm (Saad, 1996). The GEM-LAM model is parallelized with a hybrid use of MPI and OpenMP. In the parallel version of the direct solver, four global communications are used which could be very time-consuming when the number of processors increases. In the iterative solver, each processor communicates with its neighbours and global communications are limited only to calculating a global dot product.
In the following sections, EBV problem to be solved is presented and the direct and iterative methods are described. The high order diffusion is discussed in section 3 while the parallelization of direct solution is shown in section 4. Results from numerical experiments are reported and analyzed in section 5, and the paper is concluded in section 6.

2. Positive Definite Helmholtz

The problem to be solved is a 3D separable EBV problem which after a vertical separation, it is reduced to a set of horizontal positive definite Helmholtz problems (Coté et al., 1998).
To illustrate the derivation of a Helmholtz problem from an implicit time discretization of the terms responsible for the gravity wave, and to show the nature of the horizontal boundary conditions for the GEM-LAM model , the following simple 2D linear Shallow water equations is integrated in a limited area of a non-rotating sphere with radius a :

$$\begin{aligned}
&\frac{\partial U}{\partial t}+\frac{1}{a^2}\frac{\partial \phi}{\partial \lambda}=0, \\
&\frac{\partial V}{\partial t}+\frac{1}{a^2}cos(\theta)\frac{\partial \phi}{\partial \theta}=0, \\
&\frac{\partial \phi}{\partial t}+\phi^* \frac{1}{cos^2(\theta)}\left(\frac{\partial U}{\partial \lambda}+cos(\theta)\frac{\partial V}{\partial \theta}\right)=0,
\end{aligned} \tag{1}$$

where the unknowns are the wind images U, V (wind times $cos(\theta)/a$), and ϕ is the perturbation geopotential from the reference geopotential ϕ^* . Using the staggered Arakawa C-grid (Arakawa et al., 1977), the wind components are placed in the middle of the lines joining the geopotential points. By employing the Crank-Nicholson time discretization , the resulting equations at the forecast time t are:

$$\frac{U}{\tau}+\frac{1}{a^2}\frac{\partial \phi}{\partial \lambda}=RU=\left[\frac{U}{\tau}+\frac{1}{a^2}\frac{\partial \phi}{\partial \lambda}\right]^-, \tag{2}$$

$$\frac{V}{\tau}+\frac{1}{a^2}cos(\theta)\frac{\partial \phi}{\partial \theta}=RV=\left[\frac{V}{\tau}+\frac{1}{a^2}cos(\theta)\frac{\partial \phi}{\partial \theta}\right]^-, \tag{3}$$

$$\frac{\phi}{\tau}+\phi^* \frac{1}{cos^2(\theta)}\left(\frac{\partial U}{\partial \lambda}+cos(\theta)\frac{\partial V}{\partial \theta}\right)=R\phi=\left[\frac{\phi}{\tau}+\phi^* \frac{1}{cos^2(\theta)}\left(\frac{\partial U}{\partial \lambda}+cos(\theta)\frac{\partial V}{\partial \theta}\right)\right]^-. \tag{4}$$

Where $\tau=\frac{\Delta t}{2}$ and the minus (-) superscript indicates the evaluation at the previous time step. To discretize in the space let, $(\lambda_i, i=1,NI, \theta_j, j=1,NJ)$ denote the set of ϕ -grid points, $(\tilde{\lambda}_i, i=0,NI, \theta_j, j=1,NJ)$ denote the set of U-grid points and $(\lambda_i, i=1,NI, \tilde{\theta}_j, j=0,NJ)$ denote the set of V-grid points with

$$\begin{aligned}
\tilde{\lambda}_i &= \frac{(\lambda_i+\lambda_{i+1})}{2}, \\
\tilde{\theta}_i &= \frac{(\theta_j+\theta_{j+1})}{2}.
\end{aligned} \tag{5}$$

Note that the boundary conditions on U and V are applied at $\tilde{\lambda}_0, \tilde{\lambda}_N$ and $\tilde{\theta}_0 \tilde{\theta}_M$. Then apply the wall boundary conditions

$$\begin{aligned} U\left(\tilde{\lambda}_0,\theta,t\right) &= U_0(\theta) \\ U\left(\tilde{\lambda}_N,\theta,t\right) &= U_N(\theta) \\ V\left(\tilde{\lambda},\tilde{\theta}_0,t\right) &= V_0(\lambda) \\ V\left(\lambda,\tilde{\theta}_M,t\right) &= V_M(\lambda), \end{aligned} \tag{6}$$

which are provided by a global model (or a larger LAM model) for U_0, U_N, V_0 and V_M to the target limited area model. The operator Δ is defined as $\Delta\lambda_i = \lambda_{i+1} - \lambda_i$. Integrating the equations (2-4) over their specific control volume $\left(\Delta\tilde{\lambda}_{i-1} \times \Delta\theta_j\right)$, $\left(\Delta\lambda_i \times \Delta\tilde{\theta}_j\right)$ and $\left(\Delta\lambda_i \times \Delta\theta_j\right)$ will yield

$$\Delta\tilde{\lambda}_{i-1}\Delta\theta_j \frac{U_{i,j}}{\tau} + \frac{1}{a^2}\left(\phi_{i+1,j} - \phi_{i,j}\right) = \Delta\tilde{\lambda}_{i-1}\Delta\theta_j\, RU_{i,j}, \tag{7}$$

$$\Delta\lambda_i \times \Delta\tilde{\theta}_{j-1} \frac{V_{i,j}}{\tau} + \frac{1}{a^2}\left(\cos\left(\tilde{\theta}_j\right)\phi_{i,j+1} - \cos\left(\tilde{\theta}_{j-1}\right)\phi_{i,j}\right) = \Delta\lambda_i \times \Delta\tilde{\theta}_{j-1}\, RV_{i,j}, \tag{8}$$

$$\Delta\lambda_i \times \Delta\theta_j \frac{\phi_{i,j}}{\tau} + \phi^* \frac{1}{\cos^2\left(\theta_i\right)}\left(\Delta\theta_j\left(U_{i+1,j} - U_{i,j}\right) + \cos\left(\theta_j\right)\phi_{i,j+1} - \cos\left(\theta_j\right)\left(V_{i+1,j} - V_{i,j}\right)\right) = \Delta\lambda_i \times \Delta\theta_j\, R\phi_{i,j}, \tag{9}$$

with

$$\begin{aligned} RU_{0,j} &= U_{0,}(j)/\tau \\ RU_{N,j} &= U_{N,}(j)/\tau \\ RV_{i,0} &= V_{0,}(i)/\tau \\ RV_{i,N} &= V_{N,}(i)/\tau. \end{aligned} \tag{10}$$

Two equations from (7) are re-written to express at two neighbouring points *(i+1,j)* and *(i,j)* in U-grid while two equations from (8) are re-written to express at two neighbouring points *(i,j+1)* and *(i,j)* in *V*-grid. These four resulting equations are added and combined with equation (9) to obtain the following discretized elliptic equation (11) for the geopotential only. This equation is called the (positive definite) Helmholtz equation by the NWP community.

$$\mathbf{A}\phi = \mathbf{r}, \tag{11}$$

where

$$\mathbf{A} = \left[\eta\, P(\theta) \otimes P(\lambda) - P'(\theta) \otimes P_{\lambda\lambda} - P_{\theta\theta} \otimes P(\lambda)\right], \tag{12}$$

where $\eta = \dfrac{a^2}{\phi^* \tau^2}$, $\otimes$ is the notation for tensor product and

$$\mathbf{r} = P(\theta) \otimes P(\lambda) R, \tag{13}$$

with

$$P(\theta) = \begin{bmatrix} \Delta\sin\tilde{\theta}_0 & & & \\ & \Delta\sin\tilde{\theta}_1 & & \\ & & \ddots & \\ & & & \Delta\sin\tilde{\theta}_{NJ-1} \end{bmatrix}, \tag{14}$$

$$P'(\theta)=\begin{bmatrix} \dfrac{\Delta\sin\tilde{\theta}_0}{\cos^2\theta_1} & & & \\ & \dfrac{\Delta\sin\tilde{\theta}_1}{\cos^2\theta_2} & & \\ & & \ddots & \\ & & & \dfrac{\Delta\sin\tilde{\theta}_{NJ\text{-}1}}{\cos^2\theta_{NJ}} \end{bmatrix}, \tag{15}$$

$$P_{\theta\theta}=\begin{bmatrix} -\dfrac{\cos^2\tilde{\theta}_1}{\Delta\sin\theta_1} & \dfrac{\cos^2\tilde{\theta}_1}{\Delta\sin\theta_1} & & & \\ \dfrac{\cos^2\tilde{\theta}_1}{\Delta\sin\theta_1} & -\dfrac{\cos^2\tilde{\theta}_1}{\Delta\sin\theta_1}-\dfrac{\cos^2\tilde{\theta}_2}{\Delta\sin\theta_2} & \dfrac{\cos^2\tilde{\theta}_2}{\Delta\sin\theta_2} & & \\ & \ddots & \ddots & \ddots & \\ & & \ddots & -\dfrac{\cos^2\tilde{\theta}_{NJ\text{-}2}}{\Delta\sin\theta_{NJ\text{-}2}}-\dfrac{\cos^2\tilde{\theta}_{NJ\text{-}1}}{\Delta\sin\theta_{NJ\text{-}1}} & \dfrac{\cos^2\tilde{\theta}_{NJ\text{-}1}}{\Delta\sin\theta_{NJ\text{-}1}} \\ & & & \dfrac{\cos^2\tilde{\theta}_{NJ\text{-}1}}{\Delta\sin\theta_{NJ\text{-}1}} & -\dfrac{\cos^2\tilde{\theta}_{NJ\text{-}1}}{\Delta\sin\theta_{NJ\text{-}1}} \end{bmatrix}, \tag{16}$$

$$P(\lambda)=\begin{bmatrix} \Delta\tilde{\lambda}_0 & & & \\ & \Delta\tilde{\lambda}_1 & & \\ & & \ddots & \\ & & & \Delta\tilde{\lambda}_{NI\text{-}1} \end{bmatrix}, \tag{17}$$

$$P_{\lambda\lambda}=\begin{bmatrix} -\dfrac{1}{\Delta\lambda_1} & \dfrac{1}{\Delta\lambda_1} & & & \\ \dfrac{1}{\Delta\lambda_1} & -\dfrac{1}{\Delta\lambda_1}-\dfrac{1}{\Delta\lambda_2} & \dfrac{1}{\Delta\lambda_2} & & \\ & \dfrac{1}{\Delta\lambda_2} & \ddots & \ddots & \\ & & \ddots & \ddots & \dfrac{1}{\Delta\lambda_{NI-1}} \\ & & & \dfrac{1}{\Delta\lambda_{NI-1}} & -\dfrac{1}{\Delta\lambda_{NI-1}} \end{bmatrix}. \tag{18}$$

In GEM-LAM with NK vertical levels, we have NK different constants $\eta(k)$, k=1,NK which are eigenvalues of a generalized eigenvalue problem like in Eq. 21 but along the vertical direction. After expanding the variables in z-direction eigenvectors, a vertical separation is done in the direct solver, and NK Helmholtz problems like the one in Eq.11 are obtained. Since the 3D problem is vertically separable, only the horizontal aspect needs to be considered though the numerical results obtained are for the full 3D elliptic solver.

Because of the nature of the horizontal boundary conditions in GEM-LAM, a brief discussion on the discrete cosine Fourier transforms in the context of differential equations is presented in the following sub-section.

2.1 Discrete Cosine Fourier transforms

Like discrete Fourier transforms (DFTs), discrete cosine transforms (DCTs) express a function in terms of a sum of sinusoids with different frequencies and amplitudes. DCT uses only cosine functions, while DFT uses both cosine and sine in the form of complex exponentials. The DFT implies a periodic extension of the function true along the longitude axis in the GEM global atmospheric model. The expression of the matrix $P_{\lambda\lambda}$ gives a clear idea about the boundary conditions implicitly used for the Helmholtz problem in the longitudinal directions in GEM-LAM. It can be seen that an even extension of the functions, possible by the use of DCT, is needed (Denis et al., 2004). Consider the analysis of right hand side of the equation (11) for each latitude j, the discrete cosine transform is

$$\tilde{\mathbf{r}}_{k,j} = \sum_{i=0}^{NI-1} \mathbf{r}_{i,j} \cos\left[\frac{\pi}{NI}\left(i+\frac{1}{2}\right)k\right]. \tag{19}$$

This DCT used in GEM-LAM implies this following boundary condition: $\mathbf{r}_{i,j}$ is even around the grid point $i = -1/2$, even around $i = NI - 1/2$ and $\tilde{\mathbf{r}}_{k,j}$ is even around the wave-number $k = 0$ and around $k = NI$. The DCT matrix is made orthogonal by scaling with a factor $\sqrt{2/NI}$ and if NI divides properly, the Fast Fourier transform (FFT) is used.

2.2 Direct Solution of Helmholtz problem

The direct solution of (11) is obtained by exploiting its separability, and expanding ϕ in λ-direction eigenvectors that diagonalize $\mathbf{A}$, i.e.

$$\phi_{ij} = \sum_{i=1}^{NI} \psi_i^{[I]} \phi_j^{[I]}, \tag{20}$$

with

$$P_{\lambda\lambda}\,\psi^{[I]} = \varepsilon_I\, P(\lambda)\psi^{[I]}, I = 1, NI, \tag{21}$$

and the property of orthogonality in

$$\sum_{i=1}^{NI} \psi_i^{[I']} P(\lambda)_{ii} \psi_i^{[I]} = \delta_{\mathrm{II'}}, \tag{22}$$

which is used to project (11) on each mode in turn. The result can then be written in matrix form as

$$\mathbf{A}^{[I]}\phi^{[I]} + \eta\, I^{[I]}(\theta)\phi^{[I]} = \mathbf{r}^{[I]}, \tag{23}$$

where

$$\mathbf{A}^{[I]} = \left[-\varepsilon_I\, P'(\theta) - P_{\theta\theta}\right];\;\; I^{[I]}(\theta) = P(\theta). \tag{24}$$

The algorithm can then be summarized as:

1. Analysis of the right-hand side: $\mathbf{r}_j^{[I]} = \sum_{i=1}^{NI} \psi_i^{[I]} \mathbf{r}_{ij}$,

2. solution of the NI tridiagonal problems in equation (23),

3. synthesis of the solution, $\phi_{ij} = \sum_{i=1}^{NI} \psi_i^{[I]} \phi_j^{[I]}$.

It is well known that for a uniform λ-grid, the modes ψ^I are proportional to the usual Fourier modes and the analysis and synthesis steps can be implemented with a real Fourier transform, and if furthermore *NI* factorizes properly, the Fast Fourier Transform (FFT) algorithm can be used, otherwise these steps are implemented with a full matrix multiplication (MXMA). In GEM-LAM, ψ^I are the cosine functions as in equation (19).

2.3 Iterative solution of Helmholtz problem

The equation (11) can also be solved by a robust parallel preconditioned GMRES algorithm where block-Jacobi iteration is used as a preconditioner (single level additive Schwarz). The blocks correspond to a different direct solution of the local Helmholtz problem in sub-domains. The GMRES code used here is the same parallel code developed by Saad and Malevsky (Saad & Malevsky, 1995), where a reverse communication mechanism is implemented in order to avoid passing a large list of arguments to the routines and, the data structure is left suitable for all possible types of preconditioners. The code can be read as follows:

```
Icode =0
1 continue
Call gmres(_)
If (icode.eq.1) then
 Call preconditioner()
Goto 1
Else if (icode.eq.2)
Call Matrix-vector()
Goto 1
Endif.
```

For each subdomain (processor), the preconditioner is called locally as a direct solution like the paragraph above but it only uses the slow transform where the matrix multiplication (MXMA) uses local data. It is known here that the preconditioning operation involves no inter-processors communication. In the matrix-vector operation, each processor will need to communicate with its neighbours.

3. The 2D high order implicit diffusion

The problem to solve is a high order diffusion equation which takes the form of the time dependent equation

$$\frac{\partial \phi}{\partial \lambda} = \mu * (-1)^{\frac{m}{2}+1} * \nabla^m \phi, \tag{25}$$

where ϕ is any prognostic variable, the integer m can be any multiple of 2 and denotes the order. The diffusion coefficient μ is considered constant for simplicity. The diffusion is periodically applied to specific meteorological fields and its effect is equivalent to applying diffusion in the prognostic equation for a period of time. In the operational GEM-LAM, only the direct solution (sec.3.2) is implemented for the 2D high order diffusion which considers either the slow (MXMA) or fast (FFT) Fourier transforms. The work for the iterative solution has not been completed.

3.1 Temporel Discretization

Implicit discretization of the equation (25) is

$$\frac{\phi^{n+1}-\phi^{n}}{\Delta t}=\mu*(-1)^{\frac{m}{2}+1}*\nabla^{m}\phi^{n+1}. \tag{26}$$

Integration of the equation (26) gives the following equation

$$\nabla^{m}\phi^{n+1}+\frac{1}{\mu*(-1)^{\frac{m}{2}+1}\Delta t}\phi^{n+1}=\frac{1}{\mu*(-1)^{\frac{m}{2}+1}\Delta t}\phi^{n}, \tag{27}$$

i.e.,

$$\nabla^{m}\phi+\eta\phi=R, \tag{28}$$

where R is the forcing term, η is a prescribed parameter. Numerical solution of (28) on the sphere requires a conservative discretization of ∇^{m}, with a consistent treatment of the boundary condition. In this paper, with m = 4 for example, the equation (28) would become the following two second order equations to be solved:

$$\nabla^{2}Z+\eta\phi=f;\ \nabla^{2}\phi-Z=0, \tag{29}$$

where ∇^{2} operator on the sphere is

$$\nabla^{2}=\frac{1}{a^{2}\cos^{2}\theta}\frac{\partial^{2}}{\partial\lambda^{2}}+\frac{1}{a^{2}\cos\theta}\frac{\partial}{\partial\theta}\left(\cos\theta\frac{\partial}{\partial\theta}\right), \tag{30}$$

and λ is the longitude, θ is the latitude and a is the earth's radius.

3.2 Spatial discretization

The spatial discretization is on the Arakawa C-grid as described in section 2. This is a tensorial grid. The discrete form of (29) is

$$\mathbf{A}Z+\eta I(\lambda,\theta)\phi=\mathbf{r};\ \ \mathbf{A}\phi-I(\lambda,\theta)Z=0, \tag{31}$$

where

$$\mathbf{A}=\left[-P'(\theta)\otimes P_{\lambda\lambda}-P_{\theta\theta}\otimes P(\lambda)\right], \tag{32}$$

where $\otimes$ is the notation for tensor product and

$$\mathbf{r} = P(\theta)\otimes P(\lambda)R; \quad I(\lambda,\theta) = P(\theta)\otimes P(\lambda), \tag{33}$$

3.3 Direct Solution

The direct solution of (15) is obtained by exploiting the separability as in the Helmholtz problem, and expanding ϕ and Z in λ-direction eigenvectors that diagonalize $\mathbf{A}$, i.e.

$$\phi_{ij} = \sum_{i=1}^{NI} \psi_i^{[I]} \phi_j^{[I]} \quad Z_{ij} = \sum_{i=1}^{NI} \psi_i^{[I]} Z_j^{[I]}, \tag{34}$$

with

$$P_{\lambda\lambda}\,\psi^{[I]} = \varepsilon_I\, P(\lambda)\psi^{[I]}, I = 1, NI, \tag{35}$$

and the property of orthogonality

$$\sum_{i=1}^{NI} \psi_i^{[I']} P(\lambda)_{ii} \psi_i^{[I]} = \delta_{\mathrm{II'}}, \tag{36}$$

is used to project (15) on each mode in turn. The result written in matrix form is obtained as

$$\mathbf{A}^{[I]} Z^{[I]} + \eta\, I^{[I]}(\theta)\phi^{[I]} = \mathbf{r}^{[I]}; \quad \mathbf{A}^{[I]}\phi^{[I]} - I^{[I]}(\theta) Z^{[I]} = 0, \quad I = 1,..NI, \tag{37}$$

where

$$\mathbf{A}^{[I]} = \left[-\varepsilon_I\, P'(\theta) - P_{\theta\theta}\right]; \quad I^{[I]}(\theta) = P(\theta). \tag{38}$$

The algorithm can then be summarized as:

1. analysis of the right-hand side: $\mathbf{r}_j^{[I]} = \sum_{i=1}^{NI} \psi_i^{[I]} \mathbf{r}_{ij}$,
2. solution of the problems in equation (37),
3. synthesis of the solution, $\phi_{ij} = \sum_{i=1}^{NI} \psi_i^{[I]} \phi_j^{[I]}$,

As seen in the direct solution of the Helmholtz problem, a uniform λ-grid the modes ψ^I are proportional to the usual Fourier modes. The analysis and synthesis steps can then be simply implemented with a real Fourier transform, and if *NI* also factorizes properly, the Fast Fourier Transform (FFT) algorithm can be applied. If the NI cannot be divided properly, these steps would become the "slow" transform case using the full matrix multiplication (MXMA). The *NI* problems in (37) can be then transformed to *NI* block tridiagonal problems to solve. With contrast to (Yong et al., 1994) where the recursive method in (Lindzen & Kuo, 1969) is used, a block LU factorization is used in this paper.

Let $X_j = \begin{bmatrix} Z_j^{[I]} \\ \phi_j^{[I]} \end{bmatrix}$, with $X_0 = \begin{bmatrix} 0 \\ 0 \end{bmatrix} = X_{NJ+1}$, the system in (37) can be written as

$$\left[\begin{bmatrix} A^{[I]}_{j,j-1} & 0 \\ 0 & A^{[I]}_{j,j-1} \end{bmatrix} \begin{bmatrix} A^{[I]}_{j,j} & (\eta * P_{jj}(\theta)) \\ -P_{jj}(\theta) & A^{[I]}_{j,j} \end{bmatrix} \begin{bmatrix} A^{[I]}_{j,j+1} & 0 \\ 0 & A^{[I]}_{j,j+1} \end{bmatrix}\right] \begin{bmatrix} X_{j-1} \\ X_j \\ X_{j+1} \end{bmatrix} = \begin{bmatrix} r^{[I]}_j \\ 0 \end{bmatrix} \quad j=1,..NJ, \tag{39}$$

i.e.,

$$M \quad X = B, \tag{40}$$

where M is a matrix of dimension $2 * NJ$, or a block tridiagonal matrix of dimension NJ where each element is a 2 by 2 matrix. We can then represent M in the form

$$M = \begin{bmatrix} D_1 & E_1 & & & \\ F_2 & D_2 & E_3 & & \\ & F_3 & \ddots & \ddots & \\ & & \ddots & D_{NJ-1} & E_{NJ-1} \\ & & & F_{NJ} & D_{NJ} \end{bmatrix}, \tag{41}$$

where blocks E_i and F_i are 2 by 2 diagonal matrices, and D_i are 2 by 2 full matrices. Let D be the block-diagonal matrix consisting of the diagonal blocks D_i , L the block strictly-lower triangular matrix consisting of the sub-diagonal blocks F_i, and U the block strictly-upper triangular matrix consisting of the super-diagonal blocks E_i. Then the above matrix M has the form

$$M = L + D + U. \tag{42}$$

A block LU factorization of M is defined by

$$M = (L + \Delta)\Delta^{-1}(\Delta + U), \tag{43}$$

where L and U are the same as above, and Δ_i are of dimension 2 by 2 and are defined by the recurrence :

$$\Delta_1 = D_1; \quad \Delta_i = D_i - F_i \Delta_{i-1}^{-1} E_i; \quad i = 2,..NJ, \tag{44}$$

where the 2 by 2 Δ_i^{-1} matrices are explicitly and exactly calculated. It is obvious that this set up is done once and its initial cost would be amortized over many solutions. The solution consists of standard forward elimination and backward substitution for the following triangular systems:

$$(L + \Delta)Y = B; \quad (U + \Delta)X = \Delta * Y. \tag{45}$$

The algorithm can now then be summarized as:

1. analysis of the right-hand side: $\mathbf{r}^{[I]}_j = \sum_{i=1}^{NI} \psi^{[I]}_i \mathbf{r}_{ij}$,
2. solution of the NI block tridiagonal problems $M \quad X = B$,
3. synthesis of the solution, $\phi_{ij} = \sum_{i=1}^{NI} \psi^{[I]}_i \phi^{[I]}_j$.

The above algorithm has been extended to the diffusion equation of any order $m = 2,4,6,8..$ Step 1 which consists of the analysis of the right-hand side and Step 3, which is the synthesis of the solution are almost identical. The elements of block matrices L, U and D become dimensions $m/2$ by $m/2$.

4. Parallel Direct Algorithms

The domain decomposition (mapping of grid points to processors) in GEM as in most large scale weather prediction models, is purely horizontal. This means that each processor owns all the NK vertical grid points in a given horizontal sub-domain. A parallel Direct solver for Helmholtz problem has been developed in (Qaddouri et al., 1999) and the same idea is applied for the high order diffusion equation. The direct solution algorithm presented in the previous sections has a great potential for vectorization and parallelism since at each step, there is recursive work along only one direction at a time, leaving the others available for vectorization. The remapping (or transposition) method is used for interprocessors communication.

The algorithm necessitates 4 global communication steps and reads for a problem with $NI \times NJ \times NK$ grid points and $P \times Q$ processors grid:

1. transposition of the right-hand sides to bring all the λ-direction grid points in each processor, the distribution becomes in θ-z subdomains:

$$\left(\frac{NI}{P}, \frac{NJ}{Q}, NK\right) \rightarrow \left(\frac{NJ}{P}, \frac{NK}{Q}, NI\right), \tag{46}$$

2. analysis of the right-hand sides,
3. transposition of the data to bring all the θ-direction grid points in each processor, the distribution becomes in z-λ subdomains:

$$\left(\frac{NJ}{Q}, \frac{NK}{P}, NI\right) \rightarrow \left(\frac{NK}{P}, \frac{NI}{Q}, NJ\right), \tag{47}$$

4. solutions of the block tri-diagonal problems,
5. inversion of the second transpose with the solutions of step 4:

$$\left(\frac{NK}{P}, \frac{NI}{Q}, NJ\right) \rightarrow \left(\frac{NJ}{Q}, \frac{NK}{P}, NI\right), \tag{48}$$

6. synthesis of the solutions,
7. inversion of the first transposition, the solutions are again distributed in λ-θ subdomains:

$$\left(\frac{NJ}{Q}, \frac{NK}{P}, NI\right) \rightarrow \left(\frac{NI}{P}, \frac{NJ}{Q}, NK\right). \tag{49}$$

5. Numerical Tests

All numerical tests presented in this chapter are done using the current forecast model GEM-LAM. In any given meteorological site, there are always time constraints when implementing operational runs. At CMC, both MPI and OpenMP are used to parallelize the GEM model in order to gain the best performance possible. The MPI is used for the communication between the sub-domains which has a global effect on the model. The OpenMP is applied to each sub-domain on selected time consuming functions or loops where their algorithms have no data dependencies and no communication. All tests were done on the IBM p575+ cluster with 121 compute nodes where each node contains 16 processors. Within each node, the 16 processors share a memory of 52G. The timings presented in Table 1 measure all the major components of a GEM-LAM model run optimized as much as possible using the combined effect of MPI and OpenMP. The model configuration for this table is from one of CMC's operational LAM (2.5km horizontal uniform-resolution) where NI=565, NJ=494 and NK=58 and the MPI topology was set at P=6, (processors along the longitude), Q=12, (processors along the latitude) and the OpenMP configuration was set to OpenMP=4. Note that timings of the solver and of the diffusion are not negligible compared to the other model components.

Components	Time (sec)	Percentage of Total runtime
Right-Hand Side	26.29	.90
Advection	626.66	21.39
Preparation for Non-Linear	47.49	1.62
Non-Linear	125.59	4.29
Solver (fft)	**187.03**	**6.38**
Back Substitution	94.33	3.22
Physics	985.61	33.65
Horizontal Diffusion	**205.32**	**7.01**
Vertical Sponge	67.12	2.29
Vertical Diffusion	335.0	11.44
Nesting and blending	127.37	4.34
Initialization and Setup	32.5	1.11
Output dynamic fields	54.42	1.86
Output physics fields	14.56	0.50
Total	2929.29	100.0

Table 1. Breakdown of model timings in the major components of a Canadian 2.5km Limited Area Model (LAM) over the eastern part of Canada for an integration of 24 hours on 18 nodes (6 x 12 x 4 PEs) .

5.1 Numerical Tests using MPI only

The experiments are designed to test the effects of MPI and OpenMP separately on the performance for the different solvers (direct MXMA-based , direct FFT-based and Iterative) and for the FFT and MXMA in implicit horizontal diffusion. The model configuration used here for these tests is a LAM (limited area modelling) at a 2.5km horizontal resolution with a setup similar to an operational run. In the experiments to test the MPI only, the number of processors were increased using MPI and at the same time, the number of computational points were maintained the same for each tile. In other words, each tile always worked on approximately 96 by 96 points by 80 levels in order to analyze the behaviour of the communication costs as the number of processors increases. Figure 1 displays the regions of interest in the series of MPI test runs. The number of grid points along the latitude was chosen in such a way that the FFT solver could also be included in the study. Table 2 displays the timings of some of the major components of the model for the MPI test runs where the MPI topology is denoted as *P*x*Q* and the OpenMP=1. It can be seen up to 25 nodes that, the increase in timings is mostly due to communication in the solver and in the diffusion (FFT-based) whereas, in the physics and the advection modules, there were no communications at all. In the experiments using 100 nodes, almost the entire cluster was utilized. There seemed to be a dramatic increase in the timings of almost all the model components for these huge runs and it is suspected that either the memory or the communication was limited. Further investigation is needed for these large integrations as it is anticipated that this could be the size of domain needed for the future of weather forecasting.

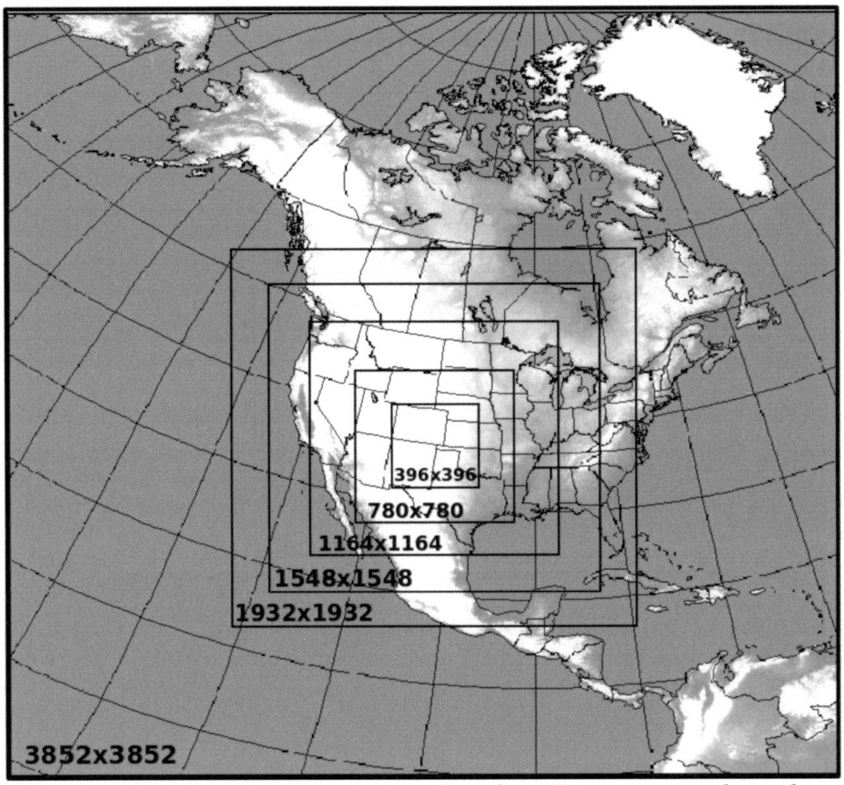

Fig. 1. LAM 2.5km resolution topography used in the MPI test runs where the results are recorded in Table 2. The number of vertical levels is 80.

Nodes	P x Q (NI x NJ pts)	# of PEs	FFT solver (secs) (count=100)	Advection (secs)	Physic (secs)	FFT Hzd (secs) (count=100)
1	4x4 (396x396)	16	23.32	149	241	47
4	8x8 (780x780)	64	30.41	153	241	52
9	12x12 (1164x1164)	144	36.7	148	238	53
16	16x16 (1548x1548)	256	44.1	152	238	61
25	20x20 (1932x1932)	400	57.0	151	240	77
100	40x40 (3852x3852)	1600	109	190	239	133

Table 2. Breakdown of model timings in the major components of the MPI test runs using a LAM grid at 2.5km resolution with 80 levels. The grid is increased to give almost the same number of points per tile for each test run (There is no OpenMP).

Applying the same MPI tests (identical configurations) but just changing the solvers, Table 3 displays the timing comparisons between using the FFT-based direct solver, the MXMA-based direct solver and the newly implemented PGMRES-based iterative solver. Note that the optimization for the iterative solver has not yet been completely refined but, it looks promising as the number of iterations required remains relatively steady.

Nodes	PxQ (NI x NJ) points	# of PEs	FFT solver (secs)	MXMA solver (secs)	Iterative solver (secs)	# of iterations
1	4x4 (396x396)	16	23.31	56.5	76.0	4
4	8x8 (780x780)	64	30.41	104.9	89.6	4
9	12x12 (1164x1164)	144	36.7	149.7	95.5	5
16	16x16 (1548x1548)	256	44.1	201.9	121.31	5
25	20x20 (1932x1932)	400	57.0	282.6	132.9	5
100	40x40 (3852x3852)	1600	109	N/A	195.85	5

Table 3. Comparison of timings between using the FFT, MXMA and the iterative Jacobi solver in the MPI test runs (The number of solver calls is 100).

A plot of the timings versus the number of nodes used per run is shown in Figure 2 and it can be seen that the timings become longer due to increased communication as more nodes were added. In the runs of the measured times in the FFT solver, there is an increase of 86 seconds from a run using one node to 100 nodes giving a factor of increase of 3.7 times over the one node run. By doing the same comparison for the runs using the iterative solver, there is an increase of 120 seconds which gives a factor increase of 1.6 times over its one node run. This shows that the communications cost more in proportion to the cost of computation in the FFT solver than in the iterative solver. It would be worth the effort to improve the performance of the iterative solver more within one node by using an approximate local solver which will diminish the computing time spent in the preconditioning operation.

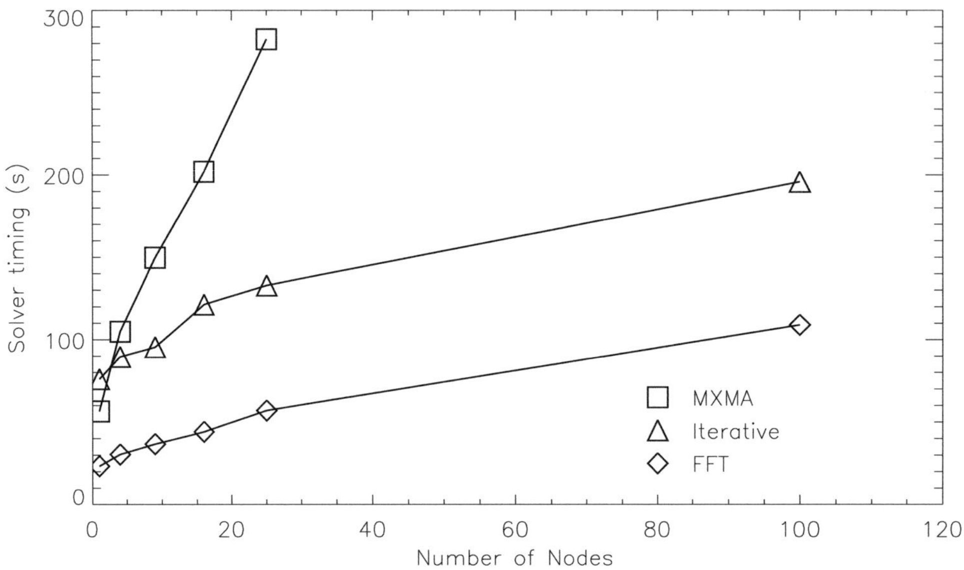

Fig. 2. Timings for FFT, MXMA and Iterative solvers in MPI test runs (computation on approximately 96 pts x 96 pts x 80 levels per processor)

Similar results are seen in Table 4 when comparing the two types of horizontal diffusion. All numerical tests presented here for the horizontal diffusion were using the sixth order implicit horizontal diffusion (m=6 in Eq.25).

Nodes	$P \times Q$ ($NI \times NJ$ points)	# of PEs	FFT diffusion (secs)	MXMA diffusion (secs)
1	4x4 (396x396)	16	47	73
4	8x8 (780x780)	64	52	129
9	12x12 (1164x1164)	144	53	179
16	16x16 (1548x1548)	256	61	252
25	20x20 (1932x1932)	400	77	360
100	40x40 (3852x3852)	1600	133	N/A

Table 4. Comparison of timings between using the FFT and MXMA in the horizontal diffusion solver within the MPI test runs (The number of diffusion calls is 100).

5.2 Numerical Tests on OpenMp

Tests for OpenMP were made using two different MPI configurations but using the same LAM grid configuration. The region of interest of the grid is shown in Figure 1 using 1548 by 1548 grid points. The FFT results are not included in this study as the OpenMP section for it was not correctly implemented. One of the OpenMP tests made is to vary the OpenMP on a MPI topology of 16 by 16 and these results are shown in Table 5. The other test is to vary the OpenMP on a MPI topology of 8 by 8 and these results are shown in Table 6. The MPI topology and OpenMP configuration is denoted by (*P*x*Q*xOpenMP). Note that with the same size LAM grid, the configuration with more MPI is more efficient than with the one with more OpenMP. Given the same number of PEs (using 256 or using 512), the MPI topology of 16 by 16 out-performs the one with more weight given to the OpenMP. This is an expected result as the model was parallelized with MPI entirely, and then with OpenMP in sub-sections of the code.

OpenMP	# of PEs	MXMA solver (secs)	MXMA Relative Speedup	Jacobi solver (secs)	Jacobi Relative Speedup
1	256	201.9	1	121.31	1
2	512	111.17	1.8	69.82	1.74
4	1024	68.13	2.96	45.53	2.6

Table 5. Comparison of timings between using the Jacobi Iterative and the MXMA solver within the OpenMP test runs where the grid is (1548x1548x80Levels) using the MPI topology of (16x16xOpenMP). The number of solver calls is 100.

OpenMP	# of PEs	MXMA solver (secs)	MXMA Relative Speedup	Jacobi solver (secs)	Jacobi Relative Speedup
1	64	1135.08	1	1443.6	1
2	128	631.04	1.8	824.89	1.72
4	256	231.25	4.9	216.71	6.66
8	512	136.21	8.33	137.73	10.46

Table 6. Comparison of timings between using the Jacobi Iterative and the MXMA solver within the OpenMP test runs where the grid is (1548x1548x80Levels) using the MPI topology of (8x8xOpenMP). The number of solver calls is 100.

6. Conclusion

In this paper, we have examined the performance of the elliptic solvers in the context of atmospheric modelling with a limited area grid. By using only the MPI paradigm (see Table.3) we can see that by increasing the grid size relative to the increase of the number of processors (in order that each processor keeps same amount of work), the number of iterations needed for the iterative solver to converge remains constant. We can say that the block-Jacobi preconditioner used in GEM-LAM is robust even though it involves no inter-processor communications and it is based on a single level additive Schwarz. We can also say that the non-scalability in real time is due to local inter-processor communications involved in matrix-vector operations and also due to the global communications (all-reduce) in the global dot product operations. It was also shown that by using the hybrid of MPI and OpenMP correctly, the parallel direct and iterative solvers present good scalability and even super-scalability in the aspect of OpenMP (Table.6). By implementing all these tests, we have also discovered that OpenMP was not well applied in the Fast Direct solver which is why the poor results are omitted from this paper. As it was noted earlier, the iterative solver needs more work in its optimization. In the future, we will introduce the second level in the additive Schwartz preconditioner (coarse grid) and we will employ a local approximate solver instead of an exact local direct solver which should reduce the computing cost.

7. References

Arakawa A. and V. R. Lamb, 1977: Computational design of the basic dynamical processes of the UCLA general circulation model. *Methods in Computational Physics*, Vol. 17, 174-267, J.Chang, Ed., Academic Press, 1977,

Coté, J., S. Gravel, A. Methot, A. Patoine, M.Roch and A. Staniford, 1998: The operational CMC-MRB Global Environmental Multiscale (GEM) model, Part I: design considerations and formulation. *Mon. Wea.* Rev. 126, 1373-1395

Denis, B., Coté, J. and R. Laprise, 2002: Spectral decomposition of two-dimensional atmospheric fields on limited-area domains using the discrete cosine transform (DCT). *Mon. Wea.* Rev. 130, 1812-1829.

Lindzen, R. S. and Kuo, H.L. 1969: *A reliable method for the numerical integration of a large class of ordinary and partial differential equations*. Mon. Wea. Rev., 97, 732-734

Qaddouri, A., J. Coté and M. Valin, 1999: A parallel direct 3D elliptic solver. *Proceedings of the 13th Annual International Symposium on High Performance Computing Systems and Applications*, Kingston, Canada, June 13-16, 1999, Kluwer Academic Publishers, 2000, 429-442

Saad, Y. and A. Malevsky, 1995: Data Structures, Computational, and Communication Kernels for Distributed Memory Sparse Iterative Solvers, *Proceedings of Parallel Computing Technologies (PaCT-95), 3rd International conference*, In: Lecture Notes in Computer Science series, Vol. 964, 252-257, ISSN 0302-9743, St. Petersburg, Russia, September 12-15, 1995, Victor Malyshkin (Ed.), Springer Verlag,

Saad, Y., 1996: Iterative Methods for Sparse Linear Systems, PWS Publishing Co International Thomson Publishing Inc, ISBN 0-534-94776-X, 1996.

Yong Li, S. Moorthi, J.R. Bates, 1994: Direct solution of the implicit formulation of fourth order horizontal diffusion for grid point models on the sphere, *NASA GLA Technical report series in atmospheric modelling and data assimilation*, Vol.2

9

A Collaborative Search Strategy to Solve Combinatorial Optimization and Scheduling Problems

Nader Azizi [a], Saeed Zolfaghari [b] and Ming Liang [a]
[a] *Department of Mechanical Engineering, University of Ottawa Ottawa, Ontario, Canada*
[b] *Department of Mechanical and Industrial Engineering, Ryerson University Toronto, Ontario, Canada*

1. Introduction

Since the creation of operations research as a discipline, a continued interest has been in the development of heuristics or approximation algorithms to solve complex combinatorial optimization problems. As many problems have been proven computationally intractable, the heuristic approaches become increasingly important in solving various large practical problems.

The most popular heuristics that have been widely studied in literature include Simulated Annealing (SA) (Kirkpatrick 1983), Tabu Search (TS) (Glover 1986), and Genetic Algorithm (GA) (Holland 1975). Simulated annealing is a stochastic search method that explores the solution space using a hill climbing process. Tabu search, on the other hand, is a deterministic search algorithm that attempts exhaustive exploration of the neighbourhood of a solution. In contrast to the local search algorithms such as SA and TS that work with one feasible solution in each iteration, GA employs a population of solutions and is capable of both local and global search in the solution space.

Despite their successes in solving many combinatorial problems, these algorithms have some limitations. For instance, SA can be easily trapped in a local optimum or may require excessive computing time to find a reasonable solution. To successfully implement a tabu search algorithm, one requires a good knowledge about the problem and its solution space to define an efficient neighbourhood structure. Genetic algorithms often converge to a local optimum prematurely and their success often relies on the efficiency of the adopted operators.

Due to the deficiencies of the conventional heuristics and ever increasing demand for more efficient search algorithms, researchers are exploring two main options, developing new methods such as nature inspired metaheuristics and investigating hybrid algorithms.

In recent years, a number of metaheuristics have been developed. Examples include the Greedy Randomized Adaptive Search Procedure (GRASP) (Feo & Resende, 1995; Aiex *et al.*, 2003), Adaptive Multi Start (Boese *et al.*, 1994), Adaptive Memory Programming (AMP)

(Taillard *et al.*, 2001), Ant System (AS) (Dorigo & Gambardella, 1997), and Particle Swarm Optimization (PSO) (Kennedy & Eberhart 1995).

Another important research domain in heuristics is *hybridization* by which a search algorithm such as GA is used in conjunction with one or more other techniques, e.g., simulated annealing and/or tabu search. Because of the complementary properties of each algorithm, hybrid approaches often outperform each individual method operating alone. However, they still require excessive computational effort.

In view of the above, this chapter presents a Collaborative Search Algorithm (CSA) for combinatorial optimization problems. The proposed approach contains two independent search algorithms, an enhanced simulated annealing with memory and a blockage removal feature (called Tabu-SA component hereafter), and a genetic algorithm (i.e., GA component). The two algorithms exchange information while consecutively run to solve a problem. The Tabu-SA algorithm utilizes a short-term memory, i.e., tabu list to avoid revisiting solutions temporarily. The purpose of the blockage removal feature in the Tabu-SA component is to resolve deadlock situation in which a (acceptable) solution is hard to find in the neighbourhood of a solution. The GA component employs two evolutionary operators, crossover and mutation operators, and a long-term memory, i.e., population list to conduct global search. The population list is constantly updated by the two algorithms, Tabu-SA and GA, as the search progresses.

The reminder of this chapter is organized as follow. In section 2, a review of the two popular hybrid algorithms, hybrid GA and hybrid SA, is presented. Section 3 describes the proposed collaborative search algorithm (CSA). In section 4, more details of its application to flow shop scheduling problem is presented. Computational results and the comparisons with other approaches followed by conclusion are presented in sections 5 and 6.

2. Review of Hybrid GA and SA Algorithms

Depending on which algorithm is selected to be the core component of the hybrid algorithms, the hybrid algorithms could be categorized as hybrid SA or hybrid GA. In a hybrid SA, the driving module of the algorithm is a simulated annealing while in a hybrid GA the driving component is a genetic algorithm.

2.1 Hybrid genetic algorithms

The popular forms of hybrid GAs are constructed by: a) including a constructive heuristic to generate one or more members of the initial population (e.g., Reeves, 1995); b) incorporating a local search heuristic to improve the quality of the solutions built by the crossover operator (e.g., Gonçalves *et al.*, 2005); and c) by combination of the former two (a and b) strategies (e.g., Wang & Zheng, 2003; Ruiz *et al.*, 2006; and Kolonko, 1999). Figure 1 illustrates the framework of the two popular hybrid genetic algorithms.

Reeves (1995) applied a genetic algorithm to the permutation flow shop scheduling problem. To generate the initial population, the author used the NEH (Newaz *et al.*, 1983) heuristic to generate the first member of the population and the rest of the population were generated randomly.

Wang and Zheng (2003) proposed a hybrid GA for the flow shop scheduling problem. In the hybrid algorithm, the NEH algorithm (Newaz *et al.*, 1983) is utilized to generate the first member of the initial population while, the rest of the individuals are generated randomly.

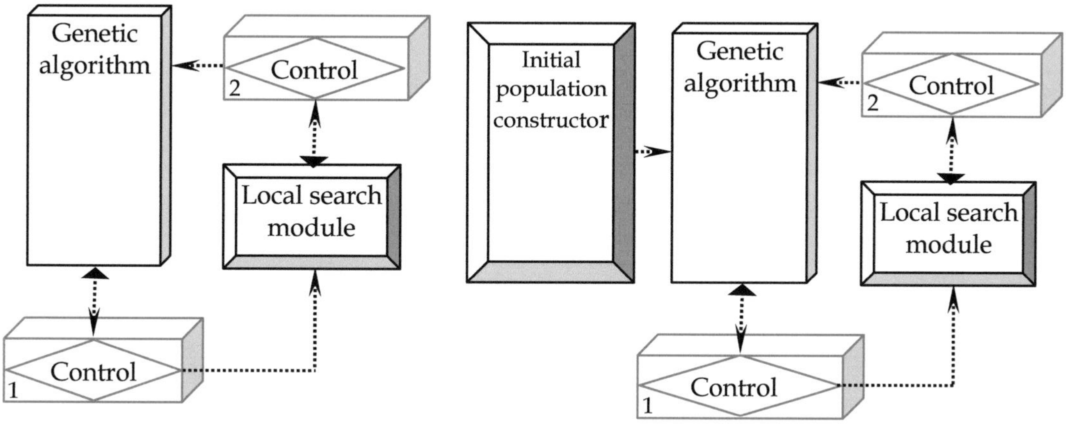

a) Hybrid GA with local search

b) Hybrid GA with local search and initial population constructor

Fig. 1. Hybrid genetic algorithm

To improve the performance of their algorithm, Wang and Zhang (2003) replaced the simple mutation operator of the plain GA with a simulated annealing module. Gonçalves *et al.*, (2005) developed a hybrid GA for job shop scheduling problem. In Gonçalves *et al.*, (2005), a local search is used to improve the quality of all individuals built by the crossover operator. Instead of using mutation operator, Gonçalves *et al.*, (2005) replaced 20 percent of the population with randomly generated schedules (i.e., chromosomes).

Ruiz *et al.*, (2006) also proposed a hybrid GA for the flow shop scheduling problem. In their method, the entire initial population is generated using a modified NEH (Newaz *et al.*, 1983) algorithm. Furthermore, each time when a new population is entirely set up, the algorithm enhances the generation by applying a local search to the best member of the new population. Kolonko (1999) proposed a hybrid GA algorithm in which members of population are independent SA runs. Each member of the population is enhanced by a SA module as long as the number of trials without improvement is less than a predetermined value. To generate a new population, two individuals are selected randomly and their schedules are crossed using a special type of crossover operator. The hybrid algorithm was favourably tested using several job shop scheduling problems.

2.2 Hybrid simulated annealing algorithms

Two common forms of hybrid SAs that have been reported in literature are built by: a) adding prohibited memory (i.e., tabu list) to simulated annealing algorithm (e.g., Osman, 1993; Zolfaghari & Liang, 1999; Azizi & Zolfaghari, 2004); and b) addition of both prohibited and reinforcement memories (e.g., El-Bouri *et al.*, 2007). Recently a new hybrid simulated annealing has been also reported in the literature that combines three algorithms, simulated annealing, genetic algorithm, and tabu search (Azizi *et al.*, 2009a and Azizi *et al.*,2009b).

Osman (1993) compared the performance of several heuristics including a hybrid simulated annealing that utilizes a tabu list. Osman (1993) concluded that the hybrid algorithm outperforms the conventional simulated annealing both in terms of solutions quality and

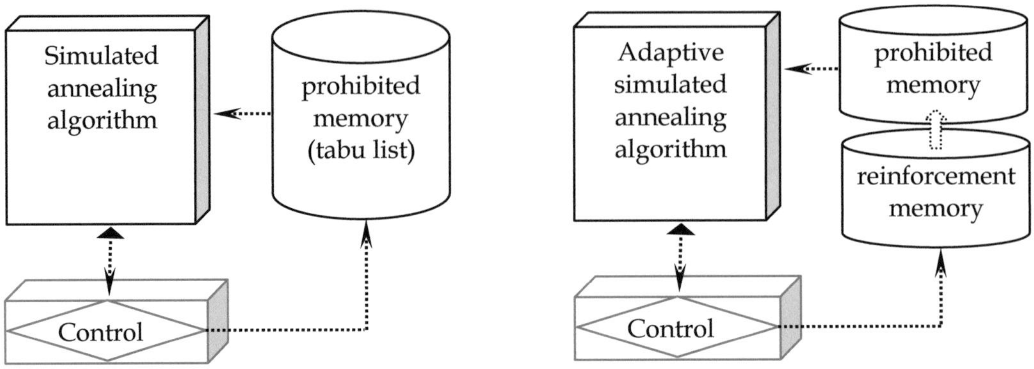

a) Tabu-simulated annealing algorithm b) Adaptive tabu-simulated annealing algorithm

Fig. 2. Hybrid simulated annealing with memory

computational time. Zolfaghari and Liang (1999) proposed a hybrid tabu-simulated annealing approach to solve the group scheduling problem. The performance of the hybrid method was tested and favourably compared with two other algorithms using tabu search and simulated annealing alone. Azizi and Zolfaghari (2004) proposed an *adaptive* simulated annealing method complemented with a tabu list. The performance of the hybrid algorithm was evaluated and compared with conventional simulated annealing using classical job shop scheduling problems. Using statistical analysis, Azizi and Zolfaghari (2004) showed that the adaptive tabu-SA algorithm outperforms a stand-alone simulated annealing algorithm.

El-Bouri *et al.*, (2007) proposed four versions of a new memory-based heuristic based on AMP and simulated annealing. The main characteristic of the proposed methods is the use of two short-term memories. The first memory is a tabu list while the second is called seed memory list that keeps tracks of the best solution visited during the last iteration. El-Bouri *et al.*, (2007) showed that the simultaneous use of prohibited and reinforcement memories in simulated annealing could significantly improve the search performance.

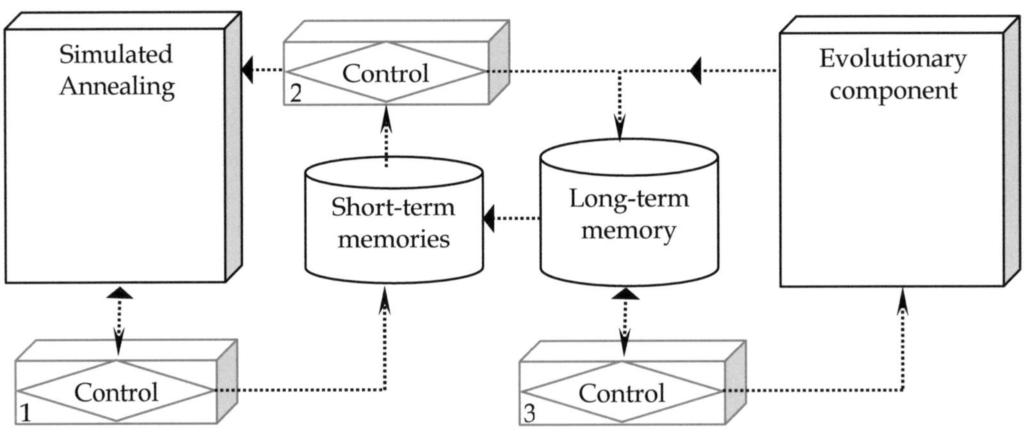

Fig. 3. The generic framework of the SAMED algorithm

Azizi *et al.*, (2009a) proposed a generic framework of a new metaheuristic, SAMED, that combines different features of several search algorithms. The framework contains several components including a simulated annealing module, three types of memories, and an evolutionary operator. Based on the generic framework, Azizi *et al.*, (2009a & 2009b) developed several search algorithms to investigate the application of the proposed framework on two popular scheduling problems, job shop and flow shop scheduling problems. Azizi *et al.*, (2009a & 2009b) showed that the new hybrid algorithms surpass the performance of the conventional heuristics as well as several hybrid genetic algorithms in both applications. The framework of the SAMED algorithm is presented in Figure 3. In the figure, control 1 verifies if the current solution is accepted, and controls 2 and 3 check if the short and long iterations are completed respectively.

For the case of job shop scheduling, Azizi *et al.* (2009a) developed another version of the new metaheuristic that includes two new components. The first component features a problem-specific local search that explores the neighbouring solutions on a critical path of a job shop scheduling solution. The second component is for blockage removal to resolve possible deadlock situations that may occur during the search (Figure 4). The algorithm is named SAMED-LB. Azizi *et al.* (2009a) showed that, in the majority of tested benchmark problems, the addition of the new components has significantly improved the computational efficiency.

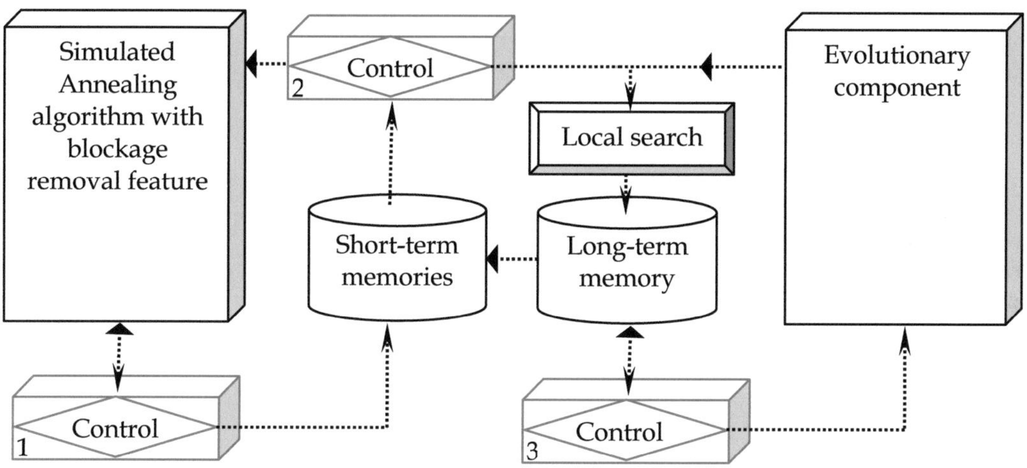

Fig. 4. The generic framework of the SAMED-LB algorithm

3. The Collaborative Search Algorithm

The CSA contains two main components, a Tabu-SA algorithm with blockage removal capability (Azizi *et al.*, 2009b) and a genetic algorithm. These two components exchange information (i.e., solutions) via a population list while consecutively run to solve a problem. In the CSA, the original population is generated randomly or by means of other heuristics. The best member of the population is selected as the initial solution for the Tabu-SA module. The Tabu-SA module begins searching the solution space with an initial solution.

Each time a solution is accepted, the quality of the solution is first compared to the overall best solution. Only if the solution improves the quality of the overall best solution, it is added to the population list. Then part of the solution that has been modified to generate the neighbouring solution is added to a tabu list. The completion of the tabu list marks the end of a short iteration. During a short iteration, the Tabu-SA also keeps track of the best solution visited during the iteration. At the end of the iteration, the tabu list is emptied and the best solution of the current iteration (if it is not the current solution) is selected as the initial solution for the next iteration. The above steps are repeated for a number of predetermined short iterations, i.e., a long iteration. Once a long iteration is completed, the performance of the search is evaluated by comparing the current (long) iteration best solution with that at the beginning of the past iteration. In the case of improvement, the Tabu-SA will continue the search; otherwise, the genetic algorithm component is called to participate in the search operations. The GA component generates a new population using the two evolutionary operators, crossover and mutation, and a copy of the current population list. The GA continues searching the solution space as long as there is improvement from one generation to another. Every time a new population is generated, GA also compares the quality of the best member of the new population with that of the overall best solution to update the original population list. Once the GA detects no improvement within its module, it will return the original population (that may have been also updated by the GA) and the best solution found during its own operations to the Tabu-SA component. The Tabu-SA utilizes the best solution (provided by GA) as the initial solution. The framework of the CSA is presented in Figure 5. In the figure, controls 1 and 5 check if the overall best solution has been improved to update the population list. Control 2 verifies the improvement within the GA component, and controls 3 and 4 test whether or not the short and long iterations are completed respectively.

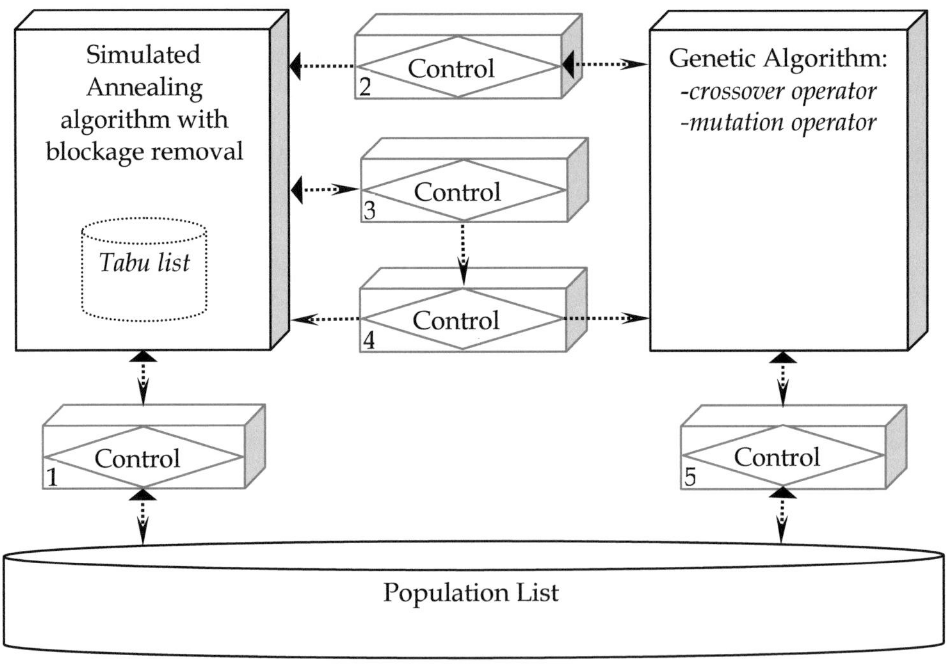

Fig. 5. Framework of the CSA

The CSA could be regarded as a variation of the SAMED algorithm proposed for the flow shop scheduling problem, SAMED-FSS (Azizi *et al.*, 2009b). However, it differs from the SAMED-FSS algorithm in several aspects. The main differences between the two algorithms have been highlighted in Table 1.

CSA(Collaborative Search Algorithm)	SAMED-FSS Algorithm
Population list is continually updated by SA and GA throughout the search	Long-term memory is updated only at the end of short iterations and is emptied at the end of long iterations
The population list is initially populated by randomly generated solutions which are gradually replaced by overall best solutions as the search progresses	Long-term memory contains the short iteration's best solutions that have been visited during the recent long iteration
Contains a complete genetic algorithm	GA component include a crossover operator
Genetic algorithm operates as long as there is improvement from one generation to another	Genetic algorithm component operates only for one generation
Once GA stops functioning, it returns the best solution found within the GA module	The new population is scanned and the first offspring whose cost is different than that of the iteration best solution might be selected.

Table 1. Differences between CSA and SAMED-FSS algorithm

4. Application of the CSA to the Permutation Flow Shop Scheduling Problem

4.1 Flow shop scheduling problem

The permutation flow shop scheduling problem studied in this paper can be described as follows. Consider a set of machines ($M_1, M_2, M_3,\ldots, M_m$) and a set of jobs ($J_1, J_2, J_2,\ldots, J_n$). Each job has to be processed on all m machines in the order given by the index of the machines. Each job consists of a sequence of m operations, O_{1j}, O_{2j} , $O_{3j},\ldots,O_{mj}$, each of them corresponding to the processing of job j on machine i during an uninterrupted processing time period $P_{i,j}$. Each machine can only process one job at a time and it is assumed that each machine processes the jobs in the same order. The objective is to find the schedule that has the minimum makespan (the duration in which all jobs are completed).

4.1.1 Solution representation

A solution of the flow shop scheduling problem is represented by a string composed of several elements each corresponding to a job number (job based scheme). The sequence of the job numbers on the string indicates the processing order of jobs on all machines.

4.1.2 Neighbouring solution

A neighbouring solution is generated by inserting a randomly selected job in front or behind another job in the string (i.e., insertion technique).

4.2 Components of CSA

As noted earlier, the CSA includes two main components, a Tabu-SA module with blockage removal and a genetic algorithm. The Tabu-SA component of the CSA is adopted from (Azizi *et al.* (2009b). The genetic algorithm component includes a random selection mechanism, a crossover operator, and a mutation operator. In order to generate a new population, two parents are selected randomly and operated by the Precedence Preservative Crossover (PPX) (Bierwirth *et al.*, 1996). To generate a new offspring by the PPX crossover operator, a template vector h of length n (n denotes the number of jobs) is filled with random elements from the set {1, 2}. This vector is then used to define the order in which elements are drawn from parent 1 and parent 2. The selected element from one parent is appended to the offspring string and then the corresponding element is deleted from both parents. This procedure repeats itself until both parent strings are emptied and the offspring contains all the involved elements.

The mutation operator selects a job randomly and inserts it in front or behind another job in the offspring chromosome. The corresponding makespans of the offspring chromosome before and after the mutation operation are compared and if the mutation deteriorates the quality of the offspring, the mutation result is revoked and then the chromosome is added to the population.

4.3 Initial population and initial solution

Both the initial population and initial solution in the CSA could be generated randomly. However, for the case of flow shop scheduling we developed a constructive heuristic based on the NEH algorithm (Newaz *et al.*, 1983) to generate portion (e.g., 50% of the members) of the population. According to this constructive heuristic, a solution is first generated randomly. Then, the solution is scanned from left to right and the first two jobs on the solution string is selected and added to a template chromosome. Following this, the positions of the two jobs is swapped and the partial makespans of the template chromosome before and after the swap is calculated. The makespans are compared and the configuration that generates shorter makespan is selected. Once the configuration of the two jobs is decided, the next job on the original solution (i.e., third job from left) is inserted in all possible positions on the template chromosome (e.g., before the first job, between job one and job two, and after job two). The lengths of the schedules associated with each configuration are calculated and the one with shorter makespan is selected. The above steps are repeated until all jobs on the randomly generated solution are transferred to the template chromosome.

The rest of the population members, i.e., the second portion, are generated randomly. The best member of the population is selected as the initial solution for the Tabu-SA algorithm.

5. Computational Results

The performance of the CSA is evaluated using 40 hard problems selected from two benchmark problem sets known as Taillard (1993) and Demirkol *et al.* (1998) benchmark problems. The algorithm is coded in Visual Basic and run on a Pentium 4 PC with 3.3 GHz CPU. The computational times as well as the parameters of the CSA including the size of tabu list (short iteration), long iteration (long-term memory), the initial temperature, the control parameter, and the maximum number of unacceptable moves are the same as those utilized in the SAMED-FSS algorithm (Azizi *et al.*, 2009b). The size of the population list is 30 for all benchmark problems except for TA21, TA22, TA24, and TA25 for which it is set to 20. For all benchmark problems, 50% of the members in each initial population are generated using the modified NEH algorithm described in section 4.2 and the remaining solutions are generated randomly.

The computational results for both benchmark problem sets are summarized in Table 2. The results presented in this table correspond to the best makespan over 10 runs and associated computing time (per second). According to the results presented in Table 2, the CSA found solutions with shorter makespans for 24 out of 28 Demirkol *et al.* (1998) benchmark problems (DMU01-DMU34) compared to those provided by the SAMED-FSS (Azizi *et al.*, 2009b). In comparison with the PSO (Liao *et al.*, 2007) algorithm, solutions found by the CSA for 22 benchmark problems are of better quality. The CSA also outperformed the conventional SA, standard GA, and hybrid genetic algorithm with local search (GA-LS) (Azizi *et al.*, 2009b) in all 28 test problems.

Furthermore, For all the 12 Taillard (1993) benchmark problems, the CSA found better quality solutions (including nine optimal) compared to those solutions found by the conventional SA, standard GA, hybrid genetic algorithm with local search (GA-LS), and the PSO (Liao *et al.*, 2007). Moreover, the CSA found the same (optimal) solutions as the SAMED-FSS for nine problems but with shorter computational times in the majority of the (nine) cases. In the remaining three problems, the CSA outperforms the SAMED-FSS both in terms of solution quality and computational times.

Figure 6 compares the standard deviation of the makespans obtained by five different methods for all the Demirkol *et al.* (1998) benchmark problems. The results presented in the figure clearly show that in the majority of the cases investigated in this study, the standard deviation of the makespans obtained by the CSA is significantly lower than those obtained by the other four techniques.

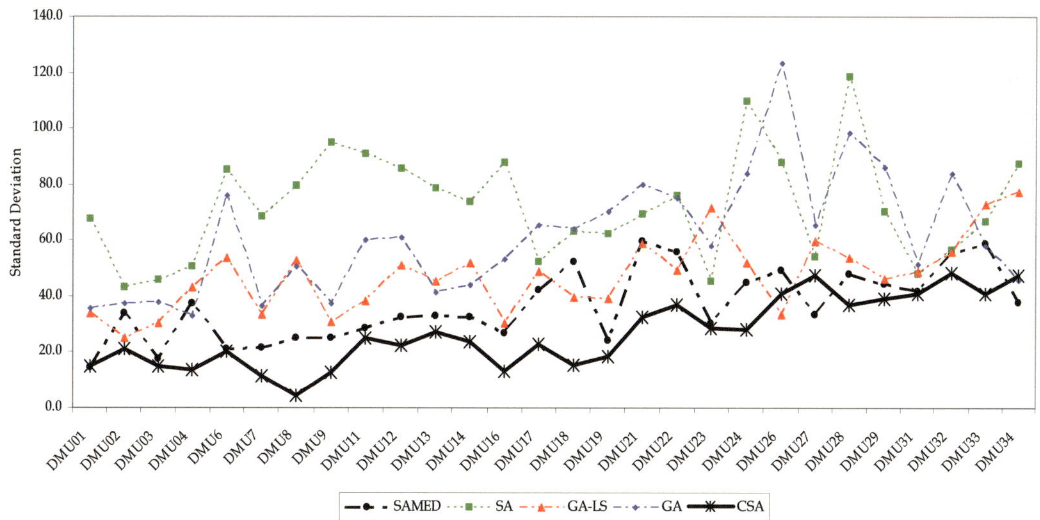

Fig. 6. Comparison of standard deviation of makespans for Demirkol *et al.*, (1998) benchmark problems

Size $(n \times m)$[a]	Problem	Optimal	Demirkol *et al.*, 1998	SA[b]	GA[b]	GA-LS[b]	PSO: Liao *et al.*, 2007	SAMED-FSS (Azizi *et al.*, 2009b)	CSA
20 × 15	DMU01	-	4437(69)	3965(5)	3981(55)	3981(5)	3937	3899(4)	**3896(13)**
	DMU02	-	4144(0.09	3838(2)	3878(2)	3833(2)	3571	3761(13)	3755(55)
	DMU03	-	3779(58)	3579(8)	3625(1)	3572(3)	3981	3534(7)	**3532(5)**
	DMU04	-	4302(67)	4097(6)	4148(25)	4094(4)	3805	4032(51)	4032(33)
20 × 20	DMU06	-	4821(159)	4609(5)	4634(78)	4577(6)	4612	4523(40)	**4523(25)**
	DMU07	-	4779(148)	4544(12)	4561(9)	4482(10)	4570	4428(23)	**4424(47)**
	DMU08	-	4944(176)	4601(6)	4604(30)	4531(8)	4504	4523(79)	4520(55)
	DMU09	-	4886(203)	4590(6)	4574(34)	4546(8)	4538	4496(48)	**4496(10)**
30 × 15	DMU11	-	5226(149)	4612(36)	4681(74)	4682(6)	4658	4582(22)	**4574(58)**
	DMU12	-	5304(163)	4742(55)	4730(79)	4725(10)	4743	4675(61)	**4669(76)**
	DMU13	-	5079(109)	4670(13)	4771(46)	4704(8)	4824	4569(99)	**4568(63)**
	DMU14	-	5605(0.17	4894(40)	5014(38)	4949(12)	4928	4836(54)	**4836(52)**
30 × 20	DMU16	-	6183(0.24	5431(48)	5494(59)	5494(19)	5782	5384(76)	**5372(87)**
	DMU17	-	6037(471)	5815(4)	5854(53)	5794(17)	5485	5718(75)	5700(28)
	DMU18	-	6241(394)	5815(4)	5856(60)	5815(22)	5486	5726(55)	5767(43)
	DMU19	-	6095(320)	5546(57)	5654(34)	5537(20)	5848	5479(68)	**5469(85)**
40 × 15	DMU21	-	6986(156)	6089(69)	6229(83)	6073(17)	6012	6026(119)	**5965(107)**
	DMU22	-	6351(224)	5797(95)	5931(101)	5829(14)	6080	5717(100)	**5702(117)**
	DMU23	-	6506(289)	5944(86)	6105(60)	5997(15)	6173	5904(40)	**5895(108)**
	DMU24	-	6845(186)	5967(33)	6081(102)	6039(13)	5855	5928(55)	5928(36)
40 × 20	DMU26	-	7154(615)	6711(31)	6771(98)	6763(34)	6730	6556(176)	**6518(167)**
	DMU27	-	7528(645)	6833(140)	6972(161)	6824(35)	6723	6704(178)	**6686(90)**
	DMU28	-	7469(674)	6965(173)	7033(160)	6962(29)	6973	6860(180)	**6842(144)**
	DMU29	-	7608(682)	6834(131)	7000(133)	6935(23)	6950	6792(166)	**6749(76)**
50 × 15	DMU31	-	7673(313)	6747(92)	6952(76)	6852(14)	6725	6747(80)	**6677(168)**
	DMU32	-	7679(299)	6740(172)	6844(118)	6761(28)	7143	6669(89)	**6614(49)**
	DMU33	-	7416(284)	6733(134)	6893(144)	6748(31)	6864	6656(138)	**6596(117)**
	DMU34	-	7548(307)	6945(149	7125(159)	6972(28)	7070	6878(101)	**6839(152)**
20 × 10	Ta11	1582	-	1593(110)	1622(3)	1586(4)	1604	1582(41)	1582(47)
	Ta12	1659	-	1676(33)	1710(4)	1692(1)	1685	1659(67)	1659(46)
	Ta13	1496	-	1524(38)	1540(1)	1515(1)	1520	1496(156)	1496(31)
	Ta14	1377	-	1384(118)	1413(10)	1396(2)	1402	1377(70)	1377(17)
20 × 20	Ta21	2297	-	2320(38)	2325(2)	2315(7)	2319	2297(12)	2297(7)
	Ta22	2099	-	2125(32)	2120(23)	2127(9)	2132	2099(18)	2099(28)
	Ta24	2223	-	2254(7)	2264(5)	2246(29)	2243	2223(17)	2223(14)
	Ta25	2291	-	2315(83)	2325(6)	2309(46)	2315	2291(43)	2291(12)
50 × 10	Ta41	2991	-	3059(208)	3116(71)	3111(21)	3080	3035(148)	**3030(146)**
	Ta42	2867	-	2921(197)	3006(77)	2975(9)	2974	2911(97)	2911(117)
	Ta44	3063	-	3071(298)	3194(71)	3121(17)	3103	3066(217)	**3063(201)**
	Ta48	3037	-	3048(230)	3121(88)	3108(10)	3085	3044(116)	**3042(164)**

Table 2. Comparison of computational results

a) $n \times m$ = n jobs and m machines, b)Conventional SA, Standard GA, and GA with Local Search (Azizi *et al.*, 2009b); **bold**= best solution.

6. Conclusion

Various scheduling problems that occur in manufacturing industries have been investigated in the literature. They are inherently complex and often referred to as combinatorial Non-Polynomial (NP) hard problems. These problems are very difficult to solve using existing heuristics or conventional techniques. This chapter presents a generic framework of a collaborative search algorithm to solve scheduling problems. The proposed framework contains two independent search modules that exchange information while consecutively run to solve a problem. Based on the proposed framework a search algorithm tailored for the flow shop scheduling is presented. The computational results for the two challenging classical problem sets clearly indicate the superior performance of the proposed method over several conventional techniques including a simulated annealing, a genetic algorithm and a hybrid genetic algorithm. The CSA results also compare favourably with those of the two newly developed algorithms, PSO (Liao *et al.*, 2007) and SAMED-FSS (Azizi *et al.*, 2009b).

7. References

Aiex, R.M.; Binato, S.; & Resende, M.G.C. (2003). Parallel GRASP with path relinking for job shop scheduling. *Parallel Computing*, 29, 393-430.

Aydin, M.E. & Fogarty, T.C. (2004). A Distributed Evolutionary Simulated Annealing Algorithm for Combinatorial Optimisation Problems. *Journal of Heuristics*, 10, 269-292.

Azizi, N. & Zolfaghari, S. (2004). Adaptive temperature control for simulated annealing: a comparative study. *Computers and Operations Research*, 31, 2439-2451.

Azizi, N.; Zolfaghari, S.; & Liang, M. (2009a). Hybrid simulated annealing with Memory: An evolution-based diversification approach, *International Journal of Production Research (IJPR)*, accepted.

Azizi, N.; Zolfaghari, S.; & Liang, M. (2009b). Hybrid Simulated Annealing in Flow-shop Scheduling: A Diversification and Intensification Approach, *International Journal of Industrial and Systems Engineering (IJISE)*, 4(3), 326-348.

Bierwirth, C.; Mattfeld, D.C.; & Kopfer, H. (1996). On Permutation Representations for Scheduling Problems, *proceeding of 4th International Conference on Parallel Problem Solving from Nature*, Lecture notes in computer science, Springer-Verlag, pp.310-318.

Demirkol, E.; Mehta, S.; & Uzsoy, R. (1998). Benchmarks for shop scheduling problems. *European Journal of Operational Research*, 109 (1), 137-141.

Dorigo, M. & Gambardella, L.M. (1997). Ant colony system: A cooperative learning approach to the travelling salesman problem. *IEEE Transaction on Evolutionary Computation*, 53-66.

El-Bouri, A.; Azizi, N.; & Zolfaghari, S. (2007). A comparative study of new metaheuristics based on simulated annealing and adaptive memory programming. *European Journal of Operations Research*, 2007, 177, 1894-1910.

Feo, T. & Resende, M. (1995). Greedy randomized adaptive search procedures. *Journal of Global Optimization*, 16, 109-133.

Gonçalves, J.F.; Mendes, J.J.M.; & Resende, M.G.C. (2005). A hybrid genetic algorithm for the job shop scheduling problem. *European Journal of Operational Research*, 2005, 167, 77-95.

Holland, J. H. (1975). *Adaptation in Natural and Artificial Systems*. The University of Michigan Press, Ann Arbor, MI.

Kennedy, J. & Eberhart, R. (1995). Particle swarm optimization. *Proceeding of. IEEE International Conference on Neural Network*, 1942–1948.

Kirkpatrick, S.; Gelatt, C.D. Jr. & Vecchi, M.P. (1983). Optimization by simulated annealing. *Science*, 220, 671-680.

Kolonko, M. (1999). Some new results on simulated annealing applied to the job shop scheduling problem. *European Journal of Operations Research*, 113, 123-136.

Liao, C.J.; Tseng, C.T.; & Luarn, P. (2007). A discrete version of particle swarm optimization for flow shop scheduling problems. *Computers & Operations Research*, 34(10), 3099-3111.

Nawaz, M.; Enscore, E. E. & Ham, I. (1983). A heuristic algorithm for the m-machine, n-job flow-shop sequencing problem. *OMEGA*, 11(1), 91-95.

Osman, I.H. (1993). Metastrategy simulated annealing and tabu search algorithms for the vehicle routing problem. *Annals of Operations Research*, 41(4), 421-451.

Reeves, C. R. (1995). A genetic algorithm for flow shop sequencing. *Computers & Operations Research*, 22(1), 5-13.

Ruiz, R. & Maroto, C. (2005). A comprehensive review and evaluation of permutation Flow shop heuristics. *European Journal of Operational Research*, 165(2), 479-494.

Taillard, E. (1993). Benchmark for basic scheduling problems. *European Journal of Operational Research*, 64(2), 278-285.

Taillard, E.D.; Gambardella, L.M.; Gendreau, M. & Potvin, J.Y. (2001). Adaptive memory programming: A unified view of metaheuristics. *European Journal of Operational Research*, 135, 1-16.

Wang, L. & Zheng, D.Z. (2003). An effective hybrid heuristic for flow shop scheduling. *International Journal of Advanced Manufacturing Technology*, 21(1), 38-44.

Zolfaghari, S. & Liang, M. (1999). Jointly solving the group scheduling and machining speed selection problems: A hybrid tabu search and simulated annealing approach. *International Journal of Production Research*, 37(10), 2377-2397.

10

Identification and Generation of Realistic Input Sequences for Stochastic Simulation with Markov Processes

Carl Sandrock
University of Pretoria
South Africa

1. Introduction

A simulation is a reproduction under controlled circumstances of a real-life situation. The term has recently become strongly associated with numeric evaluation of a computer model due to the increase in speed and availability of computing resources. This increase in speed has led to much interest in stochastic simulation, where processes with elements that are random are simulated. An attractive branch of stochastic simulation termed Monte Carlo simulation uses deterministic models driven by stochastic input sequences to approximate the distributions of output variables over time. To do this, a good deterministic model of the process is needed in addition to a good method of generating realistic input sequences.

Correct input sequences are a prerequisite for reliable results from stochastic simulation. To generate them, the modeller must either generate input sequences by hand, develop a model based on intuition or understanding of the process, or use existing data. Generating input sequences by hand is a tedious and error-prone process and intuition is not a particularly verifiable source of information. This means that data-driven model development has been gaining favour steadily as data becomes more accessible.

This chapter covers three aspects of input signal generation: First, the basic theory of Markov processes and hidden Markov models is reviewed with a view on using them as generating processes for input models. Second, signal segmentation is introduced. This is the first step in identifying state transition probabilities for discrete Markov processes. In this part, novel work done on the identification of state transitions using multi-objective optimisation is introduced and ideas for future research are posed. Third, the problem of estimating state transition probabilities from the segmented signals is discussed, touching on the issues that modellers should be aware of.

Markov processes have featured strongly in stochastic sequence identification and generation for many years, but some of the related problems are still active research fields.

2. Markov Processes

2.1 Discrete-time Markov Processes

A stochastic process with state space S has the Markov property if the current state completely determines the probability of the following state. A sequence $X_1, X_2, \ldots, X_t$ having this property is known as a Markov chain.

Stated mathematically, a Markov chain obeys the property

$$\Pr(X_{t+1} = j | X_t = i) = \Pr(X_{m+1} = j | X_m = i) = p_{ij} \tag{1}$$

in words, the probability that the next state will be equal to j given that the current state is i is only dependant on the current state.
When S is a countable set, the state transition probabilities can be written as a state transition matrix P as shown for a 3 state process in equation 2

$$P = \begin{bmatrix} p_{11} & p_{12} & p_{13} \\ p_{21} & p_{22} & p_{23} \\ p_{31} & p_{32} & p_{33} \end{bmatrix} \tag{2}$$

The probability of remaining within the state space must be unity, hence we may write

$$\sum_{j \in S} p_{ij} = 1 \; \forall \; i \in S. \tag{3}$$

Matrices with this property as well as the common-sense property that $0 \leq p_{ij} \leq 1$ (as they are probabilities) are called stochastic matrices.
The orientation of P is not unique. The arrangement with the current state in the rows and next state in the columns is known as a right transition matrix. The transpose arrangement has also been used (see for instance Bhar & Hamori (2004)) and is then described as a left transition matrix. Modern engineering usage leans toward the description used in this work.
A common way of visualising a Markov process with countable state space is by showing a directed graph with the states in the nodes and the transition probabilities on the edges as shown in Figure 1. In these representations, it is customary to neglect edges with zero probabilities.

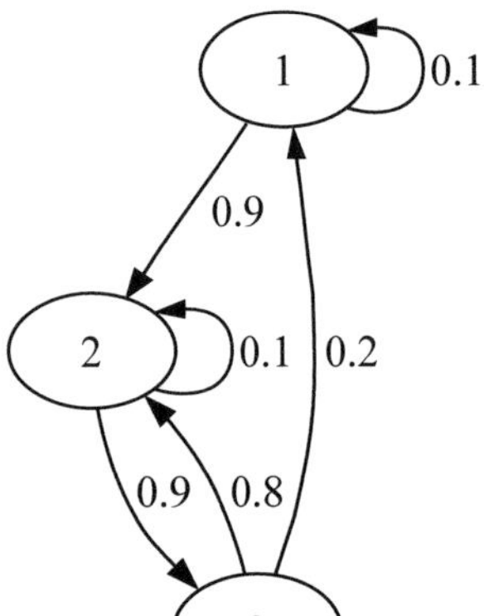

$$P = \begin{bmatrix} 0.1 & 0.9 & 0 \\ 0 & 0.1 & 0.9 \\ 0.2 & 0.8 & 0 \end{bmatrix}$$

Fig. 1. Markov process represented by a transition matrix and a graph

The state transition probabilities sufficiently describe the time dependence of the process, but the initial state can not be determined using the transition probabilities alone. The probability of the process starting out in a given state i is denoted $\pi_i, i \in S$, and the vector of initial state probabilities is called $\boldsymbol{\pi}$. It can be seen that a discrete time Markov process is completely described by its state space S, its state transition matrix P and its initial state probability vector $\boldsymbol{\pi}$. If S is countable and has N elements, $N^2 + N$ probabilities have to be known to fully characterise the process. For convenience, the model is written $\lambda = (P, \boldsymbol{\pi})$.

2.2 Hidden Markov Models

It is not always possible to observe the state (in the state space S) of a Markov process directly. It may, however, be possible to make observations from an observation space O related to the state of the process. If the probability of making a particular observation is only related to the current state of the process, the process may be described by a hidden Markov model (HMM). What is "hidden" in this case are the true values of the Markov process states.
Figure 2 shows the situation graphically. If the Markov process is in state 1, there are even odds that observation 2 or 3 will be made. In state 2, only observation 2 is made and state 3 is associated with observation 1 80% of the time and observation 2 20% of the time.

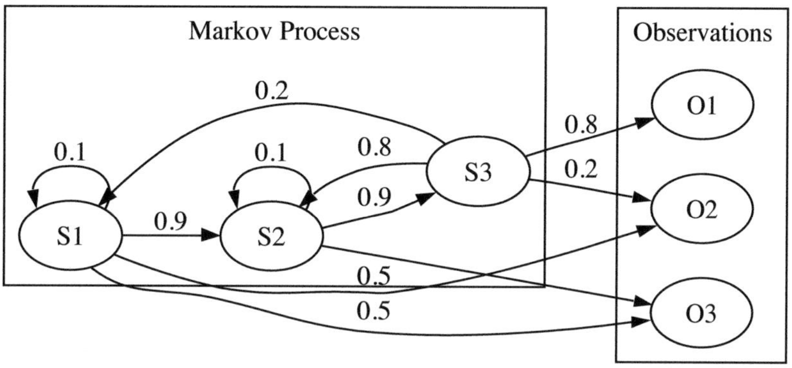

Fig. 2. Graphical representation of a finite hidden Markov model

The probabilities associated with a observation k being made when the process is in state i may be written b_{ik} and can be arranged into an observation probability matrix B in a similar fashion as was previously done for P. One difference is that, while P was an $N \times N$ square matrix, B will have N rows associated with the N states of the Markov process and M columns associated with the observation space. An HMM as described here can therefore be characterised by the same $N^2 + N$ probabilities describing the Markov process in addition to MN observation probabilities. The model description can be abbreviated to $\lambda = (P, B, \pi)$.
There are three main problems associated with HMMs (Gamerman & Lopes, 2006):

- What is the probability of generating a specific output sequence from a particular model?
- What is the most likely sequence of states that would lead to a particular output sequence?
- How do we identify the model that corresponds to a given output sequence?

2.3 Continuous-time Markov Processes

The description of discrete-time Markov processes assumed that the transition time was known or unimportant and one could imagine simulating the process by picking a state i and moving to the next state with probability p_{ij}. One shortcoming of such a description is that there is no information about the amount of time a process remains in a particular state before moving to the next (or possibly same) state.

Continuous-time Markov processes encode the transition probabilities as transition rates q_{ij} (forming a Q matrix as p_{ij} formed a P matrix), such that

$$\Pr(X(t+\Delta t) = j | X(t) = i) = \begin{cases} 1 - q_{ii}\Delta t + o(\Delta t) & \text{for } i = j \\ q_{ij}\Delta t + o(\Delta t) & \text{otherwise} \end{cases} \tag{4}$$

The idea is that, having changed to state i, the probability of changing to state j increases at a linear rate.

3. Segmentation

Segmentation aims to approximate an input signal of length N by $n < N$ events. Segmentation can be used as a compression measure, as a method of smoothing the data or to investigate underlying structure in the signal. Keogh et al. (1993) gives a good review of several segmentation algorithms applied to EKG time series. Segmentation is also used in a different sense in fields like speech recognition to mean identification of transitions in the data without explicit fitting of a curve or reduction of data. This usage will not be discussed here.
The most popular event type is straight line or piecewise-linear segmentation. However, more interesting functions like general polynomials (Arora & Khot, 2003) have been proposed.

3.1 Objectives

A good segmentation algorithm:

1. minimises the error of the segmented description (or at least satisfies some upper bound on the error),
2. uses the simplest description possible for the data (which may be in terms of the number or complexity of the identified segments) and
3. is efficient in computer time and space requirements.

If the algorithm is to be used on-line to segment signals as they are read, it is also beneficial if the algorithm can incorporate new data efficiently.
Some of these objectives are contradictory – a more complex description will almost always allow a lower segmentation error than a simpler one, for instance. Also, it is always possible to segment with zero error by simply dividing the segmented data at every single sample point, so direct minimisation of the fitting error is clearly insufficient on its own.
The next sections summarise commonly employed algorithms. The details are taken largely from Keogh et al. (1993), with some reinterpretation to fit within the structure of this document. Note that the algorithms have been significantly reworked.

3.2 Top-down methods

These methods can also be described as subdivision methods and feature a recursive subdivision of the signal that stops when an error measure has been reduced below a threshold. The algorithm described in Algorithm 1 lends itself to optimisation by dynamic programming, as the optimal subdivisions of smaller sequences can be stored as partial solutions to the larger problem. The Douglas-Peuker algorithm (Douglas & Peucker, 1973) is also an example of a top-down algorithm, although it does not search for optimal breaks recursively – it simply uses the node with the maximum perpendicular distance from the line as the break point.

Algorithm 1 Top-down algorithm

```
function TOPDOWN(T, ε)
    if approximationerror(T) < ε then
        return approximate(T)
    else
        N ← length(T)
        b ← min_i splitcost(T, i)                                  ▷ Find best split point
        return topdown(T[1 . . . b]) + topdown(T[b + 1 . . . N])
    end if
end function
```

3.3 Bottom-up methods

Bottom-up or composition methods start with segments between all data points and merge similar segments until there are no segment pairs to merge without violating an error measure.

Algorithm 2 Bottom-up algorithm

```
function BOTTOMUP(T, ε)
    N ← length(N)
    for i ∈ (1 . . . N − 1) do                          ▷ Start with lines between all points
        segments.append(segment(T[i . . . i + 1]))
    end for
    for i ∈ 1 . . . length(segments)-1 do               ▷ Find cost of merging each pair
        c(i) ←error(merge(segments[i],segments[i + 1]))
    end for
    while min(c) < ε do
        i ← minindex(c)                                 ▷ Find "cheapest" pair to merge
        segments[i] ← merge(segments[i],segments[i + 1])                   ▷ Merge them
        delete(segments[i + 1])                                      ▷ Update records
        c(i) ←error(merge(segments[i],segments[i + 1]);
        c(i − 1) ← error(merge(segments[i − 1], segments[i]));
    end while
end function
```

Algorithm 2 shows a sample algorithm for a bottom-up method.
If properly implemented, both bottom-up and top-down methods should give similar results.

3.4 Methods employing sliding windows

Sliding window or incremental methods process the signal to be segmented sequentially, in one pass. This means that they can be employed on-line, in contrast to the recursive methods discussed before, which require the entire data set to be loaded into memory before being started.
Algorithm 3 shows a possible sliding window algorithm.

3.5 Optimisation-based methods

Any one of the objectives mentioned in Section 3.1 can be rewritten as an objective function for an optimisation algorithm. This objective function could then be minimised by choosing

Algorithm 3 Sliding window algorithm

function SLIDINGWINDOW(T, ϵ)
  $a \leftarrow 1$
  segments $\leftarrow \emptyset$
  while $b < N$ **do**
    $b \leftarrow a + 1$
    while error(T[a...b]) $< \epsilon$ **do**
      $b \leftarrow b + 1$
    end while
    segments.append(T[$a \ldots b - 1$])
    $a \leftarrow b$
  end while
  return segments
end function

the number of parameters, the number of segments and the parameter values for each of the identified segments. Application of this reasoning can be seen in the direct fitting of line segments to data described in Cantoni (1971), which leads to a direct analytical solution via the pseudo-inverse, or in where numerical optimisation is employed to fit more complicated segmentation functions.

A common thread in the optimisation-based methods is that the number of line segments must be known in advance. This is required when using derivative-based optimisation, as the number of design variables fixes the dimensions of the derivative and the current position in the design space. This is a disadvantage when compared to the previous methods, which would automatically fit varying numbers of segments given different data set. Recall, however, that these methods would terminate when a certain error bound had been met, and that this bound had to be set in advance. When the error is reduced using optimisation, this bound is not required.

Another, more significant benefit of using optimisation rather than the direct methods, is that it enables a more general description of a segment to be used with very little additional effort beyond deciding on the parameters of the description. While it is clear how to approach subdivision for line segments, it is not as simple to adjust the algorithms for other functions (Waibel & Lee, 1990)

3.6 Multi-objective optimisation

The trade-off between accuracy and generality of a fit would traditionally be decided by the designer of an algorithm. Perhaps some noise reduction would be done before identifying events, or constraints on the fitting functions would be enforced to avoid over fitting (Arora & Khot, 2003; Punskaya et al., 2002). One could specify an acceptable error bound before segmentation or one could specify a number of segments.

Multi-objective optimisation provides a different approach. All the objective function values are evaluated and a solution is retained if it is better in any way than all of the solutions already encountered. Such solutions are called Pareto optimal or nondominated solutions (Steuer, 1986). The result of such an optimisation algorithm is a *list* of Pareto optimal solutions, or more properly an approximation of the Pareto front. This list is most commonly called the archive.

Evolutionary algorithms are a natural fit for multi-objective optimisation, as they are already population based. Genetic algorithms in particular have enjoyed popularity (Deb & Kalyanmoy, 2001). Recent work in Particle Swarm Optimisation has rekindled interest in using it for multi-objective optimisation.

3.6.1 Application

As an example of the results obtainable using multi-objective optimisation, the MOPSO-CD (Multi-Objective Particle Swarm Optimisation with Crowding Distance) algorithm proposed by Raquel & Naval (2005)was used to fit a first-order response prototype to input signals. The algorithm is a modification of Particle Swarm Optimisation that adds an archive of nondominated solutions and uses a crowding distance measure to prevent many similar Pareto optimal solutions from being retained in the archive.
A problem description based on a prototypical first order response was used in this study. Figure 3 shows the prototype function.

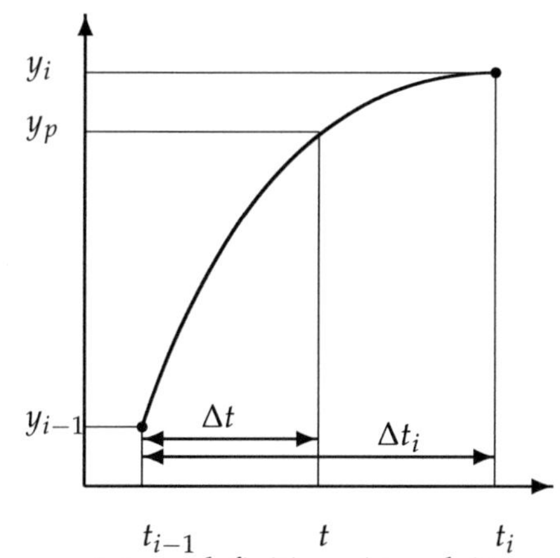

Fig. 3. First order response prototype definition. Δt and Δt_i are the times of the interpolation time and end point time relative to the prototype start.

Our goal is to find a sequence of prototypes that fits the sequence of events. We wish to fit the entire data set, so the first and last times are to coincide with the first and last times in the data set. Therefore, given that we are fitting N prototypes, we seek to find $N-1$ transition times and N parameter value sets.
A few key decisions were made to ease optimisation. Firstly, a linear term was added to the exponential response to ensure that the prototype interpolates through the initial (x_{i-1}, y_{i-1}) and final (x_i, y_i) points. This did not add any parameters to the description. The predicted value for the prototype at a given time t is shown in equation 5:

$$y_p = y_{i-1} + y_i \left(1 - \underbrace{e^{\Delta t/\tau_i}}_{\text{exponential}} + \underbrace{\frac{\Delta t}{\Delta t_i} e^{\Delta t_i/\tau_i}}_{\text{linear}} \right) \tag{5}$$

Secondly, the optimisation parameters were chosen to reduce coupling in the problem parameters by using absolute times for each starting point and constraining these times to be sequential rather than time differences constrained to be positive. This reduced the effect of any one starting point on the error produced by the remaining fit functions.

3.6.2 Objective functions

Two objectives were defined: the RMS error of the fit over all the prototypes and the "complexity" of the fit, which was calculated as

$$c = \sum_{i}^{N} \frac{1}{\tau_i}. \tag{6}$$

This complexity measure works due to the addition of the linear correction term, which dominates for large τ, meaning that as τ increases, one sees more of the linear behaviour and less of the exponential. Therefore, larger c corresponds to greater curvature of the fitting prototypes.

3.6.3 Prototype to event mapping

Each sequence of prototypes identified was mapped back to a sequence of event types by using the following heuristics:

- If the difference between the start and end values is less than a cut-off value ϵ_c, the prototype is taken to represent a constant event.
- If the time constant is larger than a cut-off time constant τ_c, it is taken as a ramp.
- If neither of these holds, the prototype is a first order response.

The values of ϵ_c and τ_c are problem-dependant and should be chosen to represent an insignificant change in y and a large time constant (in the chosen time units) respectively.

3.6.4 Results

To illustrate the type of result that is obtained using the technique, we show the results on a a signal consisting of 6 events, attempting to fit 4 events. Figure 4 shows the evolution of the Pareto front in terms of fit complexity and RMS error for different numbers of iterations.
It should be noted that, although the front seems to be converging, population based multi-objective optimisation algorithms can not guarantee convergence with a finite archive. This is due to the pruning that must inevitably be done when the archive is full. Figure 4 does, however, show that the front has not receded.

3.7 Optimisation with variable numbers of events

The optimisation methods discussed so far have a significant disadvantage: it is not possible for them to choose the "optimal" number of segments as one of the design variables, as their design space needs to have constant dimension. It is, however, possible to use genetic algorithms (GAs) for this purpose, by using a crossover operator allowing varying chromosome lengths. One such operator is the simple "cut and splice" operator, which chooses a crossover point on the chromosome of each parent independently before exchanging material. The application of multi-objective GAs with varying chromosome lengths may yield the first fully-automated optimisation for fitting events, as it allows the number of events to be included in the objective set.
Finding the Pareto-optimal set of fits in this way will enable much richer analysis of time series.

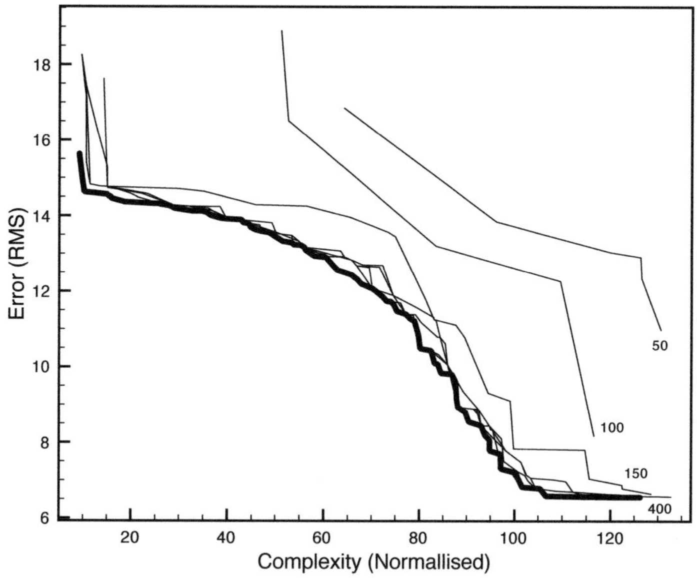

Fig. 4. Evolution of Pareto Front for 6 events being fit by 4 events.

4. Estimating state transition probabilities

The most direct method of estimating the state transition probabilities of a Markov process is to count the number of transitions in an input signal. This strategy has some problems:

1. Certain transitions may not occur in the input signal, so that these transitions will never be simulated by the identified model
2. Segmentation of the input signal may bias the event types or transitions – if a certain event is more often fit by the segmentation algorithm, that event will be over-represented in the transition matrix.

If transitions between some events are very rare, it may be advisable to introduce a small artificial probability into the matrix to ensure that the event has a chance of getting generated during the simulation. This is especially true if the repercussions of a certain event combination are significant.

Segmentation bias can be combated by generating a large unbiased test set and testing the segmentation algorithm on it. If a segmentation bias is detected, the transition probabilities can be modified to take these into account.

5. Conclusions

Markov processes provide a simple yet powerful method for generating realistic input sequences. The theory in this chapter should be enough for the interested reader to get started in this fascinating field and should enable simulation of a system with little additional reading required. The techniques for segmenting input signals and identifying model parameters are applicable to a broad range of fields and includes novel work on the employment of multi-objective optimisation to signal segmentation and estimation.

The most interesting future work suggested by this research is the use of variable-length multi-objective GAs to segment signals.

6. References

Arora, S. & Khot, S. (2003). Fitting algebraic curves to noisy data, *Special Issue on STOC 2002* **67**(2): 325âĂŞ340. http://portal.acm.org/citation.cfm?id=963875.963882.

Bhar, R. & Hamori, S. (2004). *Hidden Markov Models: Applications to Financial Economics*, Advanced studies in theoretical and applied econometrics, Kluwer Academic Publishers, Boston, Mass.

Cantoni, A. (1971). Optimal curve fitting with piecewise linear functions, *Computers, IEEE Transactions on* **C-20**(1): 59–67.

Deb, K. & Kalyanmoy, D. (2001). *Multi-Objective Optimization Using Evolutionary Algorithms*, Wiley. http://www.amazon.ca/Multi-Objective-Optimization-using-Evolutionary-Algorithms/dp/047187339X/.

Douglas, D. H. & Peucker, T. K. (1973). Algorithms for the reduction of the number of points required to represent a digitized line or its caricature, *Cartographica: The International Journal for Geographic Information and Geovisualization* **10**(2): 112–122. http://dx.doi.org/10.3138/FM57-6770-U75U-7727.

Gamerman, D. & Lopes, H. F. (2006). *Markov Chain Monte Carlo: Stochastic Simulation for Bayesian Inference*, 2nd ed edn, Chapman & Hall/CRC, Boca Raton.

Keogh, E., Chu, S., Hart, D. & Pazzani, M. (1993). Segmenting time series: A survey and novel approach, *IN AN EDITED VOLUME, DATA MINING IN TIME SERIES DATABASES. PUBLISHED BY WORLD SCIENTIFIC* pp. 1—22. http://citeseerx.ist.psu.edu/viewdoc/summary?doi=10.1.1.12.9924.

Punskaya, E., Andrieu, C., Doucet, A. & Fitzgerald, W. (2002). *Bayesian curve fitting using MCMC with applications to signal segmentation*, IEEE Press. http://citeseer.ist.psu.edu/548064.html.

Raquel, C. R. & Naval, P. C. (2005). An effective use of crowding distance in multiobjective particle swarm optimization, *GECCO '05: Proceedings of the 2005 conference on Genetic and evolutionary computation*, ACM, New York, NY, USA, p. 257âĂŞ264. http://portal.acm.org/citation.cfm?id=1068009.1068047.

Steuer, R. E. (1986). *Multiple Criteria Optimization (Probability & Mathematical Statistics)*, John Wiley & Sons Inc. http://www.amazon.ca/Multiple-Criteria-Optimization-Computation-Application/dp/047188846X/.

Waibel, A. & Lee, K. (1990). *Readings in speech recognition*.

11

TOLERANCE ANALYSIS USING JACOBIAN-TORSOR MODEL: STATISTICAL AND DETERMINISTIC APPLICATIONS

Walid Ghie
Université du Québec en Abitibi-Témiscamingue
445, Boul. de l'Université, Rouyn-Noranda, Qc
Canada, J9X 5E4
Walid.Ghie@uqat.ca

ABSTRACT
In industry, the current practice concerning geometrical specifications for mechanical parts is to include both ***dimensions*** and ***tolerances.*** The objective of these specifications is to describe a class of functionally acceptable mechanical parts that are geometrically similar. To ensure that their functionality in respected during, assembly designers have to apply tolerance analysis. A model based on either worst-case or statistical type analysis may be used.

This paper explains both types using the Jacobian-Torsor unified model. For statistical tolerance analysis we consider Monte Carlo simulation and for the worst case type we consider arithmetic intervals. Although the numerical example presented is for a three-part assembly, the method used is capable of handling three-dimensional geometry.

KEY WORDS
Tolerance, Jacobian, Torsor, Analysis, Statistical.

1. Introduction

Tolerancing decisions can profoundly impact the quality and cost of products. Thus to ensure that functional requirements for an assembly are respected, the designer determines the dimension chains and definitions for each part using the specifications described for tolerancing. The tolerance values can then be calculated using the worst-case or statistical approach. In our work we analyze how both methods can influence the results obtained, using our Jacobian-torsor model. We also describe the example we used to study these methods.

2. Related Works

Tolerance model variables are derived from a variety of tolerance models, represented either in conventional plus-minus or geometric tolerance formats. The assembly response system noted by functional requirement (FR) may also be represented in two models: closed mathematical and relative positioning. In the closed mathematical model, mathematical equations are formulated and the design function variations calculated through applying the equations directly. In the relative positioning model, an optimization model is used instead of the closed mathematical equations. Using the closed mathematical model, in previous papers a tool for deterministic tolerance analysis was presented [1], [2] which used an interval arithmetic formulation:

$$\begin{bmatrix} [\underline{u},\overline{u}] \\ [\underline{v},\overline{v}] \\ [\underline{w},\overline{w}] \\ [\underline{\alpha},\overline{\alpha}] \\ [\underline{\beta},\overline{\beta}] \\ [\underline{\delta},\overline{\delta}] \end{bmatrix}_{FR} = \left[\begin{bmatrix} J_1 J_2 J_3 J_4 J_5 J_6 \end{bmatrix}_{FE1} \cdots\cdots \begin{bmatrix} J_1 J_2 J_3 J_4 J_5 J_6 \end{bmatrix}_{FEN} \right] \bullet \begin{bmatrix} \begin{bmatrix} [\underline{u},\overline{u}] \\ [\underline{v},\overline{v}] \\ [\underline{w},\overline{w}] \\ [\underline{\alpha},\overline{\alpha}] \\ [\underline{\beta},\overline{\beta}] \\ [\underline{\delta},\overline{\delta}] \end{bmatrix}_{FE1} \\ \cdots\cdots\cdots\cdots \\ \begin{bmatrix} [\underline{u},\overline{u}] \\ [\underline{v},\overline{v}] \\ [\underline{w},\overline{w}] \\ [\underline{\alpha},\overline{\alpha}] \\ [\underline{\beta},\overline{\beta}] \\ [\underline{\delta},\overline{\delta}] \end{bmatrix}_{FEN} \end{bmatrix} \quad (1)$$

Where:

$[FR] = \begin{bmatrix} [\underline{u},\overline{u}] \\ \vdots \\ [\underline{\delta},\overline{\delta}] \end{bmatrix}_{FR}$ *and* $[FEi] = \begin{bmatrix} [\underline{u},\overline{u}] \\ \vdots \\ [\underline{\delta},\overline{\delta}] \end{bmatrix}_{FEi}$: Small displacement torsors were associated with some functional requirements (play, gap, clearance) represented as a [FR] vector or some Functional Element uncertainties (tolerance, kinematic link, etc.) were also represented as [FE] vectors; where N represents the number of torsors in a kinematic chain;

$\begin{bmatrix} J_1 \cdots J_6 \end{bmatrix}_{FEi}$: A Jacobian matrix expresses a geometrical relation between a [FR] vector and some corresponding [FE] vector;

$\underline{u}, \underline{v}, \underline{w}, \underline{\alpha}, \underline{\beta}, \underline{\delta}$: Lower limits of $u, v, w, \alpha, \beta, \delta$;

$\overline{u}, \overline{v}, \overline{w}, \overline{\alpha}, \overline{\beta}, \overline{\delta}$: Upper limits of $u, v, w, \alpha, \beta, \delta$.

In this work, the SDT or ***Small displacement torsor with interval*** scheme was adopted to represent future deviation and the ***Jacobian matrix*** has suggested for mapping all SDT in a dimensional chain. The following section describes these elements.

Small Displacement torsor with interval: The concept of the small displacement torsor (SDT) was developed in the seventies by P. Bourdet and A. Clément, in order to solve the general problem of fitting a geometrical surface model to a set of points. In its first form this concept was largely used in the field of metrology. In tolerancing we are more interested in surface or feature (axis, center, plane) variations relative to the nominal position. The components of these variations can be represented by a screw parameter, and this screw parameter is then called a small displacement screw. It may be used directly in its generic form to represent potential variations along and about all three Cartesian axes [3].

Described in [4] is an inventory of all standard tolerance zones, along with their corresponding torsor representations and geometrical constraints. For a given functional element, a torsor represents its various possible dispersions in translation (u, v, w) and in rotation (α, β, δ) as opposed to its remaining degrees of freedom (represented here by zeros). The following table shows the various classes of tolerance zones, their corresponding torsors and their constraints, as suggested by Desrochers and adapted, with minor changes, from [1,2].

<table>
<tr><th colspan="2">ZONE PLANAR</th></tr>
<tr><td colspan="2">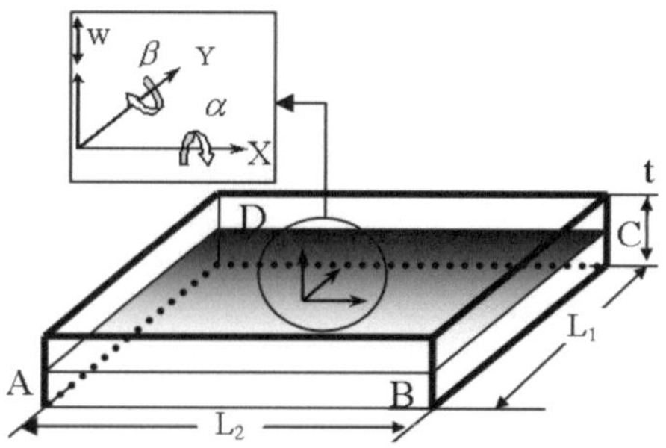
</td></tr>
<tr><td>Constraints</td><td>Torsor</td></tr>
</table>

Positional constraints $-\frac{t}{2} \le w \le +\frac{t}{2}$ **Angular constraints** $-\frac{t}{L_1} \le \alpha \le +\frac{t}{L_1}$ $-\frac{t}{L_2} \le \beta \le +\frac{t}{L_2}$	$\begin{bmatrix} [\underline{u},\bar{u}] \\ [\underline{v},\bar{v}] \\ [\underline{w},\bar{w}] \\ [\underline{\alpha},\bar{\alpha}] \\ [\underline{\beta},\bar{\beta}] \\ [\underline{\delta},\bar{\delta}] \end{bmatrix}_{FEi} = \begin{bmatrix} [0,0] \\ [0,0] \\ \left[-\frac{t}{2},+\frac{t}{2}\right] \\ \left[-\frac{t}{L_1},+\frac{t}{L_1}\right] \\ \left[-\frac{t}{L_2},+\frac{t}{L_2}\right] \\ [0,0] \end{bmatrix}_{FEi}$

Table 1. Small Displacement torsor with interval

Jacobian matrix: The purpose of the Jacobian matrix is to express the relation between the small displacement of all functional elements (FE) and the functional requirement (FR) sought. In this matrix therefore the columns are extracted from the various homogeneous transform matrices T_0^i relating the functional element (FE) reference frames to that of the functional requirement (FR).

$$T_0^i = \begin{bmatrix} [R_{3\times3}]_0^i & \vdots & [P_{3\times1}]_0^i \\ \cdots & \vdots & \cdots \\ 0 & \vdots & 1 \end{bmatrix} = \begin{bmatrix} \vec{C}_{1i} & \vec{C}_{2i} & \vec{C}_{3i} & \vec{d}_i \\ 0 & 0 & 0 & 1 \end{bmatrix}_{4\times4} \tag{2}$$

Where

$R_0^i = \left[\vec{C}_{1i}\ \vec{C}_{2i}\ \vec{C}_{3i}\right]$: These vectors represent the orientation of reference frame i with respect to 0, where the columns $\vec{C}_{1i}$, $\vec{C}_{2i}$ and $\vec{C}_{3i}$ respectively indicate the unit vectors along the axes X_i, Y_i and Z_i of reference mark i in reference mark 0.

$\vec{d}_i = \left[dx_i\ dy_i\ dz_i\right]^T$: Position vector defining the origin for the reference frame i in 0.

The Jacobian matrix is formulated by:

$$\left[J_1 \cdots J_6\right]_{FEi} = \begin{bmatrix} \left[R_0^i\right]_{3\times3} & \vdots & \left[W_i^n\right]_{3\times3} \bullet \left[R_0^i\right]_{3\times3} \\ \cdots\cdots\cdots & \vdots & \cdots\cdots\cdots\cdots\cdots\cdots \\ [0]_{3\times3} & \vdots & \left[R_0^i\right]_{3\times3} \end{bmatrix}_{6\times6} \tag{3}$$

Where $\left[W_i^n\right]_{3\times3}$ is a *Skew-symmetric* matrix [5] allowing the representation of the vector $\left[\vec{d}_n - \vec{d}_i\right]$ with $dx_i^n = dx_n - dx_i$, $dy_i^n = dy_n - dy_i$ and $dz_i^n = dz_n - dz_i$ knowing that $\vec{d}_n$ and $\vec{d}_i$ can be obtained from the transformation matrix in equation (2). $\left[W_i^n\right]_{3\times3} \bullet \left[R_0^i\right]_{3\times3}$ should be used to directly obtain the first three elements in the fourth, fifth and sixth columns of the Jacobian matrix. $\left[R_0^i\right]_{3\times3}$ represent the orientation matrix of reference frame *i* relative to *0* (from equation (2)).

The Jacobian-torsor model can be expressed as follows:

$$[FR] = [J][FE_i] \tag{4}$$

Where

$[FR]$: *6x1* small displacements torsor of the functional requirement; *6x1*small torsor displacements for the functional requirement;

$[J]$: *6xn* Jacobian matrix;

$[FE_i]$: *6x1* individual small displacements torsors of each part in the chain, i = 1 to *n;* and n represent is the total number of functional elements in the chain;

As shown, column matrix [FR] represents the dispersions around a given functional condition where the six small displacements are bounded by interval values. Similarly, the corresponding column matrix [FEs] represents the various functional elements encountered in the tolerance chain where intervals are again used to represent variations on each element. Naturally, the terms in this expression remain the same as those used in "conventional" Jacobian modeling [15, 16].

Thereafter we build on this model through applying the statistical analyses (Monte Carlo) and deterministic analysis (Worst-Case).

3. Analysis tolerances

In this method we apply deterministic and statistical tolerance analysis in order to compare the results. In our research, tolerance analysis consists of an assembly simulation with manufactured parts, *i.e.* parts with geometric variations. Deterministic and statistical tolerance analyses make use of a relationship expressed by Equation (5) where Y is the assembly response (gap or functional characteristics) and $X = \{x_1, x_2, \ldots, x_N\}$ the values of certain characteristics (such as situation deviations and/or intrinsic deviations) of the individual parts or subassemblies making up the assembly. Function f is the assembly response function. This relationship can be expressed in any form, in which a value for Y given values of X may be computed. An explicit analytic expression or an implicit analytic expression could be used, or the process could involve complex engineering calculations, conducting experiments or running simulations.

$$Y = f\left(x_1, x_2, \cdots, x_N\right) \tag{5}$$

Where :

$x_1, x_2, \cdots, x_N$	:	Parameters include dimensional chain tolerances
Y	:	Represent the functional requirement [FR];
f	:	A geometric expression relates the nominal dimension to the assembly's functionality.

3.1 Tolerances analysis deterministic

Generally in tolerance the application of functional analysis involves the entering of tolerances for all parts $x_1, x_2, \cdots, x_N$ involved in the dimensional chain, for those ratings related to the functional requirements. As output, we obtain the arithmetic value of functional requirement *Y*. Thus, when we want to apply an analysis it is assumed we will have a predetermined set of dimensional tolerances. Moreover, this analysis considers the worst possible combinations of individual tolerances and then examines the functional characteristics. In this approach the arithmetic intervals used have the highest possible maximum values [1, 2, 6].

In the deterministic analysis, we will apply the Jacobian-Torsor model (Equation (5) based on equation (1)). The application of this model is based on the arithmetic interval [1, 2, 6, 7].

3.2 Statistical analysis tolerances

Same of WC, statistical tolerance analysis uses a relationship of the form (Equation (5) based on equation (1)). In this case, the input variables $X = \{x_1, x_2, \ldots, x_N\}$ are continuous random variables.

A variety of methods and techniques allow to estimate the probability distribution of Y and the probability of the respect of the geometrical requirement. Essentially, the methods can be categorized into four classes according to the different type of function f [8-10]: Linear propagation (Root sum of squares), Non-linear propagation (Extended Taylor series), Numerical integration (Quadrature technique). Monte Carlo simulation.

So, in the case of the statistical tolerance analysis, the function *Y* is not available in analytic form, the determination of the value of *Y* involve the running simulation. Therefore, we use a Monte Carlo simulation. Indeed, Monte Carlo technique is easily the most popular tool used in tolerancing problems [9-10]. M*onte Carlo simulation* is a method for *iteratively* evaluating a deterministic model using sets of random numbers as inputs. This method is often used when the model is complex, nonlinear, or involves more than just a couple uncertain parameters.

Statistical tolerance analysis, is based on a very simple thinking: Random number generators are used to generate a sample of numbers x_1, x_2. . . x_N, belonging to the random variables X_1, X_2, . . .,x_N, respectively. The value of Y, $y_1 = f(x_1, x_2, \ldots, x_N)$, corresponding to this sample is computed. This procedure is replicated a large number of samples. This would yield a random sample $\{x_1, x2, \ldots, x_N\}$ for Y.

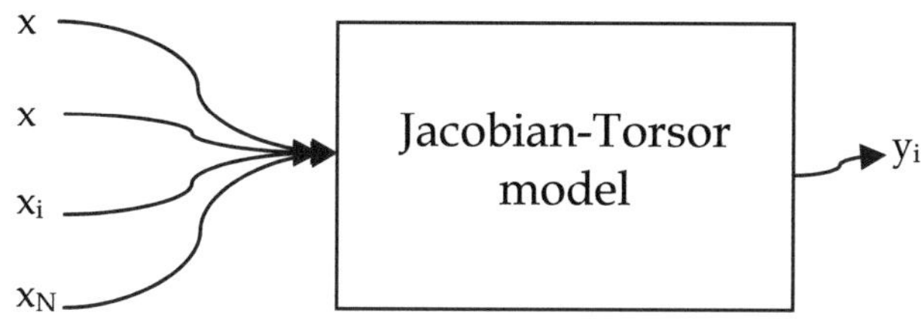

Fig. 1. Monte Carlo simulation

Clearly, if statistical tolerances are specified for the inputs (set of $(x_1, x_2, \ldots, x_N)$), a statistical tolerance can be calculated for the output (set of $(y_1, y_2, \ldots, y_N)$). This amounts to determining the average and standard deviation of the output. Simulations can always be used to predict these two values. However, there also exist a variety of methods for deriving approximate and sometimes exact equations for the average and standard deviation. Details can be found in Taylor [11, 12] in these approaches have a variety of names including statistical tolerance analysis, propagation of errors and variation transmission analysis.

Returning to the case where $Y = f(x_1, \ldots, x_n)$, equations can be derived for the average and standard deviation of Y in terms of the average and standard deviation of the x_i's.

Based on uncertain propagation theory [11, 12], the statistical tolerance for Y *(in our context* ***Y is FR$_D$****.)* can then be calculated as follows:

$$FR_D = FR_{Dm} \pm \delta FR_D \tag{6}$$

Where:

FR_D : Represents the functional requirement in direction D, with D is x, y or z. In this paper, we concentred only on the direction in translation, and did not evaluate the rotational direction.

FR_{Dm} : Best value of FR or average of FR.

δFR_D : Deviation of functional requirement, statistical is represented by standard deviation squared.

Next section shows by an example these methods.

4. Numerical example

The *centering pin mechanism* in Figures 2 to 5 was used to demonstrate the use of this tool. In these figures, we labelled some key tolerances from *ta* to *te*. The mechanism featured three parts, with two functional conditions as shown in Figures 2, 3 and 4. The purpose of this example is to explore the functional condition FR1 (Figure 5).

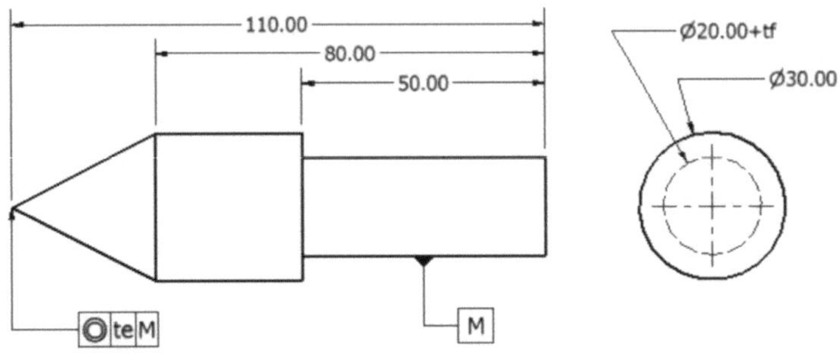

Fig. 2. Pin for centering pin mechanism

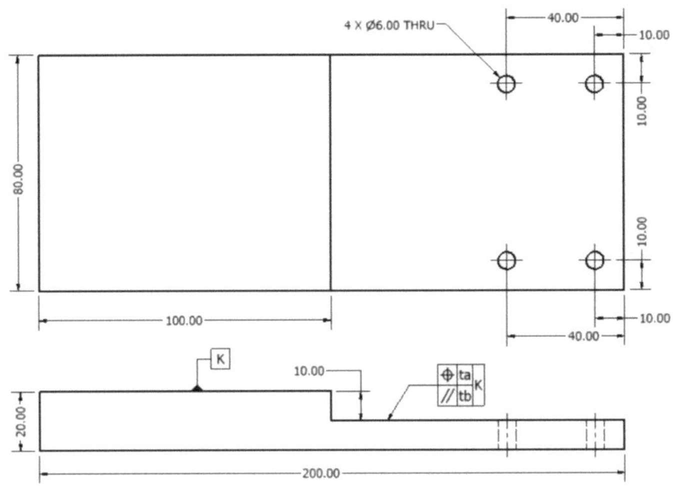

Fig. 3. Base for centering pin mechanism

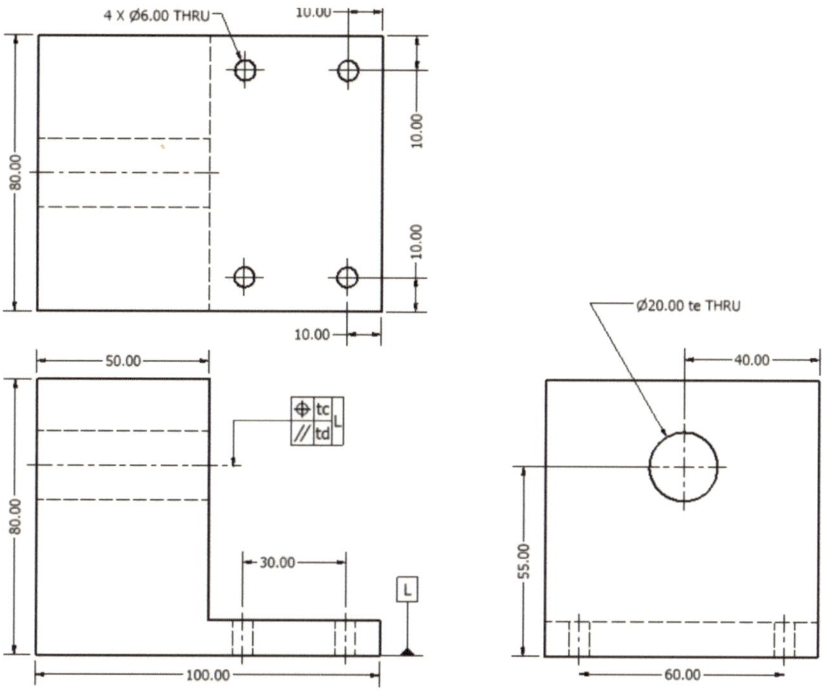

Fig. 4. Block for centering pin mechanism

The figure below shows the assembly drawing.

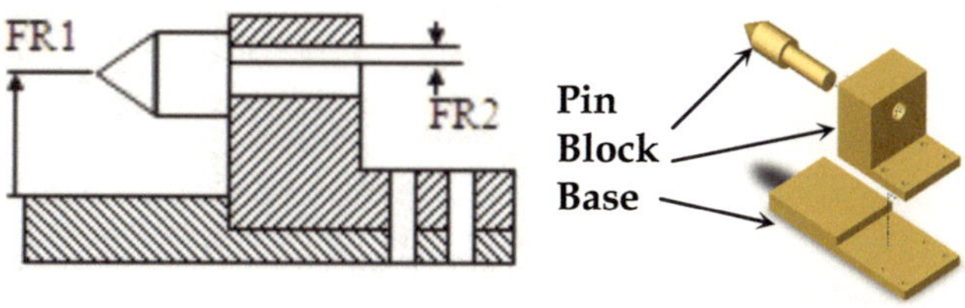

Fig. 5. Detail assembly for centering pin mechanism with two FRs

In this example, the designer specified an FR1 of ±0.5mm. (For more information, see the analysis for this example described in [14, 15]). To meet this objective the designer proposed a list of tolerances from *ta* to *tg*, as described in the table below.

For this simple example, the relevant parameters are as follows:

Tolerances values proposed							
ta	0.2	***tc***	0.2	***te***	*H11 : 0.00/0.13*	***tg***	0.1
tb	0.1	***td***	0.1	***tf***	*h8 : -0.033/0.000*		

Table 2. Assigned tolerances values

As shown in Figure 6, the contact surfaces between the parts are first identified. A connection graph is then constructed for this mechanism in order to establish the dimensional chain around the functional condition FR1.

The resulting kinematic chain contains three internal pairs (FE0, FE1), (FE2, FE3), (FE4, FE5) as well as one kinematic pair (FE1, FE2). Note that there are two FRs: FR1 applies between (FE0, FE5) and FR2 between (FE3, FE4) and that defined for functional fit 20 is H11/h8.

In this example, we assumed that the reference frames are in the middle of the tolerance or contact uncertainty zone, and are associated with the second element in the pairs defined above. The kinematic torsor for (FE1, FE2) is considered null because the contact between the two planes is assumed perfect, and form tolerances are not being considered here.

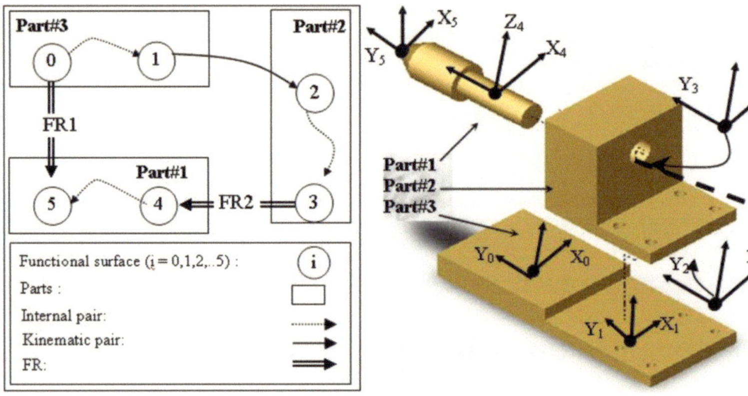

Fig. 6. Kinematic chain identification

The torsor calculation method accounts for the effect that might result when a tolerance dimension or position is imposed simultaneously on the same surface. The tables 3 and 4 list the constraints of torsors and there details that will be included in the Jacobian-Torsor model. From this, the final expression for the Jacobian-Torsor model and its intervals becomes:

$$\begin{bmatrix}[\underline{u},\overline{u}]\\ [\underline{v},\overline{v}]\\ [\underline{w},\overline{w}]\\ [\underline{\alpha},\overline{\alpha}]\\ [\underline{\beta},\overline{\beta}]\\ [\underline{\delta},\overline{\delta}]\end{bmatrix}_{FRr} = \left[\begin{bmatrix}1&0&0&0&-55&100\\0&1&0&55&0&0\\0&0&1&-100&0&0\\0&0&0&1&0&0\\0&0&0&0&1&0\\0&0&0&0&0&1\end{bmatrix}_{FE1}\begin{bmatrix}1&0&0&0&0&75\\0&1&0&0&0&0\\0&0&1&-75&0&0\\0&0&0&1&0&0\\0&0&0&0&1&0\\0&0&0&0&0&1\end{bmatrix}_{FE2}\begin{bmatrix}1&0&0&0&0&75\\0&1&0&0&0&0\\0&0&1&-75&0&0\\0&0&0&1&0&0\\0&0&0&0&1&0\\0&0&0&0&0&1\end{bmatrix}_{FE3}\begin{bmatrix}1&0&0&0&45&0\\0&1&0&-45&0&0\\0&0&1&0&0&0\\0&0&0&1&0&0\\0&0&0&0&1&0\\0&0&0&0&0&1\end{bmatrix}_{FE4}\right]\begin{bmatrix}\begin{bmatrix}[0,0]\\ [0,0]\\ [\pm0.05]\\ [\pm0.002]\\ [\pm0.0025]\\ [0,0]\end{bmatrix}_{FE1}\\ \begin{bmatrix}[\pm0.05]\\ [0,0]\\ [\pm0.05]\\ [\pm0.004]\\ [0,0]\\ [\pm0.004]\end{bmatrix}_{FE2}\\ \begin{bmatrix}[\pm0.0815]\\ [0,0]\\ [\pm0.0815]\\ [\pm0.0033]\\ [0,0]\\ [\pm0.0033]\end{bmatrix}_{FE3}\\ \begin{bmatrix}[\pm0.05]\\ [0,0]\\ [\pm0.05]\\ [\pm0.0033]\\ [0,0]\\ [\pm0.0033]\end{bmatrix}_{FE4}\end{bmatrix} \quad (7)$$

The torsor components corresponding to undetermined elements in the kinematic pair can then be replaced by null elements, because they do not affect small displacements along the analysis direction (*w* in this case, on axis Z_0). Thus, the calculated functional condition becomes. By using the approach described in [1, 2], we obtain the following deterministic method: Along the Z direction, $\mathbf{FR_Z = \pm 0.976}$ **mm.**

FE#	Constraints
FE1	$w = \pm(ta - tb)/2$ $\alpha = \pm ta/100; \beta = \pm ta/80$
FE2	$u = \pm(tc - td)/2; w = \pm(tc - td)/2$ $\alpha = \pm tc/50; \delta = \pm tc/50$
FE3[1]	$t = ES - ei \begin{cases} u = \pm t/2; w = \pm t/2 \\ \alpha = \pm t/50; \delta = \pm t/50 \end{cases}$
FE4	$u = \pm tg/2; w = \pm tg/2$ $\alpha = \pm tg/30; \delta = \pm tg/30$

Table 3. Constraints details

---

[1] FE3 : contact element between elements 3 and 4

FE#	FE1	FE2	FE3[2]	FE4
Torsors form	$\begin{bmatrix} [0,0] \\ [0,0] \\ [\underline{w},\overline{w}] \\ [\underline{\alpha},\overline{\alpha}] \\ [\underline{\beta},\overline{\beta}] \\ [0,0] \end{bmatrix}_{FE1}$	$\begin{bmatrix} [\underline{u},\overline{u}] \\ [0,0] \\ [\underline{w},\overline{w}] \\ [\underline{\alpha},\overline{\alpha}] \\ [0,0] \\ [\underline{\delta},\overline{\delta}] \end{bmatrix}_{FE2}$	$\begin{bmatrix} [\underline{u},\overline{u}] \\ [0,0] \\ [\underline{w},\overline{w}] \\ [\underline{\alpha},\overline{\alpha}] \\ [0,0] \\ [\underline{\delta},\overline{\delta}] \end{bmatrix}_{FE3}$	$\begin{bmatrix} [\underline{u},\overline{u}] \\ [0,0] \\ [\underline{w},\overline{w}] \\ [\underline{\alpha},\overline{\alpha}] \\ [0,0] \\ [\underline{\delta},\overline{\delta}] \end{bmatrix}_{FE4}$
Torsors values	$\begin{bmatrix} [0,0] \\ [0,0] \\ [\pm 0.1] \\ [\pm 0.003] \\ [\pm 0.0025] \\ [0,0] \end{bmatrix}_{FE1}$	$\begin{bmatrix} [\pm 0.05] \\ [0,0] \\ [\pm 0.05] \\ [\pm 0.004] \\ [0,0] \\ [\pm 0.004] \end{bmatrix}_{FE2}$	$\begin{bmatrix} [\pm 0.065] \\ [0,0] \\ [\pm 0.065] \\ [\pm 0.0026] \\ [0,0] \\ [\pm 0.0026] \end{bmatrix}_{FE3}$	$\begin{bmatrix} [\pm 0.05] \\ [0,0] \\ [\pm 0.05] \\ [\pm 0.0033] \\ [0,0] \\ [\pm 0.0033] \end{bmatrix}_{FE4}$

Table 4. Torsor details

In the statistical approach, the random variables generated using last column (Equation (7)). Following this generation and based on the principle described in Section 3, the dispersion based on this condition becomes functional (where *D* represents the direction along the axe *Z*):

$$FR_D = FR_{Dm} \pm \delta FR_D = \underline{\mathrm{FR}_Z = 0.00 \pm 0.27 \text{ mm.}}$$

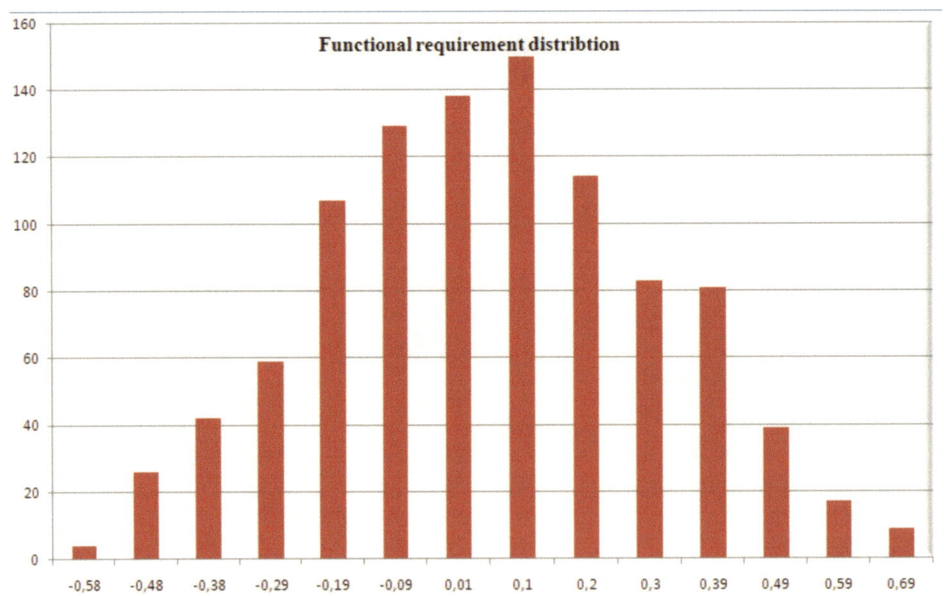

Fig. 7. Functional requirement distribution

---

[2] FE3 : contact element between elements 3 and 4

We can then see that the statistical dispersion is smaller than that of the deterministic method because:

- The deterministic method assumes that mistakes happen all at once and are most probable. By contrast, the statistical method assumes that the maximum values are generated (distribution is normally low) around the average values (in our case the average is zero);

- The best estimate functional condition is null, due to the fact that the JT model hides ratings in its nominal Jacobian matrix. The results are therefore variations around the nominal. In this way we need to extract the face value of the functional condition, which can be done by using the homogeneous matrix transformation between the first and last repository of the ratings string. This work is the subject of current research.

- We can conclude that the tolerances imposed (Table 2) may be expanded to ensure that manufacturing costs will be cheaper, even when we work with the deterministic method the results obtained for the condition are very close to the designer's limits. The statistical method enables us to enhance tolerance, but it does not provide any indication of the maximum expansion possible.

- From the figure 7, *FR* has a normally distribution: In probability theory, if $C=A+B$, if A and B are independent random variables and identically distributed random variables that are normally distributed, then C is also normally distributed. [16].

5. Conclusion

Tolerance analysis is an important step in design. Proper tolerancing ensures that parts will behave as analyzed for stress and deflection. Worst-case tolerancing tends to overestimate output variations, resulting in extra costs when output variations are overestimated. Statistical tolerancing tends to underestimate the output variations, and quality suffers when output variations are underestimated. By using process tolerancing, output behaviour may be accurately predicted, thus providing the desired quality at a lower cost.
We are currently working on a process that will provide expansion coefficients for a tolerancing method situated between the statistical and deterministic methods. In practice this should enable industry designers and fabrication personnel to handle tolerancing in a more effective manner.

Acknowledgements
The authors would like to acknowledge the Université du Québec en Abitibi-Témiscaming (**UQAT**) for their financial contribution to this ongoing project.

6. References

[1] W. Ghie, Modèle unifié Jacobien-Torseur pour le tolérancement assisté par ordinateur, *Ph.D. thesis*; Université de Sherbrooke, Canada, 2004.

[2] A. Desrochers, W. Ghie, L. Laperriere, Application of a unified Jacobian-Torsor model for tolerance analysis, *Journal of Computing and Information Science in Engineering, 1*(3), 2003, pp. 2-14.

[3] P. Bourdet, A., A. Clément, Study of optimal-criteria identification based on the small displacement screw model, *Annals of the CIRP*, 1988, vol. 37, pp.503-506.

[4] A. Desrochers, Modeling three dimensional tolerance zones using screw parameters, *CD-ROM Proceedings of ASME 25th Design Automation Conference*, 1999, Las Vegas.

[5] L. Tsai « *the mechanics of serial and parallel manipulators* », New York, N.Y. : J. Wiley and Sons, ISBN 0-471-32593-7,1999.

[6] L. Jaulin, M. Kieffer and O. Didrit « *Applied Interval Analysis With Examples in Parameter and State Estimation, Robust Control and Robotics* », World Scientific Publishing Company Incorporated ,ISBN 1852332190, 2001

[7] R. Moore « *Methods and Applications of Interval Analysis*», Society for Industrial and Applied Mathematic, ISBN 0898711614, 1979.

[8] L. Laperrière, W. Ghie and A. Desrochers,« *Statistical and deterministic Tolerance Analysis and synthesis Using a unified jacobian-torsor model*», 52nd General Assembly CIRP, San Sebastian, v. 51/1/2002 pp. 417-420.

[9] L. Laperrière, T. Kabore, Monte-Carlo simulation of tolerance synthesis equations, *International Journal of Production Research, 11*(39), 2001, pp. 2395-2406.

[10] Bjørke ø, «Computer-Aided Tolerancing», 2nd edition New York: ASME Press; 1989.

[11] Taylor J. R., Incertitudes et analyse des erreurs dans les mesures physiques avec exercices corrigés, collection Masson Sciences, Dunod, Paris, 2000.

[12]Taylor, B., Kuyatt, C., «Guidelines for Evaluating and Expressing the Uncertainty of NIST Measurement Results, NIST Technical Note 1297, Gaithersburg, MD: National Institute of Standards and Technology, September, 1994.

[13] Zhang C., Luo J. and Wang B. Statistical tolerance synthesis using distribution function zones. International Journal of Production Research 1999; 37:3995-4006.

[14] W. Ghie, , A. Desrochers, L. Laperriere, Assessment of design parameter space using tolerance *analysis, 10th International Seminar On Computer Aided Tolerancing,* (CIRP,2007, 21-23 March,, Neurburg, Germany.

[15] W. Ghie, L. Laperriere, A. Desrochers, Re-design of Mechanical Assemblies using the Jacobian–Torsor model, *Models for Computer Aided Tolerancing in Design and Manufacturing, 9th CIRP International Seminar on Computer-Aided Tolerancing*, held at Arizona State, J. K. Davidson , Springer-Verlag GmbH (Eds), 2006, ISBN: 1-4020-5437-8, PP. 95-104.

[16] William W. Hines, Douglas C. Montgomery, David M. Goldsman, Connie M. Borror, *Probabilités et statistique pour ingénieurs* (Chenelière éducation, 2005). ISBN 2-7651-0245-7.

12

Random Variational Inequalities with Applications to Equilibrium Problems under Uncertainty

Joachim Gwinner
Institut für Mathematik, Fakultät für Luft- und Raumfahrtechnik, Universität der Bundeswehr München, D-85577 Neubiberg, Germany
email: Joachim.Gwinner@unibw-muenchen.de

Fabio Raciti
Facoltà di Ingegneria dell'Università di Catania, Dipartimento di Matematica e Informatica dell'Università di Catania, 95125-Catania, Italy
email: fraciti@dmi.unict.it

Abstract. In this contribution we introduce to the topic of Random Variational Inequalities (RVI) and present some of our recent results in this field. We show how the theory of monotone RVI, where random variables occur both in the operator and the constraints set, can be applied to model nonlinear equilibrium problems under uncertainty arising from economics and operations research, including migration and transportation science. In particular we treat Wardrop equilibria in traffic networks. We describe an approximation procedure for the statistical quantities connected to the equilibrium solution and illustrate this procedure by means of some small sized numerical examples.
Keywords: Random Variational Inequality, Random Set, Monotone Operator, Averaging,Truncation, Approximation Procedure, Cassel-Wald Equilibrium, Distributed Market Equilibrium, Spatial Price Equilibrium, Migration Equilibrium, Traffic Network, Wardrop Equilibrium.

1. Introduction

Although relatively recent, the Variational Inequality (V.I.) approach to a variety of equilibrium problems arising in various fields of applied sciences, such as economics, game theory and transportation science, has developped very rapidly (see e.g. (10), (23), (8), (19)). Since the data of most of the above mentioned problems are often affected by uncertainty, the question arises of how to introduce this uncertainty, or randomness, in their V.I. formulation. In fact, while the topic of stochastic programming is already a well established field of optimization theory (see e.g.(25), (6)), the theory of random (or stochastic) variational inequalities is much less developped.

In (14) the author studied a class of V.I. with a linear random operator, presented an existence and discretization theory and applied this theory to a unilateral boundary value problem stemming from mechanics, where the coefficients of the elliptic differential operator are admitted to be random to model uncertainty in material parameters. The functional setting introduced therein, and extended in (15) in order to include randomness also in the constraints set, can also be utilized to model many finite dimensional random equilibrium problems, which only in special cases admit an optimization formulation (see e.g.(16)). Furthermore,

recently in (17), the authors have extended the theory in (15) to the monotone nonlinear case, while formulating their results in an abstract Hilbert space setting. However, apart from the generalization of the previous theory, this extension is motivated by the need to cope with the nonlinearity in many equilibrium problems arising in operations research, such as the random traffic equilibrium problem which is studied in detail in this article.
For a comparison between our approach and other ways to treat randomness in variational inequalities we refer the interested reader to (16). Here we just quote (11), (12), for the solution of stochastic variational inequalities with a (nonlinear) Fréchet differentiable mapping on a polyhedral subset in finite dimension via the sample-path method, (21) presenting a regularization method for stochastic programs with complementarity constraints, and (28), (29) for a systematic study of stochastic programs under equilibrium constraints.
The paper is structured in 6 sections. In the following Sect. 2 we specialize the abstract formulation of (17) to the case in which the deterministic variables belong to a finite dimensional space, so as to make our theory readily applicable to economics and operations research problems; in Sect. 3 we consider the special case where the deterministic and the random variables are separated; in Sect. 4 we recall and refine the approximation procedure given in (17). Then in Sect. 5, we show how the theory of monotone RVI, where random variables occur both in the operator and the constraints set, can be applied to model various nonlinear equilibrium problems under uncertainty arising from economics and operations research, including migration. In the last Sect. 6 we focus on the modelling of the nonlinear random traffic equilibrium problem and, in order to explain the role of monotonicity, we also discuss the fact that this problem (as every network equilibrium problem) can be formulated by using two different sets of variables, connected by a linear transformation. Finally we illustrate our approximation procedure by two small sized numerical examples of traffic equilibrium problems.

2. The Pointwise and the Integral Formulation

Let $(\Omega, \mathcal{A}, \mu)$ be a complete σ-finite measure space. For all $\omega \in \Omega$, let $\mathcal{K}(\omega)$ be a closed, convex and nonempty subset of $\mathbb{R}^k$. Consider a random vector λ and a Carathéodory function $F : \Omega \times \mathbb{R}^k \mapsto \mathbb{R}^k$, i.e. for each fixed $x \in \mathbb{R}^k$, $F(\cdot, x)$ is measurable with respect to $\mathcal{A}$, and for every $\omega \in \Omega$, $F(\omega, \cdot)$ is continuous. Moreover, for each $\omega \in \Omega$, $F(\omega, \cdot)$ a monotone operator on $\mathbb{R}^k$, i.e. $\langle F(\omega, x) - F(\omega, y), x - y \rangle \geq 0$, $\forall x, y \in \mathbb{R}^k$.
With these data we consider the following

Problem 1. For each $\omega \in \Omega$, find $\hat{X}(\omega) \in \mathcal{K}(\omega)$ such that

$$\langle F(\omega, \hat{X}(\omega)), x - \hat{X}(\omega) \rangle \geq \langle \lambda(\omega), x - \hat{X}(\omega) \rangle, \qquad \forall x \in \mathcal{K}(\omega). \tag{1}$$

Now we consider the set-valued map $\Sigma : \Omega \hookrightarrow \mathbb{R}^k$ which, to each $\omega \in \Omega$, associates the solution set of (1). The measurability of Σ (with respect to the algebra $\mathcal{B}(\mathbb{R}^k)$ of the Borel sets on $\mathbb{R}^k$ and to the σ-algebra $\mathcal{A}$ on Ω) has been proved in (15) for the case of a bilinear form on a general separable Hilbert space. However, the proof given therein can be adapted straightforwardly to nonlinear operators.
To progress in our analysis we shall confine ourselves to the case of strongly monotone operators, since it is known that the strong monotonicity assumption guarantees the existence of a unique solution to (1) (see (18)). Moreover we shall need the following sharpening of monotonicity.

Definition 2.1. *We call F uniformly strongly monotone, if there is some constant* $c_0 > 0$ *such that*

$$\langle F(\omega,x) - F(\omega,y), x - y \rangle \geq c_0 \|x - y\|^2 \quad \forall x,y \in \mathbb{R}^k, \forall \omega \in \Omega.$$

In many applications, such as the traffic equilibrium problem, the modelling is often done with polynomial cost functions. We are then led to require the growth condition

$$\|F(\omega,z)\| \leq \alpha(\omega) + \beta(\omega)\|z\|^{p-1} \quad \forall z \in \mathbb{R}^k, \tag{2}$$

for some $p \geq 2$.
Since our final aim is to calculate statistical quantities such as the mean value or the variance of the solution of (1), we shall use the following result which has been proved in (17):

Theorem 2.1. *Let* $(\Omega, \mathcal{A}, \mu)$ *a complete* σ*-finite measure space, and* $F(\omega, \cdot)$ *a strongly monotone operator on* $\mathbb{R}^k$ *for all* $\omega \in \Omega$*. Then the variational inequality (1) admits a unique solution* $\hat{X} : \omega \in \Omega \mapsto \hat{X}(\omega) \in \mathcal{K}(\omega)$*. Moreover, suppose that, F is uniformly strongly monotone, that the random vector* λ *belongs to* $L^p(\Omega, \mu, \mathbb{R}^k)$*, that the growth condition (2) is satisfied and that there exists* $z_0 \in L^{(p-1)p}(\Omega, \mu, \mathbb{R}^k) \bigcap L^p(\Omega, \mu, \mathbb{R}^k)$ *such that* $z_0(\omega)$ *belongs to* $\mathcal{K}(\omega)$*. Then* $\hat{X} \in L^p(\Omega, \mu, \mathbb{R}^k)$*.*

Let us now introduce a probability space $(\Omega, \mathcal{A}, P)$ and for fixed $p \geq 2$, the reflexive Banach space $L^p(\Omega, P, \mathbb{R}^k)$ of random vectors V from Ω to $\mathbb{R}^k$ such that the expectation

$$E^P \|V\|^p = \int_\Omega \|V(\omega)\|^p dP(\omega) < \infty. \tag{3}$$

Furthermore we define the convex and closed set

$$K := \{V \in L^p(\Omega, P, \mathbb{R}^k) : V(\omega) \in \mathcal{K}(\omega), \text{P-almost sure}\}.$$

Under the growth condition (2) with $\alpha \in L^p(\Omega, P), \beta \in L^\infty(\Omega, P)$, and assuming that $\lambda \in L^p(\Omega, P, \mathbb{R}^k)$, the integrals

$$\int_\Omega \langle F(\omega, U(\omega)), V(\omega) - U(\omega) \rangle dP(\omega), \int_\Omega \langle \lambda(\omega), V(\omega) - U(\omega) \rangle dP(\omega)$$

are well defined for all $U, V \in L^p(\Omega, P, \mathbb{R}^k)$. Therefore, we can consider the following

Problem 2. Find $U \in K$ such that, $\forall V \in K$,

$$\int_\Omega \langle F(\omega, U(\omega)), V(\omega) - U(\omega)) \rangle dP(\omega) \geq \int_\Omega \langle \lambda(\omega), V(\omega) - U(\omega) \rangle dP(\omega). \tag{4}$$

Under our assumptions, (4) has a unique solution $U \in L^p(\Omega, P, \mathbb{R}^k)$. Thus, by uniqueness, Problem 1 and Problem 2 are equivalent in the sense that from the integral formulation in Problem 2 we obtain a pointwise solution that is only defined P-a.e. on Ω and that coincides there with the pointwise solution of Problem 1.

3. The Separable Case

Here and in the sequel we shall posit further assumptions on the structure of the random set and on the operator. More precisely, with a matrix $A \in \mathbb{R}^{m\times k}$ and a random m - vector D being given, we consider the random set

$$M(\omega) := \{x \in \mathbb{R}^k : Ax \leq D(\omega)\},\ \omega \in \Omega.$$

Moreover, let $G, H : \mathbb{R}^k \to \mathbb{R}^k$ be two (nonlinear) maps; $b, c \in \mathbb{R}^k$ fixed vectors and R and S two real valued random variables on Ω. Thus, we simplify Problem 1 to that of finding $\hat{X} : \Omega \to \mathbb{R}^k$, such that $\hat{X}(\omega) \in M(\omega)$ (P-a.s.) and the following inequality holds for P-almost every elementary event $\omega \in \Omega$ and $\forall x \in M(\omega)$

$$\langle S(\omega)\, G(\hat{X}(\omega)) + H(\hat{X}(\omega)), x - \hat{X}(\omega)\rangle \geq \langle b + R(\omega)\, c, x - \hat{X}(\omega)\rangle . \tag{5}$$

We assume that $S \in L^\infty(\Omega)$ and $R \in L^p(\Omega)$, while the operator F defined by

$$F(\omega, x) := S(\omega)\, G(x) + H(x)$$

is uniformly strongly monotone. The uniform strong monotonicity of F is ensured by the strong monotonicity of $\underline{s}\, G$ and H , where $\underline{s}$ is a positive constant such that there holds $S \geq \underline{s}$ P - a.s. (almost sure). We also require that F satisfies the growth condition (2).
Moreover, we assume that $D \in L^p_m(\Omega) := L^p(\Omega, P, \mathbb{R}^m)$. Hence we can introduce the following closed convex nonvoid subset of $L^p_k(\Omega)$:

$$M^P := \{V \in L^p_k(\Omega) : A\, V(\omega) \leq D(\omega),\ P - a.s.\}$$

and consider the following problem:
Find $\hat{U} \in M^P$ such that, $\forall V \in M^P$,

$$\int_\Omega \langle S(\omega)\, G(\hat{U}(\omega)) + H(\hat{U}(\omega)), V(\omega) - \hat{U}(\omega)\rangle\, dP(\omega) \geq \int_\Omega \langle b + R(\omega)\, c, V(\omega) - \hat{U}(\omega)\rangle\, dP(\omega) . \tag{6}$$

The r.h.s. of (6) defines a continuous linear form on $L^p_k(\Omega)$, while the l.h.s. defines a continuous form on $L^p_k(\Omega)$ which inherits strong monotonicity from the strong monotonicity of $\underline{s}\, G + H$. Therefore, (see e.g. (18)), there exists a unique solution in M^P to problem (6). By uniqueness, problems (5) and (6) are equivalent.
In order to get rid of the abstract sample space Ω, we consider the joint distribution $\mathbb{P}$ of the random vector (R, S, D) and work with the special probability space $(\mathbb{R}^d, \mathcal{B}(\mathbb{R}^d), \mathbb{P})$, where the dimension $d := 2 + m$. To simplify our analysis we shall suppose that R, S and D are independent random vectors. Let $r = R(\omega)$, $s = S(\omega)$, $t = D(\omega)$, $y = (r, s, t)$. For each $y \in \mathbb{R}^d$, consider the set

$$M(y) := \{x \in \mathbb{R}^k : Ax \leq t\}$$

Then the pointwise version of our problem now reads:
Find $\hat{x}$ such that $\hat{x}(y) \in M(y)$, $\mathbb{P}$ - a.s., and the following inequality holds for $\mathbb{P}$ - almost every $y \in \mathbb{R}^d$ and $\forall x \in M(y)$,

$$\langle s\, G(\hat{x}(y)) + H(\hat{x}(y)), x - \hat{x}(y)\rangle \geq \langle b + r\, c, x - \hat{x}(y)\rangle . \tag{7}$$

In order to obtain the integral formulation of (7), consider the space $L^p(\mathbb{R}^d, \mathbb{P}, \mathbb{R}^k)$ and introduce the closed convex nonvoid set

$$M_{\mathbb{P}} := \{v \in L^p(\mathbb{R}^d, \mathbb{P}, \mathbb{R}^k) : Av(r,s,t) \leq t,\ \mathbb{P} - a.s.\}.$$

This leads to the problem:
Find $\hat{u} \in M_{\mathbb{P}}$ such that, $\forall v \in M_{\mathbb{P}}$,

$$\int_{\mathbb{R}^d} \langle s\,G(\hat{u}(y)) + H(\hat{u}(y)), v(y) - \hat{u}(y)\rangle \, d\mathbb{P}(y) \geq \int_{\mathbb{R}^d} \langle b + rc, v(y) - \hat{u}(y)\rangle \, d\mathbb{P}(y). \quad (8)$$

By using the same arguments as in the ω-formulation in section 2, problems (7) and (8) are equivalent.

Remark 3.1. *Our approach and analysis here and in the next section readily applies also to more general finite Karhunen-Loève expansions*

$$\lambda(\omega) \;=\; b + \sum_{l=1}^{L} R_l(\omega)\, c_l,\;\; F(\omega,x) = H(x) + \sum_{l=1}^{L_F} S_l(\omega)\, G_l(x).$$

However, such an extension does not only need a more lengthy notation, but - more importantly - leads to more computational work; see (15) for a more thorough discussion of those computational aspects.

4. An Approximation Procedure by Discretization of Distributions

Without loss of generality, we can suppose that $R \in L^p(\Omega, P)$ and $D \in L^p_m(\Omega, P)$ are nonnegative (otherwise we can use the standard decomposition in the positive part and the negative part). Moreover, we assume that the support (the set of possible outcomes) of $S \in L^\infty(\Omega, P)$ is the interval $[\underline{s}, \overline{s}) \subset (0, \infty)$. Furthermore we assume that the distributions P_R, P_S, P_D are continuous with respect to the Lebesgue measure, so that according to the theorem of Radon-Nikodym, they have the probability densities $\varphi_R, \varphi_S, \varphi_{D_i}$ $i = 1, \ldots, m$, respectively. Hence, $\mathbb{P} = P_R \otimes P_S \otimes P_D$, $dP_R(r) = \varphi_R(r)\, dr$, $dP_S(s) = \varphi_S(s)\, ds$ and $dP_{D_i}(t_i) = \varphi_{D_i}(t_i)\, dt_i$ for $i = 1, \ldots, m$. Let us note that $v \in L^p(\mathbb{R}^d, \mathbb{P}, \mathbb{R}^k)$ means that $(r,s,t) \mapsto \varphi_R(r)\varphi_S(s)\varphi_D(t)v(r,s,t)$ belongs to the standard Lebesgue space $L^p(\mathbb{R}^d, \mathbb{R}^k)$ with respect to the Lebesgue measure, where shortly $\varphi_D(t) := \prod_i \varphi_{D_i}(t_i)$. Thus we arrive at the probabilistic integral formulation of our problem:
Find $\hat{u} \in M_{\mathbb{P}}$ such that, $\forall v \in M_{\mathbb{P}}$,

$$\int_0^\infty \int_{\underline{s}}^{\overline{s}} \int_{\mathbb{R}^m_+} \langle s\,G(\hat{u}) + H(\hat{u}), v - \hat{u}\rangle\, \varphi_R(r)\varphi_S(s)\varphi_D(t)\, dy \geq$$
$$\int_0^\infty \int_{\underline{s}}^{\overline{s}} \int_{\mathbb{R}^m_+} \langle b + rc, v - \hat{u}\rangle\, \varphi_R(r)\varphi_S(s)\varphi_D(t)\, dy.$$

In order to give an approximation procedure for the solution $\hat{u}$, let us start with a discretization of the space $X := L^p(\mathbb{R}^d, \mathbb{P}, \mathbb{R}^k)$ and introduce a sequence $\{\pi_n\}_n$ of partitions of the support $Y := [0, \infty) \times [\underline{s}, \overline{s}) \times \mathbb{R}^m_+$ of the probability measure $\mathbb{P}$ induced by the random elements R, S, D. To be precise, let $\pi_n = (\pi_n^R, \pi_n^S, \pi_n^D)$, where

$$\pi_n^R := (r_n^0, \ldots, r_n^{N_n^R}),\; \pi_n^S := (s_n^0, \ldots, s_n^{N_n^S}),\; \pi_n^{D_i} := (t_{n,i}^0, \ldots, t_{n,i}^{N_n^{D_i}})$$

$$0 = r_n^0 < r_n^1 < \ldots r_n^{N_n^R} = n$$
$$\underline{s} = s_n^0 < s_n^1 < \ldots s_n^{N_n^S} = \overline{s}$$
$$0 = t_{n,i}^0 < t_{n,i}^1 < \ldots t_{n,i}^{N_n^{D_i}} = n \ (i = 1, \ldots, m)$$
$$|\pi_n^R| := \max\{r_n^j - r_n^{j-1} : j = 1, \ldots, N_n^R\} \to 0 \qquad (n \to \infty)$$
$$|\pi_n^S| := \max\{s_n^k - s_n^{k-1} : k = 1, \ldots, N_n^S\} \to 0 \qquad (n \to \infty)$$
$$|\pi_n^{D_i}| := \max\{t_{n,i}^{h_i} - t_{n,i}^{h_i-1} : h_i = 1, \ldots, N_n^{D_i}\} \to 0 \qquad (i = 1, \ldots, m; n \to \infty).$$

These partitions give rise to the exhausting sequence $\{Y_n\}$ of subsets of Y, where each Y_n is given by the finite disjoint union of the intervals:

$$I_{jkh}^n := [r_n^{j-1}, r_n^j) \times [s_n^{k-1}, s_n^k) \times I_h^n,$$

where we use the multiindex $h = (h_1, \cdots, h_m)$ and

$$I_h^n := \Pi_{i=1}^m [t_{n,i}^{h_i-1}, t_{n,i}^{h_i}).$$

For each $n \in \mathbb{N}$ let us consider the space of the $\mathbb{R}^l$-valued simple functions ($l \in \mathbb{N}$) on Y_n, extended by 0 outside of Y_n:

$$X_n^l := \{v_n : v_n(r,s,t) = \sum_j \sum_k \sum_h v_{jkh}^n 1_{I_{jkh}^n}(r,s,t), v_{jkh}^n \in \mathbb{R}^l\}$$

where 1_I denotes the $\{0,1\}$-valued characteristic function of a subset I.
To approximate an arbitrary function $w \in L^p(\mathbb{R}^d, \mathbb{P}, \mathbb{R})$ we employ the mean value truncation operator μ_0^n associated to the partition π_n given by

$$\mu_0^n w := \sum_{j=1}^{N_n^R} \sum_{k=1}^{N_n^S} \sum_h (\mu_{jkh}^n w) 1_{I_{jkh}^n}, \tag{9}$$

where

$$\mu_{jkh}^n w := \begin{cases} \dfrac{1}{\mathbb{P}(I_{jkh})} \displaystyle\int_{I_{jkh}^n} w(y)\, d\mathbb{P}(y) & \text{if } \mathbb{P}(I_{jkh}^n) > 0; \\ 0 & \text{otherwise.} \end{cases}$$

Likewise for a L^p vector function $v = (v_1, \ldots, v_l)$, we define $\mu_0^n v := (\mu_0^n v_1, \ldots, \mu_0^n v_l)$. From Lemma 2.5 in ((14)) (and the remarks therein) we obtain the following result.

Lemma 4.1. *For any fixed $l \in \mathbb{N}$, the linear operator $\mu_0^n : L^p(\mathbb{R}^d, \mathbb{P}, \mathbb{R}^l) \to L^p(\mathbb{R}^d, \mathbb{P}, \mathbb{R}^l)$ is bounded with $\|\mu_0^n\| = 1$ and for $n \to \infty$, μ_0^n converges pointwise in $L^p(\mathbb{R}^d, \mathbb{P}, \mathbb{R}^l)$ to the identity.*

This lemma reflects the well-known density of the class of the simple functions in a L^p space. It shows that the mean value truncation operator μ_0^n, which acts as a projector on $L^p(\mathbb{R}^d, \mathbb{P}, \mathbb{R}^l)$, can be understood as a conditional expectation operator introduced by Kolmogorov in 1933, see also (7), and thus our approximation method is a projection method according to the terminology of (20).
In order to construct approximations for

$$M_{\mathbb{P}} = \{v \in L^p(\mathbb{R}^d, \mathbb{P}, \mathbb{R}^k) : Av(r,s,t) \le t,\ \mathbb{P} - a.s.\}$$

we introduce the orthogonal projector $q : (r,s,t) \in \mathbb{R}^d \mapsto t \in \mathbb{R}^m$ and let, for each elementary quadrangle I^n_{jkh},

$$\overline{q}^n_{jkh} = (\mu^n_{jkh} q) \in \mathbb{R}^m, \qquad (\mu^n_0 q) = \sum_{jkh} \overline{q}^n_{jkh} 1_{I^n_{jkh}} \in X^m_n .$$

Thus we arrive at the following sequence of convex, closed sets

$$M^n_{\mathbb{P}} := \{v \in X^k_n : Av^n_{jkh} \le \overline{q}^n_{jkh},\ \forall j,k,h\} .$$

Note that the sets $M^n_{\mathbb{P}}$ are of polyhedral type. In (17) it has been proved that the sequence $\{M^n_{\mathbb{P}}\}$ approximate the set $M_{\mathbb{P}}$ in the sense of Mosco ((1), (22)), i.e.

$$\text{weak-limsup}_{n\to\infty} M^n_{\mathbb{P}} \subset M_{\mathbb{P}} \subset \text{strong-liminf}_{n\to\infty} M^n_{\mathbb{P}} .$$

Moreover we want to approximate the random variables R and S and introduce

$$\rho_n = \sum_{j=1}^{N^R_n} r_n^{j-1} 1_{[r_n^{j-1}, r_n^j)} \in X_n, \qquad \sigma_n = \sum_{k=1}^{N^S_n} s_n^{k-1} 1_{[s_n^{k-1}, s_n^k)} \in X_n .$$

We observe that $\sigma_n(r,s,t) \to \sigma(r,s,t) = s$ in $L^\infty(\mathbb{R}^d, \mathbb{P})$ while, as a consequence of the Chebyshev inequality (see e.g. (3)), $\rho_n(r,s,t) \to \rho(r,s,t) = r$ in $L^p(\mathbb{R}^d, \mathbb{P})$.
Thus we are led to consider, $\forall n \in \mathbb{N}$, the following substitute problem:
Find $\hat{u}_n \in M^n_{\mathbb{P}}$ such that, $\forall v_n \in M^n_{\mathbb{P}}$,

$$\int_{\mathbb{R}^d} \langle \sigma_n(y)\, G(\hat{u}_n(y)) + H(\hat{u}_n(y)), v_n(y) - \hat{u}_n(y)\rangle \, d\mathbb{P}(y) \ge \int_{\mathbb{R}^d} \langle b + \rho_n(y)\, c, v_n(y) - \hat{u}_n(y)\rangle \, d\mathbb{P}(y) . \tag{10}$$

We observe that (10) splits in a finite number of finite dimensional strongly monotone variational inequalities:
For $\forall n \in \mathbb{N}$, $\forall j,k,h$ find $\hat{u}^n_{jkh} \in M^n_{jkh}$ such that, $\forall v^n_{jkh} \in M^n_{jkh}$,

$$\langle \tilde{F}^n_k(\hat{u}^n_{jkh}), v^n_{jkh} - \hat{u}^n_{jkh}\rangle \ge \langle \tilde{c}^n_j, v^n_{jkh} - \hat{u}^n_{jkh}\rangle , \tag{11}$$

where

$$M^n_{jkh} := \{v^n_{jkh} \in \mathbb{R}^k : Av^n_{jkh} \le \overline{q}^n_{jkh}\},$$

$$\tilde{F}^n_k := s_n^{k-1} G + H,\ \ \tilde{c}^n_j := b + r_n^{j-1} c .$$

Clearly, this gives

$$\hat{u}_n = \sum_j \sum_k \sum_h \hat{u}^n_{jkh} 1_{I^n_{jkh}} \in X^k_n .$$

Now, we can state the following convergence result (whose proof can be found in (17)).

Theorem 4.1. *The sequence $\hat{u}_n$ generated by the substitute problems in (10) converges strongly in $L^p(\mathbb{R}^d,\mathbb{P},\mathbb{R}^k)$ for $n \to \infty$ to the unique solution $\hat{u}$ of (8).*

This theorem can be refined under the additional assumption of Lipschitz continuity, because in this case (and in virtue of uniform strong monotonicity), it is enough to solve the finite dimensional substitute problem (10) only inaccurately.

Theorem 4.2. *Suppose, both maps G and H are uniformly strongly monotone and Lipschitz continuous. Let $\varepsilon_n > 0$. Introduce the monotone operator T_n by*

$$T_n(u)(y) := \sigma_n(y)\,G(u)(y) + H(u)(y) - b - \rho_n(y)\,c$$

and the associated natural map

$$F_n^{nat}(u) = u - Proj_{M_{\mathbb{P}}^n}[u - T_n(u)],$$

both acting in $X_n^l(\mathbb{R}^d,\mathbb{P},\mathbb{R}^k)$ (where Proj is the minimum norm projection). Let $\tilde{u}_n \in M_{\mathbb{P}}^n$ satisfy

$$\|F_n^{nat}(\tilde{u}_n)\| \leq \varepsilon_n\,. \tag{12}$$

Suppose that in (12), $\varepsilon_n \to 0$ for $n \to \infty$. Then the sequence $\tilde{u}_n$ converges strongly in $L^p(\mathbb{R}^d,\mathbb{P},\mathbb{R}^k)$ to the unique solution $\hat{u}$ of (8).

Proof. It will be enough to show that $\lim_n \|\tilde{u}_n - \hat{u}_n\| = 0$.
Let us observe that obviously a zero $\hat{u}_n$ of F_n^{nat} is an exact solution of (10). Instead we solve (10) only inaccurately. In fact, we can estimate (see (8) Volume I, Theorem 2.3.3)

$$\|\tilde{u}_n - \hat{u}_n\| \leq \frac{L_n + 1}{c_n}\,\|F_n^{\mathrm{nat}}(\tilde{u}_n)\|,$$

where L_n, respectively c_n is the Lipschitz constant, respectively the uniform monotonicity constant of T_n. Since the support of the random variable $S \in L^\infty(\Omega, P)$ is the interval $[\underline{s}, \overline{s}) \subset (0,\infty)$ and $\underline{s}G + H$ is uniformly strongly monotone with some constant $c_0 > 0$, respectively $\overline{s}G + H$ is Lipschitz continuous with some constant L_0, we have $0 < c_0 \leq c_n, L_n \leq L_0 < \infty$. Therefore by construction, $\lim_n \|\tilde{u}_n - \hat{u}_n\| = 0$ follows.

□

5. Some Random Nonlinear Equilibrium Problems

In this section we describe some simple equilibria problems from economics and migration theory, while equilibrium problems using a more involved network structure are deferred to the next section. Here we discuss where uncertainty can enter in the data of the problems and show how our theory of RVI, where we can admit that random variables occur both in the operator and the constraints set, can be applied to model those nonlinear equilibrium problems under uncertainty.

5.1 A random Cassel-Wald economic equilibrium model

We follow (19) and describe a Cassel-Wald type economic equilibrium model. This model deals with n commodities and m pure factors of production. Let c_k be the price of the k-th commodity, let b_i be the total inventory of the i-th factor, and let a_{ij} be the consumption rate of the i-th factor which is required for producing one unit of the j-th commodity, so that we set $c = (c_1, \ldots, c_n)^T, b = (b_1, \ldots, b_m)^T, A = (a_{ij})_{m\times n}$. Next let x_j denote the output of the j-th commodity and p_i denote the shadow price of the i-th factor, so that $x = (x_1, \ldots, x_n)^T$ and $p = (p_1, \ldots, p_m)^T$. In this model it is assumed that the prices are dependent on the outputs, so that $c : \mathbb{R}^n_+ \to \mathbb{R}^n_+$ is a given mapping. Now in contrast to (19) we do not consider b as a fixed vector, but we admit that the total inventory vector may be uncertain and model it as a random vector $b = B(\omega)$. Thus we arrive at the following

Problem CW-1. For each $\omega \in \Omega$, find $\hat{X}(\omega) \in \mathbb{R}^n_+, \hat{P}(\omega) \in \mathbb{R}^n_+$ such that

$$\langle c(\hat{X}(\omega)), \hat{X}(\omega) - x\rangle + \langle \hat{P}(\omega), Ax - A\hat{X}(\omega)\rangle \geq 0, \quad \forall x \in \mathbb{R}^n_+;$$
$$\langle p - \hat{P}(\omega), B(\omega) - A\hat{X}(\omega)\rangle \geq 0, \quad \forall p \in \mathbb{R}^n_+.$$

This is nothing but the optimality condition for the variational inequality problem:

Problem CW-2. For each $\omega \in \Omega$, find $\hat{X}(\omega) \in \mathcal{K}(\omega)$ such that

$$\langle c(\hat{X}(\omega)), \hat{X}(\omega) - x\rangle \geq 0, \quad \forall x \in \mathcal{K}(\omega),$$

where here

$$\mathcal{K}(\omega) = \{x \in \mathbb{R}^n \mid x \geq 0, Ax \leq B(\omega)\}.$$

Both problems CW-1 and CW-2 are special instances of the general Problem 1, where randomness in CW-1 only occurs via the generally nonlinear mapping c, while randomness in CW-2 also affects the comstraints set.

5.2 A random distributed market equilibrium model

We follow (13) and consider a single commodity that is produced at n supply markets and consumed at m demand markets. There is a total supply g_i in each supply market i, where $i = 1, \ldots, n$. Likewise there is a total demand f_j in each demand market j, where $j = 1, \ldots, m$. Since the markets are spatially separated, x_{ij} units of the commodity are transported from i to j. Introducing the excess supply s_i and the excess demand t_j we must have

$$g_i = \sum_{j=1}^{m} x_{ij} + s_i, \qquad i = 1, \ldots, n; \tag{13}$$

$$f_j = \sum_{i=1}^{n} x_{ij} + t_j, \qquad j = 1, \ldots, m; \tag{14}$$

Moreover the transportation from i to j gives rise to unit costs π_{ij}. Further we associate with each supply market i a supply price p_i and with each demand market j a demand price q_j. We assume there is given a fixed minimum supply price $\underline{p}_i \geq 0$ ('price floor') for each supply market i and also a fixed maximum demand price $\bar{q}_j > 0$ ('price ceiling') for each demand market j. These bounds can be absent and the standard spatial price equilibrium model due to Dafermos ((5), see also (19)) results, where the markets are required to be cleared, i.e.

$$s_i = 0 \quad \text{for } i = 1, \ldots, n; \qquad t_j = 0 \quad \text{for } j = 1, \ldots, m$$

are required to hold. Since $s_i \geq 0$ and $t_j \geq 0$ are admitted, the model is also termed a disequilibrium model. As is common in operations research models, we also include upper bounds $\bar{x}_{ij} > 0$ for the transportation fluxes x_{ij} on our bipartite graph of distributed markets.
Let us group the introduced quantities in vectors omitting the indices i and j: We have the total supply vector $g \in \mathbb{R}^n$, the supply price vector $p \in \mathbb{R}^n$, the total demand vector $f \in \mathbb{R}^m$, the demand price vector $q \in \mathbb{R}^m$, the flux vector $x \in \mathbb{R}^{nm}$, and the unit cost vector $\pi \in \mathbb{R}^{nm}$. Thus in our constrained distibuted market model the feasible set for the unknown vector $u = [p,q,x]$ is given by the product set

$$M := \prod_{i=1}^{n} [\underline{p}_i, \infty) \times \prod_{j=1}^{m} [0, \bar{q}_j] \times \prod_{i=1}^{n} \prod_{j=1}^{m} [0, \bar{x}_{ij}] \,.$$

As soon as the given bounds are uncertain and we model these bounds as random variables, we obtain the random constraints set

$$\mathcal{M}(\omega) := \prod_{i=1}^{n} [\underline{p}_i(\omega), \infty) \times \prod_{j=1}^{m} [0, \bar{q}_j(\omega)] \times \prod_{i=1}^{n} \prod_{j=1}^{m} [0, \bar{x}_{ij}(\omega)] \,.$$

Assuming perfect equilibrium the economic market conditions take the following form

$$s_i > 0 \;\Rightarrow\; p_i = \underline{p}_i \,,\quad p_i > \underline{p}_i \Rightarrow s_i = 0 \qquad i = 1, \ldots, n; \tag{15}$$

$$t_j > 0 \;\Rightarrow\; q_j = \bar{q}_j \,,\quad q_j < \bar{q}_j \Rightarrow t_j = 0 \qquad j = 1, \ldots, m; \tag{16}$$

$$p_i + \pi_{ij} \begin{cases} \geq q_j & \text{if } x_{ij} = 0 \\ = q_j & \text{if } 0 < x_{ij} < \bar{x}_{ij} \\ \leq q_j & \text{if } x_{ij} = \bar{x}_{ij} \end{cases} \qquad i = 1, \ldots, n \,; j = 1, \ldots, m \,. \tag{17}$$

The last condition (17) extends the classic equilibrium conditions in that $p_i + \pi_{ij} < q_j$ can occur because of the flux constraint $x_{ij} \leq \bar{x}_{ij}$. As in unconstrained market equilibria ((5)) we assume that we are given the functions

$$g = \breve{g}(p) \,, f = \breve{f}(q) \,, \pi = \breve{\pi}(x) \,.$$

Then under the natural assumptions that for each $i = 1, \ldots, n; j = 1, \ldots, m$ there holds

$$q_j = 0 \Rightarrow \breve{f}_j(q) \geq 0 ; \quad x_{ij} > 0 \Rightarrow \breve{\pi}_{ij}(x) > 0 \,.$$

it can be shown (see (13)) that a market equilibrium $u = (p,q,x)$ introduced above by the conditions (13) – (17) can be characterized as a solution to the following Variational Inequality: Find $u = (p,q,x) \in M$ such that

$$\sum_{i=1}^{n} (\breve{g}_i(p) - \sum_{j=1}^{m} x_{ij})(\tilde{p}_i - p_i) \; - \; \sum_{j=1}^{m} (\breve{f}_j(q) - \sum_{i=1}^{n} x_{ij})(\tilde{q}_j - q_j)$$

$$+ \sum_{i=1}^{n} \sum_{j=1}^{m} (p_i + \breve{\pi}_{ij}(x) - q_j)(\tilde{x}_{ij} - x_{ij}) \;\geq\; 0 \,, \qquad \forall \tilde{u} = (\tilde{p}, \tilde{q}, \tilde{x}) \in M \,.$$

Now also the functions $\breve{g}, \breve{f}, \breve{\pi}$ may be not precisely known, but are affected by uncertainness, so may be modelled as random. Thus we obtain the random distributed market problem:
Problem DM. For each $\omega \in \Omega$, find $(\hat{P}, \hat{Q}, \hat{X})(\omega) \in \mathcal{M}(\omega)$ such that

$$\sum_{i=1}^{n}(\check{g}_i(\omega,\hat{P}(\omega)) - \sum_{j=1}^{m}\hat{X}_{ij}(\omega))(\tilde{p}_i - \hat{P}_i(\omega))$$

$$- \quad \sum_{j=1}^{m}(\check{f}_j(\omega,\hat{Q}(\omega)) - \sum_{i=1}^{n}\hat{X}_{ij})(\omega))(\tilde{q}_j - \hat{Q}_j(\omega))$$

$$+ \quad \sum_{i=1}^{n}\sum_{j=1}^{m}(\hat{P}_i(\omega) + \check{\pi}_{ij}(\omega,\hat{X}) - \hat{Q}_j(\omega))(\tilde{x}_{ij} - \hat{X}_{ij}(\omega)) \geq 0\,,\ \forall\tilde{u} = (\tilde{p},\tilde{q},\tilde{x}) \in \mathcal{M}(\omega)\,.$$

Obviously Problem DM is a special instance of Problem 1 with randomness both in the operator and in the constraints set.

5.3 A random migration equilibrium model

We follow (19) in simplifying a more involved migration model of (23). This model involves a set of nodes (locations) $\mathbf{N}$. For each $i \in \mathbf{N}$ let b_i denote the the initial fixed population in location i; let h_{ij} denote the value of the migration flow from i to j, and let x_i denote the current population in location i. Set $x = \{x_i | i \in \mathbf{N}\}$ and $h = \{h_{ij} | i,j \in \mathbf{N}, i \neq j\}$. Because of nonnegativity of the migration flow and due to the conservation of flows while preventing any chain migration we have the feasible set

$$\begin{aligned} M \quad := \quad & \{(x,h)\,|\,h \geq 0, \sum_{j\neq i} h_{ij} \leq b_i\,, \\ & x_i = b_i + \sum_{j\neq i} h_{ji} - \sum_{j\neq i} h_{ij}\,,\ \ \forall i \in \mathbf{N}\}\,. \end{aligned}$$

With each location i there is associated the utility u_i that is assumed to be dependent on the population, i.e. $u_i = \breve{u}_i(x)$. Also with each pair of loactions $i,j; i \neq j$ there is associated the migration cost c_{ij} that is assumed to be dependent on the migration flow, i.e. $c_{ij} = \check{c}_{ij}(h)$. Now a pair $(x,h) \in M$ is considered to be in equilibrium, if (note the similarities to the equlibrium conditions (15) and (17)!)

$$\breve{u}_i(x) - \breve{u}_j(x) + \check{c}_{ij}(h) + \mu_i \begin{cases} \geq 0 & \text{if } h_{ij} = 0, \\ = 0 & \text{if } h_{ij} > 0; \end{cases} \qquad \forall i,j \in \mathbf{N}, i \neq j;$$

$$\mu_i \begin{cases} \geq 0 & \text{if } \sum_{l\neq i} h_{il} = b_i\,, \\ = 0 & \text{if } \sum_{l\neq i} h_{il} < b_i\,; \end{cases} \qquad \forall i \in \mathbf{N}.$$

These equilibrium conditions can be equivalently expressed in the form of the variational inequality:
Find a pair $(x,h) \in M$ such that

$$\sum_{i\in\mathbf{N}} \breve{u}_i(x)(x_i - \tilde{x}_i) + \sum_{i,j\in\mathbf{N}, i\neq j} \check{c}_{ij}(h)(\tilde{h}_{ij} - h_{ij}) \geq 0\,, \qquad \forall(\tilde{x},\tilde{h}) \in M\,.$$

Now the functions $\breve{u}_i, \check{c}_{ij}$ may be not precisely known, but are affected by uncertainness, so may be modelled as random. Thus we obtain the random migration problem:

Problem M. For each $\omega \in \Omega$, find $(\hat{X},\hat{H})(\omega) \in M$ such that

$$\sum_{i\in\mathbf{N}} \breve{u}_i(\omega,\hat{X}(\omega))(\hat{X}_i(\omega)-\tilde{x}_i) + \sum_{i,j\in\mathbf{N},i\neq j} \breve{c}_{ij}(\omega,\hat{H}(\omega))(\tilde{h}_{ij}-\hat{H}_{ij}(\omega)) \geq 0, \qquad \forall(\tilde{x},\tilde{h}) \in M.$$

Obviously Problem DM is a special instance of Problem 1 now with randomness only in the operator.

6. A Random Traffic Equilibrium Problem

In this Section 6 we apply our results to network equilibrium problems. A common characteristic of these problems is that they admit two different formulations based either on link variables or on path variables. These are actually related to each other through a linear transformation; we stress that in general, in the path approach, the strong monotonicity assumption is not reasonable. However, we are able to fill this gap by proving a Mosco convergence result for the transformed sequence of sets and working in the "right" group of variables. To be more precise we need first some notation commonly used to state the standard traffic equilibrium problem from the user's point of view in the stationary case (see for instance (27), (4), (24)).

A traffic network consists of a triple (N,A,W) where $N=\{N_1,\ldots,N_p\}$, $p\in\mathbb{N}$, is the set of nodes, $A=(A_1,\ldots,A_n)$, $n\in\mathbb{N}$, represents the set of the directed arcs connecting couples of nodes and $W=\{W_1,\ldots,W_m\}\subset N\times N$, $m\in\mathbb{N}$ is the set of the origin– destination (O,D) pairs. The flow on the arc A_i is denoted by f_i, this gives the arc flow vector $f=(f_1,\ldots,f_n)$; for the sake of simplicity we shall consider arcs with infinite capacity. We call a set of consecutive arcs a path, and assume that each (O_j,D_j) pair W_j is connected by r_j, $r_j\in\mathbb{N}$, paths whose set is denoted by P_j, $j=1,\ldots,m$. All the paths in the network are grouped in a vector $(R_1,\ldots,R_k)$, $k\in\mathbb{N}$, We can describe the arc structure of the paths by using the arc–path incidence matrix

$$\Delta = (\delta_{ir})_{\substack{i=1,\ldots,n\\ r=1,\ldots,k}} \text{ with the entries } \delta_{ir} = \begin{cases} 1 & \text{if } A_i \in R_r \\ 0 & \text{if } A_i \notin R_r \end{cases}. \tag{18}$$

To each path R_r there corresponds a flow F_r. The path flows are grouped in a vector $(F_1,\ldots,F_k)$ which is called the path (network) flow. The flow f_i on the arc A_i is equal to the sum of the flows on the paths which contain A_i, so that $f=\Delta F$. Let us now introduce the unit cost of transversing A_i as a given real-valued function $c_i(f)\geq 0$ of the flows on the network, so that $c(f)=(c_1(f),\ldots,c_n(f))$ denotes the arc cost vector on the network. The meaning of the cost is usually that of the travel time. Analogously, one can define a cost on the paths as $C(F)=(C_1(F),\ldots,C_k(F))$. Usually $C_r(F)$ is just the sum of the costs on the arcs which build that path, hence $C_r(F)=\sum_{i=1}^{n}\delta_{ir}c_i(f)$ or in compact form,

$$C(F) = \Delta^T c(\Delta F). \tag{19}$$

For each (O,D) pair W_j there is a given traffic demand $D_j\geq 0$, so that $(D_1,\ldots,D_m)$ is the demand vector. Feasible flows are nonnegative flows which satisfy the demands, i.e. belong to the set

$$K = \{F\in\mathbb{R}^k :\ F_r \geq 0 \text{ for any } r=1,\ldots,k \text{ and } \Phi F = D\},$$

where Φ is the pair–path incidence matrix whose elements, say $\varphi_{jr}, j=1,\ldots,m, r=1,\ldots,k$, are

$$\varphi_{jr} = \begin{cases} 1 & \text{if the path } R_r \text{ connects the pair } W_j \\ 0 & \text{elsewhere} \end{cases}.$$

A path flow H is called an equilibrium flow or *Wardrop Equilibrium*, if and only if $H \in K$ and for any $W_j \in W$ and any $R_q, R_s \in P_j$ there holds

$$C_q(H) < C_s(H) \quad \Longrightarrow \quad H_s = 0. \tag{20}$$

This statement is equivalent (see for instance (4) and (27)) to

$$H \in K \quad \text{and} \quad \langle C(H), F - H\rangle \geq 0, \quad \forall F \in K. \tag{21}$$

Roughly speaking, the meaning of Wardrop Equilibrium is that the road users choose minimum cost paths. Let us note that condition (20) implies that all the used paths of a given (O,D) pair have the same cost.
Although the Wardrop equilibrium principle is expressed in the path variables, it is clear that the "physical" (and measured) quantities are expressed in the arc (link) variables; moreover, the strong monotonicity hypothesis on $c(f)$ is quite common, but as noticed for instance in (2) this does not imply the strong monotonicity of $C(F)$ in (19), unless the matrix $\Delta^T\Delta$ is nonsingular. Although one can give a procedure for buildings networks preserving the strong monotonicity property (see for instance (9)), the condition fails for a generic network, even for a very simple one as we shall illustrate in the sequel. Thus, it is useful to consider the following variational inequality problem:

$$h \in \Delta K \text{ and } \langle c(h), f - h\rangle \geq 0 \quad \forall f \in \Delta K. \tag{22}$$

If c is strongly monotone, one can prove that for each solution H of (21), $C(H)$ =const., i.e. all possibly nonunique solutions of (21) share the same cost. From an algorithmic point of view it is worth noting that one advantage in working in the path variables is the simplicity of the corresponding convex set but the price to be paid is that the number of paths grows exponentially with the size of the network.
Let us now consider the random version of (21) and (22), which results from an uncertain demand and uncertain costs. In the path-flow variables the random Wardrop equilibrium problem reads:
For each $\omega \in \Omega$, find $H(\omega) \in K(\omega)$ such that

$$\langle C(\omega, H(\omega)), F - H(\omega)\rangle \geq 0, \quad \forall F \in K(\omega), \tag{23}$$

where, for any $\omega \in \Omega$,

$$K(\omega) = \{F \in \mathbb{R}^k : F_r \geq 0 \text{ for any } r = 1,\ldots,k \text{ and } \Phi F = D(\omega)\},$$

Analogously in the link-flow variables the random Wardrop equilibrium problem reads:
For each $\omega \in \Omega$, find $h(\omega) \in \Delta K(\omega)$ such that

$$\langle c(\omega, h(\omega)), f - h(\omega)\rangle \geq 0, \quad \forall f \in \Delta K(\omega). \tag{24}$$

Clearly (23) is equivalent to the random Wardrop principle: For any $\omega \in \Omega$, for any $H(\omega) \in K(\omega)$, and for any $W_j \in W$, $R_q, R_s \in P_j$, there holds

$$C_q(\omega, H(\omega)) < C_s(\omega, H(\omega)) \quad \Longrightarrow \quad H_s(\omega) = 0.$$

Moreover, both problems are special instances of Problem 1 (pointwise formulation).
In order to use our approximation scheme we require the separability assumption . However this assumption is very natural in many applications where the random perturbation is treated as a *modulation* of a deterministic process. Under the above mentioned assumptions, (23) assumes the particular form:

$$S(\omega)\langle A(H(\omega)), F - H(\omega)\rangle \geq R(\omega)\langle b, F - H(\omega)\rangle, \ \forall F \in K(\omega) \tag{25}$$

In equation (25), both the l.h.s. and the r.h.s. can, be replaced with any (finite) linear combination of monotone and separable terms, where each term satisfies the hypothesis of the previous sections:

$$\sum_i S_i(\omega)\langle A_i(H(\omega)), F - H(\omega)\rangle \geq \sum_j R_j(\omega)\langle b_j, F - H(\omega), \ \forall F \in K(\omega). \tag{26}$$

In this way, in (25) $R(\omega), S(\omega)$ can be replaced by a random vector, respectively by a random matrix.
Hence, in the traffic network, we could consider the case where the random perturbation has a different weight for each path.

Remark 6.1. *When applying our theory to the random traffic equilibrium problem we shall consider the integrated form of* (25), *which, after the transformation to the image space, is defined on the feasible set:*

$$K_{\mathbb{P}} = \{F \in L^p(\mathbb{R}^d, \mathbb{P}, \mathbb{R}^k) : \Phi F(r,s,t) = t, F(r,s,t) \geq 0 \quad \mathbb{P} - a.s.\}$$

Let $K^n_{\mathbb{P}}$ be the approximate sets constructed as described in section 4. It can be easily verified that the sets $K^n_{\mathbb{P}}$ are uniformly bounded. Moreover, the arc-path incidence matrix Δ induces a linear operator mapping $L^p(\mathbb{R}^d, \mathbb{P}, \mathbb{R}^k)$ to $L^p(\mathbb{R}^d, \mathbb{P}, \mathbb{R}^n)$. This operator, which by abuse of notation is still denoted by Δ, is weak-weak, as well as strong-strong continuous. Thus, from the Mosco convergence $K^n_{\mathbb{P}} \to K_{\mathbb{P}}$ it follows easily that also $\Delta K^n_{\mathbb{P}} \to \Delta K_{\mathbb{P}}$ in Mosco's sense.

In what follows we present two examples of small size. In the first example we build a small network and we study the random variational inequality in the path-flow variables. The network is built in such a way that if the cost operator is strongly monotone in the link-flow variables, the transformed operator, is still strongly monotone in the path-flow variables. Moreover, this small network can be considered as an elementary block of an arbitrarily large network with the same property of preserving strong monotonicity. On the other hand, the second example, which we solve exactly, shows that even very simple networks can fail to preserve the strong monotonicity of the operator when passing from the link to the path-flow variables. In this last case, two possible strategies can be followed. The first possibility is to work from the beginning in the link-variables and use the previous remark to apply our approximation procedure. The other option is to regularize (in the sense of Tichonov) the problem in the path-variables. We stress the fact that if one is interested in the cost shared by the network users, it does not matter which solution is obtained from the regularized problem, because, thanks to the particular structure of the operator, the cost is constant on the whole solution set.

Example 6.1. In the network under consideration, (see Fig.1), there are 7 links and one origin-destination pair, $1-6$, which can be connected by 3 paths, namely:
$R_1 = A_1 A_2 A_7$

N	$\langle F_1 \rangle$	$\langle F_2 \rangle$	$\langle F_3 \rangle$	σ_1^2	σ_2^2	σ_3^2
10	4.5396	1.4756	4.4346	0.0153	0.0017	0.0148
100	4.5590	1.4821	4.4537	0.0154	0.0017	0.0149
1000	4.5610	1.4821	4.4556	0.0154	0.0017	0.0149
10000	4.5612	1.4828	4.4558	0.0154	0.0017	0.0149

Table 1. Mean values corresponding to various approximations for $d \in [10, 11]$ and $\rho = 0.1$

$R_2 = A_1 A_6 A_4$
$R_3 = A_5 A_3 A_4$
The traffic demand is represented by the non negative random variable d, so that $F_1 + F_2 + F_3 = d$, while link-cost functions are given by:

$$t_1 = \rho f_1^2 + f_1; \qquad t_5 = \rho f_5^2 + f_5$$
$$t_2 = \rho f_2^2 + 2f_2; \qquad t_6 = \rho f_6^2 + 2f_6$$
$$t_3 = \rho f_3^2 + f_3; \qquad t_7 = \rho f_7^2 + f_7 + 0.5 f_5$$
$$t_4 = \rho f_4^2 + 2f_4 + f_6.$$

The linear part of the operator above is represented by a nonsymmetric positive definite matrix, while the nonnegative parameter ρ represents the weight of the non linear terms. Such a functional form is quite common in many network equilibrium problems ((23)). Since we want to solve the variational inequality associated to the Wardrop Equilibrium we have to perform the transformation to the path-flow variables, which yields for the cost functions the following expressions:

$$C_1 = 3\rho F_1^2 + \rho F_2^2 + 2\rho F_1 F_2 + 4F_1 + F_2 + 0.5F_3;$$
$$C_2 = \rho F_1^2 + 3\rho F_2^2 + \rho F_3^2 + 2\rho F_1 F_2 + 2\rho F_2 F_3 + F_1 + 6F_2 + 2F_3;$$
$$C_3 = \rho F_2^2 + 3\rho F_3^2 + 2\rho F_2 F_3 + 4F_3 + 3F_2$$

For the numerical solution of the discretized, finite dimensional variational inequalities, many algorithms are available. Due to the simple structure of our example we employ the extragradient algorithm, see e.g. (8).
In the tables 3 and 4 we show mean values and variances for various choices of the parameters in the case of uniform distribution. We observe that the variances in the second table are quite large. This is due to the fact that if $\rho = 1$, when the other parameter varies the equilibrium pattern changes qualitatively. In particular, near $d = 10$ there is a zero component (H_2) in the solution, while in most of the interval the equilibrium solution has nonzero components.

Example 6.2. We consider the simple network of Fig. 2 below which consists of four arcs and one origin–destination pair, which can be connected by four different paths. Let us assume that the traffic demand between O and D is given by a random variable $t \in \mathbb{R}$, and that the link cost functions are given by $c_1 = 2f_1, c_2 = 3f_2, c_3 = f_3, c_4 = f_4$. The link flows belong to the set

$$\{f \in \mathbb{R}^4 : \exists F \in K(t),\ f = \Delta F\},$$

N	$\langle F_1 \rangle$	$\langle F_2 \rangle$	$\langle F_3 \rangle$	σ_1^2	σ_2^2	σ_3^2
10	3.1602	2.6005	4.6891	4.2853	2.3442	0.1010
100	3.6964	2.1968	4.6017	3.0077	1.6456	0.0759
1000	3.6460	2.2390	4.6143	3.1668	1.7326	0.0791
10000	3.6505	2.2436	4.6157	3.1837	1.7418	0.0794

Table 2. Mean values corresponding to various approximations for $d \in [10,11]$ and $\rho = 1$

where $K(t)$ is the feasible set in the path flow variables

$$K(t) = \{F_1, F_2, F_3, F_4 \geq 0 \text{ such that } F_1 + F_2 + F_3 + F_4 = t,\ t \in [0,T]\},$$

and Δ is the link-path matrix. Hence, if F is known, one can derive f from the equations

$$\begin{aligned} f_1 &= F_1 + F_2, \\ f_2 &= F_3 + F_4, \\ f_3 &= F_1 + F_3, \\ f_4 &= F_2 + F_4. \end{aligned}$$

The path–cost functions are given by the relations

$$\begin{aligned} C_1 &= c_1 + c_3 = 3F_1 + 2F_2 + F_3, \\ C_2 &= c_1 + c_4 = 2F_1 + 3F_2 + F_4, \\ C_3 &= c_2 + c_3 = F_1 + 4F_3 + 3F_4, \\ C_4 &= c_2 + c_4 = F_2 + 3F_3 + 4F_4 \end{aligned}$$

The associated variational inequality can be solved exactly (see e.g. (9) for a non iterative algorithm) and the solution expressed in term of the second path variable is

$$\left(\frac{3t}{5} - G(t), G(t), G(t) - \frac{t}{10}, -G(t) + \frac{t}{2}\right)$$

where $G : [0,T] \mapsto \mathbb{R}$ is any functions which satisfies the constraint $G(t) \in \left[\frac{t}{10}, \frac{t}{2}\right]$. Let us observe that for each feasible choice of $G(t)$ the cost at the corresponding solution is always equal to $\frac{17}{10}t(1,1,1,1)$. One can also solve the variational inequality in the link variables by using the relations

$$\begin{aligned} f_1 + f_2 &= t, \\ f_3 + f_4 &= t. \end{aligned}$$

We are then left with the problem:

$$(c_2 - c_1)\,(f_2 - h_2(t)) + (c_4 - c_3)\,(f_4 - h_4(t)) \geq 0,$$

which yields

$$h(t) = t\left(\frac{3}{5}, \frac{2}{5}, \frac{1}{2}, \frac{1}{2}\right).$$

As an example we assume that our random parameter follows the *lognormal distribution*. This statistical distribution is used for numerous applications to model random phenomena described by nonnegative quantities. It is also known as the Galton Mc Alister distribution and, in economics, is sometimes called the Cobb-Douglas distribution, and has been used to model production data. Thus, let:

$$g_{\mu,\sigma^2}(x) = \frac{1}{\sqrt{2\pi}\sigma} e^{-\frac{(x-\mu)^2}{2\sigma^2}}$$

the *normal* distribution, then, the *lognormal distribution* is defined by:

$$\begin{cases} (1/x) g_{\mu,\sigma^2}(\log x), & \text{if } x > 0 \\ 0, & \text{if } x \leq 0 \end{cases}$$

The numerical evaluation of the mean values and variances, corresponding to $\mu = 0$ and $\sigma = 1$ yields:

$$(\langle h_1 \rangle, \langle h_2 \rangle, \langle h_3 \rangle, \langle h_4 \rangle) = 1.64(3/5, 2/5, 1/2, 1/2)$$

$$(\sigma^2(h_1), \sigma^2(h_2), \sigma^2(h_3), \sigma^2(h_4)) = 4.68(3/5, 2/5, 1/2, 1/2).$$

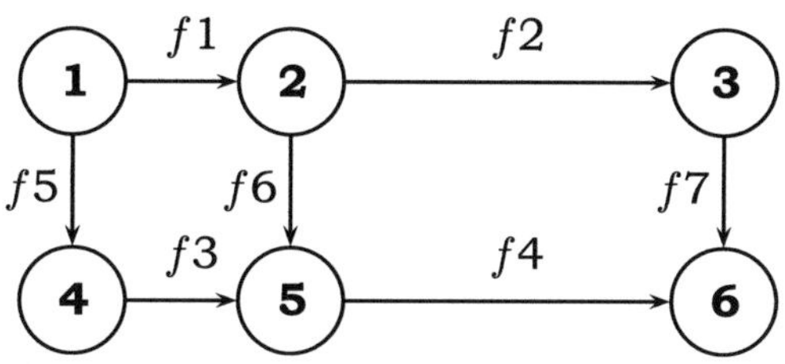

Fig. 1. Network which preserves strong monotonicity

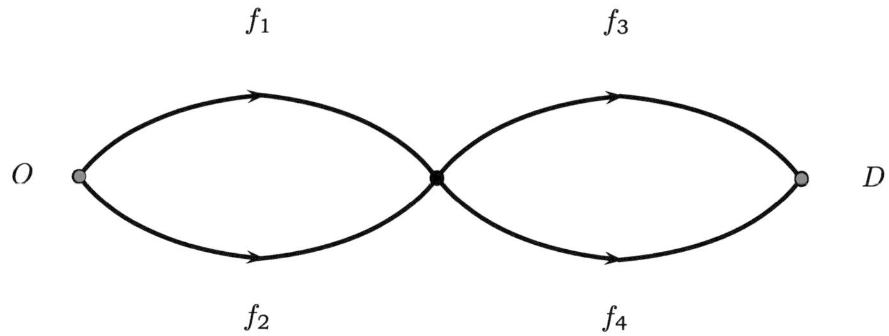

Fig. 2. Loss of strong monotonicity through a linear mapping

7. References

[1] Attouch, H.: *Variational Convergence for Functions and Operators*. Pitman, Boston, 1984.
[2] Bertsekas, D. and Gafni, E.: "Projection methods for variational inequalities with application to the traffic assignment problem", Math. Prog. Stud., **17**, pp. 139–159, 1982.
[3] Billingsley P.: *Probability and Measure*. Wiley, New York, 1995.
[4] Dafermos, S.: "Traffic equilibrium and variational inequalities", Transportation Sci., **14**, pp. 42–54, 1980.
[5] Dafermos, S.: Exchange price equilibria and variational inequalities, *Math. Programming* **46**, 391–402, 1990.
[6] Dempster, M.A.H.: Introduction to stochastic programming. Stochastic programming, Proc. int. Conf., Oxford, 3-59 (1980).
[7] Doob, J.L.: *Stochastic Processes*, Wiley, New York, 1953.
[8] Facchinei, F., Pang, J.-S.: *Finite-Dimensional Variational Inequalities and Complementarity Problems*, Two Volumes. Springer, New York, 2003.
[9] Falsaperla, P. and Raciti, F.: An improved, non-iterative algorithm for the calculation of the equilibrium in the traffic network problem. J. Optim. Theory. Appl., **133**, pp. 401–411, 2007.
[10] Giannessi, F., Maugeri, A. (Eds.): *Variational Inequalities and Network Equilibrium Problems*. Erice, 1994; Plenum Press, New York, 1995.
[11] Gürkan, G., Özge, A.Y., Robinson, S.M.: Sample-path solution of stochastic variational inequalities. Math.Program. **84**, 313–333, 1999.
[12] Gürkan, G., Özge, A.Y., Robinson, S.M.: Solving stochastic optimization problems with constraints: An application in network design. Proceedings of the 31st conference on Winter Simulation— a bridge to the future, 471–478, ACM Press, New York, 1999, Eds.: P.A. Farrington, H.B. Nembhard, D.T. Sturrock, G.W. Evans.
[13] Gwinner, J.: Stability of monotone variational inequalities with various applications, in (10), 123 – 142, 1995.
[14] Gwinner, J.: A class of random variational inequalities and simple random unilateral boundary value problems: Existence, discretization, finite element approximation. Stochastic Anal. Appl. **18**, 967–993, 2000.
[15] Gwinner J., Raciti F.: On a Class of Random Variational Inequalities on Random Sets. Numerical Functional Analysis and Optimization, **27**, pp 619-636, 2006.
[16] Gwinner J., Raciti F.: Random equilibrium problems on networks. Mathematical and Computer Modelling, **43**, pp. 880 – 891, 2006.
[17] Gwinner J., Raciti F.: On Monotone Variational Inequalities with Random Data, 11 p., to appear in Journal of Mathematical Inequalities.
[18] Kinderlehrer, D., Stampacchia, G.: *An Introduction to Variational Inequalities and their Applications*. Academic Press, New York, 1980.
[19] Konnov, I. V.: *Equilibrium Models and Variational Inequalities*. Elsevier, Amsterdam, 2007.
[20] Lepp, R.: Projection and discretization methods in stochastic programming. J. Comput. Appl. Math. 56, 55-64, 1994.
[21] Lin G.H. and Fukushima M.: Regularization method for stochastic mathematical programs with complementarity constraints. ESAIM Control Optim. Calc. Var. **11**, pp. 252–265, 2005.
[22] Mosco, U.: Convergence of convex sets and of solutions of variational inequalities. Advances in Math. **3**, 510–585 (1969).

[23] Nagurney, A.: *Network Economics: A Variational Inequality Approach*, Kluwer Academic Publishers, Dordrecht, Holland, 1993.
[24] Patriksson, M.: *The Traffic Assignment Problem*, VSP, Utrecht, The Netherlands, 1994.
[25] Prékopa, A:*Stochastic programming*. Budapest: Akadémiai Kiadó; Dordrecht: Kluwer Academic Publishers, 1995.
[26] Taji K., Fukushima M., Ibaraki T.: A globally convergent Newton method for solving strongly monotone variational inequalities. Math. Program. **58** 369–383 1993.
[27] Smith, M.J.: The existence, uniqueness and stability of traffic equilibrium. Transportation Res., **138**, pp. 295-304, 1979.
[28] Shapiro, A.:Stochastic Programming with equilibrium constraint, J.Opt.Th. Appl **128**, 223–243, 2006.
[29] Shapiro, A.: Stochastic programming approach to optimization under uncertainty. Math. Program. **112**, pp. 183–220, 2008.

Optimal control systems of second order with infinite time horizon - maximum principle*

Dariusz Idczak and Rafał Kamocki
Faculty of Mathematics and Computer Science, University of Lodz
Banacha 22, 90-238 Lodz, Poland
idczak@math.uni.lodz.pl; rafkam@math.uni.lodz.pl

Abstract

In the paper, we consider an optimal control problem for a second order control system on unbounded interval $(0, \infty)$ and an integral cost functional.
In the first part of the paper, we recall some results concerning the existence and uniqueness of a solution to the control system, corresponding to any admissible control, the continuous dependence of solutions on controls and the existence of the so-called classically optimal solution to the optimal control problem under consideration. These results has been obtained in [D. Idczak, S. Walczak, *Optimal control systems of second order with infinite time horizon - existence of solutions*, to appear in JOTA].
In the second part, some other definitions of optimality are introduced and their interrelationships, including optimality principle, are given. Two maximum principles stating necessary conditions for the introduced kinds of optimality (in general case and in a special one) are derived.

1. Introduction

As in Idczak (to appear), we consider a control system described by the following system of the second order equations

$$\ddot{x}(t) = G_x(t, x(t), u(t)),\ t \in I := (0, \infty)\ a.e, \tag{1}$$

with the initial condition

$$x(0) = 0, \tag{2}$$

where $G_x : I \times \mathbb{R}^n \times M \to \mathbb{R}^n$ is the gradient with respect to x of a function $G : I \times \mathbb{R}^n \times M \to \mathbb{R}$, $M \subset \mathbb{R}^m$ is a fixed set. In the next, we shall use notations and definitions introduced in Idczak (to appear). In particular, we assume that the controls $u(\cdot)$ belong to a set $\mathcal{U}^p := \{u \in L^p(I, \mathbb{R}^m);\ u(t) \in M \text{ for } t \in I \text{ a.e.}\}$, $p \in [1, \infty]$, and the trajectories $x(\cdot)$ - to Sobolev space $H_0^1(I, \mathbb{R}^n)$ (cf. Brezis (1983)). Since each function $x(\cdot) \in H^1(I, \mathbb{R}^n)$ possesses the limit $\lim_{t \to \infty} x(t) = 0$, therefore the problem of the existence of a solution to (1)-(2) in the space

*This work is a part of the research project N514 027 32/3630 supported by the Ministry of Science and Higher Education (Poland).

$H_0^1(I,\mathbb{R}^n)$, corresponding to a control $u(\cdot)$, is, in fact, two-point boundary value problem with boundary conditions

$$x(0) = 0,\ x(\infty) := \lim_{t\to\infty} x(t) = 0.$$

We say that a function $x_u(\cdot) \in H_0^1(I,\mathbb{R}^n)$ is a solution to (1)-(2), corresponding to control $u(\cdot)$, if

$$\int_I (\left\langle \dot{x}_u(t), \dot{h}(t) \right\rangle + \langle G_x(t, x_u(t), u(t)), h(t)\rangle)dt = 0 \tag{3}$$

for any $h(\cdot) \in H_0^1(I,\mathbb{R}^n)$.

The study of systems (1) in the space $H^1(I,\mathbb{R}^n)$ is justified because in this space both kinetic energy $E_k = \frac{1}{2}\int_I \left|\dot{x}_u(t)\right|^2 dt$ and potential one $\int_I G(t, x_u(t), u(t))dt$ of the system are finite as in the real world (in the case of potential energy - under appropriate assumptions on G). Potential form of the right-hand side of this system allows us to use a variational approach. In the case of bounded time interval I (finite horizon), classical cost functional for optimal control problems has the following integral form

$$J(x,u) = \int_I f(t, x(t), u(t))dt.$$

When $I = (0,\infty)$ (infinite horizon) assumptions guarantying the integrability of the function $I \ni t \longmapsto f(t, x(t), u(t)) \in \mathbb{R}$ are often too restrictive and they are not fulfilled in some (e.g. economical) applications. So, in such a case it is necessary to consider some other concepts of optimality. Following Carlson and Haurie (cf. Carlson (1987)) we use the notions of strong, catching-up, sporadically catching-up and finitely optimal solution to the optimal control problem under consideration and show their interrelationships. A review of the concepts of optimality for the first order problems with infinite horizon and their interrelationships are given in Carlson (1989).

In the first part of the paper, we recall main results concerning system (1)-(2), obtained in Idczak (to appear), namely, on the existence and uniqueness of a solution $x_u(\cdot) \in H_0^1(I,\mathbb{R}^n)$ to (1)-(2), corresponding to any control $u(\cdot) \in U^p$, and its continuous dependence on $u(\cdot)$ (Theorems 1, 2, 4). Next, we recall the existence results for an optimal control problem connected with (1)-(2) and a cost functional of integral type, obtained in Idczak (to appear) (Theorems 5, 6).

In the second - main part of the paper, we derive necessary conditions for optimality in the sense of the mentioned notions of optimality. Theorem 13 concerns a general form of cost functional. The proof of this theorem is based on the so called optimality principle (Theorem 9) and the maximum principle for finite horizon second order optimal control problems, obtained in Idczak (1998). Theorem 15 concerns some special case of cost functional. Proof of this theorem is based on Theorem 13.

The appropriate optimality principle and necessary optimality conditions for the first order systems with infinite horizon have been obtained in Halkin (1974) (cf. also (Carlson, 1987, Th. 2.3)).

2. Existence, uniqueness and stability

Let us denote $B_{\mathbb{R}^n}(0,r) = \{x \in \mathbb{R}^n;\ |x| \le r\}$, $B_{H_0^1(I,\mathbb{R}^n)}(0,r) = \{x(\cdot) \in H_0^1(I,\mathbb{R}^n);\ \|x(\cdot)\|_{H_0^1(I,\mathbb{R}^n)} \le r\}$ and formulate the following assumptions:

A1a. *function* $G(t,\cdot,\cdot):\mathbb{R}^n\times M\to\mathbb{R}$ *is continuous for* $t\in I$ *a.e. and function* $G(\cdot,x,u):I\to\mathbb{R}$ *is measurable in Lebesgue sense for any* $(x,u)\in\mathbb{R}^n\times M$

A1b. *function* $G_x(t,\cdot,\cdot):\mathbb{R}^n\times M\to\mathbb{R}^n$ *is continuous for* $t\in I$ *a.e. and function* $G_x(\cdot,x,u):I\to\mathbb{R}^n$ *is measurable in Lebesgue sense for any* $(x,u)\in\mathbb{R}^n\times M$

A2. *there exist constants* $b_2>0$, $c_2>0$, *functions* $b_1(\cdot)$, $c_1(\cdot)\in L^2(I,\mathbb{R})$ *and* $b_0(\cdot)$, $c_0(\cdot)\in L^1(I,\mathbb{R})$ *such that*

$$b_2\left|x\right|^2+b_1(t)\left|x\right|+b_0(t)\leq G(t,x,u)\leq c_2\left|x\right|^2+c_1(t)\left|x\right|+c_0(t)$$

for $t\in I$ *a.e.,* $x\in\mathbb{R}^n$, $u\in M$

A3. *for any* $r>0$ *there exist a constant* $d_1>0$ *and a function* $d_0(\cdot)\in L^2(I,\mathbb{R})$ *such that*

$$\left|G_x(t,x,u)\right|\leq d_1\left|x\right|+d_0(t)$$

for $t\in I$ *a.e.,* $x\in B_{\mathbb{R}^n}(0,r)$, $u\in M$.

By r_0 we mean a constant

$$r_0=\frac{\overline{b}_1+\sqrt{\overline{b}_1^2-4\overline{b}_2(\overline{b}_0-\overline{c}_0)}}{2\overline{b}_2}$$

where $\overline{b}_2=\min\{\frac{1}{2},b_2\}$, $\overline{b}_1=(\int_I\left|b_1(t)\right|^2dt)^{\frac{1}{2}}$, $\overline{b}_0=\int_I b_0(t)dt$, $\overline{c}_0=\int_I c_0(t)dt$. This constant is always nonnegative. Since the case of $r_0=0$ is not interesting (in such a case the zero function is the unique (in $H_0^1(I,\mathbb{R}^n)$) solution to (1)-(2) for any control $u(\cdot)\in\mathcal{U}^p$ (cf. (Idczak, to appear, proof of Theorem 5))), therefore we shall assume in the next that $r_0>0$.
In the next, we shall also use the following two assumptions

A4a. *function* $G(t,\cdot,u):B_{\mathbb{R}^n}(0,r_0)\to\mathbb{R}$ *is convex for* $t\in I$ *a.e. and* $u\in M$,

A4b. *function* $G(t,\cdot,u):\mathbb{R}^n\to\mathbb{R}$ *is convex for* $t\in I$ *a.e. and* $u\in M$

We have

Theorem 1. *If G satisfies assumptions A1a, A1b, A2, A3 and A4a, then, for any fixed* $u(\cdot)\in\mathcal{U}^p$, *there exists a solution* $x_u(\cdot)\in B_{H_0^1(I,\mathbb{R}^n)}(0,r_0)$ *to (1)-(2) which is unique in* $B_{H_0^1(I,\mathbb{R}^n)}(0,r_0)$. *If, additionally, G satisfies A4b, then the solution* $x_u(\cdot)$ *is unique in* $H_0^1(I,\mathbb{R}^n)$.

2.1 Stability - case of strong convergence of controls

Let us assume that G is lipschitzian with respect to $u\in M$, i.e.

A5. *there exists a function* $k(\cdot)\in L^q(I,\mathbb{R}^n)$ $(\frac{1}{p}+\frac{1}{q}=1)$ *such that*

$$\left|G(t,x,u_1)-G(t,x,u_2)\right|\leq k(t)\left|u_1-u_2\right|$$

for $t\in I$ *a.e.,* $x\in B_{\mathbb{R}^n}(0,r_0)$, $u_1,u_2\in M$.

We have

Theorem 2. *Let G satisfies assumptions A1a, A1b, A2, A3, A4a and A5. If a sequence of controls* $(u_k(\cdot))_{k\in\mathbb{N}}\subset\mathcal{U}^p$ *converges in* $L^p(I,\mathbb{R}^m)$ *to* $u_0(\cdot)\in\mathcal{U}^p$ *with respect to the norm topology, then the sequence* $(x_k(\cdot))_{k\in\mathbb{N}}$ *of corresponding solutions to (1)-(2), belonging to* $B_{H_0^1(I,\mathbb{R}^n)}(0,r_0)$, *converges weakly in* $H_0^1(I,\mathbb{R}^n)$ *to a solution* $x_0(\cdot)$ *to (1)-(2), corresponding to the control* $u_0(\cdot)$ *and belonging to* $B_{H_0^1(I,\mathbb{R}^n)}(0,r_0)$.

Remark 3. *Weak convergence of a sequence* $(x_k(\cdot))_{k\in\mathbb{N}}$ *in* $H_0^1(I,\mathbb{R}^n)$ *implies (cf. Lieb (1997)) its uniform convergence on any finite interval* $[0,T]\subset I$ *and weak convergence of sequences* $(x_k(\cdot))_{k\in\mathbb{N}}$, $(\dot{x}_k(\cdot))_{k\in\mathbb{N}}$ *in* $L^2(I,\mathbb{R}^n)$.

2.2 Stability - case of $p=\infty$ and weak-* convergence of controls

Now, we shall consider the set of controls

$$\mathcal{U}^\infty = \{u\in L^\infty(I,\mathbb{R}^m);\ u(t)\in M \text{ for } t\in I \text{ a.e.}\}$$

with the weak-* topology induced from $L^\infty(I,\mathbb{R}^m)$. We assume that function G is affine in u, i.e.

$$G(t,x,u) = G^1(t,x) + G^2(t,x)u \tag{4}$$

where functions $G^1 : I\times\mathbb{R}^n \to \mathbb{R}$, $G^2 : I\times\mathbb{R}^n\to\mathbb{R}^m$ are measurable in $t\in I$, continuous in $x\in\mathbb{R}^n$ and

A6. *there exists a function* $\gamma\in L^1(I,\mathbb{R})$ *such that*

$$\left|G^2(t,x)\right| \le \gamma(t)$$

for $t\in I$ *a.e.,* $x\in B_{\mathbb{R}^n}(0,r_0)$.

We have

Theorem 4. *Let G of the form (4) satisfies assumptions A1a, A1b, A2, A3, A4a and A6. If a sequence of controls* $(u_k(\cdot))_{k\in\mathbb{N}}\subset\mathcal{U}^\infty$ *converges in* $L^\infty(I,\mathbb{R}^m)$ *to* $u_0(\cdot)\in\mathcal{U}^\infty$ *with respect to the weak-* topology, then the sequence* $(x_k(\cdot))_{k\in\mathbb{N}}$ *of corresponding solutions to (1)-(2), belonging to* $B_{H_0^1(I,\mathbb{R}^n)}(0,r_0)$, *converges in the weak topology of* $H_0^1(I,\mathbb{R}^n)$ *to the solution* $x_0(\cdot)$ *to (1)-(2), corresponding to* $u_0(\cdot)$ *and belonging to* $B_{H_0^1(I,\mathbb{R}^n)}(0,r_0)$.

3. Optimal control - existence of solutions

3.1 Affine case

Let us consider control system

$$\ddot{x}(t) = G_x^1(t,x(t)) + G_x^2(t,x(t))u(t),\ t\in I \text{ a.e,} \tag{5}$$

with cost functional

$$J(x(\cdot),u(\cdot)) = \int_I (\langle \alpha(t),\dot{x}(t)\rangle + f(t,x(t),u(t)))dt \to \min. \tag{6}$$

By *a classical solution* to problem (5)-(6) in the set $B_{H_0^1(I,\mathbb{R}^n)}(0,r_0)\times\mathcal{U}^\infty$ ($H_0^1(I,\mathbb{R}^n)\times\mathcal{U}^\infty$) we mean a pair $(x_0(\cdot),u_0(\cdot))\in B_{H_0^1(I,\mathbb{R}^n)}(0,r_0)\times\mathcal{U}^\infty$ ($(x_0(\cdot),u_0(\cdot))\in H_0^1(I,\mathbb{R}^n)\times\mathcal{U}^\infty$) satisfying system (5) and such that

$$J(x_0(\cdot),u_0(\cdot)) \le J(x(\cdot),u(\cdot)) \tag{7}$$

for any pair $(x(\cdot),u(\cdot))\in B_{H_0^1(I,\mathbb{R}^n)}(0,r_0)\times\mathcal{U}^\infty$ ($(x(\cdot),u(\cdot))\in H_0^1(I,\mathbb{R}^n)\times\mathcal{U}^\infty$) satisfying system (5).

We assume that

A7. *a set* $M\subset\mathbb{R}^m$ *and functions* $\alpha : I\to\mathbb{R}^n$, $f : I\times B_{\mathbb{R}^n}(0,r_0)\times M\to\mathbb{R}$ *are such that*

a) *M is convex and compact*
b) $\alpha(\cdot) \in L^2(I, \mathbb{R}^n)$
c) *function f is $\mathcal{L}(I) \otimes \mathcal{B}(B_{\mathbb{R}^n}(0, r_0)) \otimes \mathcal{B}(M)$ - measurable* ($\mathcal{L}(I)$ means the σ-field of Lebesgue measurable subsets of I, $\mathcal{B}(B_{\mathbb{R}^n}(0, r_0))$, $\mathcal{B}(M)$ - the σ-fields of Borel subsets of $B_{\mathbb{R}^n}(0, r_0)$, M, respectively; $\mathcal{L}(I) \otimes \mathcal{B}(B_{\mathbb{R}^n}(0, r_0)) \otimes \mathcal{B}(M)$ is the product σ-field)
d) *for $t \in I$ a.e. function $f(t, \cdot, \cdot)$ is lower semicontinuous on $B_{\mathbb{R}^n}(0, r_0) \times M$*
e) *for $t \in I$ a.e. and any $x \in B_{\mathbb{R}^n}(0, r_0)$, function $f(t, x, \cdot)$ is convex on M*
f) *there exists a function $\beta \in L^1(I, \mathbb{R})$ such that*

$$|f(t, x, u)| \leq \beta(t)$$

for $t \in I$ a.e., $x \in B_{\mathbb{R}^n}(0, r_0)$, $u \in M$.

If the function G of the form (4) satisfies assumptions of Theorem 1 and A7 is fulfilled, then for any control $u(\cdot) \in \mathcal{U}^\infty$ there exists a unique in $B_{H_0^1(I,\mathbb{R}^n)}(0, r_0)$ solution $x_u(\cdot)$ of control system (5) and cost functional (6) has a finite value at the pair $(x_u(\cdot), u(\cdot))$ (if G satisfies A4b, then the solution $x_u(\cdot)$ is unique in $H_0^1(I, \mathbb{R}^n)$).
Moreover (cf. Idczak (to appear)), we have

Theorem 5. *If G of the form (4) satisfies assumptions A1a, A1b, A2, A3, A4a, A6 and assumption A7 is satisfied, then optimal control problem (5)-(6) has a classical solution in the set $B_{H_0^1(I,\mathbb{R}^n)}(0, r_0) \times \mathcal{U}^\infty$. If, additionally, assumption A4b is satisfied, then problem (5)-(6) has a classical solution in the set $H_0^1(I, \mathbb{R}^n) \times \mathcal{U}^\infty$.*

In Idczak (to appear), an example illustrating the above theorem is given.

3.2 Nonlinear case

Now, let us consider the nonlinear system (1) with cost functional (6). Below, by $\mathcal{U}_0^p$ ($p \in [1, \infty]$) we mean a compact (in norm topology of $L^p(I, \mathbb{R}^m)$) set of controls, contained in $\mathcal{U}^p$. We have

Theorem 6. *If G satisfies assumptions A1a, A1b, A2, A3, A4a, A5 and assumption A7 is satisfied, then optimal control problem (1)-(6) has a classical solution in the set $B_{H_0^1(I,\mathbb{R}^n)}(0, r_0) \times \mathcal{U}_0^p$. If, additionally, assumption A4b is satisfied, then problem (1)-(6) has a classical solution in the set $H_0^1(I, \mathbb{R}^n) \times \mathcal{U}_0^p$.*

Remark 7. *Definition of a classical solution to problem (1)-(6) in the set $B_{H_0^1(I,\mathbb{R}^n)}(0, r_0) \times \mathcal{U}_0^p$ is quite analogous as in the case of the problem (5)-(6) and the set $B_{H_0^1(I,\mathbb{R}^n)}(0, r_0) \times \mathcal{U}^\infty$ (with (5) replaced by (1) and $\mathcal{U}^\infty$ replaced by $\mathcal{U}_0^p$ - cf. section 3.2).*

4. Optimal control - optimality principle

In this section we assume that assumptions A1a, A1b, A2, A3 and A7 are satisfied.
Since in the next we shall consider system (1) also on a finite time interval, therefore below we give a definition of a solution to such a finite horizon system (cf. Idczak (1998)).
We say that a pair $(x_u(\cdot), u(\cdot)) \in H^1((0, T), \mathbb{R}^n) \times \mathcal{U}_{(0,T)}^\infty$ satisfies system (1) a.e. on $(0, T)$ if

$$\int_0^T \left\langle \dot{x}_u(t), \dot{h}(t) \right\rangle + \langle G_x(t, x_u(t), u(t)), h(t) \rangle \, dt = 0 \qquad (8)$$

for any $h(\cdot) \in H_0^1((0,T),\mathbb{R}^n)$, where $H_0^1((0,T),\mathbb{R}^n)$ is the classical Sobolev space of functions $h(\cdot) \in H^1((0,T),\mathbb{R}^n)$ satisfying the boundary conditions

$$h(0) = h(T) = 0$$

and $\mathcal{U}^\infty_{(0,T)} := \{u \in L^\infty((0,T),\mathbb{R}^m);\ u(t) \in M \text{ for } t \in I \text{ a.e.}\}$.
By J_T we shall mean the functional given by the formula

$$J_T(x(\cdot),u(\cdot)) = \int_0^T (\langle \alpha(t), \dot{x}(t) \rangle + f(t,x(t),u(t)))dt.$$

In the theory of infinite horizon optimal control the following concepts of optimality, different from the classical one (cf. (7)), are used (cf. (Carlson, 1987, Definition 1.2), Carlson (1989)).
By *a strong solution* of the problem (1)-(6) in the set $H_0^1(I,\mathbb{R}^n) \times \mathcal{U}^\infty$ we mean a pair $(x_0(\cdot),u_0(\cdot)) \in H_0^1(I,\mathbb{R}^n) \times \mathcal{U}^\infty$ which satisfies system (1) and

$$\lim_{T\to\infty} (J_T(x_0(\cdot),u_0(\cdot)) - J_T(x(\cdot),u(\cdot))) \leq 0$$

for any pair $(x(\cdot),u(\cdot)) \in H_0^1(I,\mathbb{R}^n) \times \mathcal{U}^\infty$ satisfying system (1).
By *a catching-up solution* of the problem (1)-(6) in the set $H_0^1(I,\mathbb{R}^n) \times \mathcal{U}^\infty$ we mean a pair $(x_0(\cdot),u_0(\cdot)) \in H_0^1(I,\mathbb{R}^n) \times \mathcal{U}^\infty$ which satisfies system (1) and

$$\limsup_{T\to\infty} (J_T(x_0(\cdot),u_0(\cdot)) - J_T(x(\cdot),u(\cdot))) \leq 0$$

for any pair $(x(\cdot),u(\cdot)) \in H_0^1(I,\mathbb{R}^n) \times \mathcal{U}^\infty$ satisfying system (1). This is equivalent to the following condition: for any pair $(x(\cdot),u(\cdot)) \in H_0^1(I,\mathbb{R}^n) \times \mathcal{U}^\infty$ satisfying system (1) and any $\varepsilon > 0$ there exists $T_0 > 0$ such that

$$J_T(x_0(\cdot),u_0(\cdot)) - J_T(x(\cdot),u(\cdot)) < \varepsilon$$

for $T > T_0$.
By *a sporadically catching-up solution* of the problem (1)-(6) in the set $H_0^1(I,\mathbb{R}^n) \times \mathcal{U}^\infty$ we mean a pair $(x_0(\cdot),u_0(\cdot)) \in H_0^1(I,\mathbb{R}^n) \times \mathcal{U}^\infty$ which satisfies system (1) and

$$\liminf_{T\to\infty} (J_T(x_0(\cdot),u_0(\cdot)) - J(x(\cdot),u(\cdot))) \leq 0$$

for any pair $(x(\cdot),u(\cdot)) \in H_0^1(I,\mathbb{R}^n) \times \mathcal{U}^\infty$ satisfying system (1). This is equivalent to the following condition: for any pair $(x(\cdot),u(\cdot)) \in H_0^1(I,\mathbb{R}^n) \times \mathcal{U}^\infty$ satisfying system (1), any $\varepsilon > 0$ and any $T > 0$ there exists $T' > T$ such that

$$J_{T'}(x_0(\cdot),u_0(\cdot)) - J_{T'}(x(\cdot),u(\cdot)) < \varepsilon.$$

By *a finitely optimal solution* of problem (1)-(6) we mean a pair $(x_0(\cdot),u_0(\cdot)) \in H_0^1(I,\mathbb{R}^n) \times \mathcal{U}^\infty$ satisfying (1) a.e. on I and such that for any $T > 0$ and any pair $(x(\cdot),u(\cdot)) \in H^1((0,T),\mathbb{R}^n) \times \mathcal{U}^\infty_{(0,T)}$ satisfying system (1) a.e. on $(0,T)$ and boundary conditions

$$x(0) = 0,\ x(T) = x_0(T),$$

we have

$$J_T(x_0(\cdot),u_0(\cdot)) \leq J_T(x(\cdot),u(\cdot)).$$

It is obvious (under our assumptions) that classical optimality implies the strong one, strong optimality implies the catching-up one, catching-up optimality implies the sporadically catching-up one. In the next theorem we shall show that sporadically catching-up optimality implies the finite one. Before we prove this theorem we shall prove the following technical lemma.

Lemma 8. *If a function* $x(\cdot) \in H^1((0,T),\mathbb{R}^n)$ *is such that* $x(0) = 0$, $v(\cdot) \in H_0^1(I,\mathbb{R}^n)$ *and* $x(T) = v(T)$, *then the function*

$$z : I \ni t \mapsto \begin{cases} x(t) \text{ for } t \in (0,T] \\ v(t) \text{ for } t \in (T,\infty) \end{cases} \in \mathbb{R}^n$$

belongs to $H_0^1(I,\mathbb{R}^n)$ *and its weak derivative* g *has the form*

$$g : I \ni t \mapsto \begin{cases} \dot{x}(t) \text{ for } t \in (0,T] \\ \dot{v}(t) \text{ for } t \in (T,\infty) \end{cases} \in \mathbb{R}^n.$$

Proof. First of all, let us point that $z(\cdot), g(\cdot) \in L^2(I,\mathbb{R}^n)$. Next, let us define the function

$$y : I \ni t \mapsto \int_T^t g(\tau)d\tau + x(T) \in \mathbb{R}^n.$$

Of course,

$$y(0) = \int_T^0 g(\tau)d\tau + x(T) = -\int_0^T g(\tau)d\tau + x(T) = -\int_0^T \dot{x}(\tau)d\tau + x(T) = -x(T) + x(T) = 0.$$

Moreover, $y(\cdot) \in L_{loc}^1(I,\mathbb{R}^n)$ and from (Brezis, 1983, Lemma VIII.2)

$$\begin{aligned} \int_0^\infty y(\tau)\dot{\varphi}(\tau)d\tau &= \int_0^\infty (\int_T^\tau g(s)ds)\dot{\varphi}(\tau)d\tau + \int_0^\infty x(T)\dot{\varphi}(\tau)d\tau \\ &= \int_0^\infty (\int_T^\tau g(s)ds)\dot{\varphi}(\tau)d\tau = -\int_0^\infty g(\tau)\varphi(\tau)d\tau \end{aligned}$$

for any $\varphi(\cdot) \in C_c^1(I,\mathbb{R}^n)$ (the space of continuously differentiable functions $\varphi : I \to \mathbb{R}^n$ with compact support $\operatorname{supp}\varphi \subset I$). This means that the weak derivative of $y(\cdot)$ exists and is equal to the function $g(\cdot)$. Now, we shall show that $y(\cdot) = z(\cdot)$. Indeed, if $t_0 \in (0,T)$, then

$$\begin{aligned} y(t_0) &= \int_T^{t_0} g(\tau)d\tau + x(T) = -\int_{t_0}^T g(\tau)d\tau + x(T) = -(\int_0^T g(\tau)d\tau - \int_0^{t_0} g(\tau)d\tau) + x(T) \\ &= -\int_0^T \dot{x}(\tau)d\tau + \int_0^{t_0} \dot{x}(\tau)d\tau + x(T) = -x(T) + x(t_0) + x(T) = x(t_0) = z(t_0). \end{aligned}$$

If $t_0 \in (T,\infty)$, then

$$\begin{aligned} y(t_0) &= \int_T^{t_0} g(\tau)d\tau + x(T) = \int_T^{t_0} \dot{v}(\tau)d\tau + v(T) = \int_T^{t_0} \dot{v}(\tau)d\tau + \int_0^T \dot{v}(\tau)d\tau = \int_0^{t_0} \dot{v}(\tau)d\tau \\ &= v(t_0) = z(t_0). \end{aligned}$$

Of course, $y(T) = x(T) = z(T)$. Thus, $z(\cdot) \in H_0^1(I,\mathbb{R}^n)$. ∎

Now, we are in the position to prove the following optimality principle that is analogous to the appropriate result for infinite horizon first order optimal control problems with initial conditions (cf. (Carlson, 1987, Theorem 2.2)).

Theorem 9 (optimality principle). *If a pair $(x_0(\cdot), u_0(\cdot)) \in H_0^1(I, \mathbb{R}^n) \times \mathcal{U}^\infty$ is a sporadically catching-up solution to (1)-(6) in the set $H_0^1(I, \mathbb{R}^n) \times \mathcal{U}^\infty$, then it is finitely optimal solution to this problem in the set $H_0^1(I, \mathbb{R}^n) \times \mathcal{U}^\infty$.*

Proof. Let us suppose that for some $T > 0$ there exists a pair $(x_*(\cdot), u_*(\cdot)) \in H^1((0,T), \mathbb{R}^n) \times \mathcal{U}^\infty_{(0,T)}$ satisfying system (1) a.e. on $[0,T]$ and such that

$$x_*(0) = 0,\ x_*(T) = x_0(T)$$

and

$$J_T(x_*(\cdot), u_*(\cdot)) < J_T(x_0(\cdot), u_0(\cdot)). \tag{9}$$

Let us define a pair $(x_+(\cdot), u_+(\cdot))$ in the following way

$$x_+ : I \ni t \mapsto \begin{cases} x_*(t) \text{ for } t \in (0,T] \\ x_0(t) \text{ for } t \in (T,\infty) \end{cases} \in \mathbb{R}^n.$$

$$u_+ : I \ni t \mapsto \begin{cases} u_*(t) \text{ for } t \in (0,T] \\ u_0(t) \text{ for } t \in (T,\infty) \end{cases} \in \mathbb{R}^n.$$

Lemma 8 implies that $x_+(\cdot) \in H_0^1(I, \mathbb{R}^n)$. Of course, $u_+(\cdot) \in \mathcal{U}^\infty$. Now, we shall check that the pair $(x_+(\cdot), u_+(\cdot))$ satisfies system (1). Since the pair $(x_*(\cdot), u_*(\cdot)) \in H^1((0,T), \mathbb{R}^n) \times \mathcal{U}^\infty_{(0,T)}$ satisfies system (1), therefore the function $x_*(\cdot)$ possesses the classical second order derivative $\ddot{x}_*(t)$ for $t \in (0,T)$ a.e. and

$$\ddot{x}_*(t) = G_x(t, x_*(t), u_*(t)),\ t \in (0,T) \text{ a.e.}$$

In the same way, the function $x_0(\cdot)$ possesses the classical second order derivative $\ddot{x}_0(t)$ for $t \in I$ a.e. and

$$\ddot{x}_0(t) = G_x(t, x_0(t), u_0(t)),\ t \in I \text{ a.e.}$$

Consequently, the function $x_+(\cdot)$ possesses the classical second order derivative $\ddot{x}_+(t)$ for $t \in I$ a.e. and

$$\ddot{x}_+(t) = G_x(t, x_+(t), u_+(t)),\ t \in I \text{ a.e.}$$

A3 implies that $\ddot{x}_+(\cdot) \in L^2(I, \mathbb{R}^n)$. Thus, for any $h(\cdot) \in H_0^1(I, \mathbb{R}^n)$, we have

$$\int_I \left\langle \ddot{x}_+(t), h(t) \right\rangle dt = \int_I \langle G_x(t, x_+(t), u_+(t)), h(t) \rangle\, dt. \tag{10}$$

The function $\dot{x}_*(\cdot)$ (more precisely, its continuous representant) is absolutely continuous on $[0,T]$ (cf. (Brezis, 1983, Theorem VIII.2)). Also, the function $\dot{x}_0(\cdot)$ is absolutely continuous on each compact subinterval of $[T,\infty)$. Consequently, the function $\dot{x}_+(\cdot)$ is absolutely continuous on each compact subinterval of I. So, integrating by parts we obtain

$$\int_I \left\langle \ddot{x}_+(t), h(t) \right\rangle dt = \lim_{P\to\infty} \int_0^P \left\langle \ddot{x}_+(t), h(t) \right\rangle dt = \lim_{P\to\infty} (\left\langle \dot{x}_+(P), h(P) \right\rangle - \left\langle \dot{x}_+(0), h(0) \right\rangle$$
$$- \int_0^P \left\langle \dot{x}_+(t), \dot{h}(t) \right\rangle dt) = - \lim_{P\to\infty} \int_0^P \left\langle \dot{x}_+(t), \dot{h}(t) \right\rangle dt = - \int_I \left\langle \dot{x}_+(t), \dot{h}(t) \right\rangle dt$$

for any $h(\cdot) \in H_0^1(I,\mathbb{R}^n)$ (we used here the fact that $\lim_{P\to\infty} \dot{x}_+(P) = \lim_{P\to\infty} \dot{x}_0(P) = 0$, which follows from Lemma 8 and the relation $\dot{x}_0(\cdot) \in H^1(I,\mathbb{R}^n)$). Putting this value to (10) we obtain

$$\int_I (\left\langle \dot{x}_+(t), \dot{h}(t) \right\rangle + \langle G_x(t, x_+(t), u_+(t)), h(t) \rangle) dt = 0$$

for any $h(\cdot) \in H_0^1(I,\mathbb{R}^n)$. This means that the pair $(x_+(\cdot), u_+(\cdot))$ satisfies (1).
Now, from (9) it follows that there exists $\varepsilon > 0$ such that

$$J_T(x_*(\cdot), u_*(\cdot)) + \varepsilon < J_T(x_0(\cdot), u_0(\cdot)).$$

From the other hand, sporadically catching-up optimality of the pair $(x_0(\cdot), u_0(\cdot))$ implies that there exists $Q > T$ such that

$$J_Q(x_0(\cdot), u_0(\cdot)) < \frac{\varepsilon}{2} + J_Q(x_+(\cdot), u_+(\cdot)).$$

But

$$\frac{\varepsilon}{2} + J_Q(x_+(\cdot), u_+(\cdot)) = \frac{\varepsilon}{2} + J_T(x_*(\cdot), u_*(\cdot)) + \int_T^Q (\left\langle \alpha(t), \dot{x}_0(t) \right\rangle + f(t, x_0(t), u_0(t)))dt$$
$$< J_T(x_0(\cdot), u_0(\cdot)) - \frac{\varepsilon}{2} + \int_T^Q (\left\langle \alpha(t), \dot{x}_0(t) \right\rangle + f(t, x_0(t), u_0(t)))dt = J_Q(x_0(\cdot), u_0(\cdot)) - \frac{\varepsilon}{2}.$$

The obtained contradiction completes the proof. ■

5. Optimal control - maximum principle

In Idczak (1998) a maximum principle for the following finite horizon optimal control problem has been obtained:

$$\frac{d}{dt}(H_{\dot{z}}(t, z(t), \dot{z}(t), u(t))) = H_z(t, z(t), \dot{z}(t), u(t)),\ t \in (0,T) \text{ a.e.}, \tag{11}$$

$$z(0) = z(T) = 0, \tag{12}$$

$$I_T(z(\cdot), u(\cdot)) = \int_0^T H_0(t, z(t), \dot{z}(t), u(t))dt \to \min. \tag{13}$$

where $H, H_0 : [0,T] \times \mathbb{R}^n \times \mathbb{R}^n \times \mathbb{R}^m \to \mathbb{R}$, $z(\cdot) \in H_0^1((0,T),\mathbb{R}^n)$, $u(\cdot) \in \mathcal{U}^\infty_{(0,T)}$, $T > 0$ is fixed.

Remark 10. *In fact, in Idczak (1998) the time interval $(0,\pi)$ was considered. Of course, it may be replaced by $(0,T)$ with any $T > 0$. In such a case in (Idczak, 1998, inequality in condition (13) and inequality (25)) the constant π should be replaced by T.*

Remark 11. *It is easy to observe that the results contained in Idczak (1998) remains true with the set $\mathbb{R}^m$ (appearing in the domains of those functions F and F_0) replaced by our set $M \subset \mathbb{R}^m$.*

We say that a pair $(z(\cdot), u(\cdot)) \in H^1((0,T),\mathbb{R}^n) \times \mathcal{U}^\infty_{(0,T)}$ satisfies (11) if

$$\int_0^T \left\langle H_{\dot{z}}(t, z(t), \dot{z}(t), u(t)), \dot{h}(t) \right\rangle dt = -\int_0^T \left\langle H_z(t, z(t), \dot{z}(t), u(t)), h(t) \right\rangle dt$$

for any $h(\cdot) \in H_0^1((0,T),\mathbb{R}^n)$.

Let us also consider the following two auxiliary problems (below, $b \in \mathbb{R}^n$ is a fixed point):

$$\frac{d}{dt}(F_{\dot{x}}(t,x(t),\dot{x}(t),u(t))) = F_x(t,x(t),\dot{x}(t),u(t)),\ t \in (0,T) \text{ a.e.}, \tag{14}$$

$$x(0) = 0,\ x(T) = b \tag{15}$$

$$J_T(x(\cdot),u(\cdot)) = \int_0^T F_0(t,x(t),\dot{x}(t),u(t))dt \to \min. \tag{16}$$

and problem (11)-(13) with functions H, H_0 given by $H(t,z,\dot{z},u) = F(t,z+\frac{b}{T}t,\dot{z}+\frac{b}{T},u)$, $H_0(t,z,\dot{z},u) = F_0(t,z+\frac{b}{T}t,\dot{z}+\frac{b}{T},u)$, i.e.

$$\frac{d}{dt}(F_{\dot{z}}(t,z(t)+\frac{b}{T}t,\dot{z}(t)+\frac{b}{T},u(t))) = F_z(t,z(t)+\frac{b}{T}t,\dot{z}(t)+\frac{b}{T},u(t)),\ t \in (0,T) \text{ a.e.}, \tag{17}$$

$$z(0) = 0,\ z(T) = 0 \tag{18}$$

$$I_T(z(\cdot),u(\cdot)) = \int_0^T F_0(t,z(t)+\frac{b}{T}t,\dot{z}(t)+\frac{b}{T},u(t))dt \to \min. \tag{19}$$

We say that a pair $(x_0(\cdot),u_0(\cdot)) \in H^1((0,T),\mathbb{R}^n) \times \mathcal{U}^\infty_{(0,T)}$ $((z_0(\cdot),u_0(\cdot)) \in H^1((0,T),\mathbb{R}^n) \times \mathcal{U}^\infty_{(0,T)})$ is the solution to problem (14)-(16) ((11)-(13)) if it satisfies (14)-(15) ((11)-(12)) and

$$\int_0^T F_0(t,x_0(t),\dot{x}_0(t),u_0(t))dt \le \int_0^T F_0(t,x(t),\dot{x}(t),u(t))dt$$

$$\left(\int_0^T H_0(t,z_0(t),\dot{z}_0(t),u_0(t))dt \le \int_0^T H_0(t,z(t),\dot{z}(t),u(t))dt\right)$$

for any pair $(x(\cdot),u(\cdot)) \in H^1((0,T),\mathbb{R}^n) \times \mathcal{U}^\infty_{(0,T)}$ satisfying (14)-(15) $((z(\cdot),u(\cdot)) \in H^1((0,T),\mathbb{R}^n) \times \mathcal{U}^\infty_{(0,T)}$ satisfying (11)-(12)).
In the proof of the maximum principle we shall use the following lemma.

Lemma 12. *If a pair $(x_0(\cdot),u_0(\cdot)) \in H^1((0,T),\mathbb{R}^n) \times \mathcal{U}^\infty_{(0,T)}$ is the solution to problem (14)-(16), then the pair $(z_0(\cdot),u_0(\cdot))$ where $z_0(t) = x_0(t) - \frac{b}{T}t$ for $t \in (0,T)$, is the solution to problem (17)-(19).*

Proof. Let as suppose that the pair $(z_0(\cdot),u_0(\cdot))$ given in the Lemma is not the solution to problem (17)-(19). So, there exists a pair $(z_*(\cdot),u_*(\cdot)) \in H^1((0,T),\mathbb{R}^n) \times \mathcal{U}^\infty_{(0,T)}$ satisfying (17)-(18) and such that

$$\int_0^T F_0(t,z_*(t)+\frac{b}{T}t,\dot{z}_*(t)+\frac{b}{T},u_*(t))dt < \int_0^T F_0(t,z_0(t)+\frac{b}{T}t,\dot{z}_0(t)+\frac{b}{T},u_0(t))dt.$$

But then the pair $(x_*(\cdot),u_*(\cdot))$ where $x_*(t) = z_*(t)+\frac{b}{T}t$ for $t \in (0,T)$, belongs to $H^1((0,T),\mathbb{R}^n) \times \mathcal{U}^\infty_{(0,T)}$, satisfies (14)-(15) and

$$\int_0^T F_0(t,x_*(t),\dot{x}_*(t),u_*(t))dt = \int_0^T F_0(t,z_*(t)+\frac{b}{T}t,\dot{z}_*(t)+\frac{b}{T},u_*(t))dt$$
$$< \int_0^T F_0(t,z_0(t)+\frac{b}{T}t,\dot{z}_0(t)+\frac{b}{T},u_0(t))dt = \int_0^T F_0(t,x_0(t),\dot{x}_0(t),u_0(t))dt.$$

This contradicts the optimality of the pair $(x_0(\cdot),u_0(\cdot))$. ■

5.1 General case

Now, we shall prove

Theorem 13 (maximum principle I). *Let assumptions A1a, A1b, A2, A3, A4b and A7 be satisfied (without A7c, A7d, A7f - cf. assumption B3 given below). Additionally, assume that G is twicely differentiable in $x \in \mathbb{R}^n$ and*

B1. *function $G_{xx}(t,\cdot,\cdot) : \mathbb{R}^n \times M \to \mathbb{R}^{n\times n}$is continuous for $t \in I$ a.e., function $G_{xx}(\cdot,x,u)$: $I \to \mathbb{R}^{n\times n}$ is measurable in Lebesgue sense for any $(x,u) \in \mathbb{R}^n \times M$*

B2. *there exist a constant $d_1 > 0$, functions $d_0(\cdot) \in L^2(I,\mathbb{R})$, $e_0(\cdot) \in L^2_{loc}(I,\mathbb{R})$ and a continuous function $a : \mathbb{R}_0^+ \to \mathbb{R}_0^+$ such that*

$$|G_x(t,x,u)| \le d_1 |x| + d_0(t),$$

$$|G_{xx}(t,x,u)| \le a(|x|)e_0(t)$$

for $t \in I$ a.e., $x \in \mathbb{R}^n$, $u \in M$

B3. *functions $f(t,\cdot,\cdot) : \mathbb{R}^n \times M \to \mathbb{R}$, $f_x(t,\cdot,\cdot) : \mathbb{R}^n \times M \to \mathbb{R}^n$ are continuous for $t \in I$ a.e.; functions $f(\cdot,x,u) : I \to \mathbb{R}$, $f_x(\cdot,x,u) : I \to \mathbb{R}^n$ are measurable in Lebesgue sense for any $(x,u) \in \mathbb{R}^n \times M$ and there exist a function $\beta \in L^1(I,\mathbb{R})$, a continuous function $b : \mathbb{R}_0^+ \to \mathbb{R}_0^+$ and a function $\gamma(\cdot) \in L^1_{loc}(I,\mathbb{R})$ such that*

$$|f(t,x,u)| \le \beta(t),$$

$$|f_x(t,x,u)| \le b(|x|)\gamma(t)$$

for $t \in I$ a.e., $x \in \mathbb{R}^n$, $u \in M$.

Let us also assume that, for $t \in I$ a.e., $x \in \mathbb{R}^n$, $u \in M$, the set

$$\{(G_x(t,x,u), f(t,x,u)) \in \mathbb{R}^n \times \mathbb{R};\ u \in M\}$$

is convex.

If a pair $(x_0(\cdot),u_0(\cdot)) \in H_0^1(I,\mathbb{R}^n) \times \mathcal{U}^\infty$ is a solution to problem (1)-(6) in the set $H_0^1(I,\mathbb{R}^n) \times \mathcal{U}^\infty$ according to any definition of optimality given in Section 4, then for any $T > 0$ there exists a function $\lambda_T \in H_0^1((0,T),\mathbb{R}^n)$ such that

$$\frac{d}{dt}(\alpha(t) + \dot{\lambda}_T(t)) = f_x(t,x_0(t),u_0(t)) + G_{xx}(t,x_0(t),u_0(t))\lambda_T(t),\ t \in (0,T) \text{ a.e.} \tag{20}$$

and

$$f(t,x_0(t),u_0(t)) + \langle G_x(t,x_0(t),u_0(t)),\lambda_T(t)\rangle = \min_{u\in M}\{f(t,x_0(t),u) + \langle G_x(t,x_0(t),u),\lambda_T(t)\rangle\} \tag{21}$$

for $t \in (0,T)$ a.e.

Proof. Using the optimality principle (if it is needed) we assert that the pair $(x_0(\cdot),u_0(\cdot))$ is finitely optimal solution to problem (1)-(6) in the set $H_0^1(I,\mathbb{R}^n) \times \mathcal{U}^\infty$. Let us fix any $T > 0$. So, the pair $(x_0(\cdot)\mid_{(0,T)}, u_0(\cdot)\mid_{(0,T)})$ is the solution to problem (14)-(16) with $b = x_0(T)$ and

$$F(t,x,\dot{x},u) = \frac{1}{2}\left|\dot{x}\right|^2 + G(t,x,u),$$

$$F_0(t,x,\dot{x},u) = \left\langle \alpha(t),\dot{x}\right\rangle + f(t,x,u).$$

From Lemma 12 it follows that the pair $(z_0(\cdot), u_0(\cdot))$ where $z_0(t) = x_0(t) - \frac{x_0(T)}{T}t$ for $t \in (0,T)$, is the solution to problem (17)-(19). This means that this pair is the solution to problem (11)-(13) with

$$H(t,z,\dot{z},u) = F(t,z+\frac{x_0(T)}{T}t,\dot{z}+\frac{x_0(T)}{T},u) = \frac{1}{2}\left|\dot{z}+\frac{x_0(T)}{T}\right|^2 + G(t,z+\frac{x_0(T)}{T}t,u)$$

$$= \frac{1}{2}\left|\dot{z}\right|^2 + \frac{1}{T}\left\langle \dot{z}, x_0(T)\right\rangle + \frac{1}{T^2}\left|x_0(T)\right|^2 + G(t,z+\frac{x_0(T)}{T}t,u),$$

$$H_0(t,z,\dot{z},u) = F_0(t,z+\frac{x_0(T)}{T}t,\dot{z}+\frac{x_0(T)}{T},u) = \left\langle \alpha(t), \dot{z}+\frac{x_0(T)}{T}\right\rangle + f(t,z+\frac{x_0(T)}{T}t,u)$$

$$= \left\langle \alpha(t),\dot{z}\right\rangle + \frac{1}{T}\left\langle \alpha(t), x_0(T)\right\rangle + f(t,z+\frac{x_0(T)}{T}t,u).$$

It is easy to check that the functions H, H_0 satisfies all of the assumptions of the maximum principle proved in Idczak (1998) (cf. Remarks 11, 14). Consequently, there exists a function $\lambda_T \in H_0^1((0,T),\mathbb{R}^n)$ such that

$$\frac{d}{dt}(\alpha(t)+\dot{\lambda}_T(t)) = f_x(t,z_0(t)+\frac{x_0(T)}{T}t,u_0(t)) + G_{xx}(t,z_0(t)+\frac{x_0(T)}{T}t,u_0(t))\lambda_T(t)$$

for $t \in (0,T)$ a.e. and

$$\left\langle \alpha(t),\dot{z}_0(t)\right\rangle + \frac{1}{T}\left\langle \alpha(t), x_0(T)\right\rangle + f(t,z_0(t)+\frac{x_0(T)}{T}t,u_0(t))$$
$$+\left\langle G_x(t,z_0(t)+\frac{x_0(T)}{T}t,u_0(t)),\lambda_T(t)\right\rangle + \left\langle \dot{z}_0(t)+\frac{1}{T}x_0(T),\dot{\lambda}_T(t)\right\rangle$$
$$= \min_{u\in M}\{\left\langle \alpha(t),\dot{z}_0(t)\right\rangle + \frac{1}{T}\left\langle \alpha(t), x_0(T)\right\rangle + f(t,z_0(t)+\frac{x_0(T)}{T}t,u)$$
$$+\left\langle G_x(t,z_0(t)+\frac{x_0(T)}{T}t,u),\lambda_T(t)\right\rangle + \left\langle \dot{z}_0(t)+\frac{1}{T}x_0(T),\dot{\lambda}_T(t)\right\rangle\}$$

for $t \in (0,T)$ a.e., i.e. (20) and (21) hold true. ■

Remark 14. *In this remark we use symbols from Idczak (1998). From assumption A4b it follows that, in our case, the matrix $C(x)$, $x \in (0,T)$ a.e., given in (Idczak, 1998, Lemma 4), is nonnegative. In such a case condition (Idczak, 1998, (25)) can be replaced by the following one*

$$\inf\{B(x)z'z';\ |z'| = 1,\ x \in S\} - 2T(\operatorname{ess\,sup}_I |A(x)|) > 0.$$

In fact, in our case, the matrix $A(x)$, $x \in (0,T)$ a.e., appearing above, is the zero matrix.

5.2 Some special case

Now, we shall prove a maximum principle in the case of integrand f not depending on x.

Theorem 15 (maximum principle II). *Let the assumptions of the previous theorem be satisfied. Additionally, assume that*

C1. *function f does not depend on x*

C2. $\alpha(\cdot) \in L^{\infty}(I, \mathbb{R}^n)$

C3. *function $G_{xx} : (0, \infty) \times \mathbb{R}^n \times M \to \mathbb{R}^{n \times n}$ is bounded and for $t \in I$ a.e., $x \in \mathbb{R}^n$, $u \in M$ the matrix $G_{xx}(t, x, u)$ is nonnegative, i.e.*

$$\langle G_{xx}(t, x, u)\lambda, \lambda \rangle \geq 0$$

for $\lambda \in \mathbb{R}^n$.

Then, if a pair $(x_0(\cdot), u_0(\cdot)) \in H_0^1(I, \mathbb{R}^n) \times \mathcal{U}^{\infty}$ is a solution to problem (1)-(6) in the set $H_0^1(I, \mathbb{R}^n) \times \mathcal{U}^{\infty}$ according to any definition of optimality given in Section 4, then there exists a function $\lambda : I \to \mathbb{R}^n$ such that $\lambda \mid_{(0,T)} \in H^1((0, T), \mathbb{R}^n)$, $\lambda(0) = 0$ and

$$\int_0^{\infty} \left\langle \alpha(t) + \dot{\lambda}(t), \dot{\varphi}(t) \right\rangle dt = \int_0^{\infty} \langle G_{xx}(t, x_0(t), u_0(t))\lambda(t), \varphi(t) \rangle \, dt \tag{22}$$

for any $\varphi(\cdot) \in C_c^1(I, \mathbb{R}^n)$,

$$f(t, u_0(t)) + \langle G_x(t, x_0(t), u_0(t)), \lambda(t) \rangle = \min_{u \in M} \{ f(t, u) + \langle G_x(t, x_0(t), u), \lambda(t) \rangle \}, \ t \in I \text{ a.e.} \tag{23}$$

Proof. Let us consider equation (22) on an interval $(0, T)$ (with a fixed $T > 0$), i.e.

$$\frac{d}{dt}(\alpha(t) + \dot{\lambda}(t)) = G_{xx}(t, x_0(t), u_0(t))\lambda(t), \ t \in (0, T) \text{ a.e.,} \tag{24}$$

with boundary conditions $\lambda(0) = \lambda(T) = 0$. It is easy to see that it is the Euler-Lagrange equation for the functional

$$\mathcal{F} : H_0^1((0, T), \mathbb{R}^n) \to \mathbb{R},$$

$$\mathcal{F}(\lambda(\cdot)) = \int_0^T \left(\frac{1}{2} \left| \dot{\lambda}(t) \right|^2 + \left\langle \alpha(t)\dot{\lambda}(t) \right\rangle + \frac{1}{2} \langle \gamma(t)\lambda(t), \lambda(t) \rangle \right) dt = \int_0^T K(t, \lambda(t), \dot{\lambda}(t)) dt$$

where $\gamma(t) = G_{xx}(t, x_0(t), u_0(t))$ and $K(t, \lambda, \dot{\lambda}) = \frac{1}{2}(\dot{\lambda})^2 + \left\langle \alpha(t)\dot{\lambda} \right\rangle + \frac{1}{2} \langle \gamma(t)\lambda, \lambda \rangle$. The function K satisfies assumptions of (Idczak, 1998, Th. 4) and is strictly convex in $(\lambda, \dot{\lambda}) \in \mathbb{R}^n \times \mathbb{R}^n$. Consequently, the function λ_T from Theorem 13 is the unique minimum point of $\mathcal{F}$. So,

$$\mathcal{F}(\lambda_T(\cdot)) < \mathcal{F}(0) = 0$$

In the same way as in Walczak (1995) we check that

$$\mathcal{F}(\lambda(\cdot)) \geq \frac{1}{2} \|\lambda(\cdot)\|^2_{H_0^1((0,T), \mathbb{R}^n)} - \|\alpha(\cdot)\|_{L^2(I, \mathbb{R}^n)} \|\lambda(\cdot)\|_{H_0^1((0,T), \mathbb{R}^n)} \cdot$$

The last two inequalities imply that

$$\left(\int_0^T \left| \dot{\lambda}_T(t) \right|^2 dt \right)^{\frac{1}{2}} = \|\lambda_T(\cdot)\|_{H_0^1((0,T), \mathbb{R}^n)} \leq 2 \|\alpha(\cdot)\|_{L^2(I, \mathbb{R}^n)} \cdot$$

for any $T > 0$.

Now, let us put $T_n = n$, $n \in \mathbb{N}$, and consider a sequence $(\lambda_n(\cdot))_{n\in\mathbb{N}}$ of solutions $\lambda_n(\cdot) = \lambda_{T_n}(\cdot)$ to system (24), belonging to $H_0^1((0,T_n),\mathbb{R}^n)$, respectively. Next, let us fix an interval $[0,T_1]$ and consider the sequence of functions $(\lambda_n(\cdot)\mid_{[0,T_1]})_{n\geq 1}$. The last inequality gives

$$\int_0^{T_1} |\lambda_n(t)|^2\,dt = \int_0^{T_1} \left|\int_0^t \dot{\lambda}_n(s)ds\right|^2 dt \leq T_1 \left\|\lambda_n(\cdot)\right\|^2_{H_0^1((0,T_n),\mathbb{R}^n)} \leq T_1\rho^2,\ n \in \mathbb{N},$$

where $\rho = 2\left\|\alpha(\cdot)\right\|_{L^2(I,\mathbb{R}^n)}$ (the constant not depending on n); of course,

$$\int_0^{T_1} \left|\dot{\lambda}_n(t)\right|^2 dt \leq \rho^2,\ n \in \mathbb{N}.$$

These inequalities mean that the sequence $(\lambda_n(\cdot)\mid_{[0,T_1]})_{n\in\mathbb{N}}$ is bounded in $H^1((0,T_1),\mathbb{R}^n)$. So, from the sequence $(\lambda_n(\cdot))_{n\in\mathbb{N}}$ one can choose a subsequence $(\lambda_n^1(\cdot))_{n\in\mathbb{N}}$ such that the sequence $(\lambda_n^1(\cdot)\mid_{[0,T_1]})_{n\in\mathbb{N}}$ is weakly convergent in $H^1((0,T_1),\mathbb{R}^n)$ to some function $\lambda_{T_1}(\cdot) \in H^1((0,T_1),\mathbb{R}^n)$. From the Arzela-Ascoli theorem and from the uniqueness of the weak limit in the space $C([0,T_1],\mathbb{R}^n)$ of continuous functions on $[0,T_1]$ it follows that we can assume, without loss of the generality, that the sequence $(\lambda_n^1(\cdot)\mid_{[0,T_1]})_{n\in\mathbb{N}}$ converges also uniformly on $[0,T_1]$ to $\lambda_{T_1}(\cdot)$. In particular, $\lambda_{T_1}(0) = 0$.
In the same way (we can assume, without loss of the generality, that the domains of the all functions $\lambda_n^1(\cdot)$, $n \in \mathbb{N}$, contain the interval $[0,T_2]$) from the sequence $(\lambda_n^1(\cdot))_{n\in\mathbb{N}}$ one can choose a subsequence $(\lambda_n^2(\cdot))_{n\in\mathbb{N}}$ such that the sequence $(\lambda_n^2(\cdot)\mid_{[0,T_2]})_{n\in\mathbb{N}}$ is weakly convergent in $H^1((0,T_2),\mathbb{R}^n)$ and uniformly on $[0,T_2]$ to some function $\lambda_{T_2}(\cdot) \in H^1((0,T_2),\mathbb{R}^n)$. Of course, $\lambda_{T_2}(\cdot)\mid_{[0,T_1]} = \lambda_{T_1}(\cdot)$.
Continuing this procedure we obtain a sequence of sequences: $(\lambda_n^1(\cdot))_{n\in\mathbb{N}}$, $(\lambda_n^2(\cdot))_{n\in\mathbb{N}}$, ..., $(\lambda_n^k(\cdot))_{n\in\mathbb{N}}$, ... such that, for any $k \in \mathbb{N}$, the sequence $(\lambda_n^{k+1}(\cdot))_{n\in\mathbb{N}}$ is a subsequence of the sequence $(\lambda_n^k(\cdot))_{n\in\mathbb{N}}$, the sequence $(\lambda_n^k(\cdot)\mid_{[0,T_k]})_{n\in\mathbb{N}}$ is weakly convergent in $H^1((0,T_k),\mathbb{R}^n)$ and uniformly on $[0,T_k]$ to a function $\lambda_{T_k}(\cdot) \in H^1((0,T_k),\mathbb{R}^n)$ and $\lambda_{T_{k+1}}(\cdot)\mid_{[0,T_k]} = \lambda_{T_k}(\cdot)$.
Let $\lambda(\cdot) : I \to \mathbb{R}^n$ be a function such that $\lambda(\cdot)\mid_{[0,T_k]} = \lambda_{T_k}(\cdot)$ for $k \in \mathbb{N}$. It is easy to see that the function $\lambda(\cdot)$ has on I the weak derivative $\dot{\lambda}(\cdot)$ and $\dot{\lambda}(\cdot)\mid_{[0,T_k]} = \left(\lambda(\cdot)\mid_{[0,T_k]}\right)^{\cdot}$. Let us consider the sequence $(\lambda_n^n(\cdot))_{n\in\mathbb{N}}$ and the sequence $(\lambda_n^n(\cdot)\mid_{[0,T_n]})_{n\in\mathbb{N}}$. Let us denote the second sequence by $(\mu_n(\cdot))_{n\in\mathbb{N}}$. On each interval $[0,T_k]$, this sequence (with a precision to the first $(k-1)$ elements) is weakly convergent in $H^1((0,T_k),\mathbb{R}^n)$ and uniformly on $[0,T_k]$ to the function $\lambda(\cdot)\mid_{[0,T_k]} \in H^1((0,T_k),\mathbb{R}^n)$
From the maximum principle I it follows that each function $\mu_n(\cdot)$ satisfies the conditions (domain of $\mu_n(\cdot)$ contains the interval $[0,T_n]$)

$$\frac{d}{dt}(\alpha(t) + \dot{\mu}_n(t)) = G_{xx}(t,x_0(t),u_0(t))\mu_n(t),\ t \in (0,T_n) \text{ a.e.,} \tag{25}$$

$$f(t,u_0(t)) + \langle G_x(t,x_0(t),u_0(t)),\mu_n(t)\rangle = \min_{u\in M}\{f(t,u) + \langle G_x(t,x_0(t),u),\mu_n(t)\rangle\},\ t \in (0,T_n) \text{ a.e.,} \tag{26}$$

The first condition is equivalent to the following one

$$\int_0^{T_n} \left\langle \alpha(t) + \dot{\mu}_n(t), \dot{\varphi}(t)\right\rangle dt = \int_0^{T_n} \langle G_{xx}(t,x_0(t),u_0(t))\mu_n(t),\varphi(t)\rangle\,dt$$

for any $\varphi(\cdot) \in C_c^1((0,T_n),\mathbb{R}^n)$ (the space of continuously differentiable functions $\varphi : (0,T_n) \to \mathbb{R}^n$ with compact support $\operatorname{supp}\varphi \subset (0,T_n)$).
Now, we shall show that (22) holds true. Indeed, let $\varphi(\cdot) \in C_c^1(I,\mathbb{R}^n)$ and $n_0 \in \mathbb{N}$ be such that $\operatorname{supp}\varphi \subset (0,T_{n_0})$. Then

$$\int_0^\infty \left\langle \alpha(t) + \dot{\lambda}(t), \dot{\varphi}(t) \right\rangle dt = \int_0^{T_{n_0}} \left\langle \alpha(t) + \dot{\lambda}(t), \dot{\varphi}(t) \right\rangle dt = \lim_{\substack{n\to\infty \\ n\geq n_0}} \int_0^{T_{n_0}} \left\langle \alpha(t) + \dot{\mu}_n(t), \dot{\varphi}(t) \right\rangle dt$$

$$= \lim_{\substack{n\to\infty \\ n\geq n_0}} \int_0^{T_{n_0}} \langle G_{xx}(t,x_0(t),u_0(t))\mu_n(t), \varphi(t)\rangle\, dt = \int_0^{T_{n_0}} \langle G_{xx}(t,x_0(t),u_0(t))\lambda(t), \varphi(t)\rangle\, dt$$

$$= \int_0^\infty \langle G_{xx}(t,x_0(t),u_0(t))\lambda(t), \varphi(t)\rangle\, dt$$

(the second equality follows from the weak convergence in $H^1((0,T_{n_0}),\mathbb{R}^n)$ of the sequence $(\mu_n(\cdot)\mid_{[0,T_{n_0}]})_{n\in\mathbb{N}}$ to the function $\lambda(\cdot)\mid_{[0,T_{n_0}]}$ and the fourth equality follows from the uniform convergence on $[0,T_{n_0}]$ of the sequence $(\mu_n(\cdot)\mid_{[0,T_{n_0}]})_{n\in\mathbb{N}}$ to the function $\lambda(\cdot)\mid_{[0,T_{n_0}]}$ and Lebesgue bounded convergence theorem). So, (22) holds true.
Now, we shall show that (23) holds true. Indeed, let $Z_n \subset (0,T_n)$, $n \in \mathbb{N}$, be a set of zero measure such that (26) does not hold on it. Let us fix a point $t \in I \setminus \bigcup_{n=1}^{\infty} Z_n$ and let $n_0 \in \mathbb{N}$ be the smallest positive integer such that $t \in (0,T_{n_0})$. We have

$$f(t,u_0(t)) + \langle G_x(t,x_0(t),u_0(t)), \mu_n(t)\rangle = \min_{u\in M}\{f(t,u) + \langle G_x(t,x_0(t),u), \mu_n(t)\rangle\}$$

for $n \geq n_0$. Since the functions

$$\varkappa_u : \mathbb{R}^n \ni \mu \longmapsto f(t,u) + \langle G_x(t,x_0(t),u), \mu\rangle \in \mathbb{R}$$

with $u \in M$ are lipschitzian with the same constant (compactness of M and continuity of G_x in $u \in M$ are important here), therefore (cf. (Łojasiewicz, 1988, Part III.2, Th. 1)) the function

$$\mathbb{R}^n \ni \mu \longmapsto \min_{u\in M} \varkappa_u(\mu) = \min_{u\in M}\{f(t,u) + \langle G_x(t,x_0(t),u), \mu\rangle\}$$

is continuous. Consequently, the fact that $\lim\limits_{\substack{n\to\infty \\ n\geq n_0}} \mu_n(t) = \lambda(t)$ implies (23). ■

6. Concluding remarks

Main results of the paper are contained in Theorems 9, 13 and 15. In Theorem 9 a connection between the notions of optimality in infinite and finite horizon cases is established. Theorem 13 contains necessary conditions for each of the introduced kinds of optimality in general case and Theorem 15 contains such conditions in some special case.
Open problems are maximum principles (in both, special and general case) stating the existence of a Lagrange multiplier $\lambda : I \to \mathbb{R}^n$ satisfying a conjugate system with the space $C_c^1(I,\mathbb{R}^n)$ replaced by $H_0^1(I,\mathbb{R}^n)$ and the minimum condition a.e. on I.

7. References

Brezis, H. (1983). *Analyse Fonctionelle. Theorie et Applications*, Masson, Paris.

Carlson, D. A. (1989). Some concepts of optimality for infinite horizon optimal control and their interrelationships, *Proceedings of Modern Optimal Control - A Conference in Honor of Solomon Lefschetz and Joseph P. LaSalle*, ed. E. O. Roxin, Marcel Dekker, Inc., New York, 13-22.

Carlson, D. A. & Haurie, A. (1987). Infinite Horizon Optimal Control. Theory and Applications, ser. *Lecture Notes in Economics and Mathematical Systems*, Springer-Verlag, Berlin, Heidelberg.

Halkin, H. (1974). Necessary conditions for optimal control problems with infinite horizon. *Econometrica*, Vol. 42, 267-273.

Idczak, D. (1998). Optimal control of a coercive Dirichlet problem, *SIAM J. Control Optim.*, Vol. 36, No. 4, 1250-1267.

Idczak, D. & Walczak, S. (to appear). Optimal control systems of second order with infinite time horizon - existence of solutions, *Journal of Optimization Theory and Applications*.

Lieb, E. H. & Loss, M. (1997). *Analysis*, American Mathematical Society, USA.

Łojasiewicz, S. (1988). *An Introduction to Theory of Real Functions*, J. Wiley & Sons, Chichester.

Walczak, S. (1995). On the continuous dependence on parameters of solutions of the Dirichlet problem. *Bulletin de la Classe des Sciences de l'Academie Royale de Belgique*, T. VI. Ser. 6, 247-261.

Optimal Control Systems with Constrains Defined on Unbounded Sets

Dorota Bors, Marek Majewski and Stanisław Walczak
University of Łódź
*Poland**

1. Introduction

We consider a quasilinear control system of the form

$$-z''(t) + A(t,u(t))z(t) + \alpha\varphi(t,z(t)) = B(t)u(t), \qquad (1)$$
$$z(0) = 0,$$

with the integral constrain of inequality type:

$$\int_I \phi(t,z(t))dt \leq l, \qquad (2)$$

and the integral quality indicator:

$$F(z,u) := \int_I f(z(t),u(t),t)dt \to \min, \qquad (3)$$

where $t \in I := [0,\infty)$, $\alpha \in \mathbb{R}$, $z(\cdot) \in H_0^1\left(I,\mathbb{R}^N\right)$, $u(\cdot) \in L^\infty\left(I,\mathbb{R}^M\right)$, $A(\cdot,\cdot) \in L^\infty\left(I \times U,\mathbb{R}^{N\times N}\right)$, $B(\cdot) \in L^1\left(I,\mathbb{R}^{N\times M}\right) \cap L^2\left(I,\mathbb{R}^{N\times M}\right)$, $\varphi(\cdot,\cdot) \in C\left(I \times \mathbb{R}^N,\mathbb{R}\right)$, $\phi(\cdot,\cdot) \in C\left(I \times \mathbb{R}^N,\mathbb{R}\right)$, $\phi(t,\cdot)$ is differentiable and $\varphi(t,\cdot) = \nabla\phi(t,\cdot)$, for $t \in I$, $U \subset \mathbb{R}^N$, $N,M \geq 1$ and $f : \mathbb{R}^N \times \mathbb{R}^M \times I \to \mathbb{R}$.

We define a space $H_0^1(I,\mathbb{R}^N)$ of trajectories as a set of functions which are absolutely continuous on any compact subinterval $I_0 \subset I$ and satisfy conditions:

$$z(0) = 0, \quad \int_I |z(t)|^2 dt < \infty \quad \text{and} \quad \int_I |z'(t)|^2 dt < \infty, \qquad (4)$$

i.e. $z(0) = 0$ and $z(\cdot),z'(\cdot) \in L^2\left(I,\mathbb{R}^N\right)$.
Let us recall that the necessary and sufficient condition for a function $z : [a,b] \to \mathbb{R}$ to be absolutely continuous is the following integral representation

$$z(t) = \int_a^t v(t)\,dt + c \qquad \text{for } t \in [a,b],$$

where $v \in L^1\left([a,b],\mathbb{R}\right)$, $c \in \mathbb{R}$ Łojasiewicz (1974). A function $z : [a,b] \to \mathbb{R}^N$ is absolutely continuous if each coordinate function $z_i(\cdot)$ is absolutely continuous. Furthermore, for almost

*This work is a part of the research project N514 027 32/3630 supported by the Ministry of Science and Higher Education (Poland).

every $t \in [a,b]$ an absolutely continuous function $z : [a,b] \to \mathbb{R}^N$ possesses finite and integrable derivative $z'(\cdot)$ (see Łojasiewicz (1974)) Moreover,

$$z'(t) = v(t) \qquad \text{for } a.e.\ t \in [a,b],$$

where

$$z(t) = \int_a^t v(t)\,dt + c.$$

(see Łojasiewicz (1974) for more details). The space of trajectories $H_0^1(I,\mathbb{R}^N)$ defined above is a Banach space with the norm

$$||z||^2 := \int_I \left(|z(t)|^2 + |z'(t)|^2\right) dt.$$

One can prove that for a function $z(\cdot) \in H_0^1(I,\mathbb{R}^N)$ we have

$$z(\infty) := \lim_{t\to\infty} z(t) = 0.$$

Moreover $H_0^1(I,\mathbb{R}^N)$ is a Hilbert space with the scalar product

$$\langle z,v\rangle := \int_I \left(\langle z(t),v(t)\rangle + \langle z'(t),v'(t)\rangle\right) dt$$

see for example Adams (1975), Kufner A (et al.) and references therein.
As a set of admissible controls we take

$$\mathcal{U} := \{u(\cdot) \in L^\infty\left(I,\mathbb{R}^M\right) : |u(t)| \le v_0(t) \wedge u(t) \in U \text{ for } a.e.\ t \in I\}, \tag{5}$$

where $v_0(\cdot) \in L^2(I,\mathbb{R})$, $U \subset \mathbb{R}^M$. The fundamental difference between above optimal control problem (1)-(5) and a classical optimal control problem is that control system (1) and functional (3) are defined on an unbounded time interval.

Differential systems of the form (1) are often referred to as the Newton's systems with an infinite time horizon. By inequalities (4), i.e. $\int_I |z(t)|^2 dt < \infty$ and $\int_I |z'(t)|^2 dt < \infty$ and some natural assumptions it may be concluded that the global kinetic energy

$$E_k = \int_0^\infty |z'(t)|^2 dt$$

and the potential energy

$$E_p = \int_0^\infty \langle A(t,u(t))z(t) + \alpha\phi(t,z(t)) - B(t)u(t), z(t)\rangle dt$$

are finite. In the real world, we meet only such a kind of the dynamical systems (see for example Lieb & Loss (2001)).

2. Existence of solutions

In this chapter we prove that the problem (1)-(2) possesses solutions for each control $u_0(\cdot) \in \mathcal{U}$. We say that for a given $u(\cdot) \in \mathcal{U}$ a function $z_u(\cdot) \in H_0^1(I,\mathbb{R}^N)$ solves (1)-(2) if there is a constant $\alpha_0 \geq 0$ that

$$-z_u''(t) + A(t,u(t))z_u(t) + \alpha_0\varphi(t,z_u(t)) = B(t)u(t) \qquad \text{for } a.e.\ t \in I,$$
$$z_u(0) = 0,$$
$$\int_I \phi(t,z_u(t))dt \leq l.$$

The above type of solution is called a Caratheodory solution.

We will make the following assumptions:

(A1) the matrix $A(t,u)$ is positively defined and symmetric for each $t \in I$ and each $u \in U$,

(A2) the function $\phi(t,\cdot)$ is strictly convex and there are a constant $a_1 > 0$ and a function $a_2(\cdot) \in L^1(I,\mathbb{R})$, such that
$$|\phi(t,z)| \leq a_1|z|^2 + a_2(t)$$
for $t \in I$ and $z \in \mathbb{R}^N$,

(A3) there is a function $\tilde{z}(\cdot) \in H_0^1(I,\mathbb{R}^N)$ such that $\int_I \phi(t,\tilde{z}(t))dt < l$,

(A4) there is a function $a_3(\cdot) \in L^\infty(I,\mathbb{R})$ such that
$$|A(t,u_1) - A(t,u_2)| \leq a_3(t)|u_1 - u_2|$$
for each $t \in I$ and each $u_1,u_2 \in U$.

The proof of the theorem on the existence of solutions to (1)-(2) is based on the following version of the well-known Lagrange multiplier rule.

Theorem 1 *Ioffe & Tihomirov (1979)Let z_* be a local minimum point for the problem*

$$\mathcal{E}(z) \to \inf,$$
$$g_i(z) \leq 0 \qquad i = 1,2,\ldots,m,$$

where $\mathcal{E}, g_i : X \to \mathbb{R}$, X is a Banach space. Assume that the functionals $\mathcal{E}$ and g_i, $i = 1,\ldots,m$ are continuous and Fréchet-differentiable on a neighborhood of z_*. Then there exist Lagrange multipliers $\lambda_i \geq 0$, $i = 0,1,\ldots,m$ not all zero, such that for $i = 1,2,\ldots,m$

$$\lambda_0\mathcal{E}'(z_*) + \sum_{i=1}^{m}\lambda_i g_i'(z_*) = 0,$$
$$\lambda_i g_i(z_*) = 0.$$

Moreover if there exists a vector $z \in X$ such that

$$g_i'(z_*)z < 0$$

for those indices $i = 1,2,\ldots,m$, for which $g_i(z_*) = 0$, then $\lambda_0 \neq 0$, and it can be assumed without loss of generality that $\lambda_0 = 1$.

Theorem 2 *If assumptions (A1)-(A3) are satisfied then for each each control $u_0(\cdot) \in \mathcal{U}$ there are exactly one $\alpha_0 \geq 0$ and exactly one function $z_{u_0}(\cdot) \in H_0^1(I, \mathbb{R}^N)$ which is a Caratheodory solution to the equation (1) with condition (2).*

Proof. Fix $u_0(\cdot) \in \mathcal{U}$. Consider the following problem

$$\mathcal{E}(z(\cdot)) := \int_I \left(\frac{1}{2} |z'(t)|^2 + \frac{1}{2} \langle A(t, u_0(t)) z(t), z(t) \rangle - \langle B(t) u_0(t), z(t) \rangle \right) dt \to \min, \quad (6)$$

$$g_1(z(\cdot)) := \int \phi(t, z(t)) dt - l \leq 0. \quad (7)$$

Let $(z_n(\cdot))_{n \in \mathbb{N}}$ be a minimizing sequence for problem (6)-(7), i.e.

$$\lim_{n \to \infty} \mathcal{E}(z_n(\cdot)) = m := \inf \left\{ \mathcal{E}(z(\cdot)) : z(\cdot) \in H_0^1(I, \mathbb{R}^N) \text{ and } \int_I \phi(t, z(t)) dt \leq l \right\},$$

$$\int_I \phi(t, z_n(t)) \leq l.$$

Since $A(t, u_0(t))$ is positively defined for each $t \in I$ and $A(\cdot, \cdot) \in L^\infty(I \times U, \mathbb{R}^{N \times N})$, it follows that there exists a function $M(\cdot) \in L^\infty(I, \mathbb{R})$ such that

$$\langle A(t, u_0(t)) z(t), z(t) \rangle \geq M(t) |z(t)|^2, \qquad a.e.\ t \in I,$$

for each $z(\cdot) \in H_0^1(I, \mathbb{R}^N)$, see for example Hestenes (1966). Thus,

$$\begin{aligned} \mathcal{E}(z_n(\cdot)) &= \int_I \left(\frac{1}{2} |z_n'(t)|^2 + \frac{1}{2} \langle A(t, u_0(t)) z_n(t), z_n(t) \rangle - \langle B(t) u_0(t), z_n(t) \rangle \right) dt \\ &\geq \int_I \frac{1}{2} |z_n'(t)|^2 dt + \int_I \frac{1}{2} M(t) |z_n(t)|^2 dt - \int_I \langle B(t) u_0(t), z_n(t) \rangle dt \\ &\geq C_1 \int_I \left(|z_n'(t)|^2 + |z_n(t)|^2 \right) dt - C_2 \left(\int_I |z_n(t)|^2 dt \right)^{\frac{1}{2}}, \end{aligned}$$

where $C_1 > 0, C_2 \in \mathbb{R}$ and both of them do not depend on n. The above inequality means that the minimizing sequence $(z_n(\cdot))_{n \in \mathbb{N}}$ is bounded. The space $H_0^1(I, \mathbb{R}^N)$ is reflexive. Hence passing if necessary to a subsequence, there exist $z_*(\cdot) \in H_0^1(I, \mathbb{R}^N)$ such that $z_n(\cdot) \rightharpoonup z_*(\cdot)$ weakly in $H_0^1(I, \mathbb{R}^N)$. The functionals $\mathcal{E}$ and g_1 are convex and continuous, and so weekly lower semicontinuous (see. Mawhin (1987), Mawhin & Willem (1989)). Therefore

$$m = \liminf_{n \to \infty} \mathcal{E}(z_n) \geq \mathcal{E}(z_*)$$

and

$$l \geq \liminf_{n \to \infty} \int_I \phi(t, z_n(t)) dt \geq \int_I \phi(t, z_*(t)).$$

Consequently $z_*(\cdot)$ is a minimum point for problem (6)-(7). Moreover, since $\mathcal{E}$ is strictly convex, the minimum point $z_*(\cdot)$ is unique. It is easy to check that the functionals $\mathcal{E}$ and g_1 are Fréchet-differentiable and for each $h(\cdot) \in H_0^1(I, \mathbb{R}^N)$

$$\mathcal{E}'(z(\cdot)) h(\cdot) = \int_I (\langle z'(t), h'(t) \rangle + \langle A(t, u_0(t)) z(t) - B(t) u_0(t), h(t) \rangle) dt,$$

$$g_1'(z(\cdot)) h(\cdot) = \int_I \langle \varphi(t, z(t)), h(t) \rangle dt.$$

By (A2), g_1 is strictly convex, and then

$$g_1(\tilde{z}(\cdot)) - g_1(z_*(\cdot)) > g_1'(z_*(\cdot))(\tilde{z}(\cdot) - z_*(\cdot)).$$

for $\tilde{z}(\cdot)$ satisfying (A3). Therefore if $g_1(z_*(\cdot)) = 0$, then

$$g_1'(z_*(\cdot))(\tilde{z}(\cdot) - z_*(\cdot)) < 0.$$

Now, by the virtue of the Lagrange multiplier rule (Theorem 1) we have that there exists $\lambda_1 \geq 0$ such that

$$\int_I \langle z'(t), h'(t)\rangle dt = -\int_I \langle A(t,u(t))z(t) - B(t)u(t) + \lambda_1\varphi(t,z(t)), h(t)\rangle dt$$

for $h(\cdot) \in H_0^1(I,\mathbb{R}^N)$. Applying the Du Bois-Reymond Lemma (see Mawhin (1987), Mawhin & Willem (1989)) we get

$$-z''(t) + A(t,u(t))z(t) + \alpha_0\varphi(t,z(t)) = B(t)u(t),$$

where $\alpha_0 = \lambda_1 \geq 0$. The uniqueness of solution follows from the fact that $\mathcal{E}$ and g_1 are strictly convex. ■

Theorem 3 *Let assumptions (A1)-(A4) are satisfied. Then, for each sequence $(u_k(\cdot))_{k\in\mathbb{N}}$ of controls tending to $u_0(\cdot)$ in $L^\infty(I,\mathbb{R}^M)$, the sequence of solutions $z_k(\cdot) := z_{u_k}(\cdot)$ tends to $z_0(\cdot) := z_{u_k}(\cdot)$ uniformly on bounded sets and $\lim_{t\to\infty} z_0(t) = 0$.*

Proof. Consider the sequence of functionals

$$\mathcal{E}_k(z(\cdot)) := \int_I \left(\frac{1}{2}|z'(t)|^2 + \frac{1}{2}\langle A(t,u_k(t))z(t), z(t)\rangle - \langle B(t)u_k(t), z(t)\rangle\right) dt.$$

By (A4), we have that

$$\begin{aligned}
&|\mathcal{E}_k(z(\cdot)) - \mathcal{E}_0(z(\cdot))| \\
&\quad\leq \int_I \frac{1}{2}|A(t,u_k(t)) - A(t,u_0(t))||z(t)|^2 dt + \int_I |B(t)||u_k(t) - u_0(t)||z(t)| dt \\
&\qquad\leq \int_I a_3(t)|u_k(t) - u_0(t)||z(t)|^2 dt + \int_I |B(t)||u_k(t) - u_0(t)||z(t)| dt. \quad (8)
\end{aligned}$$

Since $u_k(\cdot)$ tends to $u_0(\cdot)$, $\mathcal{E}_k$ tends to $\mathcal{E}_0$ uniformly on bounded sets, by (8). As $A(t,u(t))$ is positively defined for each $t \in I$ and $(A(\cdot,u_k(\cdot)))_{k\in\mathbb{N}}$ is bounded we have that there is a function $M(\cdot) \in L^\infty(I,\mathbb{R}^N)$ such that

$$\langle A(t,u_k(t))z(t), z(t)\rangle \geq M(t)|z(t)|^2, \qquad k \in \mathbb{N} \text{ and } a.e.\ t \in I,$$

for $z(\cdot) \in H_0^1(I,\mathbb{R}^N)$. Therefore,

$$\begin{aligned}
\mathcal{E}_k(z(\cdot)) &= \int_I \left(\frac{1}{2}|z'(t)|^2 + \frac{1}{2}\langle A(t,u_k(t))z(t), z(t)\rangle - \langle B(t)u_k(t), z(t)\rangle\right) dt \\
&\geq \int_I \frac{1}{2}|z'(t)|^2 dt + \int_I \frac{1}{2}M(t)|z(t)|^2 dt - \int_I \langle B(t)u_k(t), z(t)\rangle dt \\
&\qquad\geq C\int_I \left(|z'(t)|^2 + |z(t)|^2\right) dt - \bar{C}\left(\int_I |z(t)|^2 dt\right)^{\frac{1}{2}},
\end{aligned}$$

for $z(\cdot) \in H_0^1(I,\mathbb{R}^N)$, where C and $\bar{C}$ do not depend on k. Moreover, $\mathcal{E}_k(0) = 0$ for $k = 1,2,\ldots$, thus the set of minimum points for functionals $\mathcal{E}_k$, $k = 1,2,\ldots$ is bounded and consequently weakly compact in $H_0^1(I,\mathbb{R}^N)$. Let $\hat{z}(\cdot) \in H_0^1(I,\mathbb{R}^N)$ be a cluster point of the above set. Obviously, $\int \phi(t,\hat{z}(t))\,dt \leq l$. Suppose that $\hat{z}(\cdot)$ is not a minimum point of $\mathcal{E}_0$. Let $z_0(\cdot)$ be a minimum point of $\mathcal{E}_0$ (such a point exits by Theorem 2). Then

$$\mathcal{E}_0(z_0(\cdot)) - \mathcal{E}_0(\hat{z}(\cdot)) =$$
$$(\mathcal{E}_0(z_0(\cdot)) - \mathcal{E}_k(z_k(\cdot))) + (\mathcal{E}_k(z_k(\cdot)) - \mathcal{E}_0(z_k(\cdot))) + (\mathcal{E}_0(z_k(\cdot)) - \mathcal{E}_0(\hat{z}(\cdot)))$$

and passing with $k \to \infty$ we have that $\mathcal{E}_0(z(\cdot)) = \mathcal{E}_0(\hat{z}(\cdot))$, since $\mathcal{E}_k$ tends to $\mathcal{E}_0$ uniformly on bounded sets and $\mathcal{E}_0$ is weakly lower semicontinuous.
To complete the proof it is enough to apply the fact that the weak convergence in $H_0^1(I,\mathbb{R}^N)$ implies the strong convergence in $C_0(I,\mathbb{R}^N)$ (cf. Mawhin (1987)) on any bounded set and any minimum point of $\mathcal{E}_k$ is a solution and reversely. ■

If we assume that $A(t,\cdot)$ is linear with respect to u for each $t \in I$, then we can weaken the topology in the set of controls.
In that case we need the following assumption

(A5) the function $A(\cdot,\cdot)$ is of the form

$$A(t,u) = a(t)u + b(t),$$

where $a(\cdot) \in L^\infty(I,\mathbb{R}^{N\times N\times M})$, $b(\cdot) \in L^\infty(I,\mathbb{R}^{N\times N})$.

Analogously to the proof of Theorem 3, it is possible to prove

Theorem 4 *Suppose (A1)-(A5). Then, for each sequence $(u_k(\cdot))_{k\in\mathbb{N}}$ of controls tending to $u_0(\cdot)$ weakly in $L^2(I,\mathbb{R}^M)$, the sequence of solutions $z_k(\cdot) := z_{u_k}(\cdot)$ tends to $z_0(\cdot) := z_{u_0}(\cdot)$ weakly in $H_0^1(I,\mathbb{R}^N)$ and consequently uniformly on bounded sets.*

3. Existence of optimal solution

In this section we have to assume

(A6) the function $f(\cdot,\cdot,t)$ is convex with respect (z,u) for each $t \in I$,

(A7) there are a constant $b_1 > 0$ and a function $b_2(\cdot) \in L^1(I,\mathbb{R})$ such that

$$|f(z,u,t)| \leq b_1|z|^2 + b_2(t)$$

for $z \in \mathbb{R}^N$, $u \in U$ and $t \in I$.

Applying Theorem 4 one can prove that optimal control problem (1)-(5) possesses a solution.

Theorem 5 *If control problem (1)-(5) satisfies assumptions (A1)-(A7), then there exist an optimal control in the set of admissible controls $\mathcal{U}$ (cf. (5)).*

Proof. Let $(z_k(\cdot),u_k(\cdot))_{k\in\mathbb{N}} \subset H_0^1(I,\mathbb{R}^N) \times \mathcal{U}$ be a minimizing sequence for problem (1)-(3). Passing, if necessary, to a subsequence we may assume that $(u_k(\cdot))_{k\in\mathbb{N}}$ tends weakly in $L^2(I,\mathbb{R}^M)$ to some $u_0(\cdot) \in \mathcal{U}$. By Theorem 4, the sequence of trajectories $z_k(\cdot)$ tends to $z_0(\cdot)$ weakly in $H_0^1(I,\mathbb{R}^N)$. Denote by μ the optimal value, i.e. $\mu = \inf\{F(x,u)\}$ where infimum is taken over all admissible processes $(z(\cdot),u(\cdot))$ of (1)-(5). Taking into account the lower semi-continuity of the functional F we obtain

$$\mu = \lim_{k\to\infty} F(z_k(\cdot),u_k(\cdot)) \geq F(z_0(\cdot),u_0(\cdot)) \geq \mu.$$

We thus get $F(z_0(\cdot),u_0(\cdot)) = \mu$. It means that the process $(z_0(\cdot),u_0(\cdot))$ is optimal. ■

4. Remarks on Schrödinger equation

The results presented above can be extended to the case of elliptic systems of the form

$$\triangle z(x) + A(x,u(x))z(x) + \alpha\varphi(x,z(x)) = B(x)u(x),\ x \in \mathbb{R}^n,\ n \geq 2, \tag{9}$$

with the integral constraints

$$\int_{\mathbb{R}^n} \phi(x,z(x))dx \leq l \tag{10}$$

and the cost functional

$$\int_{\mathbb{R}^n} f(z(x),u(x),x)dx. \tag{11}$$

The set of admissible controls is of the form

$$\mathcal{U} := \{u(\cdot) \in L^\infty\left(\mathbb{R}^n,\mathbb{R}^M\right) : u(x) \in U \subset \mathbb{R}^M\}. \tag{12}$$

System (9)-(12) is considered in the Sobolev space $H^1\left(\mathbb{R}^n,\mathbb{R}^N\right)$, see Lieb & Loss (2001). For system (9)-(12) one can prove theorems analogous to the Theorems 3 - 5. The most interesting is the case, when $n = 3$, $M = N = 1$, $A(x,u) = -u$, $\varphi(x,z) = z$, $B = 0$ and $\phi(x,z) = \frac{1}{2}|z|^2$. In this case system (9) is reduced to the scalar elliptic equation

$$\triangle z(x) - u(x)z(x) + \alpha z(x) = 0, \tag{13}$$

with the integral condition

$$||z||^2_{L^2(\mathbb{R}^3,\mathbb{R})} = \int_{\mathbb{R}^3} |z(x)|^2 dx \leq 1, \text{ where } z(\cdot) \in H^1(\mathbb{R}^3,\mathbb{R}). \tag{14}$$

Equation (13) is the well-known stationary Schrödinger equation, see Lieb & Loss (2001) and references therein.

From theorem analogous to Theorems 3 - 5, it follows that equation (13) possesses a solution $z_u(\cdot) \in H^1(\mathbb{R}^3,\mathbb{R})$ that depends continuously on a potential $u(\cdot) \in L^\infty(\mathbb{R}^3,\mathbb{R})$. Moreover,

$$\int_{\mathbb{R}^3} |z_u(x)|^2 dx = 1$$

and

$$\alpha = \min_{z\in S} \int_{\mathbb{R}^3} \left(|\nabla z(x)|^2 + u(x)|z(x)|^2\right) dx,$$

where $S := \{z \in H^1(\mathbb{R}^3,\mathbb{R}) : \int_{\mathbb{R}^3} |z_u(x)|^2 dx = 1\}$.

The existence of solution to the Schrödinger equation was proved many years ago by applying direct, variational or topological methods. However, as far as we know, the result presented above and concerning continuous dependence of solutions on varying potential $u(x)$ is new.

5. Remarks on biological oscillators

In the work presented above we obtain some results related to the technical or physical applications. Similar methods we can apply to the biological oscillators which are considered, among others, in Murray (2002).
The mathematical models of the oscillators are given by differential systems of the form

$$\frac{dz^1(t)}{dt} = f(z^n(t)) - k_1 z^1(t) \tag{15}$$
$$\frac{dz^r(t)}{dt} = z^{r-1}(t) - k_r z^r(t), \quad r = 2,3,\ldots,n$$

where f is a continuous function, $k_i > 0$, $i = 1,2,\ldots,n$.
System (15) is investigated with the Cauchy initial conditions or the Dirichlet boundary conditions.
In particular cases system (15) may be reduced to the scalar differential equation

$$v^{(n)}(t) + a_{n-2}v^{(n-2)}(t) + \ldots + a_2 v''(t) = \varphi(t, v(t)) \tag{16}$$

where n is an even natural number, $a_i \in \mathbb{R}$, $\varphi(t,\cdot)$ is a continuous function. Systems of this form are often referred to as the Newton system of the $n-$th order. (If $n = 2$, we have classical Newton system $a_2 v''(t) = \varphi(t, v(t))$ with $a_2 \neq 0$). The differential equation of the form (16) can be investigated by means of variational methods, in a similar way to equation (1).

6. Remarks on systems with variable mass

The variational method presented in the paper might be applied to the investigation of systems with variable mass. Let us consider an object Q with $k \geq 1$ engines I_s that emit gases with velocities $v_s = v_s(t)$, $s = 1,2,...,k$; $t \in [0,T]$ for a fixed $T > 0$. For example Q might be an airplane, a rocket and the like, see for example Meriam & Kraige (2002).
A motion of the object Q in $\mathbb{R}^n$ may be described by the equation

$$m(t)\frac{dv(t)}{dt} = \sum_{s=1}^{k}(v_s(t) - v(t))\frac{dm_s(t)}{dt} + f(t, x(t), u(t)) \tag{17}$$

where $m(t)$ is the mass of the object Q at time $t \in [0,T]$; $v_s(t)$ stands for the velocity of the emitted gas by the engine I_s; $v(t)$ denotes the velocity of the object Q; $m_s(t)$ is the mass of the engine I_s; f denotes an external force (for example the gravity force) acting on the object Q that may depend on the location of object $x(t) = x(0) + \int_0^t v(\tau)d\tau$, and finally $u(t)$ is a control.
The equation (17) is so called the Meščerskii equation and appears in mathematical models of systems with variable mass (see Kosmodemianskii (1966), Peraire (2002), Meščerskii (1962)). In a particular case, if we assume that $f = 0$, $k = 1$ and $v_1(t) - v(t) = const$, then the equation (17) reduces to the Tsiolkovskii equation of the form

$$m(t)\frac{dv(t)}{dt} = c\frac{dm(t)}{dt}. \tag{18}$$

Integrating the equation (18), we obtain

$$v(t) - v(0) = c\ln\frac{m(t)}{m(0)}. \tag{19}$$

The equation (19) describes the dependence of the increase in the velocity of the object Q and the loss in its mass. In the same way we can interpret a solution to the equation (17). From the equation (19) it follows that the increase in velocity is a nonlinear function of mass.
If $v(t) = x'(t)$ and $v_s(t) - v(t) = c(t)$, then the equation (17) has the form

$$x''(t) = F(t, x(t), \mu(t), u(t)) \tag{20}$$

where $x(t)$ stands for the location of the object Q at time $t \in [0, T]$, $\mu = (\mu_1, \mu_2, ..., \mu_k)$ with $\mu_s(t) = \frac{dm_s(t)}{dt}$, $s = 1, 2, ..., k$, $u(\cdot)$ is some external control and the function F is given by

$$F(t, x, \mu, u) = \frac{1}{m(t)} \left[\sum_{s=1}^{k} c_s(t) \mu_s(t) + f(t, x(t), u(t)) \right].$$

Let us assume that a relative velocity of the emitted gas is a given function $c_s(t) = v_s(t) - v(t)$ for any $s = 1, 2, ..., k$ and $t \in [0, T]$. Moreover, for any $s = 1, 2, ..., k$, the function μ_s controls the power of the engine I_s on the interval $[0, T]$.
The equation (20) may be considered with the boundary conditions of the Dirichlet type

$$x(0) = x_0,\ x(T) = x_T, \tag{21}$$

and with the constrains on controls

$$\mu(\cdot) \in \mathcal{M} = \left\{ \mu(\cdot) \in L^\infty\left([0, T], \mathbb{R}^k\right); \mu(t) \in M \subset \mathbb{R}^k \right\}, \tag{22}$$
$$u(\cdot) \in \mathcal{U} = \{ u(\cdot) \in L^\infty([0, T], \mathbb{R}^m); \mu(t) \in U \subset \mathbb{R}^m \}$$

and state coordinates

$$\int_0^T \varphi(t, x(t))\, dt \le l. \tag{23}$$

Let us consider the cost functional of the form

$$G(x, \mu, u) = \int_0^T g(t, x(t), \mu(t), u(t))\, dt. \tag{24}$$

We impose the following assumptions:

(M1) the function $f : [0, T] \times \mathbb{R}^n \times \mathbb{R}^m \to \mathbb{R}^n$ is continuous and linear with respect to u,

(M2) the function $\varphi : [0, T] \times \mathbb{R}^n \to \mathbb{R}$ is continuous and convex with respect to x,

(M3) the integrand $g : [0, T] \times \mathbb{R}^n \times \mathbb{R}^k \times \mathbb{R}^m \to \mathbb{R}$ is continuous and convex with respect to (μ, u).

Applying the method presented in the first section of the chapter we can prove the theorem on the existence of optimal processes to system (20) – (24) that is analogous to Theorem 5.

7. References

Adams, R. A. (1975). *Sobolev spaces,* Academic Press, New York.

Hestenes, M. R. (1966). *Calculus of Variations and Optimal Control Theory,* John Wiley and Sons, New York.

Ioffe, A. D. & Tihomirov, V. M. (1979). *Theory of Extremal Problems,* North-Holland Publishing Company, Amsterdam, New York, Oxford.

Kufner, A., John, O. & Fučik, S. (1977). *Function spaces,* Academia, Prague, and Noordhoff, Leyden.

A.A. Kosmodemianskii, A. A. (1966). *The course of theoretical mechanics,* Moscow (in Russian).

Lieb, E. H. & Loss, M. (2001). *Analysis,* AMS, 2001.

Łojasiewicz, S. (1974). *An Introduction to the Theory of Real Functions,* John Willey and Sons Ltd., Chichester.

Mawhin, J. (1987). *Problémes de Dirichlet Variationnels Non-Linéaires.* Les Presses de L'Universté de Montréal, Canada.

Mawhin, J. & Willem, M. (1989). *Critical Point Theory and Hamiltonian Systems,* Springer-Verlag, New York.

Meriam J. L. & Kraige, L. G. (2002). *Engineering mechanics, Dynamics,*5th edition, John Wiley & Sons.

Meščerskii I. V. (1962). *Works on mechanics of the variable mass,* Moscow (in Russian).

Murray, J. D. (2002). *An Introduction to Mathematical Biology,* Springer-Verlag.

Peraire, J. (2004). *Variable mass systems: the rocket equation,* MIT OpenSourceWare, Massachusetts Institute of Technology, available online.

15

Factorization of overdetermined boundary value problems

Jacques Henry[1], Bento Louro[2] and Maria Orey[2]
[1]*INRIA Bordeaux - Sud-Ouest*
France
[2]*Universidade Nova de Lisboa*
Portugal

1. Introduction

The purpose of this chapter is to present the application of the factorization method of linear elliptic boundary value problems to overdetermined problems. The factorization method of boundary value problems is inspired from the computation of the optimal feedback control in linear quadratic optimal control problems. This computation uses the invariant embedding technique of R. Bellman (1): the initial problem is embedded in a family of similar problems starting from the current time with the current position. This allows to express the optimal control as a linear function of the current state through a gain that is built using the solution of a Riccati equation. The idea of boundary value problem factorization is similar with a space-wise invariant embedding. The method has been presented and justified in (5) in the simple situation of a Poisson equation in a cylinder. In this case the family of spatial subdomains is simply a family of subcylinders. The method can be generalized to other elliptic operators than the laplacian (7) and more general spatial embeddings (6). The output of the method is to furnish an equivalent formulation of the boundary value problem as the product of two uncoupled Cauchy initial value problems that are to be solved successively in a spatial direction in opposite ways. These problems need the knowledge of a family of operators that satisfy a Riccati equation and that relate on the boundaries of the subdomains the Dirichlet and Neumann boundary conditions. This factorization can be viewed as an infinite dimensional generalization of the block Gauss *LU* factorization. It inherits the same properties: once the factorization is done (i.e. the Riccati equation has been solved), solving the same problem with new data needs only the integration of the two Cauchy problems.
Here we consider the situation where one wants to simulate a phenomenon described by a model using an elliptic operator with physical boundary conditions but using also an additional information that may come from boundary measurements. In general this extra information is not compatible with the model and one explains it as a small disturbance of the data of the model that is to be minimized. That is to say that we want to solve the model satisfying all the boundary conditions but the equation is to be solved in the least mean square sense. Then the factorization method is applied to the normal equations for this least square problem. It will need now the solution of two equations for operators: one is the same Riccati equation as for the well-posed problem and the second is a linear Lyapunov equation. It preserves the

property of reducing the solution of the problem for extra sets of data or measurements to two Cauchy problems.
This chapter is organized in the following way: section 2 states the well-posed and overdetermined problems to be solved. Section 3 gives a reformulation of the well-posed problem as a control problem which gives a clue to the factorization method. In section 5 the normal equations for the problem with additional boundary conditions are derived. In section 4 the factorization method for the well-posed elliptic problem is recalled. Section 6 gives the main result of the chapter with the derivation of the factorization of the normal equation of the overdetermined problem. Section 7 presents mathematical properties of the operators P and Q and of the equations they satisfy.

2. Position of the problem

Let Ω be the cylinder $\Omega =]0,1[\times\mathcal{O}$, $x' = (x,y) \in \mathbb{R}^n$, where x is the coordinate along the axis of the cylinder and $\mathcal{O}$, a bounded open set in $\mathbb{R}^{n-1}$, is the section of the cylinder. Let $\Sigma =]0,1[\times\partial\mathcal{O}$ be the lateral boundary, $\Gamma_0 = \{0\}\times\mathcal{O}$ and $\Gamma_1 = \{1\}\times\mathcal{O}$ be the faces of the cylinder.
We consider the following Poisson equation with mixed boundary conditions

$$(\mathcal{P}_0)\begin{cases} -\Delta z = -\dfrac{\partial^2 z}{\partial x^2} - \Delta_y z = f \quad \text{in}\,\Omega, \\ z|_\Sigma = 0, \\ -\dfrac{\partial z}{\partial x}|_{\Gamma_0} = z_0, \quad z|_{\Gamma_1} = z_1. \end{cases} \tag{1}$$

If $f \in L^2(\Omega)$, $z_0 \in (H_{00}^{1/2}(\mathcal{O}))'$ and $z_1 \in H_{00}^{1/2}(\mathcal{O})$, problem $(\mathcal{P}_0)$ has an unique solution in

$$\mathcal{Z} = \{z \in H^1(\Omega) : \Delta z \in L^2(\Omega), z|_\Sigma = 0\}.$$

We also assume that we want to simulate a system satisfying the previous equation but we want also to use an extra information we have on the "real" system which is a measurement of the flux on the boundary Γ_1. The problem is now overdetermined so, we will impose to satisfy both Dirichlet and Neumann boundary conditions on Γ_1, the state equation being satisfied only in the mean square sense. That will define problem $(\mathcal{P}_1)$ that we shall make precise in section 5.

3. Associated control problem

In this section, for the sake of simplicity, we consider $z_0 = 0$. We define an optimal control problem that we will show to be equivalent to $(\mathcal{P}_0)$. The control variable is v and the state z verifies equation (2) below. Let $\mathcal{U} = L^2(\mathcal{O})$ be the space of controls. For each $v \in \mathcal{U}$, we represent by $z(v)$ the solution of the problem:

$$\begin{cases} \dfrac{\partial z}{\partial x} = v \quad \text{in}\,\Omega, \\ z(1) = z_1. \end{cases} \tag{2}$$

We consider the following set of admissible controls:

$$\mathcal{U}_{ad} = \{v \in \mathcal{U} : z(v) \in X_{z_1}\}$$

where

$$X_{z_1} = \{h \in L^2(0,1;H_0^1(\mathcal{O})) \cap H^1(0,1;L^2(\mathcal{O})) : h(1) = z_1\}.$$

The cost function is

$$J(v) = \|z(v) - z_d\|^2_{L^2(0,1;H_0^1(\mathcal{O}))} + \|v\|^2_{L^2(\Omega)} = \int_0^1 \|\nabla_y z(v) - \nabla_y z_d\|^2_{L^2(\mathcal{O})} dx +$$
$$+ \int_0^1 \int_{\mathcal{O}} v^2 dxdy, \quad v \in \mathcal{U}_{ad}.$$

The desired state z_d is defined in each section by the solution of

$$\begin{cases} -\Delta_y \varphi(x) = f(x) \ \text{ in } \mathcal{O}, \\ \varphi|_{\partial\mathcal{O}} = 0, \end{cases} \tag{3}$$

where $\varphi \in L^2(0,1;H_0^1\mathcal{O})$. Consequently, we have

$$z_d = (-\Delta_y)^{-1} f \in L^2(0,1;H_0^1(\mathcal{O})).$$

Now we look for $u \in \mathcal{U}_{ad}$, such that

$$J(u) = \inf_{v \in \mathcal{U}_{ad}} J(v).$$

Taking into account that $\mathcal{U}_{ad}$ is not a closed subset in $L^2(\Omega)$, we cannot apply the usual techniques to solve the problem, even it is not clear under that form that this problem has a solution. Nevertheless we can rewrite it as an equivalent minimization problem with respect to the state

$$\mathcal{U}_{ad} = \left\{ \frac{\partial h}{\partial x} : h \in X_{z_1} \right\}$$

and, consequently

$$J(u) = \inf_{v \in \mathcal{U}_{ad}} J(v) = \inf_{h \in X_{z_1}} \bar{J}(h) = \bar{J}(z)$$

where $\frac{\partial z}{\partial x} = u$, and

$$\bar{J}(h) = \|h - z_d\|^2_{L^2(0,1;H_0^1(\mathcal{O}))} + \|\frac{\partial h}{\partial x}\|^2_{L^2(\Omega)} = \int_0^1 \|\nabla_y h - \nabla_y z_d\|^2_{L^2(\mathcal{O})} dx +$$
$$+ \int_0^1 \int_{\mathcal{O}} \left|\frac{\partial h}{\partial x}\right|^2 dxdy.$$

We remark that X_{z_1} is a closed convex subset in the Hilbert space

$$X = L^2(0,1;H_0^1(\mathcal{O})) \cap H^1(0,1;L^2(\mathcal{O}))$$

and $(\bar{J}(h))^{\frac{1}{2}}$ is a norm equivalent to the norm in X. Then by Theorem 1.3, chapter I, of (8), there exists a unique $z \in X_{z_1}$, such that:

$$\bar{J}(z) = \inf_{h \in X_{z_1}} \bar{J}(h)$$

which is uniquely determined by the condition

$$\bar{J}'(z)(h-z) \geq 0, \forall h \in X_{z_1}.$$

But X_0 is a subspace, and so the last condition is equivalent to

$$\bar{J}'(z)(h) = 0, \forall h \in X_0. \tag{4}$$

Now we have

$$\bar{J}'(z)(h) = 0 \Leftrightarrow \lim_{\theta \to 0^+} \frac{1}{\theta}[\bar{J}(z+\theta h) - \bar{J}(z)] = 0 \Leftrightarrow \int_0^1 \int_{\mathcal{O}} \nabla_y(z - z_d).\nabla_y h dxdy +$$
$$+ \int_0^1 \int_{\mathcal{O}} \frac{\partial z}{\partial x}\frac{\partial h}{\partial x} dxdy = 0, \forall h \in X_0$$

which implies that

$$\int_0^1 \langle -\Delta_y(z - z_d), h \rangle_{H^{-1}(\mathcal{O}) \times H_0^1(\mathcal{O})} dx + \int_0^1 \int_{\mathcal{O}} \frac{\partial z}{\partial x}\frac{\partial h}{\partial x} dxdy = 0, \forall h \in X_0.$$

Then, taking into account that $z_d = (-\Delta_y)^{-1} f$, we obtain

$$\int_0^1 \langle -\Delta_y(z) - f, h \rangle_{H^{-1}(\mathcal{O}) \times H_0^1(\mathcal{O})} dx + \int_0^1 \int_{\mathcal{O}} \frac{\partial z}{\partial x}\frac{\partial h}{\partial x} dxdy = 0, \forall h \in X_0.$$

If we consider $h \in \mathcal{D}(\Omega)$, then

$$\left\langle -\Delta_y z - \frac{\partial^2 z}{\partial x^2} - f, h \right\rangle_{\mathcal{D}'(\Omega) \times \mathcal{D}(\Omega)} = 0, \forall h \in \mathcal{D}(\Omega)$$

so, we may conclude that $-\Delta z = f$ in the sense of distributions. But $f \in L^2(\Omega)$, and so we deduce that $z \in Y$, where

$$Y = \left\{ v \in X_{z_1} : \Delta v \in L^2(\Omega) \right\}.$$

We now introduce the adjoint state:

$$\begin{cases} \frac{\partial p}{\partial x} = -\Delta_y z - f \ \text{ in } \Omega, \\ p(0) = 0. \end{cases}$$

We know that $-\Delta_y z - f \in L^2(0,1; H^{-1}(\mathcal{O}))$. For each $h \in X_0$

$$\int_0^1 \langle -\Delta_y z - f, h \rangle_{H^{-1}(\mathcal{O}) \times H_0^1(\mathcal{O})} dx = \int_0^1 \left\langle \frac{\partial p}{\partial x}, h \right\rangle_{H^{-1}(\mathcal{O}) \times H_0^1(\mathcal{O})} dx =$$
$$= - \int_0^1 \int_{\mathcal{O}} p \frac{\partial h}{\partial x} dxdy$$

and so $p \in L^2(\Omega)$. Using the optimality condition (4), we obtain:

$$\int_0^1 \int_{\mathcal{O}} \left(-p + \frac{\partial z}{\partial x} \right) \frac{\partial h}{\partial x} dxdy = 0, \forall h \in X_0,$$

which implies

$$-p+\frac{\partial z}{\partial x}\in H^1(0,1;L^2(\mathcal{O}))\subset C([0,1]\,;L^2(\mathcal{O}))$$

and

$$\frac{\partial}{\partial x}(-p+\frac{\partial z}{\partial x})=0.$$

Then there exists $c(y)\in L^2(\mathcal{O})$, such that:

$$(-p+\frac{\partial z}{\partial x})|_{\Gamma_s}=c(y),\forall s\in[0,1]\,.$$

On the other hand, integrating by parts, we obtain:

$$\int_{\mathcal{O}} c(y)\,h|_{\Gamma_0}(y)dy=0,\forall h\in X_0,$$

and consequently $c(y)=0$. It follows that $-p+\dfrac{\partial z}{\partial x}=0$.
We have thus shown that problem

$$(\mathcal{P}_{1,z_1})\begin{cases}\dfrac{\partial z}{\partial x}=p\ \text{ in }\Omega,\ \ z\,(1)=z_1,\\ \dfrac{\partial p}{\partial x}=-\Delta_y z-f\ \text{ in }\Omega,\ \ p\,(0)=0,\end{cases}\tag{5}$$

admits a unique solution $\{z,p\}\in H_0^1(\Omega)\times L^2(\Omega)$, where z is the solution of $(\mathcal{P}_0)$.
We can represent the optimality system (5) in matrix form as follows:

$$\mathcal{A}\begin{pmatrix}p\\ z\end{pmatrix}=\begin{pmatrix}0\\ f\end{pmatrix},\ z(1)=z_1,\ p(0)=0,\tag{6}$$

with

$$\mathcal{A}=\begin{pmatrix}-I & \frac{\partial}{\partial x}\\ -\frac{\partial}{\partial x} & -\Delta_y\end{pmatrix}.$$

4. Factorization of problem $(\mathcal{P}_0)$ by invariant embedding

Following R. Bellman (1), we embed problem $(\mathcal{P}_{1,z_1})$ in the family of similar problems defined on $\Omega_s=]0,s[\times\mathcal{O},0<s\leq 1$:

$$(\mathcal{P}_{s,h})\begin{cases}\dfrac{\partial\varphi}{\partial x}-\psi=0\ \text{ in }\Omega_s,\ \ \varphi(s)=h,\\ \varphi|_{\Sigma}=0,\\ -\dfrac{\partial\psi}{\partial x}-\Delta_y\varphi=f\ \text{ in }\Omega_s,\ \ \psi(0)=-z_0,\end{cases}\tag{7}$$

where h is given in $H_{00}^{1/2}(\mathcal{O})$. When $s = 1$ and $h = z_1$ we obtain problem $(\mathcal{P}_{1,z_1})$. Due to the linearity of the problem, the solution $\{\varphi_{s,h}, \psi_{s,h}\}$ of $(\mathcal{P}_{s,h})$ verifies

$$\psi_{s,h}(s) = P(s)h + r(s), \tag{8}$$

where $P(s)$ and $r(s)$ are defined as follows:
1) We solve

$$\begin{cases} \dfrac{\partial \beta}{\partial x} - \gamma = 0 \text{ in } \Omega_s, \quad \beta(s) = h, \\ \beta|_{\Sigma} = 0, \\ -\dfrac{\partial \gamma}{\partial x} - \Delta_y \beta = 0 \text{ in } \Omega_s, \quad \gamma(0) = 0. \end{cases} \tag{9}$$

This defines $P(s)$ as:

$$P(s)h = \gamma(s).$$

We remark that $P(s)$ is the Dirichlet-to-Neumann operator on Γ_s relative to the domain Ω_s.
2) We solve

$$\begin{cases} \dfrac{\partial \eta}{\partial x} - \xi = 0 \text{ in } \Omega_s, \quad \eta(s) = 0, \\ \eta|_{\Sigma} = 0, \\ -\dfrac{\partial \xi}{\partial x} - \Delta_y \eta = f \text{ in } \Omega_s, \quad \xi(0) = -z_0. \end{cases} \tag{10}$$

The remainder $r(s)$ is defined by:

$$r(s) = \xi(s).$$

Furthermore, the solution $\{z, p\}$ of $(\mathcal{P}_{1,z_1})$ restricted to $]0, s[$ satisfies $(\mathcal{P}_{s,z|_{\Gamma_s}})$, for $s \in]0, 1[$, and so one has the relation

$$p(x) = P(x)z(x) + r(x), \forall x \in]0, 1[. \tag{11}$$

>From (11) and the boundary conditions at $x = 0$, we easily deduce that

$$P(0) = 0, \quad r(0) = -z_0.$$

Formally, taking the derivative with respect to x on both sides of equation (11), we obtain:

$$\frac{\partial p}{\partial x}(x) = \frac{dP}{dx}(x)z(x) + P(x)\frac{\partial z}{\partial x}(x) + \frac{dr}{dx}(x)$$

and, substituting from (5) and (11) we conclude that:

$$\begin{aligned} &-\Delta_y z - f = \frac{dP}{dx}(x)z(x) + P(x)(P(x)z(x) + r(x)) + \frac{dr}{dx} \Leftrightarrow \\ &(\frac{dP}{dx} + P^2 + \Delta_y)z + \frac{dr}{dx} + Pr + f = 0. \end{aligned} \tag{12}$$

Then, taking into account that $z(x) = h$ is arbitrary, we obtain the following decoupled system:

$$\frac{dP}{dx} + P^2 + \Delta_y = 0, \quad P(0) = 0, \tag{13}$$

$$\frac{\partial r}{\partial x} + Pr = -f, \quad r(0) = -z_0, \tag{14}$$

$$\frac{\partial z}{\partial x} - Pz = r, \quad z(1) = z_1, \tag{15}$$

where P and r are integrated from 0 to 1, and finally z is integrated backwards from 1 to 0. We remark that P is an operator on functions defined on $\mathcal{O}$ verifying a Riccati equation.
We have factorized problem $(\mathcal{P}_0)$ as:

$$\text{“}-\Delta\text{”} = -\left(\frac{d}{dx} + P\right)\left(\frac{d}{dx} - P\right).$$

This decoupling of the optimality system (5) may be seen as a generalized block LU factorization. In fact, for this particular problem, we may write

$$\mathcal{A} = \begin{pmatrix} I & 0 \\ -P & -\frac{d}{dx} - P \end{pmatrix} \begin{pmatrix} -I & I \\ I & 0 \end{pmatrix} \begin{pmatrix} I & -P \\ 0 & \frac{d}{dx} - P \end{pmatrix}.$$

We will see in section 7 that P is self adjoint. So, the first and third matrices are adjoint of one another and are, respectively, lower triangular and upper triangular.

5. Normal equations for the overdetermined problem

>From now on, we suppose $z_0 \in H_{00}^{1/2}(\mathcal{O})$, $z_1 \in H_0^{3/2}(\mathcal{O})$, $z_2 \in H_{00}^{1/2}(\mathcal{O})$, $f \in H^{5/2}(\Omega)$ and $(\Delta f)|_\Sigma = 0$.
Assuming we have an extra information, given by a Neumann boundary condition at point 1, we consider the overdetermined system

$$\mathcal{A}\begin{pmatrix} p \\ z \end{pmatrix} = \begin{pmatrix} 0 \\ f \end{pmatrix}, \; z(1) = z_1, \; p(0) = -z_0, \; \frac{\partial z}{\partial x}(1) = z_2. \tag{16}$$

If the data are not compatible with (5), this system should be satisfied in the least square sense. We introduce a perturbation,

$$\mathcal{A}\begin{pmatrix} p \\ z \end{pmatrix} = \begin{pmatrix} \delta g \\ f + \delta f \end{pmatrix}, \; z(1) = z_1, \; p(0) = -z_0, \; \frac{\partial z}{\partial x}(1) = z_2. \tag{17}$$

We want to minimize the norm of the perturbation,

$$J(\delta f, \delta g) = \frac{1}{2}\int_0^1 \left(\|\delta f\|^2_{L^2(\mathcal{O})} + \|\delta g\|^2_{L^2(\mathcal{O})}\right) dx, \tag{18}$$

subject to the constraint given by (17). This defines problem $(\mathcal{P}_1)$.
We remark that, like in section 3, this is an ill-posed problem. We could solve it by regularization, taking $\frac{\partial \delta g}{\partial x} \in L^2(\Omega)$, $\delta g(0) = \delta g(1) = 0$ and considering the problem of the minimization of the functional

$$J_\varepsilon(\delta f, \delta g) = J(\delta f, \delta g) + \frac{\varepsilon}{2} \int_0^1 \left\| \frac{\partial \delta g}{\partial x} \right\|^2_{L^2(\mathcal{O})} dx, \tag{19}$$

subject to the constraint given by (17), which is a well-posed problem.
However, like in section 3, the final optimality problem is well-posed. >From now on we consider the final problem and take the corresponding Lagrangian.
Taking, for convenience, the Lagrange multiplier of the second equation of (17) as $\bar{z} - f$,

$$\begin{aligned} L(\delta f, \delta g, z, p, \bar{z}, \bar{p}) = J(\delta f, \delta g) + \int_0^1 \left(\bar{p}, \frac{\partial z}{\partial x} - p - \delta g \right)_{L^2(\mathcal{O})} dx + \\ + \int_0^1 \left(\bar{z} - f, -\frac{\partial p}{\partial x} - \Delta_y z - f - \delta f \right)_{L^2(\mathcal{O})} dx + \left(\mu, \frac{\partial z}{\partial x}(1) - z_2 \right)_{L^2(\mathcal{O})}. \end{aligned} \tag{20}$$

Taking into account that $\frac{\partial z}{\partial x}(1) = p(1) + \delta g(1)$, we obtain

$$\left(\frac{\partial L}{\partial z}, \varphi \right) = \int_0^1 (\bar{z} - f, -\Delta_y \varphi)_{L^2(\mathcal{O})} dx + \int_0^1 \left(\bar{p}, \frac{\partial \varphi}{\partial x} \right)_{L^2(\mathcal{O})} dx, \ \forall \varphi \in \mathcal{Y},$$

where

$$\mathcal{Y} = \left\{ \varphi \in \mathcal{Z} : \frac{\partial \varphi}{\partial x}(0) = 0, \ \varphi(1) = 0 \right\}$$

and, integrating by parts, we derive

$$\left(\frac{\partial L}{\partial z}, \varphi \right) = \int_0^1 (-\Delta_y(\bar{z} - f), \varphi)_{L^2(\mathcal{O})} dx - (\bar{p}(0), \varphi(0)) + \int_0^1 \left(-\frac{\partial \bar{p}}{\partial x}, \varphi \right)_{L^2(\mathcal{O})} dx.$$

Now, if $\bar{p}(0) = 0$, and because all the functions are null on Σ, we conclude that:

$$\frac{\partial L}{\partial z} = 0 \Leftrightarrow -\frac{\partial \bar{p}}{\partial x} - \Delta_y \bar{z} = -\Delta_y f.$$

On the other hand

$$\begin{aligned} \left(\frac{\partial L}{\partial p}, \psi \right) = \int_0^1 \left(\bar{z} - f, -\frac{\partial \psi}{\partial x} \right)_{L^2(\mathcal{O})} dx + \int_0^1 (\bar{p}, -\psi)_{L^2(\mathcal{O})} dx + \\ (\mu, \psi(1))_{L^2(\mathcal{O})} = \int_0^1 \left(\frac{\partial(\bar{z} - f)}{\partial x}, \psi \right)_{L^2(\mathcal{O})} dx + (\bar{z}(0) - f(0), \psi(0)) - \\ - (\bar{z}(1) - f(1), \psi(1)) + \int_0^1 (-\bar{p}, \psi)_{L^2(\mathcal{O})} dx + (\mu, \psi(1)) \end{aligned}$$

and, if $\psi(0) = 0$ and $\bar{z}(1) - f(1) = \mu$ arbitrary, then

$$\frac{\partial L}{\partial p} = 0 \Leftrightarrow \frac{\partial \bar{z}}{\partial x} - \bar{p} = \frac{\partial f}{\partial x}.$$

We have thus obtained:

$$\left\{\begin{array}{l}\dfrac{\partial \bar{z}}{\partial x}-\bar{p}=f_1:=\dfrac{\partial f}{\partial x},\quad \bar{z}\,(1)\ \text{arbitrary},\\ -\dfrac{\partial \bar{p}}{\partial x}-\Delta_y \bar{z}=f_2:=-\Delta_y f,\quad \bar{p}\,(0)=0.\end{array}\right. \tag{21}$$

We finally evaluate the optimal values for δf and δg. We have:

$$\left(\frac{\partial L}{\partial(\delta f)},\gamma\right)=\int_0^1(\delta f,\gamma)_{L^2(\mathcal{O})}dx+\int_0^1(\bar{z}-f,-\gamma)_{L^2(\mathcal{O})}dx,\ \ \forall\gamma\in L^2(\Omega)$$

and for all $\xi \in L^2(\Omega)$ such that $\frac{\partial\xi}{\partial x}\in L^2(\Omega)$,

$$\left(\frac{\partial L}{\partial(\delta g)},\xi\right)=\int_0^1(\delta g,\xi)_{L^2(\mathcal{O})}dx+\int_0^1(\bar{p},-\xi)_{L^2(\mathcal{O})}dx.$$

At the minimum, we must have

$$\frac{\partial L}{\partial(\delta f)}=0\Leftrightarrow \delta f=\bar{z}-f$$

and

$$\frac{\partial L}{\partial(\delta g)}=0\Leftrightarrow \delta g=\bar{p}.$$

In conclusion, we obtain

$$\mathcal{A}\begin{pmatrix}p\\ z\end{pmatrix}=\begin{pmatrix}\delta g\\ f+\delta f\end{pmatrix}=\begin{pmatrix}\bar{p}\\ \bar{z}\end{pmatrix}, \tag{22}$$

and the normal equation is given by

$$\mathcal{A}^2\begin{pmatrix}p\\ z\end{pmatrix}=\begin{pmatrix}f_1\\ f_2\end{pmatrix},\ p(0)=-z_0,\ z(1)=z_1,\ \frac{\partial z}{\partial x}(1)=z_2,\ -\frac{\partial z}{\partial x}(0)=z_0. \tag{23}$$

>From (23), we have

$$-\Delta\bar{z}=-\frac{\partial^2\bar{z}}{\partial x^2}-\Delta_y\bar{z}=\frac{\partial^2 f}{\partial x^2}-\Delta_y f=-\Delta f \tag{24}$$

and, from (23) and (24),

$$\begin{aligned}-\Delta f=-\Delta\bar{z}&=-\Delta\left(-\frac{\partial p}{\partial x}-\Delta_y z\right)=-\Delta\left(\frac{\partial\bar{p}}{\partial x}-\frac{\partial^2 z}{\partial x^2}-\Delta_y z\right)\\&=-\Delta\left(-\Delta_y\bar{z}+\Delta_y f-\Delta z\right)=\Delta^2 z+\Delta_y\left(\Delta\bar{z}-\Delta f\right)=\Delta^2 z\end{aligned}$$

We now notice that

$$\frac{\partial^2\bar{p}}{\partial x^2}=\frac{\partial}{\partial x}\left(\Delta_y f-\Delta_y\bar{z}\right)=\Delta_y\left(\frac{\partial f}{\partial x}-\frac{\partial\bar{z}}{\partial x}\right)=-\Delta_y\bar{p}$$

and, remarking that $\bar{p}(0) = 0$, we derive $-\Delta_y \bar{p}(0) = 0$ which implies that

$$\frac{\partial(\Delta z)}{\partial x}(0) = \frac{\partial^2 p}{\partial x^2}(0) - \frac{\partial \bar{z}}{\partial x}(0) = -\Delta_y \bar{p}(0) - \bar{p}(0) - \frac{\partial f}{\partial x}(0) = -\frac{\partial f}{\partial x}(0)$$

Now we can write the normal equation as

$$(\mathcal{P}_2) \begin{cases} \Delta^2 z = -\Delta f, \quad \text{in } \Omega, \\ z|_\Sigma = 0, \quad \Delta z|_\Sigma = 0, \\ -\dfrac{\partial z}{\partial x}(0) = z_0, \quad \dfrac{\partial \Delta z}{\partial x}(0) = -\dfrac{\partial f}{\partial x}(0), \\ z(1) = z_1, \; \dfrac{\partial z}{\partial x}(1) = z_2. \end{cases} \tag{25}$$

6. Factorization of the normal equation by invariant embedding

In order to factorize problem (25) we consider an invariant embedding using the family of problems $(\mathcal{P}_{s,h,k})$ defined in $\Omega_s =]0,s[\times\mathcal{O}$, for each $h \in H^{\frac{3}{2}}(\mathcal{O})$ and each $k \in (H_{00}^{\frac{1}{2}}(\mathcal{O}))'$. These problems can be factorized in two second order boundary value problems. Afterwards we will show the relation between $(\mathcal{P}_{s,h,k})$ for $s = 1$ and problem (25).

$$(\mathcal{P}_{s,h,k}) \begin{cases} \Delta^2 z = -\Delta f, \quad \text{in } \Omega_s, \\ z|_\Sigma = 0, \quad \Delta z|_\Sigma = 0, \\ -\dfrac{\partial z}{\partial x}(0) = z_0, \quad \dfrac{\partial \Delta z}{\partial x}(0) = -\dfrac{\partial f}{\partial x}(0), \\ z|_{\Gamma_s} = h, \; \Delta z|_{\Gamma_s} = k. \end{cases} \tag{26}$$

Due to the linearity of the problem, for each $s \in]0,1]$, h, k, the solution of $(\mathcal{P}_{s,h,k})$ verifies:

$$\frac{\partial z}{\partial x}(s) = P(s)h + Q(s)k + \tilde{r}(s). \tag{27}$$

In fact, let us consider the problem

$$\begin{cases} \Delta^2 \gamma_1 = 0, \quad \text{in } \Omega_s, \\ \gamma_1|_\Sigma = 0, \quad \Delta\gamma_1|_\Sigma = 0, \\ \dfrac{\partial \gamma_1}{\partial x}(0) = 0, \quad \dfrac{\partial \Delta\gamma_1}{\partial x}(0) = 0, \\ \gamma_1|_{\Gamma_s} = h, \; \Delta\gamma_1|_{\Gamma_s} = 0. \end{cases} \tag{28}$$

This problem reduces to:

$$\begin{cases} \Delta \gamma_1 = 0, \quad \text{in } \Omega_s, \\ \gamma_1|_\Sigma = 0, \\ \dfrac{\partial \gamma_1}{\partial x}(0) = 0, \quad \gamma_1|_{\Gamma_s} = h. \end{cases} \tag{29}$$

Setting $P_1(s)h = \frac{\partial \gamma_1}{\partial x}(s)$, from (9) we may conclude that $P_1 = P$. On the other hand, given

$$\begin{cases} \Delta^2 \gamma_2 = 0, & \text{in } \Omega_s, \\ \gamma_2|_\Sigma = 0, \quad \Delta\gamma_2|_\Sigma = 0, \\ \frac{\partial \gamma_2}{\partial x}(0) = 0, \quad \frac{\partial \Delta\gamma_2}{\partial x}(0) = 0, \\ \gamma_2|_{\Gamma_s} = 0, \ \Delta\gamma_2|_{\Gamma_s} = k, \end{cases} \tag{30}$$

we define:

$$Q(s)k = \frac{\partial \gamma_2}{\partial x}(s).$$

Problem (30) can be decomposed in two second order boundary value problems. Finally, we solve:

$$\begin{cases} \Delta^2 \beta = -\Delta f, & \text{in } \Omega_s, \\ \beta|_\Sigma = \Delta\beta|_\Sigma = 0, \\ -\frac{\partial \beta}{\partial x}(0) = z_0, \quad \frac{\partial \Delta\beta}{\partial x}(0) = -\frac{\partial f}{\partial x}(0), \\ \beta|_{\Gamma_s} = \Delta\beta|_{\Gamma_s} = 0 \end{cases} \tag{31}$$

and set:

$$\tilde{r}(s) = \frac{\partial \beta}{\partial x}(s).$$

Then, the solution of the normal equation restricted to $]0, s[$, verifies $(\mathcal{P}_{s, z|_{\Gamma_s}, \Delta z|_{\Gamma_s}})$, for $s \in]0,1[$. So, one has the relation

$$\frac{\partial z}{\partial x}|_{\Gamma_s} = P(s)z|_{\Gamma_s} + Q(s)\Delta z|_{\Gamma_s} + \tilde{r}(s). \tag{32}$$

>From (32), it is easy to see that $Q(0) = 0$ and $\tilde{r}(0) = -z_0$. On the other hand, we may consider the following second order problem on Δz as a subproblem of problem (26)

$$\begin{cases} \Delta(\Delta z) = -\Delta f, & \text{in } \Omega_s, \\ \Delta z|_\Sigma = 0, \\ \frac{\partial \Delta z}{\partial x}(0) = -\frac{\partial f}{\partial x}(0), \\ \Delta z|_{\Gamma_1} = c, \end{cases} \tag{33}$$

where c is to be determined later, in order to be compatible with the other data. >From (14) and (15), it admits the following factorization:

$$\begin{cases} \frac{\partial t}{\partial x} + Pt = -\Delta f, \quad t(0) = -\frac{\partial f}{\partial x}(0), \\ -\frac{\partial \Delta z}{\partial x} + P\Delta z = -t, \quad \Delta z(1) = c. \end{cases} \tag{34}$$

Formally, taking the derivative with respect to x on both sides of (32), we obtain:

$$\frac{\partial^2 z}{\partial x^2}(x) = \frac{dP}{dx}(x)z(x) + P(x)\frac{\partial z}{\partial x}(x) + \frac{dQ}{dx}(x)\Delta z(x) + Q(x)\frac{\partial \Delta z}{\partial x}(x) + \frac{d\tilde{r}}{dx}(x)$$

and, substituting from (32) and (34), we obtain:

$$\Delta z - \Delta_y z = \frac{dP}{dx} z + P(Pz + Q\Delta z + \tilde{r}) + \frac{dQ}{dx}\Delta z + Q(P\Delta z + t) + \frac{d\tilde{r}}{dx} \tag{35}$$

or which is equivalent

$$(\frac{dP}{dx} + P^2 + \Delta_y) + (\frac{dQ}{dx} + PQ + QP - I)\Delta z + \frac{d\tilde{r}}{dx} + P\tilde{r} + Qt = 0. \tag{36}$$

Now, taking into account that $z|_{\Gamma_s} = h$ and $\Delta z|_{\Gamma_s} = k$ are arbitrary, we derive

$$\frac{dP}{dx} + P^2 + \Delta_y = 0, \quad P(0) = 0, \tag{37}$$

$$\frac{dQ}{dx} + PQ + QP = I, \quad Q(0) = 0, \tag{38}$$

$$\frac{\partial t}{\partial x} + Pt = -\Delta f, \quad t(0) = -\frac{\partial f}{\partial x}(0), \tag{39}$$

$$\frac{\partial \tilde{r}}{\partial x} + P\tilde{r} = -Qt, \quad \tilde{r}(0) = -z_0, \tag{40}$$

$$\frac{\partial \Delta z}{\partial x} - P\Delta z = t, \quad \Delta z(1) = c, \tag{41}$$

$$\frac{\partial z}{\partial x} - Pz = Q\Delta z + \tilde{r}, \quad z(1) = z_1. \tag{42}$$

It is easy to see, from the definition, that $Q(1)$ is a bijective operator from $(H_{00}^{\frac{1}{2}}(\mathcal{O}))'$ to $H^{\frac{1}{2}}(\mathcal{O})$, so we can define $(Q(1))^{-1}$. >From (27) and the regularity assumptions made at beginning of this section, we can define:

$$c = (Q(1))^{-1}(z_2 - P(1)\, z_1 - \tilde{r}(1)). \tag{43}$$

Once again we can remark the interest of the factorized form if the same problem has to be solved many times for various sets of data (z_1, z_2). Once the problem has been factorized, that is P and Q have been computed, and t and $\tilde{r}$ are known, the solution for a data set (z_1, z_2) is obtained by solving (43) and then the Cauchy initial value problems (41), (42) backwards in x. We have factorized problem $(\mathcal{P}_2)$. We may write

$$\mathcal{A}^2 = \begin{pmatrix} -\frac{d}{dx} - P & 0 \\ -Q & -\frac{d}{dx} - P \end{pmatrix} \begin{pmatrix} 0 & -I \\ -I & 0 \end{pmatrix} \begin{pmatrix} \frac{d}{dx} - P & -Q \\ 0 & \frac{d}{dx} - P \end{pmatrix}.$$

We will see in section 7 that P and Q are self adjoint. So, the first and third matrices are adjoint of one another and are, respectively, lower triangular and upper triangular.

7. Some properties of P and Q

The Riccati equation (37) was studied in (3), using a Yosida regularization.
1– For each $s \in [0,1]$, $P(s) \in \mathcal{L}(H_0^1(\mathcal{O}), L^2(\mathcal{O}))$.
2– For each $s \in [0,1]$, $P(s)$ is a self-adjoint and positive operator. In fact, the property is obviously true when $s = 0$. On the other hand, let $s \in]0,1]$, $h_1, h_2 \in L^2(\mathcal{O})$, and $\{\beta_1, \gamma_1\}$,$\{\beta_2, \gamma_2\}$

the corresponding solutions of (9) to h_1 and h_2. From the definition of P we may conclude that $P(s)h_i = \frac{\partial \beta_i}{\partial x}|_{\Gamma_s}$, where β_i is the solution of:

$$\begin{cases} -\Delta\beta_i = 0 \quad \text{in } \Omega_s, \\ \beta_i|_{\Sigma} = 0, \\ -\frac{\partial \beta_i}{\partial x}|_{\Gamma_0} = 0, \quad \beta_i|_{\Gamma_s} = h_i. \end{cases}$$

We then have that:

$$0 = \int_{\Omega_s} (-\Delta\beta_1)\beta_2 dxdy = \int_{\Omega_s} \nabla\beta_1 \nabla\beta_2 dxdy - \int_{\partial\Omega_s} \frac{\partial \beta_1}{\partial x}\beta_2 d\sigma$$

and, taking into account that $\beta_2|_{\Sigma} = 0, \frac{\partial \beta_1}{\partial x}|_{\Gamma_0} = 0$ and $\beta_2|_{\Gamma_s} = h_2$, we conclude that:

$$(P(s)h_1, h_2) = \int_{\Gamma_s} \frac{\partial \beta_1}{\partial x}(s)\beta_2(s)d\sigma = \int_{\Omega_s} \nabla\beta_1 \nabla\beta_2 dxdy$$

which shows that $P(s)$ is a self-adjoint and positive operator.
3−

$$\|P(s)h\|_{L^2(\mathcal{O})} \leq \|h\|_{H_0^1(\mathcal{O})}, \forall h \in H_0^1(\mathcal{O}), \forall s \in [0,1].$$

4− For each $s \in [0,1]$, $Q(s)$ is an operator from $(H_{00}^{1/2}(\mathcal{O}))'$ into $H_{00}^{1/2}(\mathcal{O})$ and from $L^2(\mathcal{O})$ into $H_0^1(\mathcal{O})$.
5− For each $s \in [0,1]$, $Q(s)$ is a linear, self-adjoint, non negative operator in $L^2(\mathcal{O})$, and it is positive if $s \neq 0$. In fact, the result is obviously verified if $s = 0$. On the other hand, if $s \in]0,1]$, $k_i \in L^2(\mathcal{O})$, and γ_i are the solutions of the problems:

$$\begin{cases} \Delta^2\gamma_i = 0, \quad \text{in } \Omega_s, \\ \gamma_i|_{\Sigma} = 0, \quad \Delta\gamma_i|_{\Sigma} = 0, \\ \frac{\partial \gamma_i}{\partial x}(0) = 0, \quad \frac{\partial \Delta\gamma_i}{\partial x}(0) = 0, \\ \gamma_i|_{\Gamma_s} = 0, \ \Delta\gamma_i|_{\Gamma_s} = k_i, \ \ i = 1,2, \end{cases} \tag{44}$$

then, by Green's formula, noticing that $\gamma_1|_{\Sigma} = \gamma_1|_{\Gamma_s} = 0$ and $\frac{\partial \Delta\gamma_2}{\partial x}(0) = 0$, we have:

$$0 = \int_{\Omega_s} \gamma_1 \Delta^2\gamma_2 dxdy = -\int_{\Omega_s} \nabla\gamma_1 \nabla(\Delta\gamma_2) dxdy$$

and, again by Green's formula, remarking that $\Delta\gamma_2|_{\Sigma} = 0$ and $\frac{\partial \gamma_1}{\partial x}(0) = 0$, we obtain

$$(Q(s)k_1, k_2) = \int_{\Gamma_s} \frac{\partial \gamma_1}{\partial x}(s)\Delta\gamma_2(s)d\sigma = \int_{\Omega_s} \Delta\gamma_1 \Delta\gamma_2 dxdy$$

which shows that $Q(s)$ is a self-adjoint non negative operator in $L^2(\mathcal{O})$. On the other hand

$$\langle Q(s)k,k\rangle = 0 \Leftrightarrow \int_{\Omega_s}(\Delta\gamma)^2 dxdy = 0 \Rightarrow \Delta\gamma = 0 \text{ in } \Omega_s \Rightarrow k = \Delta\gamma|_{\Gamma_s} = 0$$

and so $Q(s)$ is positive for $s \in]0,1]$.
6– For each $x \in [0,1]$, $-P(x)$ is the infinitesimal generator of a strongly continuous semigroup of contractions in $L^2(\mathcal{O})$.
In fact we know that, for each $x \in [0,1]$, $P(x)$ is an unbounded and self-adjoint operator from $L^2(\mathcal{O})$ into $L^2(\mathcal{O})$ with domain $H_0^1(\mathcal{O})$. By (4), proposition II.16, page 28, $-P(x)$ is a closed operator. On the other hand

$$(-P(x)h,h) \leq 0, \forall h \in H_0^1(\mathcal{O})$$

so, $-P(x)$ is a dissipative operator. Finally, by (9), Corollary 4.4, page 15, $-P(x)$ is the infinitesimal generator of a strongly continuous semigroup of contractions in $L^2(\mathcal{O})$, $\{\exp(-tP(x)\}_{t\geq 0}$.

It is easy to see that the family $\{-P(x)\}_{x\in[0,1]}$ verifies the conditions of Theorem 3.1, with the slight modification of remark 3.2, of (9). This implies that there exists a unique evolution operator $U(x,s)$ in $L^2(\mathcal{O})$, that is, a two parameter family of bounded linear operators in $L^2(\mathcal{O})$, $U(x,s)$, $0 \leq s < x \leq 1$, verifying $U(x,x) = I$, $U(x,r)U(r,s) = U(x,s), 0 \leq s \leq r \leq x \leq 1$, and $(x,s) \longmapsto U(x,s)$ is strongly continuous for $0 \leq s \leq x \leq 1$. Moreover, $\|U(x,s)\|_{\mathcal{L}(L^2(\mathcal{O}))} \leq 1$ and

$$\frac{\partial}{\partial s}U(x,s)h = U(x,s)P(s)h, \quad \forall h \in H_0^1(\mathcal{O}), \text{ a.e. in } 0 \leq s \leq x \leq 1.$$

Formally, from equation (38), we have:

$$\frac{\partial}{\partial s}(U(x,s)Q(s)U^*(x,s)) = U(x,s)U^*(x,s).$$

Integrating from 0 to x, and remarking that $Q(0) = 0$,

$$Q(x) = \int_0^x U(x,s)U^*(x,s)\,ds.$$

We define a mild solution of (38) by

$$(Q(x)h,\bar{h}) = \int_0^x (U^*(x,s)h, U^*(x,s)\bar{h})\,ds, \quad \forall h,\bar{h} \in H_0^1(\mathcal{O}).$$

By the preceeding remarks, equation (38) has a unique mild solution.

Again formally, from equation (39), we have

$$\frac{\partial}{\partial s}(U(x,s)t(s)) = U(x,s)\frac{\partial t}{\partial s} + U(x,s)P(s)t = -U(x,s)\Delta f,$$

so we define a mild solution of (39) by

$$t(x) = -U(x,0)\frac{\partial f}{\partial x}(0) - \int_0^x U(x,s)\Delta f\,ds.$$

For equations (40), (41) and (42) we proceed in a similar way, noting that for (41) and (42) the integral is taken between x and 1.

8. References

[1] R. Bellman, Dynamic Programming, Princeton University Press, Princeton, 1957.

[2] A. Bensoussan, G. Da Prato, M. Delfour and S. Mitter, *Representation and Control of Infinite Dimensional Systems*, Birkhäuser, 2007.

[3] N. Bouarroudj, J. Henry, B. Louro and M. Orey, On a direct study of an operator Riccati equation appearing in boundary value problems factorization. Appl. Math. Sci. (Ruse), Vol. 2, no. 46 (2008), 2247–2257

[4] H. Brézis, *Analyse fonctionnelle*, Dunod, 1999.

[5] J. Henry and A. M. Ramos, Factorization of Second Order Elliptic Boundary Value Problems by Dynamic Programming, *Nonlinear Analysis. Theory, Methods & Applications*, **59**, (2004) 629-647.

[6] J. Henry, B. Louro and M. C. Soares, A factorization method for elliptic problems in a circular domain, *C. R. Acad. Sci. Paris*, série 1, **339** (2004) 175-180.

[7] J. Henry, *On the factorization of the elasticity system by dynamic programming* "Optimal Control and Partial Differential Equations" en l'honneur d'A. Bensoussan. ed J.L. Menaldi, E. Rofman, A. Sulem, IOS Press 2000, p 346-352.

[8] J. L. Lions, *Optimal Control of Systems Governed by Partial Differential Equations*, Springer Verlag, 1971.

[9] A. Pazy, *Semigroups of Linear Operators and Applications to Partial Differential Equations*, Springer Verlag, 1983.

16

Cellular automata simulations - tools and techniques

Henryk Fukś
Brock University
Canada

1. Introduction

The purpose of this chapter is to provide a concise introduction to cellular automata simulations, and to serve as a starting point for those who wish to use cellular automata in modelling and applications. No previous exposure to cellular automata is assumed, beyond a standard mathematical background expected from a science or engineering researcher.

Cellular automata (CA) are dynamical systems characterized by discreteness in space, time, and in state variables. In general, they can be viewed as cells in a regular lattice updated synchronously according to a local interaction rule, where the state of each cell is restricted to a finite set of allowed values. Unlike other dynamical systems, the idea of cellular automaton can be explained without using any advanced mathematical apparatus. Consider, for instance, a well-known example of the so-called majority voting rule. Imagine a group of people arranged in a line line who vote by raising their right hand. Initially some of them vote "yes", others vote "no". Suppose that at each time step, each individual looks at three people in his *direct neighbourhood* (himself and two nearest neighbours), and updates his vote as dictated by the majority in the neighbourhood. If the variable $s_i(t)$ represents the vote of the i-th individual at the time t (assumed to be an integer variable), we can write the *CA rule* representing the voting process as

$$s_i(t+1) = \text{majority}\{s_{i-1}(t), s_i(t), s_{i+1}(t)\}. \quad (1)$$

This is illustrated in Figure 1, where periodic boundary conditions are used, that is, the right

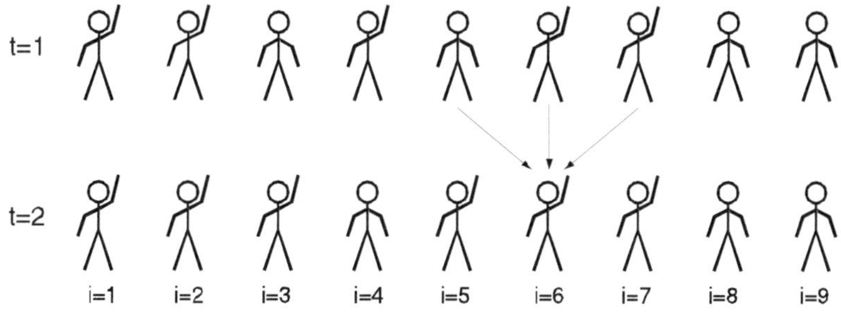

Fig. 1. Example of CA: majority voting rule.

neighbour of $i = 9$ is considered to be $i = 1$, and similarly for $i = 1$. If eq. (1) is iterated many times for $t = 1, 2, 3, \ldots$, we have a discrete-time dynamical system, often referred to as one-dimensional cellular automaton. Of course, in a general case, instead of eq. (1) we can use another rule, and instead of one-dimensional lattice we may consider higher-dimensional structures. Voting rule in 2-dimensions, for example, could be defined as

$$s_{i,j}(t+1) = \text{majority}\{s_{i-1,j}(t), s_{i+1,j}(t), s_{i,j}(t), s_{i,j-1}(t), s_{i,j+1}(t)\}, \quad (2)$$

where the variable $s_{i,j}(t)$ represents the vote of the individual located at (i, j) at time t, assuming that i, j and t are all integer variables. Again, by iterating the above rule for $t = 1, 2, 3, \ldots$, we obtain a two-dimensional dynamical system, known as two-dimensional majority-voting cellular automaton.

Given the simplicity of CA definition, it is not surprising that cellular automata enjoy tremendous popularity as a modelling tool, in a number of diverse fields of science and engineering. While it is impossible to list all applications of CA in this short chapter, we will mention some monographs and other publications which could serve as a starting point for exploring CA-based models. The first serious area of applications of CA opened in mid-80's, when the development of lattice gas cellular automata (LGCA) for hydrodynamics initiated an extensive growth of CA-based models in fluid dynamics, including models of Navier-Stokes fluids and chemically reacting systems. Detailed discussion of these models, as well as applications of CA in nonequilibrium phase transition modelling can be found in (Chopard and Drozd, 1998). In recent years, the rise of fast and inexpensive digital computers brought a new wave of diverse applications of CA in areas ranging from biological sciences (e.g., population dynamics, immune system models, tumor growth models, etc.) to engineering (e.g. models of electromagnetic radiation fields around antennas, image processing, interaction of remote sensors, traffic flow models, etc.) An extensive collection of articles on applications of cellular automata can be found in a series of conference volumes produced bi-annually in connection with International Conference on Cellular Automata for Research and Industry (Bandini et al., 2002; Sloot et al., 2004; Umeo et al., 2008; Yacoubi et al., 2006) as well as in Journal of Cellular Automata, a new journal launched in 2006 and dedicated exclusively to CA theory and applications. Among the applications listed above, traffic flow models should be singled out as one of the most important and extensively studies areas. A good albeit already somewhat dated review of these models can be found in (Chowdhury et al., 2000). For readers interested in the theory of cellular automata, computational aspects of CA are discussed in (Ilachinski, 2001; Wolfram, 1994; 2002), while more mathematical approach is presented in Kari (2005).

Discrete nature of cellular automata renders CA-based models suitable for computer simulations and computer experimentation. One can even say that computer simulations are almost mandatory for anyone who wants to understand behavior of CA-based model: apparent simplicity of CA definition is rather deceiving, and in spite of this simplicity, dynamics of CA can be immensely complex. In many cases, very little can be done with existing mathematical methods, and computer simulations are the only choice.

In this chapter, we will describe basic problems and methods for CA simulations, starting from the definition of the "simulation" in the context of CA, and followed by the discussion of various types of simulations, difficulties associated with them, and methods used to resolve these difficulties. Most ideas will be presented using one-dimensional examples for the sake of clarity.

2. Cellular automata

We will start from some remarks relating CA to partial differential equations, which are usually more familiar to modelers that CA. Cellular automata are often described as fully discrete analogs of partial differential equations (PDEs). In one dimension, PDE which is first-order in time can be written as

$$u_t(x,t) = F(u, u_x, u_{xx}, \ldots), \tag{3}$$

where $u(x,t)$ is the unknown function, and subscripts indicate differentiation. Informally, cellular automata can be obtained by replacing derivatives in (3) by difference quotients

$$u_t \rightarrow \frac{u(x,t+\epsilon) - u(x,t)}{\epsilon}, \tag{4}$$

$$u_x \rightarrow \frac{u(x+h,t) - u(x-h,t)}{2h}, \tag{5}$$

$$u_{xx} \rightarrow \frac{u(x+2h,t) - 2u(x,t) + u(x-2h,t)}{4h^2}, \tag{6}$$

etc. With these substitutions, and by taking $h = \epsilon = 1$ one can rewrite (3) as

$$u(x,t+1) = u(x,t) + F\left(u, \frac{u(x+1,t) - u(x-1,t)}{2}, \frac{u(x+2,t) - 2u(x,t) + u(x-2,t)}{4}, \ldots\right). \tag{7}$$

One can now see that the right hand side of the above equation depends on

$$u(x,t), u(x \pm 1, t), u(x \pm 2, t), \ldots \tag{8}$$

and therefore we can rewrite rewrite (7) as

$$u(x,t+1) = f(u(x-r,t), u(x-r+1,t), \ldots, u(x+r,t)), \tag{9}$$

where f is called a *local function* and the integer r is called a *radius* of the cellular automaton. The local function for cellular automata is normally restricted to take values in a finite set of symbols $\mathcal{G}$. To reflect this, we will use symbol $s_i(t)$ to denote the value of the (discrete) state variable at site i at time t, that is,

$$s_i(t+1) = f\Big(s_{i-r}(t), s_{i-r+1}(t), \ldots, s_{i+r}(t)\Big). \tag{10}$$

In the case of binary cellular automata, which are the main focus of this chapter, the local function takes values in the set $\{0,1\}$, so that $f : \{0,1\} \rightarrow \{0,1\}^{2r+1}$. Binary rules of radius 1 are called elementary rules, and they are usually identified by their Wolfram number $W(f)$, defined as

$$W(f) = \sum_{x_1,x_2,x_3=0}^{1} f(x_1,x_2,x_3) 2^{(2^2x_1+2^1x_2+2^0x_3)}. \tag{11}$$

In what follows, the set of symbols $\mathcal{G} = \{0,1,...N-1\}$ will be be called *a symbol set*, and by $\mathcal{S}$ we will denote the set of all bisequences over $\mathcal{G}$, where by a bisequence we mean a function on $\mathbb{Z}$ to $\mathcal{G}$. The set $\mathcal{S}$ will also be called the *configuration space*. Most of the time, we shall assume that $\mathcal{G} = \{0,1\}$, so that the configuration space will usually be a set of bi-infinite binary strings. Corresponding to f (also called *a local mapping*) we can define a *global mapping* $F : \mathcal{S} \rightarrow \mathcal{S}$ such that $(F(s))_i = f(s_{i-r}, \ldots, s_i, \ldots, s_{i+r})$ for any $s \in \mathcal{S}$.

Comparing (3) and (10), we conclude that r plays a similar role in CA as the degree of the highest derivative in PDEs. We should stress, however, that the PDE defined by (3) and the cellular automaton (10) obtained by the above "discretization procedure" have usually very little in common. There exist discretization schemes (such as ultradiscretization) which seem to preserve some features of the dynamics while passing from PDE to CA, but they are beyond the scope of this chapter. We merely want to indicate here that conceptually, cellular automata are closely related to PDEs, although in contrast to PDEs, all variables in CA are discrete. Moreover, dependent variable u is bounded in the case of CA – a restriction which is not normally imposed on the dependent variable of a PDE.

2.1 Deterministic initial value problem

For PDEs, an initial value problem (also called a Cauchy problem) is often considered. It is the problem of finding $u(x,t)$ for $t > 0$ subject to

$$\begin{aligned} u_t(x,t) &= F(u, u_x, u_{xx}, \ldots), \quad \text{for } x \in \mathbb{R}, t > 0, \\ u(x,0) &= G(x) \quad \text{for } x \in \mathbb{R}, \end{aligned} \tag{12}$$

where the function $G : \mathbb{R} \to \mathbb{R}$ represents the given initial data. A similar problem can be formulated for cellular automata: given

$$\begin{aligned} s_i(t+1) &= f\Big(s_{i-r}(t), s_{i-r+1}(t), \ldots, s_{i+r}(t)\Big), \\ s_i(0) &= g(i), \end{aligned} \tag{13}$$

find $s_i(t)$ for $t > 0$, where the initial data is represented by the given function $g : \mathbb{Z} \to \mathcal{G}$. Here comes the crucial difference between PDEs and CA. For the initial value problem (12), we can in some cases obtain an exact solution in the sense of a formula for $u(x,t)$ involving $G(x)$. To give a concrete example, consider the classical Burgers equation

$$u_t = u_{xx} + u u_x. \tag{14}$$

If $u(x,0) = G(x)$, one can show that for $t > 0$

$$u(x,t) = 2\frac{\partial}{\partial x} \ln \left\{ \frac{1}{\sqrt{4\pi t}} \int_{-\infty}^{\infty} \exp\left[-\frac{(x-\xi)^2}{4t} - \frac{1}{2}\int_0^{\xi} G(\xi')d\xi' \right] d\xi \right\}, \tag{15}$$

which means that, at least in principle, knowing the initial condition $u(x,0)$, we can compute $u(x,t)$ for any $t > 0$. In most cases, however, no such formula is known, and we have to resort to numerical PDE solvers, which bring in a whole set of problems related to their convergence, accuracy, stability, etc.

For cellular automata, obtaining an exact formula for the solution of the initial value problem (13) analogous to (15) is even harder than for PDEs. No such formula is actually known for virtually any non-trivial CA. At best, one can find the solution if $g(i)$ is simple enough. For example, for the majority rule defined in eq. (1), if $g(i) = i \bmod 2$, then one can show without difficulty that

$$s_i(t) = (i+t) \bmod 2, \tag{16}$$

but such result can hardly be called interesting.[1]

[1] By $a \bmod 2$ we mean the integer remainder of division of a by 2, which is 0 for even a and 1 for odd a.

Nevertheless, for CA, unlike for PDEs, it is very easy to find the value of $s_i(t)$ for any $i \in \mathbb{Z}$ and any $t \in \mathbb{N}$ by direct iteration of the cellular automaton equation (10). Thus, in algorithmic sense, problem (13) is always solvable – all one needs to do is to take the initial data $g(x)$ and perform t iterations. In contrast to this, initial value problem for PDE cannot be solved exactly by direct iteration – all we can usually do is to obtain some sort of numerical approximation of the solution.

2.2 Probabilistic initial value problem

Before we address basic simulation issues for CA, we need to present an alternative, and usually more useful, way of posing the initial value problem for CA. Often we are interested in a range of initial conditions, with a given probability distribution. How to handle the initial value problem in such cases? This is best achieved by using some basic concepts of probability theory, namely the notion of the cylinder set and the probability measure. A reader unfamiliar with these concepts can skip to the end of this subsection.

An appropriate mathematical description of an initial distribution of configurations is a probability measure μ on $\mathcal{S}$, where $\mathcal{S}$ is the set of all possible configurations, i.e., bi-infinite strings of symbols.

Such a measure can be formally constructed as follows. If b is a block of symbols of length k, that is, $b = b_0 b_1 \dots b_{k-1}$, then for $i \in \mathbb{Z}$ we define a cylinder set as

$$C_i(b) = \{s \in \mathcal{S} : s_i = b_0, s_{i+1} = b_1 \dots, s_{i+k-1} = b_{k-1}\}. \tag{17}$$

The cylinder set is thus a set of all possible configurations with fixed values at a finite number of sites. Intuitively, the measure of the cylinder set given by the block $b = b_0 \dots b_{k-1}$, denoted by $\mu[C_i(b)]$, is simply a probability of occurrence of the block b in a position starting at i. If the measure μ is shift-invariant, that is, $\mu(C_i(b))$ is independent of i, we can drop the index i and simply write $\mu(C(b))$.

The Kolmogorov consistency theorem states that every probability measure μ satisfying the consistency condition

$$\mu[C_i(b_1 \dots b_k)] = \sum_{a \in \mathcal{G}} \mu[C_i(b_1 \dots b_k, a)] \tag{18}$$

extends to a shift invariant measure on $\mathcal{S}$. For $p \in [0,1]$, the Bernoulli measure defined as $\mu_p[C(b)] = p^j(1-p)^{k-j}$, where j is a number of ones in b and $k-j$ is a number of zeros in b, is an example of such a shift-invariant (or spatially homogeneous) measure. It describes a set of random configurations with the probability that a given site is in state 1 equal to p.

Since a cellular automaton rule with global function F maps a configuration in $\mathcal{S}$ to another configuration in $\mathcal{S}$, we can define the action of F on measures on $\mathcal{S}$. For all measurable subsets E of $\mathcal{S}$ we define $(F\mu)(E) = \mu(F^{-1}(E))$, where $F^{-1}(E)$ is an inverse image of E under F.

The probabilistic initial value problem can thus be formulated as follows. If the initial configuration was specified by μ, what can be said about $F^t\mu$ (i.e., what is the probability measure after t iterations of F)?

Often in practical applications we do not need to know $F^t\mu$, but given a block b, we want to know what is the probability of the occurrence of this block in a configuration obtained from a random configuration (sampled, for example, according to the measure μ_p) after t iterations of a given rule. In the simplest case, when $b = 1$, we will define the *density of ones* as

$$\rho(t) = (F^n \mu_p)(C(1)). \tag{19}$$

3. Simulation problems

The basic problem in CA simulations is often called the forward problem: given the initial condition, that is, the state of cells of the lattice at time $t = 0$, what is their state at time $t > 0$? On the surface, this is an easy question to answer: just iterate the CA rule t of times, and you will find the answer. Nevertheless, upon closer inspection, some potential problems emerge.

- **Infinite lattice problem:** In the initial value problem (13), the initial condition is an infinite sequence of symbols. How do we compute an image of an infinite sequence under the cellular automaton rule?
- **Infinite time problem:** If we are interested in $t \to \infty$ behavior, as we usually do in dynamical system theory, how can simulations be used to investigate this?
- **Speed of simulations:** What if the lattice size and the number of iterations which interest us are both finite, but large, and the running time of the simulation is too long? Can we speed it up?

Some of these problems are interrelated, as will become clear in the forthcoming discussion.

4. Infinite lattice problem

In statistical and solid state physics, it is common to use the term "bulk properties", indicating properties of, for example, infinite crystal. Mathematically bulk properties are easier to handle, because we do not have to worry about what happens on the surface, and we can assume that the underlying physical system has a full translational invariance.
In simulations, infinite system size is of course impossible to achieve, and periodic boundary conditions are used instead. In cellular automata, similar idea can be employed. Suppose that we are interested in solving an initial value problem as defined by eq. (13). Obviously, it is impossible to implement direct simulation of this problem because the initial condition $s_i(0)$ consists of infinitely many cells. Once can, however, impose boundary condition such that $g(i + L) = g(i)$. This means that the initial configuration is periodic with period L. It is easy to show that if $s_i(0)$ is periodic with period L, then $s_i(t)$ is also periodic with the same period. This means than in practical simulations one needs to store only the values of cells with $i = 0, 1, 2, \ldots, L - 1$, that is, a finite string of symbols.
If one is interested in some bulk property P of the system being simulated, it is advisable to perform a series of simulations with increasing L, and check how P depends on L. Quite often, a clear trend can be spotted, that is, as L increases, P converges to the "bulk" value. One has to be aware, however, that some finite size effects are persistent, and may be present for any L, and disappear only on a truly infinite lattice.
Consider, as a simple example, the well-know rule 184, for which the local rule is defined as

$$\begin{aligned} &f(0,0,0) = 0,\ f(0,0,1) = 0,\ f(0,1,0) = 0,\ f(0,1,1) = 1,\\ &f(1,0,0) = 1,\ f(1,0,1) = 1,\ f(1,1,0) = 0,\ f(1,1,1) = 1, \end{aligned} \tag{20}$$

or equivalently

$$s_i(t+1) = s_{i-1}(t) + s_i(t)s_{i+1}(t) - s_{i-1}(t)s_i(t). \tag{21}$$

Suppose that as the initial condition we take

$$s_i(0) = i \bmod 2 + \delta_{i,0} - \delta_{i,1}, \tag{22}$$

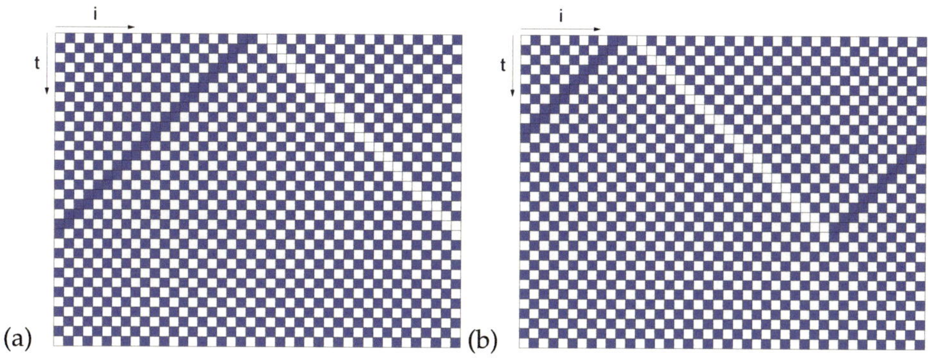

Fig. 2. Spread of defects in rule 184.

where $\delta_{i,j} = 1$ if $i = j$ and $\delta_{i,j} = 0$ otherwise. One can show that under the rule 184, at time $t > 1$ we have the following solution of the initial value problem given by (21, 22),

$$s_i(t) = (i+t) \bmod 2 + \sum_{k=0}^{t} \delta_{-t+2k,i} - \sum_{k=0}^{t} \delta_{-t+2k+1,i}. \tag{23}$$

This can be verified by substituting (23) into (21). It is also straightforward to verify that in $s_i(t)$ a pair of adjacent ones is always present, since $s_{-t-1}(t) = s_{-t}(t) = 1$ for all $t \geq 0$, that is, at time t, sites with coordinates $i = -t-1$ and $i = -t$ are in state 1.

Let us say that we are interested in the number of pairs 11 present in the configuration in the limit of $t \to \infty$, and we want to find it our by a direct simulation. Since the initial string $s_i(0)$ consists of 1100 preceded and followed by infinite repetition of 10, that is, $s_i(0) = \ldots 1010101100101010\ldots$, we could take as the initial condition only part of this string corresponding to $i = -L$ to $L+1$ for a given L, impose periodic boundary conditions on this string, and compute t consecutive iterations, taking t large enough, for example, $t = 2L$. It turns out that by doing this, we will always obtain a string which does not have any pair 11, no matter how large L we take! This is illustrated in Figure 2a, where first 30 iterations of a string given by eq. (22) with $i = -20$ to 21 and periodic boundary conditions is shown. Black squares represent 1, and white 0. The initial string ($t = 0$) is shown as the top line, and is followed by consecutive iterations, so that t increases in the downward direction. It is clear that we have two "defects", 11 and 00, moving in opposite direction. On a truly infinite lattice they would never meet, but on a periodic one they do meet and annihilate each other. This can be better observed in Figure 2b, in which the location of the initial defect has been shifted to the left, so that the annihilation occurs in the interior of the picture.

The disappearance of 11 (and 00) is an artifact of periodic boundaries, which cannot be eliminated by increasing the lattice size. This illustrates that extreme caution must be exercised when we draw conclusions about the behaviour of CA rules on infinite lattices from simulations of finite systems.

5. Infinite time problem

In various papers on CA simulations one often finds a statement that simulations are to be performed for long enough time so that the system "settles into equilibrium". The notion of equilibrium is rarely precisely defined, and this is somewhat understandable: mathematically, the definition of the "equilibrium" in spatially extended dynamical system such as CA is far from obvious.

The idea of the "equilibrium" can be better understood if we note that it has its roots in dynamical systems theory. Consider a difference equation $x_{n+1} = f(x_n)$, where f is a given function. Point a which has the property $f(a) = a$ is called a fixed point. In many applications and mathematical models, the prevailing type of fixed points is the so-called hyperbolic fixed point, satisfying $|f'(a)| \neq 1$. Suppose that a is hyperbolic with $|f'(a)| < 1$. One can then show (Devaney, 1989) that for every initial value x_0 in some open interval around a, if we iterate $x_{n+1} = f(x_n)$ starting from that initial value, we have $\lim_{n\to\infty} x_n = a$, and that there exists nonnegative $A < 1$ such that

$$|x_n - a| \leq A^n |x_0 - a|. \tag{24}$$

This indicates that x_n approaches the fixed point a *exponentially fast* (or faster). It turns out that the hyperbolicity is a very common feature of dynamical systems, even in higher dimensions, and that exponential approach to a fixed point is also a very typical behavior.

In cellular automata, the notion of the fixed point can be formulated in the framework of both deterministic and probabilistic initial value problem. The deterministic fixed point of a given CA rule f is simply a configuration s such that the if the rule f is applied to s, one obtains the same configuration s. Deterministic fixed points in CA are common, but they are usually not that interesting.

A far more interesting is the fixed point in the probabilistic sense, that is, a probability measure μ which remains unchanged after the application of the rule. Using a more practical language, we often are interested in a probability of some block of symbols, and want to know how this probability changes with t. In the simplest case, this could be the probability of occurrence of 1 in a configuration at time t, which is often referred to as the density of ones and denoted by $\rho(t)$. In surprisingly many cases, such probability tends to converge to some fixed value, and the convergence is of the hyperbolic type.

Consider, as an example, a rule which has been introduced in connection with models of the spread of innovations (Fukś and Boccara, 1998). Let us assume that, similarly as in the majority voting rule, we have a group of individuals arranged on an infinite line. Each individual can be in one of two states: adopter (1) and non-adopter (0). Suppose that each time step, each non-adopter becomes adopter if and only if exactly one of his neighbours is an adopter. Once somebody becomes adopter, he stays in this state forever. Local function for this rule is defined by $f(1,0,1) = f(0,0,0) = 0$, and $f(x_0, x_1, x_2) = 1$ otherwise.

Let us say that we are interested in the density of ones, that is, the density of adopters at time t, to be denoted by $\rho(t)$. Assume that we start with a random initial configuration with the initial density of adopters equal to $p < 1$. This defines a probabilistic initial value problem with an initial Bernoulli measure μ_p. In (Fukś and Boccara, 1998) it has been demonstrated that

$$\rho(t) = 1 - p^2(1-p) - p\frac{(1-p)^3}{2-p} - \left[1 - p^2 + \frac{p(1-p)^2}{p-2}\right](1-p)^{2t+1}, \tag{25}$$

and

$$\lim_{t\to\infty} \rho(t) = 1 - p^2(1-p) - p\frac{(1-p)^3}{2-p}. \tag{26}$$

It is now clear that $\rho(\infty) - \rho(t) \sim A^t$, where $A = (1-p)^2$, meaning that $\rho(t)$ approaches $\rho(\infty)$ exponentially fast, similarly as in the case of hyperbolic fixed point discussed above. If

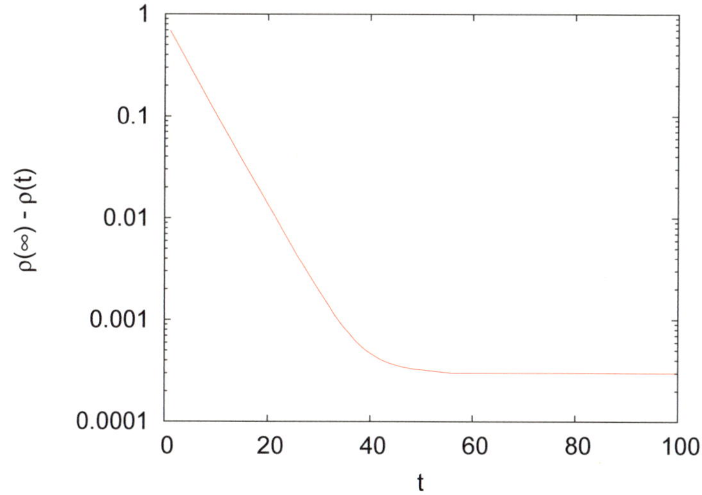

Fig. 3. Plot of $\rho(\infty) - \rho(t)$ as a function of time for simulation of rule 222 on a lattice of length 50000 starting from randomly generated initial condition with initial density $p = 0.1$.

we now simulate this rule on a finite lattice, $\rho(t)$ will initially exponentially decrease toward $\rho(\infty)$, so that $\rho(\infty) - \rho(t)$ plotted as a function of t in a semi-log graph will follow a straight line, and then, due to finite size of the lattice, it will level off, as shown in Figure 3. This plateau level is usually referred to as an "equilibrium". Note that the plateau is reached very quickly (in less then 60 iterations in this example), but it corresponds to a value of $\rho(t)$ slightly below the "true" value of $\rho(\infty)$. This is an extremely common behavior encountered in many CA simulations: we reach the plateau very quickly, but it is slightly off the "true" value. A proper way to proceed, therefore, is to record the value of the plateau for many different (and increasing) lattice sizes L, and from there to determine what happens to the plateau in the limit of $L \to \infty$. This is a much more prudent approach than simply "iterating until we reach the equilibrium", as it is too often done.

Of course, in addition to the behaviour analogous to the convergence toward a hyperbolic fixed point, we also encounter in CA another type of behaviour, which resembles a non-hyperbolic dynamics. Again, in order to understand this better, let us start with one-dimensional dynamical system. This time, consider the logistic difference equation

$$x_{t+1} = \lambda x_t (1 - x_t), \tag{27}$$

where λ is a given parameter $\lambda \in (0, 2)$. This equation has two fixed points $x^{(1)} = 0$ and $x^{(2)} = 1 - 1/\lambda$. For any initial value $x_0 \in (0, 1)$, when $\lambda < 1$, x_t converges to the first of these fixed points, that is, $x_t \to 0$, and otherwise it converges to the second one, so that $x_t \to 1 - 1/\lambda$ as $t \to \infty$.

In the theory of iterations of complex analytic functions, it is possible to obtain an approximate expressions describing the behavior of x_t near the fixed point as $t \to \infty$. This is done using a method which we will not describe here, by conjugating the difference equation with an appropriate Möbius transformation, which moves the fixed point to ∞. Applying this method, one obtains formulas for the asymptotic behavior of x_t which can be summarized as follows:

$$x_t - x_\infty \sim \begin{cases} \lambda^t & \text{if } \lambda < \lambda_c, \\ 1/t & \text{if } \lambda = \lambda_c, \\ (2-\lambda)^t & \text{if } \lambda > \lambda_c, \end{cases} \tag{28}$$

where $\lambda_c = 1$. We can see that the approach toward the fixed point is exponential if $\lambda \neq 1$, and that it slows down as λ is getting closer to 1. At $\lambda = 1$, the decay toward the fixed point is not exponential, but takes a form of a power law, indicating that the fixed point is non-hyperbolic. This phenomenon, which is called a *transcritical bifurcation*, has a close analog in dynamics of cellular automata. In order to illustrate this, consider the following problem. Let s be an infinite string of binary symbols, i.e., $s = \ldots s_{-1}s_0s_1\ldots$. We will say that the symbol s_i has a *dissenting right neighbour* if $s_{i-1} = s_i \neq s_{i+1}$. By *flipping* a given symbol s_i we will mean replacing it by $1 - s_i$. Suppose that we simultaneously flip all symbols which have dissenting right neighbours, as shown in the example below.

$$\begin{array}{cccccccccccccc} \cdots & 0 & 0 & 1 & 0 & 0 & 1 & 1 & 1 & 0 & 1 & 0 & 1 & \cdots \\ & & \downarrow & & & \downarrow & & & \downarrow & & & & & \\ \cdots & 0 & 1 & 1 & 0 & 1 & 1 & 1 & 0 & 0 & 1 & 0 & 1 & \cdots \end{array} \tag{29}$$

Assuming that the initial string is randomly generated, what is the probability $P_{dis}(t)$ that a given symbol has a dissenting right neighbour after t iterations of the aforementioned procedure?

It is easy to see that the process we have described is nothing else but a cellular automaton rule 142, with the following local function

$$\begin{aligned} f(0,0,0) = 0, f(0,0,1) = 1, f(0,1,0) = 1, f(0,1,1) = 1, \\ f(1,0,0) = 0, f(1,0,1) = 0, f(1,1,0) = 0, f(1,1,1) = 1, \end{aligned} \tag{30}$$

which can also be written in an algebraic form

$$f(x_0, x_1, x_2) = x_1 + (1 - x_0)(1 - x_1)x_2 - x_0x_1(1 - x_2). \tag{31}$$

In (Fukś, 2006), it has been demonstrated that the desired probability $P_{dis}(t)$ is given by

$$P_{\text{dis}}(t) = 1 - 2q - \sum_{j=1}^{t+1} \frac{j}{t+1} \binom{2t+2}{t+1-j} (2q)^{t+1-j}(1-2q)^{t+1+j}, \tag{32}$$

where $q \in [0, 1/2]$ is the probability of occurrence of the block 10 in the initial string. It is possible to show that in the limit of $t \to \infty$

$$\lim_{t\to\infty} P_{\text{dis}}(t) = \begin{cases} 2q & \text{if } q < 1/4, \\ 1-2q & \text{otherwise,} \end{cases} \tag{33}$$

indicating that $q = 1/4$ is a special value separating two distinct "phases".

Suppose now that we perform a simulation of rule 142 as follows. We take a finite lattice with randomly generated initial condition in which the proportion of blocks 10 among all blocks of length 2 is equal to q. We iterate rule 142 starting from this initial condition t times, and we count what is the proportion of sites having dissenting neighbours. If we did this, we would

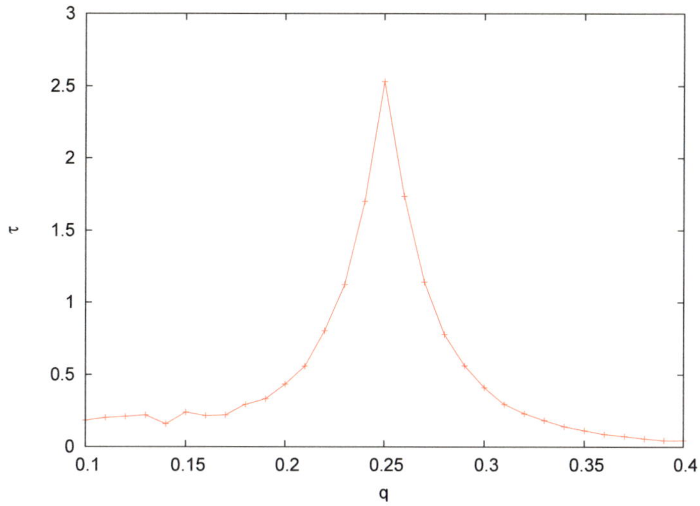

Fig. 4. Decay time as a function of q for rule 142.

observe that most of the time the number of dissenting neighbours behaves similarly to what we have seen in rule 222 (Figure 3), that is, quickly reaches a plateau. However, when q gets closer and closer to $1/4$, it takes longer and longer to get to this plateau.
A good way to illustrate this phenomenon is by introducing a quantity which can be called a decay time,

$$\tau = \sum_{t=0}^{\infty} |P_{dis}(t) - P_{dis}(\infty)|. \tag{34}$$

Decay time will be finite if $P_{dis}(t)$ decays exponentially toward $P_{dis}(\infty)$, and will become infinite when the decay is non-exponential (of power-law type). One can approximate τ in simulations by truncating the infinite sum at some large value t_{max}, and by using the fraction of sites with dissenting neighbours in place of $P_{dis}(t)$. An example of a plot of τ obtained this way as a function of q for simulations of rule 142 is show in Figure 4. We can see that around $q = 1/4$, the decay shows a sign of divergence, and indeed for larger values of t_{max} the height of the peak at $q = 1/4$ would increase. Such divergence of the decay indicates that at $q = 1/4$ the convergence to "equilibrium" is no longer exponential, but rather is analogous to an approach to a non-hyperbolic fixed point. In fact, it has been demonstrated (Fukś, 2006) that at $q = 1/4$ we have $|P_{dis}(t) - P_{dis}(\infty)| \sim t^{-1/2}$. Similar divergence of the decay time is often encountered in statistical physics in systems exhibiting a phase transition, and it is sometimes called "critical slowing down".
This example yields the following practical implications for CA simulations. If the CA rule or initial conditions which one investigates depend on a parameter which can be varied continuously, it is worthwhile to plot the decay time as a function of this parameter to check for signs of critical slowing down. Even if there is no critical slowing down, the decay time is an useful indicator of the rate of convergence to "equilibrium" for different values of the parameter, and it helps to discover non-hyperbolic behavior.
One should also note at this point that in some cellular automata, decay toward the "equilibrium" can be much slower than in the $q = 1/4$ case in the above example. This is usually

the case when the rule exhibits complex propagating spatiotemporal structures. For example, it has been found that in rule 54, the number of some particle-like spatiotemporal structures tends to zero as approximately $t^{-0.15}$ (Boccara et al., 1991). In cases like this, simulations are computationally very expensive, that is, very large number of iterations is required in order to get sufficiently close to the "equilibrium".

6. Improving simulation performance

If the decay toward the equilibrium is non-hyperbolic, the speed of simulations becomes an issue. The speed of simulations can be improved either in software, or by using a specialized hardware. We will discuss only selected software methods here, only mentioning that specialized CA hardware has been build in the past (for example, CAM-6 and CAM-8 machines, field programmable gate arrays), and some novel hardware schemes have been proposed or speculated upon (implementation of CA using biological computation, nanotechnology, or quantum devices). Additionally, CA simulations are very suitable for parallel computing environments – a topic which deserves a separate review, and therefore will not be discussed here.

Typically, CA simulations are done using integer arrays to store the values of $s_i(t)$. A basic and well-know method for computing $s_i(t+1)$ knowing $s_i(t)$ is to use a lookup table – that is, table of values of the local function f for all possible configurations of the neighbourhood. Two arrays are needed, one for $s_i(t)$ (let us call it "s") and one for $s_i(t+1)$ ("snew"). Once "s" is computed using the lookup table, one only needs to swap pointers to "s" and "snew". This avoids copying of the content of "snew" to "s", which would decrease simulation performance.

Beyond these basic ideas, there are some additional methods which can improve the speed of simulations, and they will be discussed in the following subsections.

6.1 Self-composition

If f and g are CA rules of radius 1, we can define a composition of f and g as

$$(f \circ g)(x_0, x_1, x_2, x_3, x_4) = f(g(x_0, x_1, x_2), g(x_1, x_2, x_3), g(x_2, x_3, x_4)). \tag{35}$$

Similar definition can be given for rules of higher radius. If $f = g$, $f \circ f$ will be called a self-composition. Multiple composition will be denoted by

$$f^n = \underbrace{f \circ f \circ \cdots \circ f}_{n \text{ times}}. \tag{36}$$

The self-composition can be used to speed-up CA simulations. Suppose that we need to iterate a given CA t times. We can do it by iterating f t times, or by first computing f^2 and iterate it $t/2$ times. In general, we can compute f^n first, and then perform t/n iterations of f^n, and in the end we will obtain the same final configuration. Obviously, this decreases the number of iterations and, therefore, can potentially speed-up simulations. There is, however, some price to pay: we need to compute f^n first, which also takes some time, and, moreover, iterating f^n will be somewhat slower due to the fact that f^n has a longer lookup table than f. It turns out that in practice the self-composition is advantageous if n is not too large. Let us denote by T_n the running time of the simulation performed using f^n as described above. The ratio T_n/T_1 (to be called a speedup factor) as a function of n for simulation of rule 18 on a lattice of 10^6 sites is shown in Figure 5. As one can see, the optimal value of n appears to be 7, which

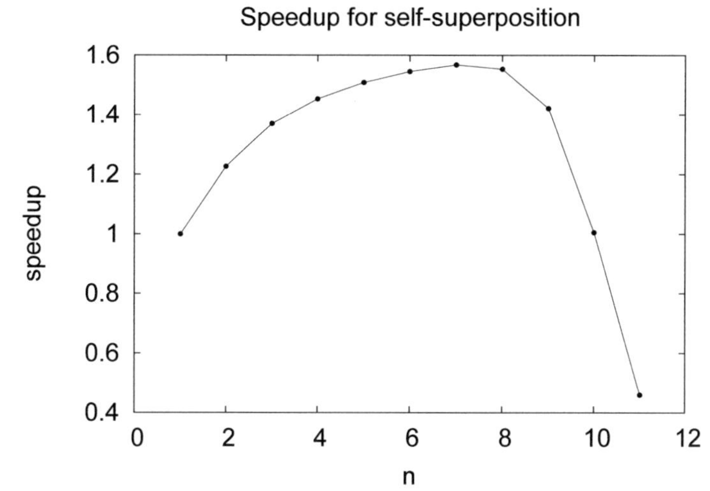

Fig. 5. Plot of the speedup factor T_n/T_1 as a function of n for self-composition of rule 18.

speeds up the simulation by 58%. Increasing n beyond this value does not bring any further improvement – on the contrary, the speedup factor rapidly decreases beyond $n = 7$, and at $n = 10$ we actually see a significant *decrease* of the running time compared to $n = 1$.
The optimal value of $n = 7$ is, of course, not universal, and for different simulations and different rules it needs to be determined experimentally. Self-composition is especially valuable if one needs to iterate the same rule over a large number of initial conditions. In such cases, it pays off to determine the optimal n first, then pre-compute f^n, and use it in all subsequent simulations.

6.2 Euler versus Langrage representation

In some cases, CA may posses so-called additive invariants, and these can be exploited to speed-up simulations. Consider again the rule 184 defined in eq (20) and (21). The above definition can also be written in a form

$$s_i(t+1) = s_i(t) + J(s_{i-1}(t), s_i(t)) - J(s_i(t), s_{i+1}(t)), \tag{37}$$

where $J(x_1, x_2) = x_1(1 - x_2)$. Clearly, for a periodic lattice with N sites, when the above equation is summed over $i = 1 \dots N$, one obtains

$$\sum_{i=1}^{N} s_i(t+1) = \sum_{i=1}^{N} s_i(t), \tag{38}$$

due to cancellation of terms involving J. This means that the number of sites in state 1 (often called "occupied" sites) is constant, and does not change with time. This is an example of additive invariant of 0-th order. Rules having this property are often called number-conserving rules.
Since the number-conserving CA rules conserve the number of occupied sites, we can label each occupied site (or "particle") with an integer $n \in \mathbb{Z}$, such that the closest particle to the

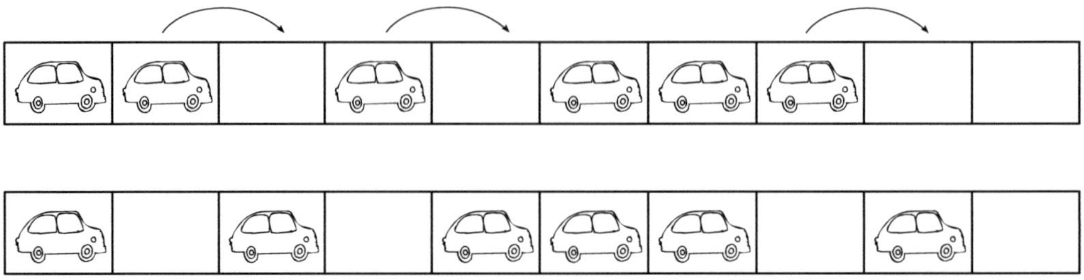

Fig. 6. Motion representation of rule 184 interpreted as a simplified road traffic model. The upper row represents configuration of cars/particles at time t, and the lower row at time $t+1$.

right of particle n is labeled $n+1$. If $y_n(t)$ denotes the position of particle n at time t, we can then specify how the position of the particle at the time step $t+1$ depends on positions of the particle and its neighbours at the time step t. For rule 184 one obtains

$$y_n(t+1) = y_n(t) + \min\{y_{n+1}(t) - y_n(t) - 1, 1\}. \tag{39}$$

This can be described in very simple terms: if a "particle" is followed by an empty site, it moves to the right, otherwise it stays in the same place. This is illustrated in Figure 6, where "particles" are depicted as "cars". Although this can hardly be called a realistic traffic flow model, it nevertheless exhibits some realistic features and can be further extended (Chowdhury et al., 2000).

Equation (39) is sometimes referred to as the motion representation. For arbitrary CA rule with additive invariant it is possible to obtain the motion representation by employing an algorithm described in (Fukś, 2000). The motion representation is analogous to Lagrange representation of the fluid flow, in which we observe individual particles and follow their trajectories. On the other hand, eq. (37) could be called Euler representation, because it describes the process at a fixed point in space (Matsukidaira and Nishinari, 2003).

Since the number of "particles" is normally smaller than the number of lattice sites, it is often advantageous to use the motion representation in simulations. Let ρ be the density of particles, that is, the ratio of the number of occupied sites and the total number of lattice sites. Furthermore, let T_L and T_E be, respectively, the execution time of one iteration for Lagrange and Euler representation. A typical plot of the speedup factor T_E/T_L as a function of ρ for rule 184 is shown in Figure 7. One can see that the speedup factor is quite close to $1/\rho$, shown as a continuous line in Figure 7. For small densities of occupied sites, the speedup factor can be very significant.

6.3 Bitwise operators

One well known way of increasing CA simulation performance is the use of bitwise operators. Typically, CA simulations are done using arrays of integers to store states of individual cells. In computer memory, integers are stored as arrays of bits, typically 32 or 64 bits long (to be called *MAXBIT*). If one wants to simulate a binary rule, each bit of an integer word can be set independently, thus allowing to store *MAXBIT* bit arrays in a single integer array.

In C/C++, one can set and read individual bits by using the following macros:

```
#define GETBIT(x, n) ((x>>n)&1)
#define SETBIT(x, n) (x | (1<<n))
```

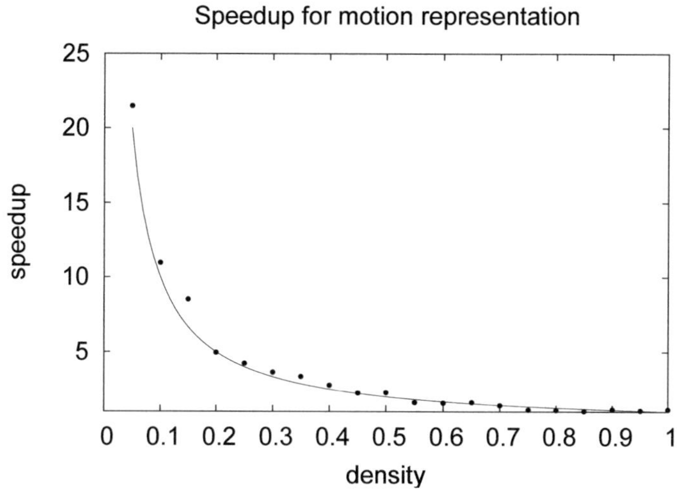

Fig. 7. Plot of the speedup factor T_E/T_L as a function of density ρ for rule 184.

```
#define ZEROBIT(x,n)  (x & (~(1<<n)))
```

For example, if x is an integer variable, then

```
x=SETBIT(x,5)
x=ZEROBIT(x,4)
```

sets respectively the 5-th bit of x to value 1 and the 4-th bit to 0. Using these macros, we can, for instance, prepare *MAXBIT* different initial conditions, and store them in one integer array. The main advantage of such bit packing lies in the fact that we can then use bitwise operators to perform operations on all bits *simultaneously*. Consider, as an example, rule 184 again, as defined in eq. (20). It is easy to check that the local function for this rule can be written using logical "and" ($\wedge$) and "or" ($\vee$) operators,

$$f(x_0, x_1, x_2) = (x_0 \wedge \overline{x}_1) \vee (x_1 \wedge x_2), \tag{40}$$

where $\overline{x}$ denotes the negation of x. In C/C++ program, we can apply this rule to all BITMAX bits of the array as follows:

```
for(i=0; i<L; i++)
     snew[i]=(s[i-1] & ~s[i]) | (s[i] & s[i+1])
```

where L is the length of the lattice, s[i] denotes the state of site i, and snew[i] is the new state of this site. This method can potentially speed up simulations BITMAX times.

7. HCELL CA simulation library

Many software tools exist which are suitable for CA simulations, ranging from very specialized ones to very broad simulation environments. Partial list of these programs can be found in (Ilachinski, 2001). Most of these packages are great for "visual" explorations of CA, but they usually miss functions which a more mathematically inclined user would require.

For speed and flexibility in simulations, it is usually best to write the simulation in a compiled language, such as C/C++. For one dimensional cellular automata, the author developed a C++ library named HCELL, which is freely available under GNU Public License (Fukś, 2005). It allows fast simulation of deterministic and probabilistic CA, supports Wolfram rule numbering, four basic symmetry transformations, composition of rules (using operator overloading), totalistic rules, minimal rules etc. Spatial set entropy and spatial measure entropy can be computed for a given lattice configuration, assignment operator can be used for rules and lattices, rules can be tested for additive invariants, currents of additive quantities are computed in a symbolic form. Although this is not a visualization package, spatiotemporal patterns can be exported as EPS and Asymptote files.
HCELL allows to create two types of objects, *CA rules* and *lattices*. These objects can be manipulated using member functions and operators, and rules can be applied to lattices. Various global functions taking as arguments rules and lattices are also defined. In order to illustrate the use of HCELL in practical simulations, we will give some examples.

7.1 Example 1: the parity problem

As a first example, consider solution of the so-called parity problem for CA. For a finite binary string s, parity of s equals to 1 if the number of ones in the string is odd, otherwise it is zero. The parity problem is to find a CA which, when iterated starting from s and using periodic boundary conditions, will converge to all 1's if the parity of s is 1, otherwise it will converge to all 0's. Although it has been proven that there does not exist a single CA which would perform this task, in (Lee et al., 2001) a solution involving more than one rule has been found. For instance, if the lattice size is $L = 2q$ and q is odd, then applying the operator

$$G = F_{254}^{\lfloor L/2 \rfloor} F_{76} (F_{132}^{\lfloor L/2 \rfloor} F_{222}^{\lfloor L/2 \rfloor})^{\lfloor L/2 \rfloor} \tag{41}$$

to s produces a configuration with the desired property, that is, consisting of all 0's if the parity of s is 0, and consisting of all 1's otherwise. In the above, F_m denotes the global function associated with elementary cellular automaton rule with Wolfram number m. The following C++ program utilizing HCELL generates a random string or length 90, applies G to it, and prints the resulting configuration:

```
#include <hcell/hcell.h>
#include <iostream>
#include <math.h>
using namespace std;

int main()
{
 //define needed rules
 CArule1d r254(1,254), r76(1,76), r132(1,132), r222(1,222);
 //create lattice
 int L=90;  Lattice lat(L);
 //initialize RNG
 r250_init(1234);
 //seed lattice randomly to get exactly 10 % sites occupied
 lat.PreciseSeed(0.1);
 int i, j;
for(j=0; j<L/2; j++)
 {
  for(i=0; i<L/2 ; i++) Evolve(&lat, r222);
```

```
020    for(i=0; i<L/2 ; i++) Evolve(&lat, r132);
021   }
022   Evolve(&lat, r76);
023   for(i=0; i<L/2 ; i++) Evolve(&lat, r254);
024   //print the resulting configuration
025   lat.Print();
026
027 return 0;
028 }
```

As we can see, all required operations are encapsulated. Elementary cellular automata rules are constructed by the statement `CArule1d r254(1,254)`, which is equivalent to "construct 1D CA rule with radius 1 and rule number 254, and name it r254". Applying a given rule to a lattice requires only a simple call to "Evolve" function, as shown in lines 19, 20 and 23. Figure 8 shows an example of a spatiotemporal patterns generated from five different initial conditions by applying the operator given by eq. (41). This figure has been produced by `ca2asy` tool included with HCELL. As expected, configurations with the parity 1 converge to all ones, and those with the parity 0 converge to all zeros.

7.2 Example 2: operations on rules

HCELL also allows various operations on rules. One can, in particular, construct composition of rules by using the overloaded $\star$ operator. For example, in order to verify that

$$f_{60} \circ f_{43} = f_{184} \circ f_{60}, \tag{42}$$

one only needs to check that the Hamming distance between rule tables $f_{60} \circ f_{43}$ and $f_{184} \circ f_{60}$ is zero, which in HCELL is as simple as

```
CArule1d r60(1,60), r184(1,184), r43(1,43);
cout << Hamming(r60*r43, r184*r60);
```

In addition to the composition, two other operators are overloaded as well: $+$ can be used to add rules (mod 2), and $=$ can be used as an assignment operator for both rules and lattices. This allows to write formulas for rules in a natural fashion. For example, one could define a new rule $f = f_{60} \circ f_{43} \oplus f_{184} \circ f_{60}$, where $\oplus$ represents mod 2 addition. Using HCELL, this could be achieved as

```
CArule1d r60(1,60), r184(1,184), r43(1,43), r;
r=r60*r43 + r184*r60;
```

One can also obtain transformed rules very easily, by calling appropriate member functions of `CArule1d`, for example,

```
rr=r.Reflected(void);
rc=r.Conjugated(void);
```

This constructs, respectively, the spatially reflected rule `rr` and the conjugated rule `rc`, where by Boolean conjugation we mean the interchange of 0's and 1's in the rule table.

Fig. 8. Parity problem solution for lattice of length 14 and initial configuration with 1 (a), 2 (b), 3 (c), 6 (d) and 9 (e) sites in state 1.

7.3 Example 3: probabilistic density classification

In addition to these and many other capabilities for deterministic CA, HCELL also supplies a basic functionality for handling of probabilistic rules. To demonstrate this, let us denote by

$$P(s_i(t+1))|s_{i-1}(t), s_i(k), s_{i+1}(t)) \tag{43}$$

the probability that the site $s_i(t)$ with nearest neighbors $s_{i-1}(k), s_{i+1}(k)$ changes its state to $s_i(t+1)$ in a single time step. Consider a special probabilistic CA rule which is known to solve the so-called probabilistic density classification problem. If this rule is iterated starting from some initial string, the probability that all sites become eventually occupied is equal to the density of occupied sites in the initial string (Fukś, 2002). The following set of transition probabilities defines the aforementioned CA rule:

$$\begin{aligned} &P(1|0,0,0) = 0 \quad P(1|0,0,1) = p \quad P(1|0,1,0) = 1-2p \quad P(1|0,1,1) = 1-p \\ &P(1|1,0,0) = p \quad P(1|1,0,1) = 2p \quad P(1|1,1,0) = 1-p \quad P(1|1,1,1) = 1, \end{aligned} \tag{44}$$

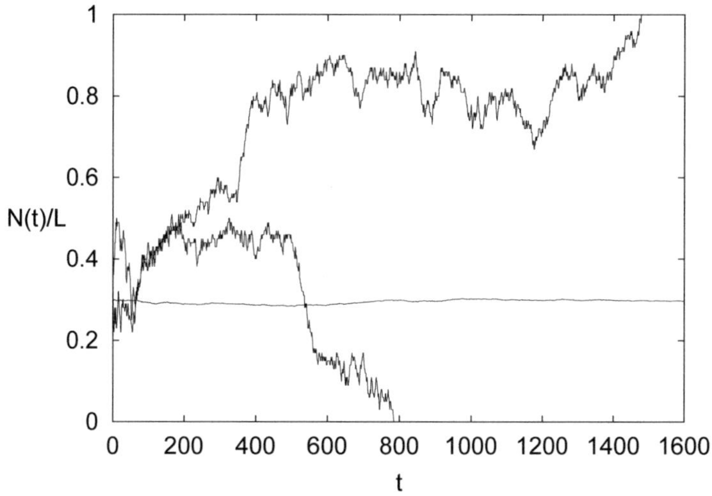

Fig. 9. Fraction of sites in state 1 $N(t)/L$ as a function of time t for two sample trajectories starting from initial configurations with $N(0) = 30$, $L = 100$, $p = 0.3$. The third line (almost horizontal) represents average of 1000 trajectories.

where $p \in (0, 1/2]$. The remaining eight transition probabilities can be obtained using $P(0|a,b,c) = 1 - P(1|a,b,c)$ for $a,b,c \in \{0,1\}$. In HCELL, this rule can be defined as

```
ProbabilisticRule1d r(1); //rule of radius 1
double p=0.25;
r.lookuptable[0]=0.0;
r.lookuptable[1]=p;
r.lookuptable[2]=1.0-2.0*p;
r.lookuptable[3]=1.0-p;
r.lookuptable[4]=p;
r.lookuptable[5]=2.0*p;
r.lookuptable[6]=1.0-p;
r.lookuptable[7]=1.0;
```

where we choose $p = 0.25$. The consecutive entries in the "lookuptable" are simply probabilities of eq. (44), in order of increasing neighbourhood code. Once the probabilistic rule is defined, it can be applied to a lattice `lat` by invoking the function `Evolve(&lat,r)`, just as in the case of deterministic rules. All the required calls to the random number generator are encapsulated and invisible to the user. Figure 9 shows two sample plots of $N(t)/L$ as a function of time, where $N(t)$ is the number of sites in state 1 and L is the length of the lattice. The value of $N(t)/L$ has been obtained by using the member function `Lattice.Density()` at every time step. The third line in Figure 9 represents an average of 1000 realizations of the process, and one can clearly see that indeed the probability of being in state 1 for any site is equal to the fraction of "occupied" sites in the initial condition, which is 0.3 in the illustrated case. These curves can be generated by HCELL in less than 20 line of code.
It is worthwhile to mention at this point that in HCELL, probabilistic rules can also be reconstructed from lattices. Suppose that `lat1` is the lattice state at time t, and `lat2` at time $t+1$,

where `lat2` has been obtained from `lat1` by applying an unknown rule *r*. Rule *r* can then be reconstructed by calling a special form of the constructor of probabilistic rules,

```
ProbabilisticRule1d r(&la1, &lat2, rad);
```

where `rad` is the desired rule radius. Of course, such reconstruction will only be approximate, and the accuracy of reconstruction will increase with the lattice size.
Many other features of HCELL, not mentioned here, are described in the documentation and examples which accompany source files. New version is currently under development. It will remove some limitations of the existing version. In particular, support for non-binary rules and numbering schemes for arbitrary rules is planned (current version supports Wolfram numbering for rules up to radius 2).

8. Conclusions

We presented an overview of basic issues associated with CA simulations, concentrating on selected problems which, in the mind of the author, deserve closer attention. We also demonstrated how HCELL can be used to perform some typical CA simulation tasks.
Obviously, many important topics have been omitted. In particular, the issue of dimensionality of space has not been addressed, and yet many important CA models require 2D, 3D, and higher dimensional lattices. Some collective phenomena in CA can only occur in high dimensions, and in terms of mathematical theory, dimensions higher than one often require quite different approach than 1D case. The reader is advised to consult the literature mentioned in the introduction to learn more about these topics.

9. References

Stefania Bandini, Bastien Chopard, and Marco Tomassini, editors. *Cellular Automata, 5th International Conference on Cellular Automata for Research and Industry, ACRI 2002, Geneva, Switzerland, October 9-11, 2002, Proceedings*, volume 2493 of *Lecture Notes in Computer Science*, 2002. Springer.

N. Boccara, J. Nasser, and M. Roger. Particle-like structures and interactions in spatio-temporal patterns generated by one-dimensional determinsitic cellular automaton rules. *Phys. Rev. A*, 44, July 1991.

B. Chopard and M. Drozd. *Cellular automata modeling of physical systems*. Cambridge UP, Cambridge, 1998.

D. Chowdhury, L. Santen, and A. Schadschneider. Statistical physics of vehicular traffic and some related systems. *Physics Reports*, 329:199–329, 2000.

R. L. Devaney. *An introduction to chaotic dynamical systems*. Addison-Wesley, Reading, MA, 1989.

H. Fukś. HCELL library for cellular automata simulations, 2005. URL `http://hcell.sourceforge.net`.

H. Fukś. A class of cellular automata equivalent to deterministic particle systems. In A. T. Lawniczak S. Feng and R. S. Varadhan, editors, *Hydrodynamic Limits and Related Topics*, Fields Institute Communications Series, Providence, RI, 2000. AMS.

H. Fukś. Non-deterministic density classification with diffusive probabilistic cellular automata. *Phys. Rev. E*, 66:066106, 2002.

H. Fukś. Dynamics of the cellular automaton rule 142. *Complex Systems*, 16:123–138, 2006.

H. Fukś and N. Boccara. Modelling diffusion of innovations with probabilistic cellular automata. In M. Delorme and J. Mazoyer, editors, *Cellular Automata: A Parallel Model*. Kluwer, Dordrecht, 1998.

Andrew Ilachinski. *Cellular Automata: A Discrete Universe*. World Scientific, Singapore, 2001.

J. Kari. Theory of cellular automata: a survey. *Theor. Comput. Sci.*, 334:3–33, 2005.

K. M. Lee, Hao Xu, and H. F. Chau. Parity problem with a cellular automaton solution. *Phys. Rev. E*, 64:026702, 2001.

J. Matsukidaira and K. Nishinari. Euler-Lagrange correspondence of cellular automaton for traffic-flow models. *Phys. Rev. Lett.*, 90:art. no.–088701, 2003.

Peter M. A. Sloot, Bastien Chopard, and Alfons G. Hoekstra, editors. *Cellular Automata, 6th International Conference on Cellular Automata for Research and Industry, ACRI 2004, Amsterdam, The Netherlands, October 25-28, 2004*, volume 3305 of *Lecture Notes in Computer Science*, 2004. Springer.

Hiroshi Umeo, Shin Morishita, Katsuhiro Nishinari, Toshihiko Komatsuzaki, and Stefania Bandini, editors. *Cellular Automata, 8th International Conference on Cellular Automata for Reseach and Industry, ACRI 2008, Yokohama, Japan, September 23-26, 2008*, volume 5191 of *Lecture Notes in Computer Science*, 2008. Springer.

S. Wolfram. *Cellular Automata and Complexity: Collected Papers*. Addison-Wesley, Reading, Mass., 1994.

Stephen Wolfram. *A New Kind of Science*. Wolfram Media, 2002.

Samira El Yacoubi, Bastien Chopard, and Stefania Bandini, editors. *Cellular Automata, 7th International Conference on Cellular Automata, for Research and Industry, ACRI 2006, Perpignan, France, September 20-23, 2006*, volume 4173 of *Lecture Notes in Computer Science*, 2006. Springer.

A survey for descriptor weakly nonlinear dynamic systems with applications

Athanasios D. Karageorgos[1], Athanasios A. Pantelous[1,2,3] and Grigoris I. Kalogeropoulos[1]
[1]Department of Mathematics, University of Athens, Greece
[2]School of Engineering and Mathematical Sciences, City University, London, UK
[3]Department of Mathematical Sciences, University of Liverpool, UK

1. Introduction

In many and very significant applications, for instance in mechanical, electrical and chemical engineering, in economy (the famous input-output Leondief model and its several important extensions, see Leontief (1986), Luenberger (1977), Campbell (1980) at al.), in actuarial science, Pantelous et al. (2008), in ecology and growth population (the Leslie growth population model and backward population projections, see Leslie (1945)), the descriptor dynamic systems' framework is required for the modelling procedure.

Example 1.1 For instance, practically speaking, we can consider a simple *circuit* network, as shown in **Figure 1**, Dai (1989) p. 10, where the voltage source $V_s(t)$ is the control input. R, L and C stand for the resistor, the inductor, and the capacity, respectively. Moreover, their voltages are denoted by $V_R(t)$, $V_L(t)$ and $V_C(t)$, respectively.

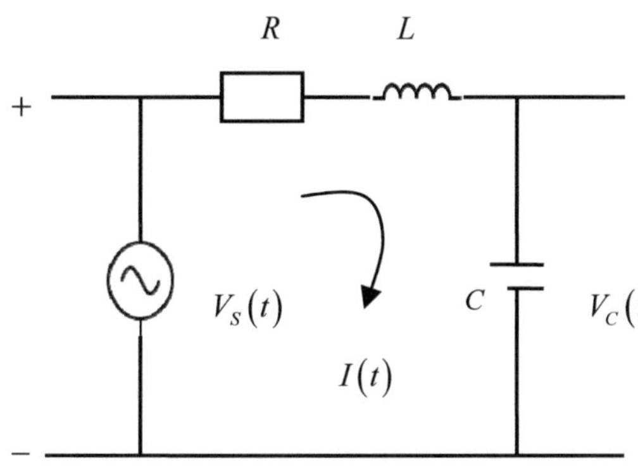

Fig. 1. A simple circuit network

Then, following Kirchoff's laws, we have the following systems of circuit equations

$$V_L(t)+V_C(t)+V_R(t)=V_S(t) \tag{1.1}$$

$$V_L(t)=L\cdot i'(t) \tag{1.2}$$

$$V_R(t)=R\cdot i(t) \tag{1.3}$$

$$V_C(t)=\frac{1}{C}\int i(\tau)d\tau\ . \tag{1.4}$$

Moreover, if we assume that

$$\underline{x}(t)=\begin{bmatrix} i(t)\\ V_L(t)\\ V_C(t)\\ V_R(t)\end{bmatrix},$$

as the state variable, we obtain

$$\begin{bmatrix} L & 0 & 0 & 0\\ 0 & 0 & 1 & 0\\ 0 & 0 & 0 & 0\\ 0 & 0 & 0 & 0\end{bmatrix}\begin{bmatrix} i'(t)\\ V_L'(t)\\ V_C'(t)\\ V_R'(t)\end{bmatrix}=\begin{bmatrix} 0 & 1 & 0 & 0\\ \frac{1}{C} & 0 & 0 & 0\\ -R & 0 & 0 & 1\\ 0 & 1 & 1 & 1\end{bmatrix}\begin{bmatrix} i(t)\\ V_L(t)\\ V_C(t)\\ V_R(t)\end{bmatrix}+\begin{bmatrix} 0\\ 0\\ 0\\ 1\end{bmatrix}V_S(t)\ .$$

Then, the following dynamic system is derived

$$F\underline{x}'(t)=G\underline{x}(t)+B\underline{u}(t), \tag{1.5a}$$

where

$$F=\begin{bmatrix} L & 0 & 0 & 0\\ 0 & 0 & 1 & 0\\ 0 & 0 & 0 & 0\\ 0 & 0 & 0 & 0\end{bmatrix},\ G=\begin{bmatrix} 0 & 1 & 0 & 0\\ \frac{1}{C} & 0 & 0 & 0\\ -R & 0 & 0 & 1\\ 0 & 1 & 1 & 1\end{bmatrix}\ \text{and}\ B=\begin{bmatrix} 0\\ 0\\ 0\\ 1\end{bmatrix}.$$

Example 1.2 (Analog-computer simulation) (Grispos, 1991)

$$\begin{cases} F\underline{x}'(t)=G\underline{x}(t)+B\underline{u}(t)\\ \underline{y}(t)=C\underline{x}(t)+D\underline{u}(t)\end{cases}, \tag{1.5b}$$

where $\det F=0$ or $\det F\neq 0$.

In **figure 2**, an analog-computer simulation of a relevant descriptor non-autonomous dynamic system is sketched, which is accelerated by the use of *integrator* ($\int$). Moreover, in the above figure, an *adder* ($\oplus$) is included, where the output vector is equal to the sum of input vectors and the *amplifier* (or *attenuator*) $\boxed{A}$. This simulation of system (1.5b) is true if we assume that the vector $F\underline{x}'(t)$ *does* exist.

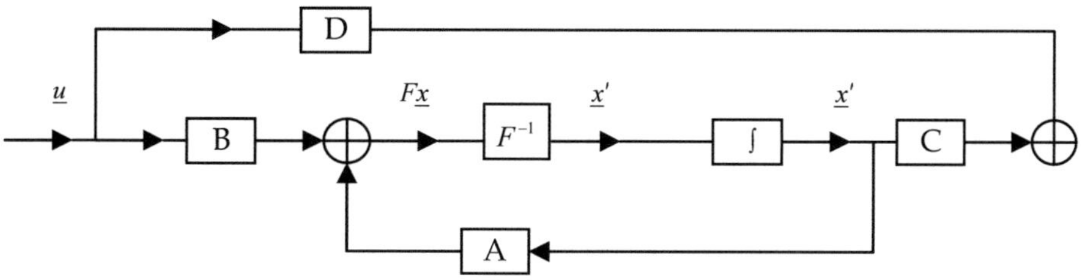

Fig. 2. Analog-computer simulation

As we can see, the systems (1.5a) and (1.5b) are linear descriptor differential systems. However, several of those electrical applications can be represented more effectively by combining linear and nonlinear parts of differential equations known, in the literature, as *weakly nonlinear differential systems*.
Weakly nonlinear (or semi-linear) regular differential systems of type (1.6) are investigated in this book chapter, see also Kalogeropoulos et al. (2008 a,b), Karageorgos et al. (2009), i.e.

$$F\underline{x}'(t) = G\underline{x}(t) + \underline{f}(t, \underline{x}(t)), \tag{1.6}$$

where $F, G \in \mathbb{C}^{n \times n}$ are time-invariant matrices, with $\det F = 0$, and $\underline{f}(t, \underline{x}(t))$ is a sufficiently differentiable n-vector function of t; $\underline{x}(t)$, for $t \geq 0$ and $\|\underline{x}\| < \infty$.
This mixture of linear and nonlinear parts is a very productive in many applications of engineering including electrical circuits and networks; power system; aerospace engineering; nonlinear mechanical phenomena; cheap control, etc. Since 1970s, this kind of systems has attracted the attention of many researchers. However, more theoretical analysis of (1.6) is needed. This chapter is a step in that direction.
In the classical literature of generalized linear regular differential systems, see Campbell (1980, 1983), Karcanias (1981), Kalogeropoulos (1985) et al., one of the important features is that not every initial condition $\underline{x}(t_o)$ admits a functional solution.
This chapter is organized as follows: Section 2 provides some preliminary concepts and definitions from Matrix Pencil theory. In Section 3, the solution of weakly nonlinear regular differential systems is derived. The solution is provided for (non-) consistent initial conditions. The asymptotic stability is investigated for the solution of weakly nonlinear regular differential systems. Some important conditions are available in Section 4. Section 5 provides a standard linearization technique and the solution of the regular linearized system is provided. Finally, section 6 concludes the paper. Several extensions and interesting fields of research are also provided.

2. Mathematical Background – Elements of Matrix Pencil Theory

This preliminary section introduces some basic concepts and definitions from Matrix Pencil theory those are used throughout the paper.

Definition 2.1 Given $F,G \in \mathbb{C}^{m\times n}$ and an indeterminate s, the matrix pencil $sF-G$ is called regular when $m=n$ and $\det(sF-G)\neq 0$, where 0 is the zero polynomial. In any other case, the pencil will be called singular.

In the case where $sF-G$ is a regular pencil, the elementary divisors of the following type is obtained:

- e.d. of the type s^{π} are called zero finite elementary divisors (**z.e.d.**)
- e.d. of the type $(s-\lambda_j)^p$, $\lambda_j \neq 0$ are called nonzero finite elementary divisors (**nz. f.e.d.**)
- e.d. of the type $\hat{s}^q$ are called infinite elementary divisors (**i.e.d**)

Theorem 2.1 (Gantmacher, 1959) (**complex Weierstrass canonical form**)

For a regular matrix pencil $sF-G$, there exist non singular $\mathbb{C}^{n\times n}$ matrices P and Q such that.

$$PFQ = F_w = \begin{bmatrix} I_p & \mathbb{O}_{p,q} \\ \mathbb{O}_{q,p} & H_q \end{bmatrix} \tag{2.1}$$

$$PGQ = G_w = \begin{bmatrix} J_p & \mathbb{O}_{p,q} \\ \mathbb{O}_{q,p} & I_q \end{bmatrix} \tag{2.2}$$

Then, the complex Weierstrass canonical form $sF_w - Q_w$ of the regular matrix pencil $sF-G$, is given by

$$sF_w - Q_w \triangleq block\ diag\{sI_p - J_p, sH_q - I_q\},$$

where the first normal Jordan type block $sI_p - J_p$ is uniquely defined by the set of f.e.d.

$$(s-\lambda_1)^{p_1}, \ldots (s-\lambda_v)^{p_v},\ \sum_{j=1}^{v} p_j = p$$

of $sF-G$ and has the form $sI_p - J_p \triangleq block\ diag\{sI_{p_1} - J_{p_1}(\lambda_1), \ldots, sI_{p_v} - J_{p_v}(\lambda_v)\}$.

And the q blocks of the second uniquely defined block $sH_q - I_q$ correspond to the i.e.d.

$$(\hat{s})^{q_1}, \ldots, (\hat{s})^{q_\mu},\ \sum_{j=1}^{\mu} q_j = q$$

of $sF-G$ and has the form $sH_q - I_q \triangleq block\ diag\{sH_{q_1} - I_{q_1}, \ldots, sH_{q_\mu} - I_{q_\mu}\}$,

where I_{p_j}, $J_{p_j}(\lambda_j)$, H_{q_j}, are given by (2.3) on the field of $\mathbb{C}$.

$$I_{p_j} = \begin{bmatrix} 1 & 0 & \cdots & 0 \\ 0 & 1 & \cdots & 0 \\ \vdots & \vdots & \ddots & \vdots \\ 0 & 0 & \cdots & 1 \end{bmatrix}_{p_j\times p_j},\ J_{p_i}(\lambda_i) = \begin{bmatrix} \lambda_i & 1 & 0 & \cdots & 0 \\ 0 & \lambda_i & 1 & \cdots & 0 \\ \vdots & \vdots & \ddots & \vdots & \vdots \\ 0 & 0 & 0 & \lambda_i & 1 \\ 0 & 0 & 0 & 0 & \lambda_i \end{bmatrix}_{p_i\times p_i} \text{ and } H_{q_j} = \begin{bmatrix} 0 & 1 & 0 & \cdots & 0 \\ 0 & 0 & 1 & \cdots & 0 \\ \vdots & \vdots & \ddots & \vdots & \vdots \\ 0 & 0 & 0 & 0 & 1 \\ 0 & 0 & 0 & 0 & 0 \end{bmatrix}_{q_j\times q_j} \tag{2.3}$$

the H_{q_j} is a nilpotent matrix of index $q^* = \max\{q_j : j = 1,2,\ldots,\sigma\}$, where

$$H_{q_j}^{q_*^*} = \mathbb{O}. \quad (2.4)$$

3. Solving weakly nonlinear regular differential systems

In this section, we are interested in solving weakly nonlinear regular differential systems by using the matrix pencil approach. However, before we go further, the following definition is necessary to be stated.

Definition 3.1 We shall call $\underline{x}_o$ *a consistent initial condition* for (1.6) at t_o, if there is a differentiable solution to (1.6) defined on some interval $[t_o, t_o + \gamma]$, $\gamma > 0$ such that $\underline{x}(t_o) = \underline{x}_o$, see Campbell (1983).

Consider, now, an electrical circuit which is in use at time $t < t_o$. Moreover, at the exact time t_o, the system has initial condition

$$\underline{x}(t_o^-) = \lim_{t \to t_o^-} \underline{x}(t) \neq \lim_{t \to t_o^+} \underline{x}(t) = \underline{x}(t_o^+),$$

which is profoundly non-consistent with the (new) system. This result is due to the impulse behaviour of the system (1.6) at time t_o, which is translated to an effort to change (almost) instantly, i.e. in zero time, the state of the system in a new initial condition. From mathematical point of view, this approach can be modelled efficiently by using δ-function of Dirac and its derivatives. In this chapter, both cases are considered and discussed. The following lemma divides our initial system (1.6) into two equivalent, lower order differential systems.

Lemma 3.1 System (1.6) is divided into two subsystems

$$\underline{y}_p'(t) = J_p \underline{y}_p(t) + P_{p,n} \underline{f}(t, Q\underline{y}(t)) \quad (3.1)$$

with initial conditions $\underline{y}_p(t_o)$, and

$$H_q \underline{y}_q'(t) = \underline{y}_q(t) + P_{q,n} \underline{f}(t, Q\underline{y}(t)) \quad (3.2)$$

with initial conditions $\underline{y}_q(t_o)$.

Proof. We make the transformation

$$\underline{x}(t) = Q\underline{y}(t). \quad (3.3)$$

Then, the system (1.6) is transformed to

$$FQ\underline{y}'(t) = GQ\underline{y}(t) + \underline{f}(t, Q\underline{y}(t)).$$

Multiplied by left by the nonsingular matrix P, we obtain

$$PFQ\underline{y}'(t) = PGQ\underline{y}(t) + P\underline{f}(t, Q\underline{y}(t)) \Leftrightarrow F_w \underline{y}'(t) = G_w \underline{y}(t) + P\underline{f}(t, Q\underline{y}(t)) \Leftrightarrow$$

$$\begin{bmatrix} I_p & \mathbb{O}_{p,q} \\ \mathbb{O}_{q,p} & H_q \end{bmatrix} \begin{bmatrix} \underline{y}_p'(t) \\ \underline{y}_q'(t) \end{bmatrix} = \begin{bmatrix} J_p & \mathbb{O}_{p,q} \\ \mathbb{O}_{q,p} & I_q \end{bmatrix} \cdot \begin{bmatrix} \underline{y}_p(t) \\ \underline{y}_q(t) \end{bmatrix} + \begin{bmatrix} P_{p,n} \\ P_{q,n} \end{bmatrix} \underline{f}(t, Q\underline{y}(t)).$$

Then, eqs. (3.1) and (3.2) derive.

Now, the initial conditions is obtained

$$\underline{x}(t_o) = Q\underline{y}(t_o) \Leftrightarrow \underline{y}(t_o) = Q^{-1}\underline{x}(t_o).$$

The $\underline{y}(t_0)=\begin{bmatrix}\underline{y}_p(t_0)\\ \underline{y}_q(t_0)\end{bmatrix}$. Thus, the initial conditions for system (3.1) is given by $\underline{y}_p(t_o)$ and for system (3.2) is provided by $\underline{y}_q(t_o)$.

Following the results of Lemma 3.1, the system (1.6) has been divided into two equivalent subsystems (3.1) and (3.2). Contrary to the matrix coefficients of the initial system (1.6), those systems have specified matrix coefficients, i.e. nilpotent, Jordan and identical matrices. This equivalence is very significant, since it provides the appropriate framework for a deeper system's analysis. The following Remarks and Lemmas provide us with the solution of system (1.6) with consistent and non-consistent initial conditions.

Remark 3.1 System (3.1) with initial conditions $\underline{y}_p(t_o)$ can be solved using some classical methods, and

$$\underline{y}_p(t)=e^{J_p(t-t_0)}\underline{y}_p(t_0)+\int_{t_0}^{t}e^{J_p(t-s)}P_{p,n}\underline{f}(s,Q\underline{y}(s))ds\,. \tag{3.4}$$

In this part of the sections, we will solve the subsystem (3.3).

Lemma 3.2 Considering that

$$\underline{y}_q(t_0)=-\sum_{j=0}^{q^*-1}H_q^jP_{q,n}\frac{d^j}{dt^j}\underline{f}(t,Q\underline{y}(t))\bigg|_{t=t_0}\,, \tag{3.5}$$

the solution of subsystem (3.3) is given by

$$\underline{y}_q(t)=-\sum_{j=0}^{q^*-1}H_q^jP_{q,n}\frac{d^j}{dt^j}\underline{f}(t,Q\underline{y}(t))\,. \tag{3.6}$$

Proof. We start by observing that –as is well known– there exists a $q^*\in\mathbb{N}$ such that $H_q^{q^*}=\mathbb{O}$, i.e. the q^* is the annihilation index of H_q. We obtain

$$H_q\underline{y}_q'(t)=\underline{y}_q(t)+P_{q,n}\underline{f}(t,Q\underline{y}(t)) \tag{3.7}$$

whereby differentiating, and multiplying by H_q, we get

$$H_q^2\underline{y}_q''(t)=H_q\underline{y}_q'(t)+H_qP_{q,n}\frac{d}{dt}\underline{f}(t,Q\underline{y}(t)) \tag{3.8}$$

and substituting (3.7) into (3.8), we have

$$H_q^2\underline{y}_q''(t)=\underline{y}_q(t)+P_{q,n}\underline{f}(t,Q\underline{y}(t))+H_qP_{q,n}\frac{d}{dt}\underline{f}(t,Q\underline{y}(t))\,. \tag{3.9}$$

By differentiating and multiplying by H_q again expression (3.9), we obtain

$$H_q^3\underline{y}_q^{(3)}(t)=H_q\underline{y}_q(t)+H_qP_{q,n}\frac{d}{dt}\underline{f}(t,Q\underline{y}(t))+H_q^2P_{q,n}\frac{d^2}{dt^2}\underline{f}(t,Q\underline{y}(t))\,.$$

Repeating this argument a sufficient number of times we end up with

$$H_q^{q^*}\underline{y}_q^{(q^*)}(t)=\underline{y}_q(t)+\sum_{k=0}^{q^*-1}H_q^kP_{q,n}\frac{d^k}{dt^k}\underline{f}(t,Q\underline{y}(t))\,. \tag{3.10}$$

Taking into consideration that $H_q^{q^*}=\mathbb{O}$ and all the other similar relations up to and including (3.10), we arrive at (3.6), where

$$H_q^0 = I_q \text{ and } \frac{d^0}{dt^0}\left(\underline{f}\left(t, Q\underline{y}(t)\right)\right) = \underline{f}\left(t, Q\underline{y}(t)\right).$$

The solution of system (3.2) has consistent initial conditions, since at $t = t_o$, we obtain (3.5). The expression (3.5) is very crucial, since the consistency of the initial conditions is finally satisfied. Thus, a very smooth functional solution is provided.

Remark 3.2 Stepping on the previous results and considering eq. (3.3), the solution of system (1.6) with consistent initial conditions is given by

$$\begin{bmatrix} \underline{y}_p(t) \\ \underline{y}_q(t) \end{bmatrix} = \begin{bmatrix} e^{J_p(t-t_0)}\underline{y}_p(t_o) + \int_{t_0}^{t} e^{J_p(t-s)} P_{p,n}\underline{f}\left(s, Q\underline{y}(s)\right)ds \\ -\sum_{j=0}^{q^*-1} H_q^j P_{q,n} \frac{d^j}{dt^j}\underline{f}\left(t, Q\underline{y}(t)\right) \end{bmatrix}. \tag{3.11}$$

Denote that the matrix $Q = \left[Q_{n,p} \;\; Q_{n,q}\right];\ p + q = n$, then

$$\underline{x}(t) = Q\underline{y}(t) = \left[Q_{n,p} \;\; Q_{n,q}\right]\begin{bmatrix} \underline{y}_p(t) \\ \underline{y}_q(t) \end{bmatrix} = Q_{n,p}\underline{y}_p(t) + Q_{n,q}\underline{y}_q(t) \Leftrightarrow$$

$$\underline{x}(t) = Q_{n,p}e^{J_p(t-t_o)}\underline{y}_p(t_o) + Q_{n,p}\int_{t_0}^{t} e^{J_p(t-s)}P_{p,n}\underline{f}\left(s, Q\underline{y}(s)\right)ds - Q_{n,q}\sum_{j=0}^{q^*-1} H_q^j P_{q,n}\frac{d^j}{dt^j}\underline{f}\left(t, Q\underline{y}(t)\right) \tag{3.12}$$

with initial conditions at time $t = t_o$

$$\underline{x}_0 = Q_{n,p}\underline{y}_p(t_o) - Q_{n,q}\sum_{j=0}^{q^*-1} H_q^j P_{q,n}\frac{d^j}{dt^j}\underline{f}\left(t, Q\underline{y}(t)\right)\Big|_{t=t_0} \Leftrightarrow \underline{x}_0 = Q\begin{bmatrix} \underline{y}_p(t_o) \\ \underline{y}_q(t_o) \end{bmatrix}.$$

Now, we assume that vector function $\underline{f}\left(t, \underline{x}(t)\right)$ is $C^{q^*-1}[0,\infty)$, where q^* is the nilpotent matrix of H_q, see section 2, with the restricted condition that

$$\left.\frac{d^k}{dt^k}\underline{f}\left(t, \underline{x}(t)\right)\right|_{t=t_o} = 0, \text{ and } \underline{x}(t_o) = \underline{0}$$

for all $k = 0,1,...,q^* - 1$. The function $\underline{f}\left(t, \underline{x}(t)\right)$ can be a polynomial of type

$$\underline{f}\left(t, \underline{x}(t)\right) = \sum_{k=2}^{n} a_k(t)\left(\underline{x}(t) - \underline{x}(t_o)\right)^k, \text{ where } n \geq q^* - 1$$

and $a_k(t)$, $k = 2,...,q^* - 1$, are sufficiently differentiable functions of t. Denote also that

$$\left(\underline{x}(t) - \underline{x}(t_o)\right)^k \triangleq \left[\left(x_1(t) - x_1(t_o)\right)^k \;\; \cdots \;\; \left(x_n(t) - x_n(t_o)\right)^k\right]^T.$$

Example 3.1 (Kalogeropoulos et al. 2008a) Consider the dynamic differential system,

$$\dot{x}_2 - \dot{x}_3 + \dot{x}_5 + \dot{x}_6 - x_1 - x_2 + x_3 + x_4 + x_6 + x_7 - x_1^2 = 0$$

$$-\dot{x}_1 - 2\dot{x}_2 + \dot{x}_3 - \dot{x}_5 - \dot{x}_6 + 3x_1 + 4x_2 + 3x_3 - x_4 - 2x_5 - 4x_6 - 5x_7 - x_2^2 - x_4^2 = 0$$

$$\dot{x}_1 - \dot{x}_2 + \dot{x}_3 - \dot{x}_4 - \dot{x}_6 - \dot{x}_7 + x_1 - 2x_2 - x_4 + 2x_5 + x_6 - x_7 - x_4^2 = 0$$

$$-\dot{x}_2 + \dot{x}_3 - \dot{x}_5 - \dot{x}_6 + x_1 + x_2 + x_3 - x_4 - x_6 - 2x_7 - x_6^2 = 0$$

$$-x_3 + x_5 + x_6 - x_5^2 = 0$$

$$\dot{x}_3 - \dot{x}_5 - \dot{x}_6 + x_1 - x_2 - x_3 - x_4 - x_6 - x_7 - x_6^2 = 0$$
$$-\dot{x}_1 - \dot{x}_2 + \dot{x}_6 + 3x_1 + 2x_2 + 3x_3 - x_4 - 2x_5 - 3x_6 - 4x_7 - x_7^2 = 0$$

or in a matrix form, where $\underline{f}(t,\underline{x}(t)) = E\underline{x}^2(t)$, and

$$\textbf{(S)} \qquad F\underline{x}'(t) = G\underline{x}(t) + E\underline{x}^2(t).$$

Note that $\underline{x}^2(t) \triangleq \begin{bmatrix} x_1^2(t) & x_2^2(t) & x_3^2(t) & x_4^2(t) & x_5^2(t) & x_6^2(t) & x_7^2(t) \end{bmatrix}^T$,

with initial condition $\underline{x}(0) = \underline{x}_o = \begin{bmatrix} 0 & 0 & 0 & 0 & 0 & 0 & 0 \end{bmatrix}^T$,

where

$$F = \begin{bmatrix} 0 & 1 & -1 & 0 & 1 & 1 & 0 \\ -1 & -2 & 1 & 0 & -1 & -1 & 0 \\ 1 & -1 & 1 & -1 & 0 & -1 & -1 \\ 0 & -1 & 1 & 0 & -1 & -1 & 0 \\ 0 & 0 & 0 & 0 & 0 & 0 & 0 \\ 0 & 0 & 1 & 0 & -1 & -1 & 0 \\ -1 & -1 & 0 & 0 & 0 & 0 & 1 \end{bmatrix}, \; G = \begin{bmatrix} 1 & 1 & -1 & -1 & 0 & -1 & -1 \\ -3 & -4 & -3 & 1 & 2 & 4 & 5 \\ -1 & 2 & 0 & 1 & -2 & -1 & 1 \\ -1 & -1 & -1 & 1 & 0 & 1 & 2 \\ 0 & 0 & 1 & 0 & -1 & -1 & 0 \\ -1 & 1 & 1 & 1 & 0 & 1 & 1 \\ -3 & -2 & -3 & 1 & 2 & 3 & 4 \end{bmatrix}$$

and

$$E = \begin{bmatrix} 1 & 0 & 0 & 0 & 0 & 0 & 0 \\ 0 & 1 & 0 & 1 & 0 & 0 & 0 \\ 0 & 0 & 0 & 1 & 0 & 0 & 0 \\ 0 & 0 & 0 & 0 & 0 & 1 & 0 \\ 0 & 0 & 0 & 0 & 1 & 0 & 0 \\ 0 & 0 & 0 & 0 & 0 & 1 & 0 \\ 0 & 0 & 0 & 0 & 0 & 0 & 1 \end{bmatrix}.$$

From the regularity of $sF - G$, there exist non singular $\mathbb{C}^{n \times n}$ matrices

$$P = \begin{bmatrix} 0 & 0 & 0 & 1 & 0 & 0 & -1 \\ 1 & 0 & 0 & 0 & 0 & 1 & 0 \\ 0 & -1 & 0 & 1 & 0 & 0 & 1 \\ 1 & 0 & 0 & 1 & 0 & 0 & 0 \\ 0 & 0 & -1 & 0 & 1 & 0 & 0 \\ 0 & 0 & 0 & 0 & 1 & 0 & 0 \\ 0 & 0 & 0 & 0 & 1 & 0 & 0 \end{bmatrix} \text{ and } Q = \begin{bmatrix} 1 & 0 & 0 & 1 & 0 & 0 & -1 \\ 0 & 1 & 0 & 0 & 0 & 0 & 0 \\ 0 & 1 & 0 & 0 & 1 & 1 & 1 \\ 1 & 0 & 1 & 0 & 1 & 1 & 0 \\ 0 & 1 & 1 & 0 & 1 & 0 & 0 \\ 0 & 0 & -1 & 0 & 0 & 1 & 0 \\ 0 & 0 & 0 & 1 & 0 & 0 & 0 \end{bmatrix},$$

such that

$$PFG = F_w = \begin{bmatrix} I_2 & \mathbb{O}_{5,2} \\ \mathbb{O}_{5,2} & H_5 \end{bmatrix}, \text{ and } PGQ = G_w = \begin{bmatrix} J_2(2) & \mathbb{O}_{5,2} \\ \mathbb{O}_{5,2} & I_5 \end{bmatrix},$$

where I_2, $J_2(2)$, H_5 are given by (2.3).

Moreover, taking into consideration the transformation (3.3) for

$$\underline{f}(t,\underline{x}(t)) = E\underline{x}^2(t) = E(Q\underline{y}(t))^2 = \begin{bmatrix} (y_1(t)+y_4(t)-y_7(t))^2 \\ y_2^2(t) \\ (y_2(t)+y_5(t)+y_6(t)+y_7(t))^2 \\ (y_1(t)+y_3(t)+y_5(t)+y_6(t))^2 \\ (y_2(t)+y_3(t)+y_5(t))^2 \\ (-y_3(t)+y_6(t))^2 \\ y_4^2(t) \end{bmatrix}$$

and multiplying by P, then

$$B(t) \triangleq \begin{bmatrix} B_2(t) \\ B_5(t) \end{bmatrix} = \begin{bmatrix} (-y_3(t)+y_6(t))^2 - y_4^2(t) \\ (y_1(t)+y_4(t)-y_7(t))^2 + (-y_3(t)+y_6(t))^2 \\ \\ -y_2^2(t) - (y_1(t)+y_3(t)+y_5(t)+y_6(t))^2 + (-y_3(t)+y_6(t))^2 + y_4^2(t) \\ (y_1(t)+y_4(t)-y_7(t))^2 + (-y_3(t)+y_6(t))^2 \\ -(y_1(t)+y_3(t)+y_5(t)+y_6(t))^2 + (y_2(t)+y_3(t)+y_5(t))^2 \\ (-y_3(t)+y_6(t))^2 \\ (y_2(t)+y_3(t)+y_5(t))^2 \end{bmatrix}.$$

The above system can be divided into the following two subsystems

$$\textbf{(S1)} \quad \underline{y}_2'(t) = \begin{bmatrix} 2 & 1 \\ 0 & 2 \end{bmatrix} \underline{y}_2(t) + B_2(t) \text{ and } \textbf{(S2)} \quad \begin{bmatrix} 0 & 1 & 0 & & \\ 0 & 0 & 1 & & \\ 0 & 0 & 0 & & \\ & & & 0 & 1 \\ & & & 0 & 0 \end{bmatrix} \underline{y}_5'(t) = \underline{y}_5(t) + B_5(t).$$

Now, we consider the initial conditions

$$\underline{y}(0) = Q^{-1}\underline{x}_o = \begin{bmatrix} \underline{y}_2(0) \\ \underline{y}_5(0) \end{bmatrix} = \begin{bmatrix} 0 & 0 & 0 & 0 & 0 & 0 & 0 \end{bmatrix}^T.$$

Note also that

$$Q = \begin{bmatrix} 1 & 0 & 0 & 1 & 0 & 0 & -1 \\ 0 & 1 & 0 & 0 & 0 & 0 & 0 \\ 0 & 1 & 0 & 0 & 1 & 1 & 1 \\ 1 & 0 & 1 & 0 & 1 & 1 & 0 \\ 0 & 1 & 1 & 0 & 1 & 0 & 0 \\ 0 & 0 & -1 & 0 & 0 & 1 & 0 \\ 0 & 0 & 0 & 1 & 0 & 0 & 0 \end{bmatrix} \triangleq \begin{bmatrix} Q_{7,2} & \vdots & Q_{7,5} \end{bmatrix}.$$

Finally, it is not difficult to verify that $H_5^3 = \mathbb{O}_5$, i.e. $q^* = 3$.

According to Remark 3.2, and the relevant expressions, the solution of the system **(S)** is given by

$$\underline{x}(t)=Q_{7,2}\left\{e^{J_2(2)(t-t_o)}\underline{y}_2(0)+\int_0^t e^{J_2(2)(t-s)}B_2(s)ds\right\}-Q_{7,5}\left\{B_5(t)+H_5\frac{d}{dt}B_5(t)+H_5^2\frac{d^2}{dt^2}B_5(t)\right\}$$

or equivalently, if we consider the initial condition then

$$\underline{x}(t)=Q_{7,2}\int_{t_o}^t e^{J_2(2)(t-s)}B_2(s)ds-Q_{7,5}\left\{B_5(t)+H_5\frac{d}{dt}B_5(t)+H_5^2\frac{d^2}{dt^2}B_5(t)\right\}.$$

Up to now, we have considered that system (1.6) has consistent initial conditions. If this assumption eliminated then subsystem (3.2) had non-consistent initial conditions, i.e.

$$\underline{y}_q(t_0)\neq-\sum_{j=0}^{q^*-1}H_q^iP_{q,n}\frac{d^j}{dt^j}f(t,Q\underline{y}(t))\,|_{t=t_0}\,, \tag{3.13}$$

then the solution of (3.2) can be found as follows.

Lemma 3.3 (Kalogeropoulos et al., 2008a) Assume that the condition (3.13) is true. The solution of the system (3.2) is given by

$$\underline{y}_q(t)=-\sum_{j=1}^{q^*-1}\delta^{(j-1)}(t)H_q^j\underline{y}_q(t_o)-\sum_{j=0}^{q^*-1}H_q^jP_{q,n}(\underline{f}*\delta^{(j)})(t)\,, \tag{3.14}$$

where $\underline{f}*\delta^{(j)}$ is the convolution between two functionals

$$(\underline{f}*\delta^{(j)})(t)=\begin{bmatrix}(f_1*\delta^{(j)})(t)\\(f_2*\delta^{(j)})(t)\\\vdots\\(f_n*\delta^{(j)})(t)\end{bmatrix} \tag{3.15}$$

and

$$(f_i*\delta^{(j)})(t)=\int_0^t f_i\left(s,Q\underline{y}(s)\right)\delta^{(j)}(t-s)ds\,, \tag{3.16}$$

where $\delta(t)$ is the Dirac function for every $j=1,2,\ldots,q^*-1$.

Proof. Let us start by observing that the q^* is the annihilation index of H_q. Whereby taking the Laplace transformation of (3.2), the following expression derives

$$H_q\Im\{\underline{y}_q'(t)\}=\Im\{\underline{y}_q(t)\}+P_{q,n}\Im\{\underline{f}(t,Q\underline{y}(t))\}$$

and by defining $\Im\{\underline{y}_q(t)\}=X_q(s)$, $\Im\{y_q'(t)\}=sX_q(s)-\underline{y}_q(t_o)$,

we obtain

$$H_q\left(sX_q(s)-\underline{y}_q(t_o)\right)=X_q(s)+P_{q,n}\Im\{\underline{f}(t,Q\underline{y}(t))\}$$

or equivalently

$$\left(sH_q-I_q\right)X_q(s)=H_q\underline{y}_q(t_o)+P_{q.n}\Im\{\underline{f}(t,Q\underline{y}(t))\}\,. \tag{3.17}$$

Since q^* is the annihilation index of H_q, it is known that $\left(sH_q-I_q\right)^{-1}=-\sum_{j=0}^{q^*-1}\left(sH_q\right)^j$, where $H_q^0=I_q$, see for instance Kalogeropoulos (1985) and Meyer (2001). Thus, substituting the above expression into the (3.17), the following equation is taken

$$X_q(s) = -\sum_{j=0}^{q^*-1}(sH_q)^j H_q \underline{y}_q(t_o) - \sum_{j=0}^{q^*-1}(sH_q)^j P_{q,n}\Im\{\underline{f}(t, Q\underline{y}(t))\} =$$

$$= -\sum_{j=0}^{q^*-1} s^j H_q^{j+1} \underline{y}_q(t_o) - \sum_{j=0}^{q^*-1} s^j H_q^j P_{q,n}\Im\{\underline{f}(t, Q\underline{y}(t))\} =$$

$$= -\left(H_q + sH_q^2 + \ldots + s^{q^*-1}H_q^{q^*}\right)\underline{y}_q(t_o) - \sum_{j=0}^{q^*-1} s^j H_q^j P_{q,n}\Im\{\underline{f}(t, Q\underline{y}(t))\} \ \left(note\ H_q^{q^*} = \mathbb{O}\right) =$$

$$= -\left(H_q + sH_q^2 + \ldots + s^{q^*-2}H_q^{q^*-1}\right)\underline{y}_q(t_o) - \sum_{j=0}^{q^*-1} s^j H_q^j P_{q,n}\Im\{\underline{f}(t, Q\underline{y}(t))\} \Leftrightarrow$$

$$X_q(s) = -\sum_{j=1}^{q^*-1} s^{j-1} H_q^j \underline{y}_q(t_o) - \sum_{j=0}^{q^*-1}(sH_q)^j P_{q,n}\Im\{\underline{f}(t, Q\underline{y}(t))\}. \tag{3.18}$$

Since $\Im\{\delta^{(j)}(t)\} = s^j$, the expression (3.18) is transformed into (3.19)

$$X_q(s) = -\sum_{j=1}^{q^*-1}\Im\{\delta^{(j-1)}(t)\} H_q^j \underline{y}_q(t_o) - \sum_{j=0}^{q^*-1} H_q^j P_{q,n}\Im\{\delta^{(j)}(t)\}\Im\{\underline{f}(t, Q\underline{y}(t))\} \tag{3.19}$$

Now, by applying the inverse Laplace transformation into (3.19), we obtain

$$\Im^{-1}\left(\Im\{\delta^{(j)}(t)\}\Im\{\underline{f}(t, Q\underline{y}(t))\}\right) = \Im^{-1}\left(\Im\{\delta^{(j)}(t)\}\begin{bmatrix}\Im\{f_1(t, Q\underline{y}(t))\}\\ \Im\{f_2(t, Q\underline{y}(t))\}\\ \vdots \\ \Im\{f_n(t, Q\underline{y}(t))\}\end{bmatrix}\right) =$$

$$= \Im^{-1}\left(\begin{bmatrix}\Im\{\delta^{(j)}(t)\}\Im\{f_1(t, Q\underline{y}(t))\}\\ \Im\{\delta^{(j)}(t)\}\Im\{f_2(t, Q\underline{y}(t))\}\\ \vdots \\ \Im\{\delta^{(j)}(t)\}\Im\{f_n(t, Q\underline{y}(t))\}\end{bmatrix}\right) = (\underline{f} * \delta^{(j)})(t).$$

Because

$$\Im^{-1}\left(\Im\{\delta^{(j)}(t)\}\cdot\Im\{f_i(t, Q\underline{y}(t))\}\right) = (f_i * \delta^{(j)})(t) \quad for\ every\ i = 1, 2, \ldots, n.$$

Moreover,

$$\underline{y}_q(t) = -\sum_{j=1}^{q^*-1}\delta^{(j-1)}(t) H_q^j \underline{y}_q(t_o) - \sum_{j=0}^{q^*-1} H_q^j P_{q,n}\left(\underline{f} * \delta^{(j)}\right)(t),$$

where the convolution of the two time function is

$$\left(\underline{f} * \delta^{(j)}\right)(t) \triangleq \begin{bmatrix} \left(f_1 * \delta^{(j)}\right)(t) \\ \left(f_2 * \delta^{(j)}\right)(t) \\ \vdots \\ \left(f_n * \delta^{(j)}\right)(t) \end{bmatrix},$$

and $\left(f_i * \delta^{(j)}\right)(t) = \int_0^t f_i\left(\tau, Q\underline{y}(\tau)\right)\delta^{(j)}(t-\tau)\,d\tau$, for $i = 1,2,\ldots,n$.

Remark 3.3 The solution of system (1.6) is given by (3.21) when the assumption (3.13) is considered.

$$\underline{x}(t) = Q\underline{y}(t) = \left[Q_{n,p}\ Q_{n,q}\right]\begin{bmatrix} \underline{y}_p(t) \\ \underline{y}_q(t) \end{bmatrix} \Leftrightarrow \underline{x}(t) = Q_{n,p}e^{J_p(t-t_o)}\underline{y}_p(t_0) +$$

$$\int_{t_0}^{t} Q_{n,p}e^{J_p(t-s)}P_{p,n}\underline{f}\left(s, Q\underline{y}(s)\right)ds - Q_{n,q}\sum_{j=1}^{q^*-1}\delta^{(j-1)}(t)H_q^j\underline{y}_q(t_o) - Q_{n,q}\sum_{j=0}^{q^*-1}H_q^jP_{q,n}(\underline{f} * \delta^{(j)})(t) \quad (3.21)$$

In the next section, the asymptotic stability of systems (1.6) with consistent initial condition is considered.

4. The asymptotic stability of weakly nonlinear regular differential systems

In the beginning of this section, some fundamental elements of asymptotic stability are introduced and discussed.

Definition 4.1 Considering a system of ordinary differential equations, then the solution $\underline{x}(t)$ is asymptotically stable (see figure 3) if for every other solution $\underline{\tilde{x}}(t)$, the following condition is satisfied

$$\lim_{t\to+\infty}\left\|\underline{x}(t) - \underline{\tilde{x}}(t)\right\| = 0.$$

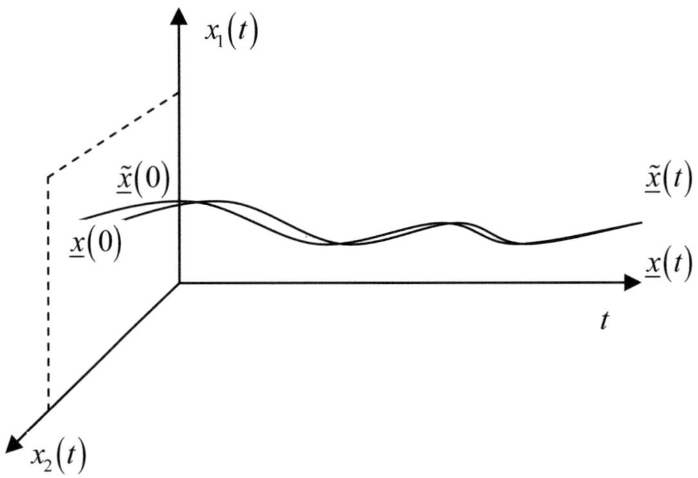

Fig. 3. The asymptotic stability of two-dimension vector $\underline{x}(t)$

Consequently, some elements of norms for rectangular matrices are needed.

Definition 4.2 Consider the function $v:\mathbb{C}^{m\times n}\to\mathbb{R}$ which is called norm in the space $\mathbb{C}^{m\times n}$ or matrix norm, if the following conditions are satisfied simultaneously.

1. $A\neq\mathbb{O}\Rightarrow v(A)>0$

2. $v(\alpha A)=|\alpha|v(A)$

3. $v(A+B)\leq v(A)+v(B)$

Definition 4.3 The matrix $A\in\mathbb{C}^{m\times n}$. Denote the **Frobenius** norm of matrix A,

$$\|A\|_F=\sqrt{\sum_{i=1}^{m}\sum_{j=1}^{n}|\alpha_{ij}|^2}=trace(A^HA)^{1/2} \tag{4.1}$$

where $A^H=\left(\overline{A}\right)^t$ (the conjugate transpose of matrix A).

Remark 4.1 The Frobenius norm has a significant property, which does not appear in other norms for rectangular matrices. Analytically, consider the matrices $A\in\mathbb{C}^{m\times p}$ and $B\in\mathbb{C}^{p\times n}$ then

$$\|A\cdot B\|_F\leq\|A\|_F\cdot\|B\|_F \tag{4.2}$$

In the next lines of this chapter, we are using the Frobenius norm. If contrary, it will be mentioned. First, we consider the asymptotic stability of system (1.6) with consistent initial conditions. Thus, we assume that $\underline{\tilde{x}}(t)$ is a different solution of system (1.6) with the initial conditions $\underline{\tilde{x}}(t_o)=\underline{\tilde{x}}_o$, and

$$\underline{\tilde{x}}(t)=Q\underline{\tilde{y}}(t)=Q\begin{bmatrix}\underline{\tilde{y}}_p(t)\\ \underline{\tilde{y}}_q(t)\end{bmatrix}.$$

Following the results of section 3, the solution of (1.6) is given by

$$\underline{\tilde{x}}(t)=Q_{n,p}e^{J_p(t-t_o)}\underline{\tilde{y}}_p(t_o)+Q_{n,p}\int_{t_0}^{t}e^{J_p(t-s)}P_{p,n}\underline{f}\left(s,Q\underline{\tilde{y}}(s)\right)ds-Q_{n,q}\sum_{j=0}^{q^*-1}H_q^jP_{q,n}\frac{d^j}{dt^j}\left(\underline{f}(t,Q\underline{\tilde{y}}(t))\right).$$

Moreover, we obtain

$$\|\underline{x}(t)-\underline{\tilde{x}}(t)\|=\Big\|Q_{n,p}e^{J_p(t-t_o)}\left(\underline{y}_p(t_o)-\underline{\tilde{y}}_p(t_o)\right)+Q_{n,p}\int_{t_0}^{t}e^{J_p(t-s)}P_{p,n}\left(\underline{f}(s,Q\underline{y}(s))-\underline{f}(s,Q\underline{\tilde{y}}(s)\right)ds$$
$$-Q_{n,q}\sum_{j=0}^{q^*-1}H_q^jP_{q,n}\left(\frac{d^j}{dt^j}\left(\underline{f}(t,Q\underline{y}(t))-\underline{f}(t,Q\underline{\tilde{y}}(t))\right)\right)\Big\|.$$

Afterwards, using some properties for norms and the eq. (4.2), we obtain

$$\|\underline{x}(t)-\underline{\tilde{x}}(t)\|\leq\|Q_{n,p}\|\cdot\|e^{J_p(t-t_o)}\|\cdot\|\underline{y}_p(t_0)-\underline{\tilde{y}}_p(t_0)\|$$
$$+\|Q_{n,p}\|\cdot\int_{t_0}^{t}\|e^{J_p(t-s)}\|\cdot\|P_{p,n}\|\cdot\left\|\underline{f}(s,Q\underline{y}(s))-\underline{f}(s,Q\underline{\tilde{y}}(s))\right\|ds$$
$$+\|Q_{n,q}\|\cdot\sum_{j=0}^{q^*-1}\|H_q^j\|\cdot\|P_{q,n}\|\cdot\left\|\frac{d^j}{dt^j}\left(\underline{f}(t,Q\underline{y}(t))-\underline{f}(t,Q\underline{\tilde{y}}(t))\right)\right\|. \tag{4.3}$$

Continuing the section, some significant Lemmas are proven. These results are consequence of important properties of norm.

Lemma 4.1 The following inequality holds

$$\left\|e^{J_p(t-t_0)}\right\| \le \sum_{i=1}^{\nu}\left(e^{\lambda_i(t-t_0)}\left(\sum_{j=0}^{p_i-1}(p_i-j)\frac{\left|(t-t_0)^{2j}\right|}{\left|(j!)^2\right|}\right)^{1/2}\right). \tag{4.4}$$

Proof. Since, we have used the Frobenius norm, we have

$$e^{J_p(t-t_0)} = block\ diag\left\{e^{J_{p_1}(\alpha_1)(t-t_0)}, \ldots, e^{J_{p_\nu}(\alpha_\nu)(t-t_0)}\right\}$$

where

$$e^{J_{p_i}(\alpha_i)(t-t_0)} = \begin{bmatrix} e^{\alpha_i(t-t_0)} & e^{\alpha_i(t-t_0)}(t-t_0) & e^{\alpha_i(t-t_0)}\frac{(t-t_0)^2}{2!} & \cdots & e^{\alpha_i(t-t_0)}\frac{(t-t_0)^{p_i}}{p_i!} \\ & e^{\alpha_i(t-t_0)} & & & e^{\alpha_i(t-t_0)}\frac{(t-t_0)^{p_i-1}}{(p_i-1)!} \\ & & \ddots & & \\ \mathbb{O} & & & & e^{\alpha_i(t-t_0)} \end{bmatrix}_{p_i\times p_i}$$

for every $i = 1, \ldots, \nu$. Thus

$$\left\|e^{J_p(t-t_0)}\right\| = \left(\sum_{i=1}^{\nu}\sum_{j=0}^{p_i-1}(p_i-j)\left|e^{\alpha_i(t-t_0)}\frac{(t-t_0)^j}{j!}\right|^2\right)^{1/2} = \left(\sum_{i=1}^{\nu}\left(\left|e^{2\alpha_i(t-t_0)}\right|\sum_{j=0}^{p_i-1}(p_i-j)\left|\frac{(t-t_0)^{2j}}{(j!)^2}\right|\right)\right)^{1/2} =$$

$$= \left(\left|e^{2\alpha_1(t-t_0)}\right|\sum_{j=0}^{p_1-1}(p_1-j)\left|\frac{(t-t_0)^{2j}}{(j!)^2}\right| + \ldots + \left|e^{2\alpha_\nu(t-t_0)}\right|\sum_{j=0}^{p_\nu-1}\frac{\left|(t-t_0)^{2j}\right|}{\left|(j!)^2\right|}\right)^{1/2} \le$$

$$\le \left|e^{2\alpha_1(t-t_0)}\right|^{1/2}\left(\sum_{j=0}^{p_1-1}(p_1-j)\frac{\left|(t-t_0)^{2j}\right|}{\left|(j!)^2\right|}\right)^{1/2} + \ldots + \left|e^{2\alpha_\nu(t-t_0)}\right|^{1/2}\left(\sum_{j=0}^{p_\nu-1}(p_\nu-j)\frac{\left|(t-t_0)^{2j}\right|}{\left|(j!)^2\right|}\right)^{1/2} =$$

(The inequality is due to the expression $\sqrt{x+y} \le \sqrt{x} + \sqrt{y}$)

$$= \left|e^{\alpha_1(t-t_0)}\right|\left(\sum_{j=0}^{p_1-1}(p_1-j)\frac{\left|(t-t_0)^{2j}\right|}{\left|(j!)^2\right|}\right)^{1/2} + \ldots + \left|e^{\alpha_\nu(t-t_0)}\right|\left(\sum_{j=0}^{p_\nu-1}(p_\nu-j)\frac{\left|(t-t_0)^{2j}\right|}{\left|(j!)^2\right|}\right)^{1/2}.$$

The factor $e^{\alpha_i(t-t_0)} = e^{(\lambda_i+\theta m_i)(t-t_0)}$, where $a_i = \lambda_i + \theta m_i$, $\theta^2 = -1$ (the imagine unit) and λ_i, $m_i \in \mathbb{R}$ for every $i = 1, 2, \ldots, \nu$. Then,

$$e^{\alpha_i(t-t_0)} = e^{\lambda_i(t-t_0)}e^{\theta m_i(t-t_0)} = e^{\lambda_i(t-t_0)}\left(\cos\left(m_i(t-t_0)\right) + \theta\sin\left(m_i(t-t_0)\right)\right),$$

for every $i = 1, 2, \ldots, \nu$. Thus

$$\left|e^{\alpha_i(t-t_0)}\right| = \left|e^{\lambda_i(t-t_0)}\right|\left|\cos\left(m_i(t-t_0)\right) + \theta\sin\left(m_i(t-t_0)\right)\right| = e^{\lambda_i(t-t_0)}\cdot 1 = e^{\lambda_i(t-t_0)}$$

for every $i = 1, 2, \ldots, \nu$. Consequently,

$$\left\|e^{J_p(t-t_0)}\right\| \le e^{\lambda_1(t-t_0)}\left(\sum_{j=0}^{p_1-1}(p_1-j)\frac{\left|(t-t_0)^{2j}\right|}{\left|(j!)^2\right|}\right)^{1/2} + \ldots + e^{\lambda_\nu(t-t_0)}\left(\sum_{j=0}^{p_\nu-1}(p_\nu-j)\frac{\left|(t-t_0)^{2j}\right|}{\left|(j!)^2\right|}\right)^{1/2} \Leftrightarrow$$

$$\Leftrightarrow \left\| e^{J_p(t-t_0)} \right\| \leq \sum_{i=1}^{\nu} \left(e^{\lambda_i(t-t_0)} \left(\sum_{j=0}^{p_i-1} (p_i - j) \frac{\left|(t-t_0)^{2j}\right|}{\left|(j!)^2\right|} \right)^{1/2} \right).$$

Remark 4.2 Considering the results of Lemma 4.1, we obtain

$$\left\| e^{J_p(t-s)} \right\| \leq \sum_{i=1}^{\nu} \left(e^{\lambda_i(t-s)} \left(\sum_{j=0}^{p_i-1} (p_i - j) \frac{\left|(t-s)^{2j}\right|}{\left|(j!)^2\right|} \right)^{1/2} \right) \tag{4.5}$$

with $t_0 \leq s \leq t$.

Remark 4.3 Assuming, now, that $t \geq t_0$ and $s \in [t_0, t]$, then the (4.4) and (4.5) are transposed to the following expressions, respectively

$$\left\| e^{J_p(t-t_0)} \right\| \leq \sum_{i=1}^{\nu} \left(e^{\lambda_i(t-t_0)} \left(\sum_{j=0}^{p_i-1} (p_i - j) \frac{(t-t_0)^{2j}}{(j!)^2} \right)^{1/2} \right), \tag{4.6}$$

and

$$\left\| e^{J_p(t-s)} \right\| \leq \sum_{i=1}^{\nu} \left(e^{\lambda_i(t-s)} \left(\sum_{j=0}^{p_i-1} (p_i - j) \frac{(t-s)^{2j}}{(j!)^2} \right)^{1/2} \right). \tag{4.7}$$

Furthermore, using the above two expressions, the eq. (4.3) is benefited as following

$$\left\| \underline{x}(t) - \underline{\tilde{x}}(t) \right\| \leq \left\| Q_{n,p} \right\| \cdot \sum_{i=1}^{\nu} \left(e^{\lambda_i(t-t_0)} \left(\sum_{j=0}^{p_i-1} (p_i - j) \frac{(t-t_0)^{2j}}{(j!)^2} \right)^{1/2} \right) \cdot \left\| \underline{y}_p(t_0) - \underline{\tilde{y}}_p(t_0) \right\| +$$

$$+ \left\| Q_{n,p} \right\| \cdot \int_{t_0}^{t} \sum_{i=1}^{\nu} \left(e^{\lambda_i(t-s)} \left(\sum_{j=0}^{p_i-1} (p_i - j) \frac{(t-s)^{2j}}{(j!)^2} \right)^{\frac{1}{2}} \right) \cdot \left\| P_{p,n} \right\| \cdot \left\| \underline{f}\left(s, Q\underline{y}(s)\right) - \underline{f}\left(s, Q\underline{\tilde{y}}(s)\right) \right\| ds +$$

$$+ \left\| Q_{n,q} \right\| \cdot \sum_{j=0}^{q^*-1} \left\| H_q^j \right\| \cdot \left\| P_{q,n} \right\| \cdot \left\| \frac{d^j}{dt^j} \left(\underline{f}\left(t, Q\underline{y}(t)\right) - \underline{f}\left(t, Q\underline{\tilde{y}}(t)\right) \right) \right\|. \tag{4.8}$$

Remark 4.3 Looking beyond the lines, the eq. (4.8) says clearly that if $\underline{f}(t, \underline{x}(t))$ is an arbitrary vector function then the asymptotic stability is not obtained. Thus, our main target is to determine the necessary conditions such as the asymptotic stability derives for system (1.6). Consequently, the following properties are taken. Note that these properties are quite general.

(i) $$\lambda_i < 0 \text{ for every } i = 1, 2, \ldots, \nu. \tag{4.9}$$

(ii) $$\left\| \underline{f}(t, \underline{x}_1(t)) - \underline{f}(t, \underline{x}_2(t)) \right\| \leq \Pi(t), \tag{4.10}$$

where $\Pi(t) = \sum_{\kappa=1}^{\sigma} \beta_\kappa t^{\gamma_\kappa}$ with $\beta_\kappa \in \mathbb{R}$ (or $\mathbb{C}$) και $\gamma_\kappa \in \mathbb{R}$, γ_κ = finite for every $\kappa = 1,\ldots,\sigma$ and σ = finite for every $\underline{x}_1(t), \underline{x}_2(t) \in \mathbb{R}^n$ (or $\mathbb{C}^n$) and every $t \geq t_0$.

(iii) $$\lim_{t \to \infty} \left\| \frac{d^j}{dt^j} \left(\underline{f}(t, \underline{x}_1(t)) - \underline{f}(t, \underline{x}_2(t)) \right) \right\| = 0, \tag{4.11}$$

for every $\underline{x}_1(t), \underline{x}_2(t) \in \mathbb{R}^n$ (or $\mathbb{C}^n$).

Lemma 4.2

$$\int_{t_0}^{t}\sum_{i=1}^{\nu}\left(e^{\lambda_i(t-s)}\left(\sum_{j=0}^{p_i-1}(p_i-j)\frac{(t-s)^{2j}}{(j!)^2}\right)^{1/2}\right)\cdot\left\|P_{q,n}\right\|\cdot\left\|\underline{f}\left(s,Q\underline{y}(s)\right)-\underline{f}\left(s,Q\underline{\tilde{y}}(s)\right)\right\|ds\le$$

$$\le\left\|P_{q,n}\right\|\cdot\sum_{i=1}^{\nu}e^{\lambda_i(t-t_0)}\left(\sum_{j=0}^{p_i-1}(p_i-j)\frac{(t-t_0)^{2j}}{(j!)^2}\right)^{1/2}\cdot\int_{t_0}^{t}\Pi(s)ds\,. \tag{4.12}$$

Proof. It is known that both $e^{\lambda_i(t-s)}$ when $\lambda_i<0$ and $\sum_{j=0}^{p_i-1}(p_i-j)\frac{(t-s)^{2j}}{(j!)^2}$ when s ∈ [t₀ , t] are decreasing functions. Thus,

$$e^{\lambda_i(t-s)}\le e^{\lambda_i(t-t_0)}\quad\text{and}\quad\sum_{j=0}^{p_i-1}(p_i-j)\frac{(t-s)^{2j}}{(j!)^2}\le\sum_{j=0}^{p_i-1}(p_i-j)\frac{(t-t_0)^{2j}}{(j!)^2}.$$

Moreover, we have that if the inequality $f(x)\le g(x)$ exists and $\Pi(x)$ is a positive function, then

$$f(x)\Pi(x)\le g(x)\Pi(x)\Rightarrow\int_{\alpha}^{\beta}f(x)\Pi(x)dx\le\int_{\alpha}^{\beta}g(x)\Pi(x)dx\,.$$

Consequently,

$$\int_{t_0}^{t}\sum_{i=1}^{\nu}\left(e^{\lambda_i(t-s)}\left(\sum_{j=0}^{p_i-1}(p_i-j)\frac{(t-s)^{2j}}{(j!)^2}\right)^{1/2}\right)\cdot\left\|P_{q,n}\right\|\cdot\left\|\underline{f}\left(s,Q\underline{y}(s)\right)-\underline{f}\left(s,Q\underline{\tilde{y}}(s)\right)\right\|ds\le$$

$$\le\int_{t_0}^{t}\sum_{i=1}^{\nu}\left(e^{\lambda_i(t-s)}\left(\sum_{j=0}^{p_i-1}(p_i-j)\frac{(t-s)^{2j}}{(j!)^2}\right)^{1/2}\right)\cdot\left\|P_{q,n}\right\|\cdot\Pi(s)ds\le$$

$$\le\left\|P_{q,n}\right\|\cdot\int_{t_0}^{t}\sum_{i=1}^{\nu}\left(e^{\lambda_i(t-t_0)}\left(\sum_{j=0}^{p_i-1}(p_i-j)\frac{(t-t_0)^{2j}}{(j!)^2}\right)^{1/2}\right)\Pi(s)ds=$$

$$=\left\|P_{q,n}\right\|\cdot\sum_{i=1}^{\nu}\left(e^{\lambda_i(t-t_0)}\left(\sum_{j=0}^{p_i-1}(p_i-j)\frac{(t-t_0)^{2j}}{(j!)^2}\right)^{1/2}\right)\cdot\int_{t_0}^{t}\Pi(s)ds.$$

Using the results of Lemma 4.2, the eqs (4.9) and (4.10), the condition (4.8) is transformed to the following.

$$\left\|\underline{x}(t)-\underline{\tilde{x}}(t)\right\|\le\left\|Q_{n,p}\right\|\cdot\sum_{i=1}^{\nu}\left(e^{\lambda_i(t-t_0)}\left(\sum_{j=0}^{p_i-1}(p_i-j)\frac{(t-t_0)^{2j}}{(j!)^2}\right)^{1/2}\right)\cdot\left\|\underline{y}_p(t_0)-\underline{\tilde{y}}_p(t_0)\right\|+$$

$$+\left\|Q_{n,p}\right\|\cdot\left\|P_{q,n}\right\|\cdot\sum_{i=1}^{\nu}\left(e^{\lambda_i(t-t_0)}\left(\sum_{j=0}^{p_i-1}(p_i-j)\frac{(t-t_0)^{2j}}{(j!)^2}\right)^{1/2}\right)\cdot\int_{t_0}^{t}\Pi(s)ds+$$

$$+\left\|Q_{n,q}\right\|\cdot\sum_{j=0}^{q^*-1}\left\|H_q^i\right\|\cdot\left\|P_{q,n}\right\|\cdot\left\|\frac{d^j}{dt^j}\left(\underline{f}\left(t,Q\underline{y}(t)\right)-\underline{f}\left(t,Q\underline{\tilde{y}}(t)\right)\right)\right\|=$$

$$=\left\|Q_{n,p}\right\|\cdot\sum_{i=1}^{\nu}\left(e^{\lambda_i(t-t_0)}\left(\sum_{j=0}^{p_i-1}(p_i-j)\frac{(t-t_0)^{2j}}{(j!)^2}\right)^{1/2}\right)\left[\left\|\underline{y}_p(t_0)-\underline{\tilde{y}}_p(t_0)\right\|+\left\|P_{q,n}\right\|\cdot\int_{t_0}^{t}\Pi(s)ds\right]+$$

$$+\left\|Q_{n,q}\right\|\cdot\sum_{j=0}^{q^*-1}\left(\left\|H_q^j\right\|\cdot\left\|P_{q,n}\right\|\cdot\left\|\frac{d^j}{dt^j}\left(\underline{f}\left(t,Q\underline{y}(t)\right)-\underline{f}\left(t,Q\underline{\tilde{y}}(t)\right)\right)\right\|\right). \tag{4.13}$$

Lemma 4.3 Consider that $\lambda < 0$ and $\theta(t)=\sum_{\kappa=1}^{\mu} d_{\kappa} t^{c_{\kappa}}$ with $c_{\kappa} \in \mathbb{R}$ (finite real powers) for every $\kappa = 1,\ldots,\mu$ and $d_{\kappa} \in \mathbb{R}$, with finite μ, then $\lim_{t\to\infty}(e^{\lambda t}\theta(t))=0$.

Proof. Calculating the $\lim_{t\to+\infty}(e^{\lambda t}t^{c})$ with $\lambda < 0$, and c finite, then using c-times De L' Hospital law, we take

$$\lim_{t\to+\infty}(e^{\lambda t}t^{c})=0.$$

A straightforward generalization of the above result is given below

$$\lim_{t\to+\infty}\left(e^{\lambda t}\theta(t)\right)=0.$$

Remark 4.4 The factor, which is included in eq. (4.13),

$$\left(\sum_{j=0}^{p_i-1}(p_i-j)\frac{(t-t_0)^{2j}}{(j!)^2}\right)^{1/2}\left[\left\|\underline{y}_p(t_0)-\underline{\tilde{y}}_p(t_0)\right\|+\left\|P_{q,n}\right\|\cdot\int_{t_0}^{t}\Pi(s)ds\right]\triangleq\Delta(t)$$

where $\Delta(t)$ is constructed equivalently to $\Pi(t)$, has a greatest power index

$$p_i-1+\gamma_{\kappa}+1=p_i+\gamma_{\kappa}.$$

Following the results of Lemma 4.3

$$\lim_{t\to+\infty}\left(e^{\lambda_i(t-t_0)}\Delta(t)\right)=0.$$

Proposition 4.1 The solution of system (1.6) with *consistent* initial conditions is asymptotically stable when expressions (4.9), (4.10) and (4.11) exist simultaneously.

Proof. Considering the eq. (4.13), the Remark 4.4 and the condition (4.11), we have

$$\lim_{t\to+\infty}\left\|\underline{x}(t)-\underline{\tilde{x}}(t)\right\|\leq\lim_{t\to+\infty}\left[\left\|Q_{n,p}\right\|\cdot\sum_{i=1}^{\nu}e^{\lambda_i(t-t_0)}\Delta(t)+\right.$$

$$\left.+\left\|Q_{n,q}\right\|\cdot\sum_{j=0}^{q^*-1}\left\|H_q^j\right\|\cdot\left\|P_{q,n}\right\|\cdot\left\|\frac{d^j}{dt^j}\left(\underline{f}\left(t,Q\underline{y}(t)\right)-\underline{f}\left(t,Q\underline{\tilde{y}}(t)\right)\right)\right\|\right]=$$

$$=\left\|Q_{n,p}\right\|\cdot\sum_{i=1}^{\nu}\lim_{t\to+\infty}\left(e^{\lambda_i(t-t_0)}\Delta(t)\right)+\left\|Q_{n,q}\right\|\cdot\left\|P_{q,n}\right\|\cdot\sum_{j=0}^{q^*-1}\left(\left\|H_q^j\right\|\cdot\left(\lim_{t\to+\infty}\left\|\frac{d^j}{dt^j}\left(\underline{f}\left(t,Q\underline{y}(t)\right)-\underline{f}\left(t,Q\underline{\tilde{y}}(t)\right)\right)\right\|\right)\right)=$$

$$=\left\|Q_{n,p}\right\|\cdot 0+\left\|Q_{n,q}\right\|\cdot\left\|P_{q,n}\right\|\cdot 0=0.$$

Thus

$$\lim_{t\to+\infty}\left\|\underline{x}(t)-\underline{\tilde{x}}(t)\right\|=0.$$

Afterwards, in this part of the section, the asymptotic stability when the system (1.6) has non-consistent initial conditions is studied. The solution of the system (1.6), as we have already seen in Remark 3.3, is given by

$$\underline{x}(t)=Q_{n,p}e^{J_p(t-t_0)}\underline{y}_p(t_0)+\int_{t_0}^{t}Q_{n,p}e^{J_p(t-s)}P_{p,n}\underline{f}\left(s,Q\underline{y}(s)\right)ds-$$

$$-Q_{n,q}\sum_{j=1}^{q^*-1}\delta^{(j-1)}(t)H_q^j\underline{y}_q(t_0)-Q_{n,q}\sum_{j=0}^{q^*-1}H_q^jP_{q,n}(\underline{f}*\delta^{(j)})(t).$$

We take a different second solution $\underline{\tilde{x}}(t)$ of the system (1.6). Then

$$\underline{\tilde{x}}(t)=Q_{n,p}e^{J_p(t-t_0)}\underline{\tilde{y}}_p(t_0)+\int_{t_0}^{t}Q_{n,p}e^{J_p(t-s)}P_{p,n}\underline{f}\left(s,Q\underline{\tilde{y}}(s)\right)ds-$$

$$-Q_{n,q}\sum_{j=1}^{q^*-1}\delta^{(j-1)}(t)H_q^j\underline{\tilde{y}}_q(t_0)-Q_{n,q}\sum_{j=0}^{q^*-1}H_q^jP_{q,n}(\underline{\tilde{f}}*\delta^{(j)})(t). \tag{4.14}$$

Remark 4.5 The

$$(\underline{\tilde{f}}*\delta^{(j)})(t)=\begin{bmatrix}(\tilde{f}_1*\delta^{(j)})(t)\\(\tilde{f}_2*\delta^{(j)})(t)\\\vdots\\(\tilde{f}_n*\delta^{(j)})(t)\end{bmatrix}$$

and

$$(\tilde{f}_i*\delta^{(j)})(t)=\int_0^t f_i\left(s,Q\underline{\tilde{y}}(s)\right)\cdot\delta^{(j)}(t-s)ds\,. \tag{4.15}$$

The factor $\underline{\tilde{f}}$ is indifferent to $\underline{f}$, since $\underline{\tilde{f}}$ depends on $\underline{\tilde{y}}(s)$ while $\underline{f}$ on $\underline{y}(s)$. Moreover, we are interested on the difference

$$\|\underline{x}(t)-\underline{\tilde{x}}(t)\|=$$

$$=\Big\|Q_{n,p}e^{J_p(t-t_0)}\left(\underline{y}_p(t_0)-\underline{\tilde{y}}_p(t_0)\right)+\int_{t_0}^t Q_{n,p}e^{J_p(t-s)}P_{p,n}\left[\underline{f}\left(s,Q\underline{y}(s)\right)-\underline{f}\left(s,Q\underline{\tilde{y}}(s)\right)\right]ds-$$

$$-Q_{n,q}\sum_{j=1}^{q^*-1}\delta^{(j-1)}(t)H_q^j\left[\underline{y}_q(t_0)-\underline{\tilde{y}}_q(t_0)\right]-Q_{n,q}\sum_{j=0}^{q^*-1}H_q^jP_{q,n}\left((\underline{f}*\delta^{(j)})(t)-(\underline{\tilde{f}}*\delta^{(j)})(t)\right)\Big\|\,. \tag{4.16}$$

Considering some basic properties of Frobenius norm, we obtain

$$\|\underline{x}(t)-\underline{\tilde{x}}(t)\|\le\|Q_{n,p}\|\cdot\|e^{J_p(t-t_0)}\|\cdot\|\underline{y}_p(t_0)-\underline{\tilde{y}}_p(t_0)\|+$$

$$+\int_{t_0}^t\|Q_{n,p}\|\cdot\|e^{J_p(t-s)}\|\cdot\|P_{p,n}\|\cdot\left\|\underline{f}\left(s,Q\underline{y}(s)\right)-\underline{f}\left(s,Q\underline{\tilde{y}}(s)\right)\right\|ds+$$

$$+\|Q_{n,q}\|\cdot\sum_{j=1}^{q^*-1}|\delta^{(j-1)}(t)|\cdot\|H_q^j\|\cdot\|\underline{y}_q(t_0)-\underline{\tilde{y}}_q(t_0)\|+\|Q_{n,q}\|\cdot\sum_{j=0}^{q^*-1}\|H_q^j\|\cdot\|P_{q,n}\|\cdot\|(\underline{f}*\delta^{(j)})(t)-(\underline{\tilde{f}}*\delta^{(j)})(t)\|.$$

In order to find the $\lim_{t\to\infty}\|\underline{x}(t)-\underline{\tilde{x}}(t)\|$, the following Lemmas are significant.

Lemma 4.4

$$\|(\underline{f}*\delta^{(j)})(t)-(\underline{\tilde{f}}*\delta^{(j)})(t)\|=\left(\sum_{i=1}^n\left|\int_0^t\left[f_i\left(s,Q\underline{y}(s)\right)-f_i\left(s,Q\underline{\tilde{y}}(s)\right)\right]\delta^{(j)}(t-s)ds\right|^2\right)^{1/2}. \tag{4.17}$$

Proof. It is easy to verify that

$$\|(\underline{f}*\delta^{(j)})(t)-(\underline{\tilde{f}}*\delta^{(j)})(t)\|=\left\|\begin{bmatrix}\int_0^t\left[f_1\left(s,Q\underline{y}(s)\right)-f_1\left(s,Q\underline{\tilde{y}}(s)\right)\right]\delta^{(j)}(t-s)ds\\\vdots\\\int_0^t\left[f_n\left(s,Q\underline{y}(s)\right)-f_n\left(s,Q\underline{\tilde{y}}(s)\right)\right]\delta^{(j)}(t-s)ds\end{bmatrix}\right\|=$$

$$=\left(\sum_{i=1}^n\left|\int_0^t\left[f_i\left(s,Q\underline{y}(s)\right)-f_i\left(s,Q\underline{\tilde{y}}(s)\right)\right]\cdot\delta^{(j)}(t-s)ds\right|^2\right)^{1/2}.$$

Denote that

$$f_i\left(s,Q\underline{y}(s)\right)-f_i\left(s,Q\underline{\tilde{y}}(s)\right)=R_i(s) \tag{4.18}$$

where $R_i(s)$ is a function which is n-times differentiable in $[0, +\infty)$.

Lemma 4.5
$$\int_0^t R_i(s)\delta^{(j)}(t-s)ds = -\left(R_i^{(j)}(t) + \sum_{\kappa=1}^{j} R_i^{(\kappa-1)}(t)\delta^{(j-\kappa)}(0)\right). \tag{4.19}$$

Proof. We have
$$\int_0^t R_i(s)\delta^{(j)}(t-s)ds = \left[R_i(s)(-1)\delta^{(j-1)}(t-s)\right]_0^t - \int_0^t R_i'(s)(-1)\delta^{(j-1)}(t-s)ds =$$
$$= -R_i(t)\delta^{(j-1)}(0) + R_i(0)\delta^{(j-1)}(t) + \int_0^t R_i'(s)\delta^{(j-1)}(t-s)ds.$$
However, for $t \neq 0$, $\delta(t) = 0$, and $\delta^{(j-1)}(t) = 0$. Consequently, we obtain
$$\int_0^t R_i(s)\delta^{(j)}(t-s)ds = -R_i(t)\delta^{(j-1)}(0) + \int_0^t R_i'(s)\delta^{(j-1)}(t-s)ds.$$
Continuing as above, we have
$$\int_0^t R_i(s)\delta^{(j)}(t-s)ds = -R_i(t)\delta^{(j-1)}(0) - R_i^{(1)}(t)\delta^{(j-2)}(0) - R_i^{(2)}(t)\delta^{(j-3)}(0) - \ldots -$$
$$- R_i^{(j-1)}(t)\delta(0) + \int_0^t R_i^{(j)}(s)\delta(t-s)ds.$$
Since $\int_0^t R_i^{(j)}(s)\delta(t-s)ds = -R_i^{(j)}(t)$. We finally take
$$\int_0^t R_i(s)\delta^{(j)}(t-s)ds = -\sum_{\kappa=1}^{j} R_i^{(\kappa-1)}(t)\delta^{(j-\kappa)}(0) - R_i^{(j)}(t).$$

Remark 4.6 Since the eq. (4.19) includes the elements $\delta^{(j-\kappa)}(0)$ for every $\kappa = 1, 2, \ldots, j$, then the $\lim_{t\to+\infty} \int_0^t R_i(s)\delta^{(j)}(t-s)ds$ is not zero. Thus, we have
$$\lim_{t\to+\infty} \left\|\underline{x}(t) - \underline{\tilde{x}}(t)\right\| \neq 0.$$
Therefore, the solution of system (1.6) with non-consistent initial conditions is not asymptotically stable.
However, under the following assumptions, we can have asymptotic stability.

1. The real parts of finite elementary divisors of matrix pencil $sF - G$ are negative numbers, i.e. the condition (4.9) is true.
2. The vector function $\underline{f}$ is only *t*-time variable, i.e. $\underline{f}(t)$.

Analytically, we consider the above assumption, the eq. (4.17) is
$$\left\|(\underline{f} * \delta^{(j)})(t) - (\underline{\tilde{f}} * \delta^{(j)})(t)\right\| = 0$$
because
$$f_i\left(s, Q\underline{y}(s)\right) - f_i\left(s, Q\underline{\tilde{y}}(s)\right) = 0 \text{ for every } i = 1, 2, \ldots, n.$$
Moreover, the eq. (4.16) is given by
$$\left\|\underline{x}(t) - \underline{\tilde{x}}(t)\right\| = \left\|Q_{n,p}e^{J_p(t-t_0)}\left(\underline{y}_p(t_0) - \underline{\tilde{y}}_p(t_0)\right) - Q_{n,q}\sum_{j=1}^{q^*-1}\delta^{(j-1)}(t)H_q^j\left[\underline{y}_q(t_0) - \underline{\tilde{y}}_q(t_0)\right]\right\|.$$
Then
$$\left\|\underline{x}(t) - \underline{\tilde{x}}(t)\right\| \leq \left\|Q_{n,p}\right\| \cdot \left\|e^{J_p(t-t_0)}\right\| \cdot \left\|\underline{y}_p(t_0) - \underline{\tilde{y}}_p(t_0)\right\| + \left\|Q_{n,q}\right\| \cdot \sum_{j=1}^{q^*-1}\left|\delta^{(j-1)}(t)\right| \cdot \left\|H_q^j\right\| \cdot \left\|\underline{y}_q(t_0) - \underline{\tilde{y}}_q(t_0)\right\|. \tag{4.21}$$

Lemma 4.6 Assuming that the condition (4.9) is true then $\lim_{t\to+\infty}\left\|e^{J_p(t-t_0)}\right\| = 0$.

Proof. We have proved in Lemma 4.1 that

$$\left\|e^{J_p(t-t_0)}\right\| \le \sum_{i=1}^{v}\left(e^{\lambda_i(t-t_0)}\left(\sum_{j=0}^{p_i-1}(p_i-j)\frac{\left|(t-t_0)^{2j}\right|}{\left|(j!)^2\right|}\right)^{1/2}\right).$$

Since $\lambda_i < 0$. Then,

$$\lim_{t\to+\infty}\sum_{i=1}^{v}\left(e^{\lambda_i(t-t_0)}\left(\sum_{j=0}^{p_i-1}(p_i-j)\frac{\left|(t-t_0)^{2j}\right|}{\left|(j!)^2\right|}\right)^{1/2}\right)=0.$$

Finally, $\lim_{t\to+\infty}\left\|e^{J_p(t-t_0)}\right\| = 0$.

Lemma 4.7 The $\lim_{t\to+\infty}\left\|Q_{n,q}\right\|\cdot\sum_{j=1}^{q^*-1}\left|\delta^{(j-1)}(t)\right|\cdot\left\|H_q^j\right\|\cdot\left\|\underline{y}_q(t_0)-\underline{\tilde{y}}_q(t_0)\right\|=0$.

Proof. This result is a straightforward application of the definition of Dirac δ-function, i.e. $\lim_{t\to+\infty}\left|\delta^{(m)}(t)\right| = 0$ for every m = 0, 1, 2,….

We conclude the section by considering the following Proposition.

Proposition 4.2 The solution of the system (1.6) with *non-consistent* initial conditions is asymptotically stable when the results (1) (or (4.9)) and (2) of Remark 4.6 hold.

Proof. Considering the Remark 4.6 and Lemmas 4.6 and 4.7, the asymptotic stability of the solution of the system (1.6) with non-consistent initial conditions is derived.

5. Studying the linearized solution of weakly nonlinear regular differential systems

In order to solve nonlinear systems, it is very common to apply a linearization technique. In this section, a standard approach for the study of nonlinear dynamical systems based on classical linearization's technique (Taylor expansion for time t) is provided, see Kalogeropoulos et al. (2008b). Analytically

$$\underline{f}(t,\underline{x}(t)) = (\underline{\omega}\circ\underline{x})(t), \tag{5.1}$$

where $\underline{\omega}:\mathbb{R}^n\to\mathbb{R}^n$, such as $\underline{\omega}=\begin{bmatrix}\underline{\omega}_1^T & \cdots & \underline{\omega}_n^T\end{bmatrix}^T\in\mathbb{R}^{n^2}$ and $\omega_i:\mathbb{R}^n\to\mathbb{R}$ for $i=1,2,\ldots,n$.

The linearized approach of $\underline{f}(t,\underline{x}(t))$ is given by the Taylor expansion method using the following expression

$$\underline{f}(t,\underline{x}(t)) \cong \underline{f}(t_0,\underline{x}(t_0)) + \begin{bmatrix} \frac{\theta\omega_1}{\theta x_1}(\underline{x}(t_0)), & \frac{\theta\omega_1}{\theta x_2}(\underline{x}(t_0)), & \cdots & \frac{\theta\omega_1}{\theta x_n}(\underline{x}(t_0)) \\ \vdots & & & \\ \vdots & & & \\ \frac{\theta\omega_n}{\theta x_1}(\underline{x}(t_0)), & \cdots & \cdots & \frac{\theta\omega_n}{\theta x_n}(\underline{x}(t_0)) \end{bmatrix}\begin{bmatrix} x_1'(t_0) \\ x_2'(t_0) \\ \vdots \\ x_n'(t_0)\end{bmatrix}(t-t_0). \tag{5.2}$$

Define

$$J(t_0)=\begin{bmatrix}\frac{\theta\omega_1}{\theta x_1}(\underline{x}(t_0)), & \dots & \frac{\theta\omega_1}{\theta x_n}(\underline{x}(t_0))\\ \vdots & & \\ \frac{\theta\omega_n}{\theta x_1}(\underline{x}(t_0)), & \dots & \frac{\theta\omega_n}{\theta x_n}(\underline{x}(t_0))\end{bmatrix} \quad and \quad \underline{x}'(t_0)=\begin{bmatrix}x'_1(t_0)\\ x'_2(t_0)\\ \vdots \\ x'_n(t_0)\end{bmatrix}$$

Thus, we obtain

$$\underline{f}(t,\underline{x}(t))\cong\underline{f}(t_0,\underline{x}(t_0))+J(t_0)\underline{x}'(t_0)(t-t_0)\,. \tag{5.3}$$

Consequently, taking into account (5.3) the system (1.6) is transformed to a linear as follows

$$F\underline{x}'(t)=G\underline{x}(t)+J(t_0)\underline{x}'(t_0)(t-t_0)+\underline{f}(t_0,\underline{x}(t_0)) \tag{5.4}$$

with initial conditions $\underline{x}(t_o)=\underline{x}_o$.

As we have already discussed in section 2, there exist non-singular matrices P, Q, such as

$$PFQ=F_w=\begin{bmatrix}I_p & \mathbb{O}_{p,q}\\ \mathbb{O}_{q,p} & H_q\end{bmatrix} \quad and \quad PGQ=G_w=\begin{bmatrix}J_p & \mathbb{O}_{p,q}\\ \mathbb{O}_{q,p} & I_q\end{bmatrix}.$$

Then, equivalently as in section 3, the following lemmas derive.

Lemma 5.1 The system (5.4) is divided into two subsystems as follows

$$\underline{y}'_p(t)=J_p\underline{y}_p(t)+P_{p,n}\left(J(t_0)Q\underline{y}'(t_0)(t-t_0)+\underline{f}(t_0,Q\underline{y}(t_0))\right) \tag{5.5}$$

with initial conditions $\underline{y}_p(t_o)$,

$$H_q\underline{y}'_q(t)=\underline{y}_q(t)+P_{q,n}\left[J(t_0)Q\underline{y}'(t_0)(t-t_0)+\underline{f}(t_0,Q\underline{y}(t_0))\right] \tag{5.6}$$

with initial conditions $\underline{y}_q(t_o)$.

Proof. We apply the same transformation (3.3) in (5.4)

$$\underline{x}(t)=Q\underline{y}(t)\,.$$

Then, the system (5.4) is transposed to

$$FQ\underline{y}'(t)=GQ\underline{y}(t)+J(t_0)Q\underline{y}'(t_0)(t-t_0)+\underline{f}(t_0,Q\underline{y}(t_0))\,.$$

Multiplied by left by the non-singular matrix P, we obtain

$$PFQ\underline{y}'(t)=PGQ\underline{y}(t)+P\left[J(t_0)Q\underline{y}'(t_0)(t-t_0)+\underline{f}(t_0,Q\underline{y}(t_0))\right]\Leftrightarrow$$

$$\Leftrightarrow F_w\underline{y}'(t)=G_w\underline{y}(t)+P\left[J(t_0)Q\underline{y}'(t_0)(t-t_0)+\underline{f}(t_0,Q\underline{y}(t_0))\right]\Leftrightarrow$$

$$\begin{bmatrix}I_p & \mathbb{O}_{p,q}\\ \mathbb{O}_{q,p} & H_q\end{bmatrix}\cdot\begin{bmatrix}\underline{y}'_p(t)\\ \underline{y}'_q(t)\end{bmatrix}=\begin{bmatrix}J_p & \mathbb{O}_{p,q}\\ \mathbb{O}_{q,p} & I_q\end{bmatrix}\cdot\begin{bmatrix}\underline{y}_p(t)\\ \underline{y}_q(t)\end{bmatrix}+\begin{bmatrix}P_{p,n}\\ P_{q,n}\end{bmatrix}\left(J(t_0)Q\underline{y}'(t_0)(t-t_0)+\underline{f}(t_0,Q\underline{y}(t_0))\right).$$

Then, eqs. (5.5) and (5.6) derive. Now, the initial conditions is obtained

$$\underline{x}(t_o)=Q\underline{y}(t_o)\Leftrightarrow\underline{y}(t_o)=Q^{-1}\underline{x}(t_o)\,.$$

The $\underline{y}(t_0)=\begin{bmatrix}\underline{y}_p(t_0)\\ \underline{y}_q(t_0)\end{bmatrix}$. Thus, the initial conditions for system (5.5) is given by $\underline{y}_p(t_o)$ and for system (5.6) is provided by $\underline{y}_q(t_o)$.

Remark 5.1 System (5.5) with initial conditions $\underline{y}_p(t_o)$ can be solved using the classical methods, and

$$\underline{y}_p(t) = e^{J_p(t-t_0)}\underline{y}_p(t_0) + \int_{t_0}^{t} e^{J_p(t-s)}P_{p,n}\Big[J(t_0)Q\underline{y}'(t_0)(s-t_0) + \underline{f}\big(t_0, Q\underline{y}(t_0)\big)\Big]ds. \quad (5.7)$$

In this part of the sections, we will solve the subsystem (5.6).

Lemma 5.2 The solution of subsystem (5.6) is given by

$$\underline{y}_q(t) = -\big((t-t_0)I_q + H_q\big)P_{q,n}J(t_0)Q\underline{y}'(t_0) - P_{q,n}\underline{f}\big(t_0, Q\underline{y}(t_0)\big), \quad (5.8)$$

when the following condition is satisfied

$$\underline{y}_q(t_0) = -H_qP_{q,n}J(t_0)Q\underline{y}'(t_0) - P_{q,n}\underline{f}\big(t_0, Q\underline{y}(t_0)\big) \quad (5.9)$$

i.e. we have consistent initial conditions.

Proof. Equivalently as in section 3, we differentiate the expression (5.6)

$$H_q\underline{y}_q''(t) = \underline{y}_q'(t) + P_{q,n}J(t_0)Q\underline{y}'(t_0).$$

Multiply by left with the nilpotent matrix H_q, we obtain

$$H_q^2\underline{y}_q''(t) = H_q\underline{y}_q'(t) + H_qP_{q,n}J(t_0)Q\underline{y}'(t_0) \Leftrightarrow$$

$$\Leftrightarrow H_q^2\underline{y}_q''(t) = \underline{y}_q(t) + P_{q,n}\underline{f}\big(t_0, Q\underline{y}(t_0)\big) + P_{q,n}J(t_0)Q\underline{y}'(t_0)(t-t_0) + H_qP_{q,n}J(t_0)Q\underline{y}'(t_0).$$

Continuing the above procedure we obtain the following recursive expression,

$$H_q^{q^*}\underline{y}_q^{(q^*)}(t) = \underline{y}_q(t) + P_{q,n}\underline{f}\big(t_0, Q\underline{y}(t_0)\big) + P_{q,n}J(t_0)Q\underline{y}'(t_0)(t-t_0) + H_qP_{q,n}J(t_0)Q\underline{y}'(t_0).$$

However, since q^* is the annihilation index of matrix H_q, i.e. $H_q^{q^*} = \mathbb{O}$. Then

$$\underline{y}_q(t) = -P_{q,n}J(t_0)Q\underline{y}'(t_0)(t-t_0) - H_qP_{q,n}J(t_0)Q\underline{y}'(t_0) - P_{q,n}\underline{f}\big(t_0, Q\underline{y}(t_0)\big),$$

for $t = t_0$, we obtain

$$\underline{y}_q(t_0) = -H_qP_{q,n}J(t_0)Q\underline{y}'(t_0) - P_{q,n}\underline{f}\big(t_0, Q\underline{y}(t_0)\big)$$

and finally expression (5.8) is derived.

Lemma 5.3 The solution of subsystem (5.7) for non-consistent initial conditions, i.e.

$$\underline{y}_q(t_0) \neq -H_qP_{q,n}J(t_0)Q\underline{y}'(t_0) - P_{q,n}\underline{f}\big(t_0, Q\underline{y}(t_0)\big)$$

is given by

$$\underline{y}_q(t) = -\sum_{\kappa=0}^{q^*-3}\delta^{(\kappa)}(t)H_q^{\kappa+1}\Big\{\underline{y}_q(t_0) + (-t_0I_q + H_q)P_{q,n}J(t_0)Q\underline{y}'(t_0)\Big\} -$$

$$-\delta^{(q^*-2)}(t)H_q^{q^*-1}\big(\underline{y}_q(t_0) - t_0P_{q,n}J(t_0)Q\underline{y}'(t_0)\big) + (t_0I_q - H_q)P_{q,n}J(t_0)Q\underline{y}'(t_0) - tP_{q,n}J(t_0)Q\underline{y}'(t_0) -$$

$$-\sum_{\kappa=1}^{q^*-1}\delta^{(\kappa-1)}(t)P_{q,n}H_q^{\kappa}\underline{f}\big(t_0, Q\underline{y}(t_0)\big) - P_{q,n}\underline{f}\big(t_0, Q\underline{y}(t_0)\big). \quad (5.10)$$

Proof. First, we apply in eq. (5.7) the Laplace transformation. Thus, we obtain

$$H_q\Im\{\underline{y}_q'(t)\} = \Im\{y_q(t)\} + P_{q,n}J(t_0)Q\underline{y}'(t_0)\Im\{t-t_0\} + P_{q,n}\underline{f}\big(t_0, Q\underline{y}(t_0)\big)\Im\{1\}.$$

Since

$$\Im\{\underline{y}_q(t)\} = X_q(s),\ \Im\{t-t_0\} = \frac{1-t_0 s}{s^2},\ \Im\{y_q'(t)\} = sX_q(s) - \underline{y}_q(t_0) \ \ and \ \ \Im\{1\} = \frac{1}{s}.$$

we obtain

$$H_q\left(sX_q(s) - \underline{y}_q(t_0)\right) = X_q(s) + P_{q,n}J(t_0)Q\underline{y}'(t_0)\frac{1-t_0 s}{s^2} + P_{q,n}\underline{f}\left(t_0, Q\underline{y}(t_0)\right)\frac{1}{s} \Leftrightarrow$$

$$\Leftrightarrow (sH_q - I_q)X_q(s) = H_q\underline{y}_q(t_0) + P_{q,n}J(t_0)Q\underline{y}'(t_0)\frac{1-t_0 s}{s^2} + P_{q,n}\underline{f}\left(t_0, Q\underline{y}(t_0)\right)\frac{1}{s}.$$

Moreover, we have $H_q^{q^*} = \mathbb{O}$ and

$$(sH_q - I_q)^{-1} = -\sum_{\kappa=0}^{q^*-1}(sH_q)^{\kappa},\ \ where\ \ H_q^0 = I_q.$$

Thus, we obtain

$$X_q(s) = -\left(\sum_{\kappa=0}^{q^*-1} s^{\kappa}H_q^{\kappa}\right)H_q\underline{y}_q(t_0) - \left(\sum_{\kappa=0}^{q^*-1} s^{\kappa}H_q^{\kappa}\right)P_{q,n}J(t_0)Q\underline{y}'(t_0)\frac{1-t_0 s}{s^2} - \left(\sum_{\kappa=0}^{q^*-1} s^{\kappa}H_q^{\kappa}\right)P_{q,n}\underline{f}\left(t_0, Q\underline{y}(t_0)\right)\frac{1}{s} =$$

$$= -\sum_{\kappa=0}^{q^*-1} s^{\kappa}H_q^{\kappa+1}\underline{y}_q(t_0) - \sum_{\kappa=0}^{q^*-1} s^{\kappa-2}H_q^{\kappa}P_{q,n}J(t_0)Q\underline{y}'(t_0) +$$

$$+ t_0\sum_{\kappa=0}^{q^*-1} s^{\kappa-1}H_q^{\kappa}P_{q,n}J(t_0)Q\underline{y}'(t_0) - \sum_{\kappa=0}^{q^*-1} s^{\kappa-1}H_q^{\kappa}P_{q,n}\underline{f}\left(t_0, Q\underline{y}(t_0)\right). \tag{5.11}$$

Now, we are working with the following sum

$$-\sum_{\kappa=0}^{q^*-1} s^{\kappa}H_q^{\kappa+1}\underline{y}_q(t_0) = -\sum_{\kappa=0}^{q^*-3} s^{\kappa}H_q^{\kappa+1}\underline{y}_q(t_0) - s^{q^*-2}H_q^{q^*-1}\underline{y}_q(t_0) -$$

$$-s^{q^*-1}H_q^{q^*}\underline{y}_q(t_0) \overset{(H_q^{q^*}=\mathbb{O})}{=\!=\!=} \sum_{\kappa=0}^{q^*-3} s^{\kappa}H_q^{\kappa+1}\underline{y}_q(t_0) - s^{q^*-2}H_q^{q^*-1}\underline{y}_q(t_0).$$

Then

$$\sum_{\kappa=0}^{q^*-1} s^{\kappa-2}H_q^{\kappa} = \sum_{m=-2}^{q^*-3} s^m H_q^{m+2} = \sum_{m=0}^{q^*-3} s^m H_q^{m+2} + s^{-1}H_q + s^{-2}I_q,$$

$$\sum_{\kappa=0}^{q^*-1} s^{\kappa-1}H_q^{\kappa} = \sum_{m=-1}^{q^*-2} s^m H_q^{m+1} = \sum_{m=0}^{q^*-3} s^m H_q^{m+1} + s^{q^*-2}H_q^{q^*-1} + s^{-1}I_q.$$

Thus, considering the above results the eq. (5.11) is given by

$$X_q(s) = -\sum_{\kappa=0}^{q^*-3} s^{\kappa}H_q^{\kappa+1}\underline{y}_q(t_0) - s^{q^*-2}H_q^{q^*-1}\underline{y}_q(t_0) -$$

$$-\sum_{\kappa=0}^{q^*-3} s^{\kappa}H_q^{\kappa+2}P_{q,n}J(t_0)Q\underline{y}'(t_0) - s^{-1}H_qP_{q,n}J(t_0)Q\underline{y}'(t_0) - s^{-2}P_{q,n}J(t_0)Q\underline{y}'(t_0) +$$

$$+ t_0\sum_{\kappa=0}^{q^*-3} s^{\kappa}H_q^{\kappa+1}P_{q,n}J(t_0)Q\underline{y}'(t_0) + t_0 s^{q^*-2}H_q^{q^*-1}P_{q,n}J(t_0)Q\underline{y}'(t_0) +$$

$$+ t_0 s^{-1}P_{q,n}J(t_0)Q\underline{y}'(t_0) - \sum_{\kappa=0}^{q^*-1} s^{\kappa-1}H_q^{\kappa}P_{q,n}\underline{f}\left(t_0, Q\underline{y}(t_0)\right) =$$

$$= -\sum_{\kappa=0}^{q^*-3} s^{\kappa} H_q^{\kappa+1}\left(\underline{y}_q(t_0) + H_q P_{q,n} J(t_0) Q \underline{y}'(t_0) - t_0 P_{q,n} J(t_0) Q \underline{y}'(t_0)\right) -$$

$$- s^{q^*-2} H_q^{q^*-1}\left(\underline{y}_q(t_0) - t_0 P_{q,n} J(t_0) Q \underline{y}'(t_0)\right)$$

$$+ s^{-1}(t_0 I_q - H_q) P_{q,n} J(t_0) Q \underline{y}'(t_0) - s^{-2} P_{q,n} J(t_0) Q \underline{y}'(t_0) -$$

$$- \sum_{\kappa=1}^{q^*-1} s^{\kappa-1} H_q^{\kappa} P_{q,n} \underline{f}\left(t_0, Q\underline{y}(t_0)\right) - \frac{1}{s} P_{q,n} \underline{f}\left(t_0, Q\underline{y}(t_0)\right).$$

Since, it is known that $\Im\{\delta^{(\kappa)}(t)\} = s^{\kappa}$, we take

$$X_q(s) = -\sum_{\kappa=0}^{q^*-3} \Im\{\delta^{(\kappa)}(t)\} H_q^{\kappa+1}\left(\underline{y}_q(t_0) + H_q P_{q,n} J(t_0) Q \underline{y}'(t_0) - t_0 P_{q,n} J(t_0) Q \underline{y}'(t_0)\right) -$$

$$- \Im\{\delta^{(q^*-2)}(t)\} H_q^{q^*-1}\left(\underline{y}_q(t_0) - t_0 P_{q,n} J(t_0) Q \underline{y}'(t_0)\right) +$$

$$+ \Im\{1\}(t_0 I_q - H_q) P_{q,n} J(t_0) Q \underline{y}'(t_0) - \Im\{t\} P_{q,n} J(t_0) Q \underline{y}'(t_0) -$$

$$- \sum_{\kappa=1}^{q^*-1} \Im\{\delta^{(\kappa-1)}(t)\} H_q^{\kappa} P_{q,n} \underline{f}\left(t_0, Q\underline{y}(t_0)\right) - \Im\{1\} P_{q,n} \underline{f}\left(t_0, Q\underline{y}(t_0)\right).$$

Applying the inverse Laplace transformation, eq. (5.10) derives.

Remark 5.2 The solution of the linearized system (5.4) with consistent initial conditions is given by

$$\underline{x}(t) = Q_{n,p}\left[e^{J_p(t-t_0)} \underline{y}_p(t_0) + \int_{t_0}^{t} e^{J_p(t-s)} P_{p,n}\left[J(t_0) Q \underline{y}'(t_0)(s-t_0) + \underline{f}\left(t_0, Q\underline{y}(t_0)\right)\right] ds -\right.$$

$$\left. - Q_{n,q}\left[(t-t_0) I_q + H_q\right] P_{q,n} J(t_0) Q \underline{y}'(t_0) - Q_{n,q} P_{q,n} \underline{f}\left(t_0, Q\underline{y}(t_0)\right)\right]. \tag{5.12}$$

Proof. It is true that

$$\underline{x}(t) = Q\underline{y}(t) \Leftrightarrow \underline{x}(t) = \begin{bmatrix} Q_{n,p} & Q_{n,q} \end{bmatrix} \begin{bmatrix} \underline{y}_p(t) \\ \underline{y}_q(t) \end{bmatrix} \Leftrightarrow x(t) = Q_{n,p} \underline{y}_p(t) + Q_{n,q} \underline{y}_q(t).$$

Using the eqs. (5.7) and (5.8), we obtain (5.12).

Remark 5.3 The solution of the linearized system (5.4) with non-consistent initial conditions is given by

$$\underline{x}(t) = Q_{n,p}\left[e^{J_p(t-t_0)} \underline{y}_p(t_0) + \int_{t_0}^{t} e^{J_p(t-s)} P_{p,n}\left[J(t_0) Q \underline{y}'(t_0)(s-t_0) + \underline{f}\left(t_0, Q\underline{y}(t_0)\right)\right] ds -\right.$$

$$- Q_{n,q} \sum_{\kappa=0}^{q^*-3} \delta^{(\kappa)}(t) H_q^{\kappa+1}\left\{\underline{y}_q(t_0) + (H_q - t_0 I_q) P_{q,n} J(t_0) Q \underline{y}'(t_0)\right\} -$$

$$- Q_{n,q} \delta^{(q^*-2)}(t) H_q^{q^*-1}\left(\underline{y}_q(t_0) - t_0 P_{q,n} J(t_0) Q \underline{y}'(t_0)\right) +$$

$$+ Q_{n,q}(t_0 I_q - H_q) P_{q,n} J(t_0) Q \underline{y}'(t_0) - t Q_{n,q} P_{q,n} J(t_0) Q \underline{y}'(t_0) -$$

$$\left. - Q_{n,q} \sum_{\kappa=1}^{q^*-1} \delta^{(\kappa-1)}(t) H_q^{\kappa} P_{q,n} \underline{f}\left(t_0, Q\underline{y}(t_0)\right) - Q_{n,q} P_{q,n} \underline{f}\left(t_0, Q\underline{y}(t_0)\right)\right]. \tag{5.13}$$

Proof. It is known that

$$\underline{x}(t) = Q\underline{y}(t) = \begin{bmatrix} Q_{n,p} & Q_{n,q} \end{bmatrix} \begin{bmatrix} \underline{y}_p(t) \\ \underline{y}_q(t) \end{bmatrix} = Q_{n,p}\underline{y}_p(t) + Q_{n,q}\underline{y}_q(t)$$

Using the eqs. (5.7) and (5.10), we obtain (5.13).

6. Conclusion

In this chapter, the class of weakly nonlinear (regular) differential systems is investigated. This kind of systems has a great importance in the modelling procedure of several applications in many scientific fields (engineering, population growth models, finance, actuarial science models etc). Thus, the analytic solution is provided, considering consistency and non-consistency in the initial conditions. Moreover, the asymptotic stability is discussed. Some necessary conditions are derived in order to obtain the asymptotic stabilization. In both cases, Propositions summarize the necessary conditions, which have not only to do with the real part of the eigenvalues, as it happens in non-descriptor systems.

Furthermore, using a classical linearization technique (Taylor expansion) and the complex Weierstrass canonical form, the linearized system is decomposed into two subsystems, whose solutions are also obtained.

Finally, the forms of solutions for the (non-) consistent initial conditions are provided. Practically speaking, the results of this chapter can be constructed and simulated. Although, there is in abstract mathematical format, the comparison of the solutions provides a first step for extending further our knowledge. Some numerical examples are also appeared. Moreover, the simulation of the linearized solution can be constructed using Matlab m-files (see for instance, Matlab DAE suite, Shampine et al. 1999).

Finally, it should be stressed some possible directions for further research. Firstly, we can transposed the system (1.6) into a control problem by introducing an input vector $\underline{u}(t)$. So,

$$F\underline{x}'(t) = G\underline{x}(t) + B\underline{u}(t) + \underline{f}(t, \underline{x}(t))$$

Thus, the controllability, the observability, the pole assignment, the elimination of impulse behaviour, and so on, can be examined. Moreover, since the system above can include a fixed, finite input $\underline{u}(t)$ (that is a step), then any resulting oscillations in the output will decay, and the output will tend asymptotically to a new final, steady-state value. If in the system, a Dirac delta impulse is given as an input, then the induced oscillations will die away and the system will return to its previous value. If the oscillations do not die away, or the system does not return to its original output when an impulse is applied, then does the system be marginally stable? Those questions are practically very important and very few things are really known.

Furthermore, a better approximation (instead of the Taylor expansion) of the nonlinear parameter can be considered. Under this approximation, a new linear system derives. Many questions about this approach can also be stated.

The last direction considers the introduction of a stochastic point of view for the system (1.6) by

$$F\underline{x}'(t) = G\underline{x}(t) + B\underline{u}(t) + \underline{f}(t, \underline{x}(t)) + B\underline{\xi}(t)$$

where the input $\underline{\xi}$ is a (fractional) white noise. This approach transforms the deterministic dynamic system into a stochastic one.

7. References

S. Ahmad and M.R.M. Rao (1999), *Theory of ordinary differential equations: with applications in Biology and Engineering*, Affiliated East-West Press Private Limited, New Delhi, India.

S.L. Campbell (1980), *Singular systems of differential equations*, Pitman Publishing.

S.L. Campbell (1983), Consistent initial conditions for singular nonlinear systems. *Circuits Systems Signal Process*, Vol. 2, pp. 45-55.

C. Chicone (2006), *Ordinary differential equations with applications* (Texts in Applied Mathematics), Springer, U.S.A.

L Dai (1989), *Singular control systems*, Springer-Verlag, Berlin, Heidelberg.

R.F. Gantmacher (1959), *The theory of matrices*, Vol. I and II, Chelsea, New York.

E.S. Grispos (1991), *Studying generalized linear differential systems using the matrix theory approach*, PhD thesis, Department of Mathematics, University of Athens.

G.I. Kalogeropoulos (1985), *Matrix Pencils and Linear Systems*, Ph.D Thesis, City University, London, UK.

G.I. Kalogeropoulos, A.D. Karageorgos and A.A. Pantelous (2008a), On generalized weakly nonlinear regular differential systems, *Proceedings of 27th IASTED International Conference MIC*, February 2008, Innsbruck, Austria, pp. 172-177.

G.I. Kalogeropoulos, A.D. Karageorgos and A.A. Pantelous (2008b), The study of the linearized solution of a class of descriptor weakly nonlinear systems, *Proceedings of 17th IASTED International Conference ASM*, June 2008, Corfu, Greece, pp. 94-99.

A.D. Karageorgos, A.A. Pantelous and G.I. Kalogeropoulos, (2009), On generalized weakly nonlinear regular differential systems, *Proceedings of 28th IASTED International Conference MIC*, February 2009, Innsbruck, Austria, pp. 248-253

N. Karcanias and G.E. Hayton, Generalized autonomous differential systems, algebraic duality, and geometric theory, *Proceedings of IFAC VIII, Triennial World Congress*, Kyoto, Japan, 1981.

P. Kunkel and V. Mehrmann (2006), *Differential-Algebraic equations: analysis and numerical solution*, European Mathematical Society.

W. Leontief, *Input-Output Economics*. 2nd ed., New York: Oxford University Press, 1986.

P.H. Leslie (1945), *On the use of matrices in certain population mathematics*, Biometrika, Vol. 35, pp. 183-212.

D.G. Luenberger (1977), Time-invariant descriptor systems, *Proceedings of Automatic Control Conference, San Francisco, U.S.A.* (also in Automatica 14, 1978, 473-480).

D.G. Luenberger and A. Arbel (1977), *Singular dynamic Leontief systems*, Econometrica, Vol. 45, pp. 991-995.

C.D. Meyer (2001), Jr. *Matrix Analysis and Applied Linear Algebra*, SIAM, Package edition.

P.C. Müller (2000), Descriptor systems: pros and cos of system modelling by differential - algebraic equations, *Mathematics and Computers in Simulation*, Vol. 53, pp. 273-279.

A.A. Pantelous, A.A. Zimbidis and G.I Kalogeropoulos (2008), *A generalized linear discrete time model for managing the solvency interaction and singularities arising from potential regulatory constraints imposed within a portfolio of different insurance products*, Proceedings of 38th ASTIN colloquium, Manchester, U.K.
S. Sastry (1999), *Nonlinear systems: Analysis, Stability and Control*, Interdisciplinary Applied Mathematics Springer, U.S.A..
L.F. Shampine, M.W. Reichelt, and J.A. Kierzenka (1999), Solving index 1 DAEs in Matlab and Simulink, *SIAM Review*, Vol. 41 (3), pp. 538-552.

18

Modelling and Simulation of 6 Pulse GTO Thyristor Converter

Muhamad Zahim Sujod
University Malaysia Pahang
Malaysia

1. Introduction

Conventional thyristor (known as SCR) has being used in various applications such as in power converter of high voltage direct current (hvdc) transmission system and as a dc speed controller for dc motor application (F. Schettler et al., 2000). Conventional thyristor can only be turned on with two conditions, that is when the device is in forward blocking state or when positive gate current is applied at the gate. This thyristor cannot be turned off by applying negative gate current. It can only be turned off if anode current goes negative (reverse). This happens when negative portion of the sine wave occurs (natural commutation). Another method of turning off is known as "forced commutation" where anode current is "diverted" to another circuitry. Alternatively, we have Gate Turn-Off (GTO) thyristor to overcome the disadvantage of conventional thyristor. GTO thyristor behave like conventional thyristor, but can be turned off using gate signal. It needs very large reverse gate current (normally 1/5 of anode current) to turn-off. Since a GTO thyristor converter is self-commutated, it can be used to supply power to a week ac system, and even to a "load-only" system. At the same time, it is able to control reactive power from lead to lag to keep an ac bus voltage constant.

In this paper, we create a model of GTO thyristor with its operation circuit and gate circuit using OrCAD PSPICE simulator and make an analysis of their switching characteristics at different anode currents. Then, this GTO thyristor model is use and implement in the 6 pulse converter circuit. Finally, we compare the simulation results of dc output voltage with mathematical calculation results.

2. GTO thyristor model

In the library of OrCAD PSPICE simulator, GTO thyristor model is not included. So, we use two transistor models to create GTO thyristor model for the simulation. The monolithic pnpn structure of GTO thyristor can be conceptualized as comprising an npn transistor and a pnp transistor, interconnected as shown in Figure 1.

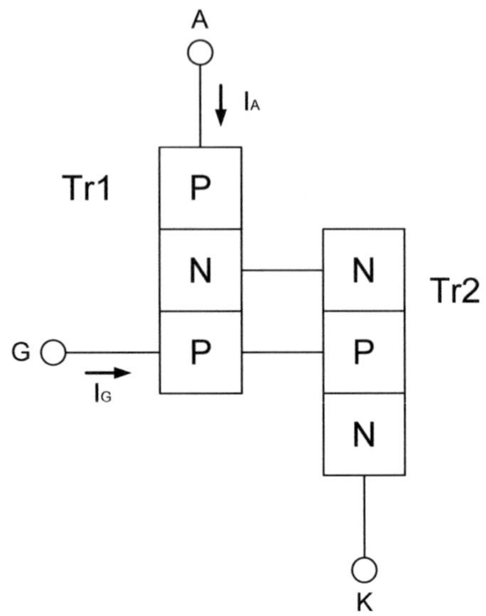

Fig. 1. Two transistor model

Here, the collector of the npn transistor provides base-drive to the pnp, while the collector of the pnp, along with any externally supplied gate current, furnishes base current to the npn. In this positive feedback arrangement, regeneration occurs once the loop gain exceeds one, when each transistor drives its "mate" into saturation.
The GTO thyristor model is then connected to the gate circuit with its operation circuit parameters, shown in Figure 2 and Table 1.

Operation Circuit	Ld	1μH
	Rd	20Ω, 10Ω, 5Ω
	Vd	100V
GTO	PNP	SMBT3906
	NPN	SMBTA06
	R	1Ω
Gate Circuit	Von	10V
	Voff	-60V
	Ron	40Ω
	Roff	22Ω, 10Ω, 5Ω

Table 1. Operation circuit parameters of GTO thyristor

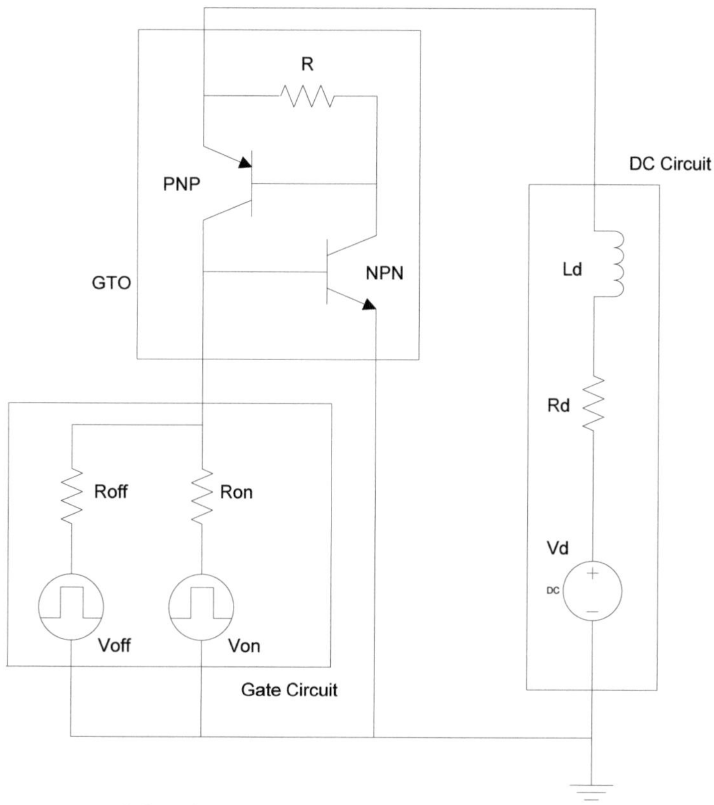

Fig. 2. GTO thyristor model and its operation circuit

In this simulation, we are using the Texas Instrument of SMBTA06 and SMBT3906 for the NPN and PNP transistors. Turn-on and turn-off of GTO thyristor model are controlled by connecting the gate terminal to the gate circuit. GTO thyristor will turned on when positive gate pulse current is applied. Small gate pulse current is enough to turn it on. Here, we set the gate pulse current 5% of the anode current. Meanwhile, GTO thyristor will turned off when negative gate pulse current is applied. Here, we set the gate pulse current 60% of the anode current. Normally, the gate current required to turn it off may be as much as 20% of the anode current. In this paper, we want to consider the turn-off time, where at 60% of anode current, the turn-off time is smaller than at 20% of anode current.
Simulation has been done with PSPICE simulator, and Figure 3, Figure 4 and Figure 5 show the waveform characteristics of the GTO thyristor with anode current 5A, 10A and 20A, respectively. Here, we applied 100V of anode-cathode voltage to the GTO thyristor model. From the figures, we measured the storage time, fall time, tail time and turn-off time. All the measured values are stated in Table 2. We set the turn-on time delay at 2.0us and turn-off time delay at 10us. These time delay settings are very important in the switching operation of 6 pulse GTO thyristor converter circuit. From these results, we know that GTO thyristor can be turned on and turned off in the range current of 5A ~ 20A with a small turn-off time. This GTO thyristor model will be used and implemented in the 6 pulse converter circuit.

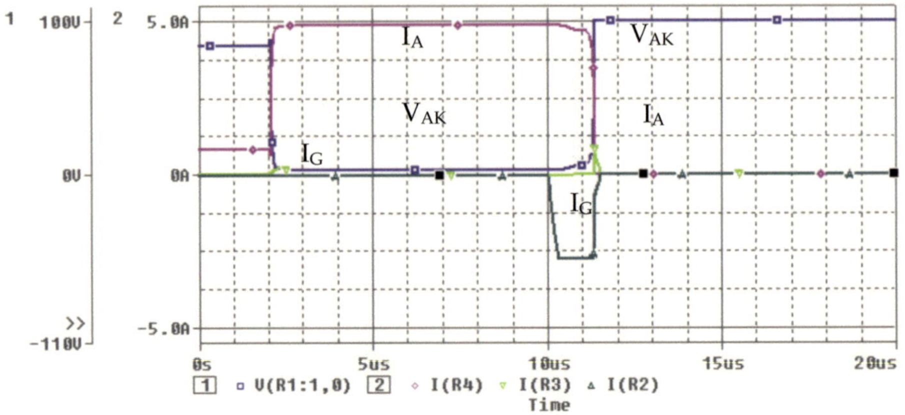

Fig. 3. Turn-on and turn-off characteristics of GTO thyristor (Id=5A)

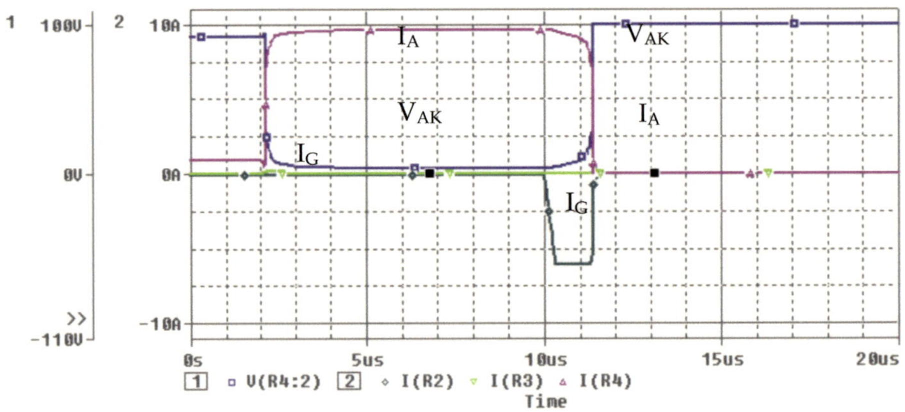

Fig. 4. Turn-on and turn-off characteristics of GTO thyristor (Id=10A)

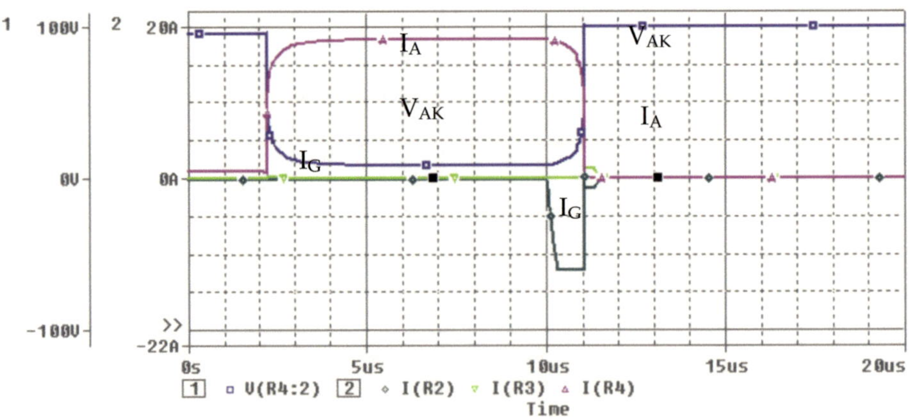

Fig. 5. Turn-on and turn-off characteristics of GTO thyristor (Id=20A)

Anode Current [A]	Storage Time [μs]	Fall Time [μs]	Tail Time [μs]	Turn-off Time [μs]
5	1.191	0.140	0.002	1.333
10	0.977	0.396	0.002	1.375
20	0.573	0.830	0.002	1.405

Table 2. Storage time, fall time, tail time and turn-off time for a different anode current

3.6 pulse converter circuit

Consider the Figure 6 in which a 3 phase, 6 pulse converter supplies power to a load. Each three single phase power supply, V_x, V_y and V_z fed 50V and 50Hz of ac voltage and frequency. The other parameters in the ac side are shown in Table 3. 6 pulse converter circuit consist of 6 GTO thyristors, and each GTO thyristors are triggered by the gate circuit G1 ~ G6. The gate circuit parameters for this simulation are the same as in Table 1, explained above. At the dc side, the load is composed of a dc voltage V_d and a variable resistor Rd in series with a smoothing inductor L_d. The parameters of these components are also shown in Table 3. The value of variable resistor is varying to fix a value of dc output current at one level. 6 pulse converter can be functioned as a rectifier and an inverter depend on the firing angle, α. It is function as a rectifier when the firing angle is in the range of 0^0 ~ 90^0. When the firing angle is advance from 90^0, the converter will function as an inverter. Therefore, dc voltage, Vd is required during the inverter operation. So, the dc voltage value is varying in the range of 1μV ~ 200V for this simulation.

3 Phase Circuit (AC Side)	Rx, Ry, Rz	0.1mΩ
	Lx, Ly, Lz	0.1mH
	Vx, Vy, Vz	50V, 50Hz
6 Pulse Converter	G1 ~ G6	Gate Circuit
DC Side	Rd	Variable
	Ld	1mH
	Vd	1μV ~ 200V

Table 3. Parameters of 6 pulse converter circuit

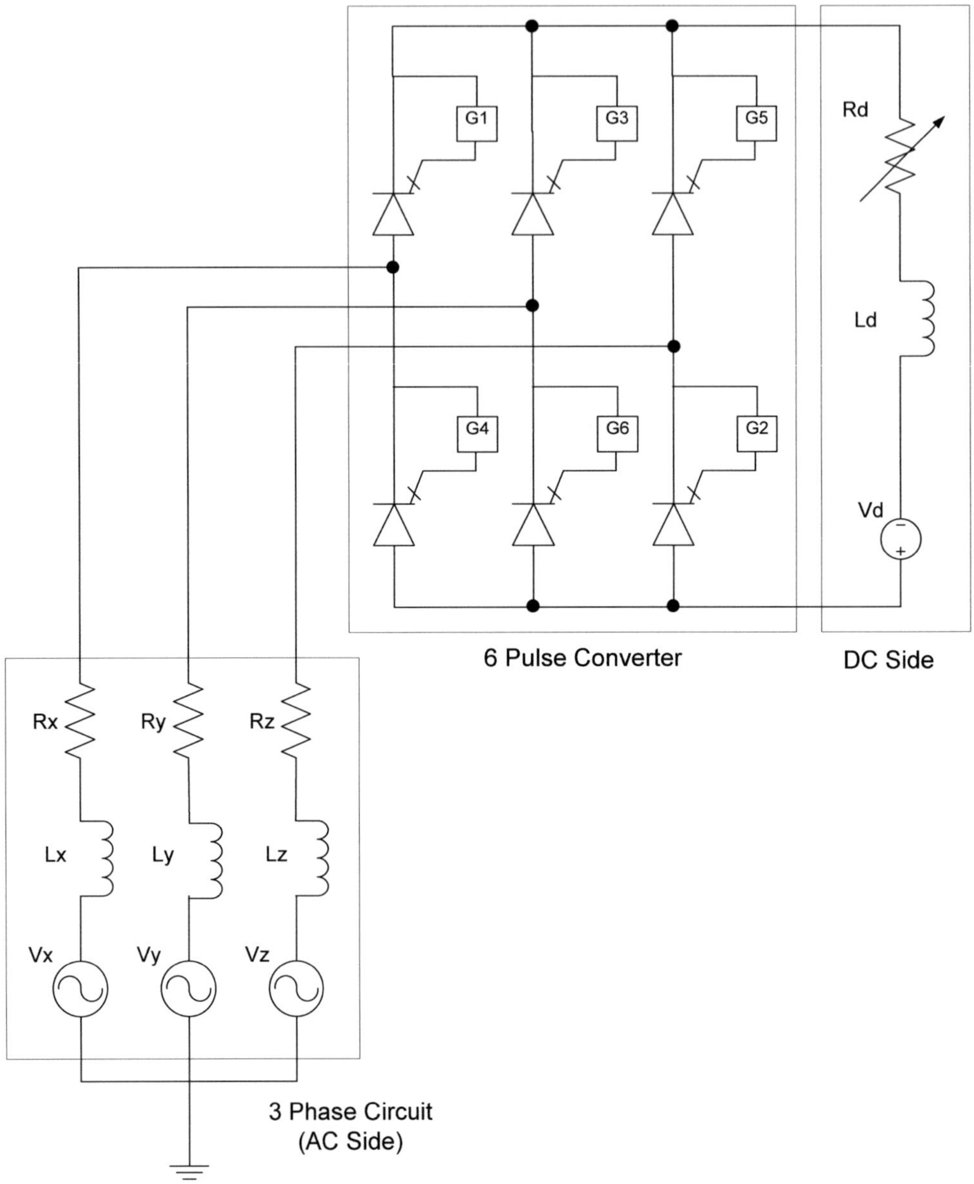

Fig. 6. 6 pulse converter circuit

Figure 7 shows some examples of dc output voltages at different firing angles and the dc output current is fixed to 5A. The time delays are setting depend on the required firing angle. For example, if we want to turn-on GTO thyristor with gate circuit G1 at firing angle $\alpha = 15^0$, we need to fired a positive gate current at time delay, TD=2.5ms. The simple equation is given as (T. Wildi, 2006),

$$TD = \frac{\alpha + 30^0}{360^0} \times \frac{1}{f} \tag{1}$$

where, f : supply frequency

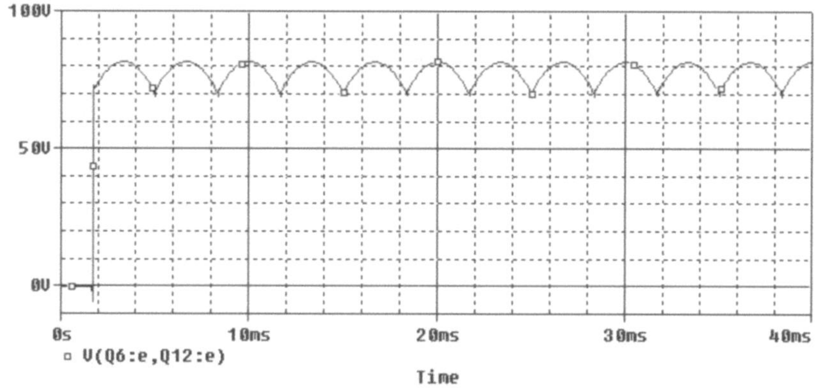

(a) α = 0⁰

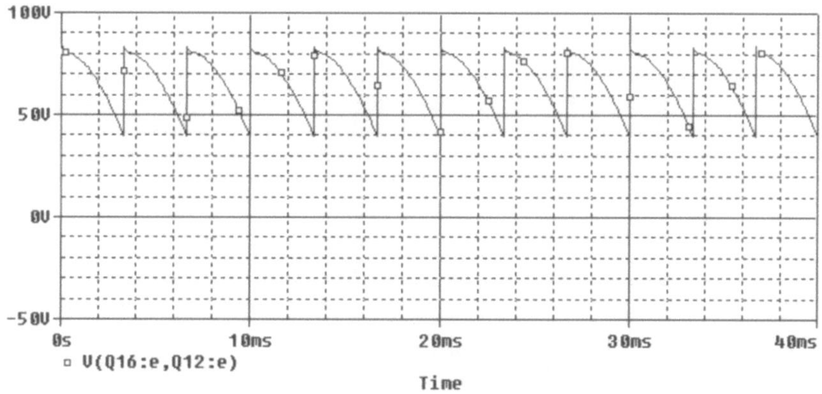

(b) α = 30⁰

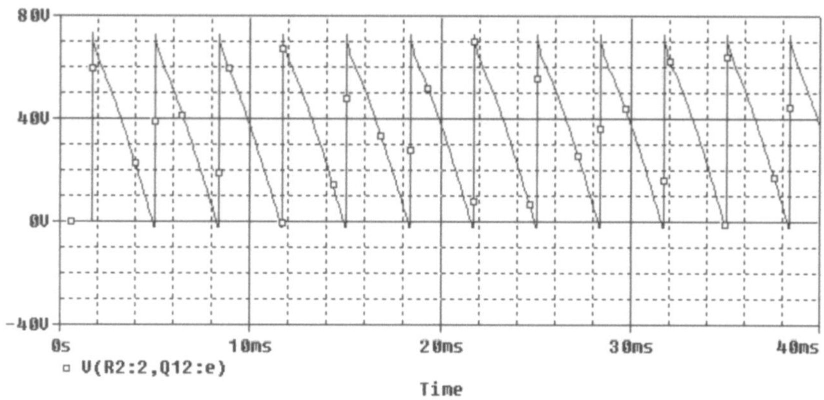

(c) α = 60⁰

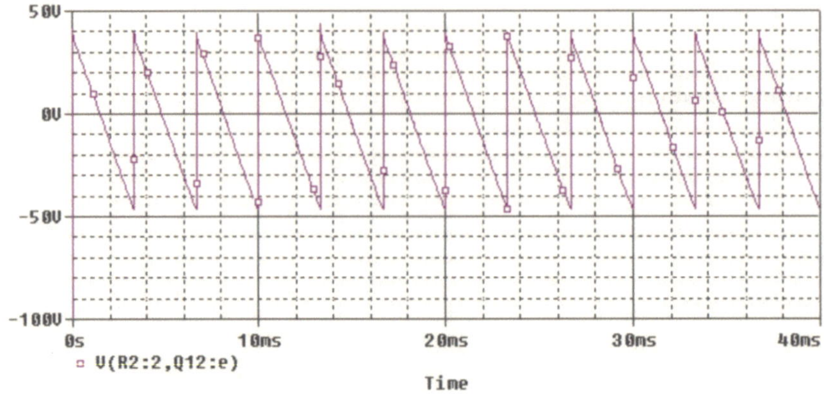

(d) α = 90^0

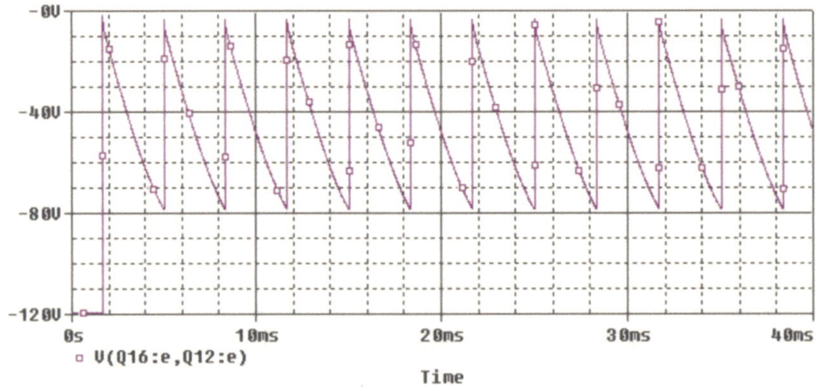

(e) α = 120^0

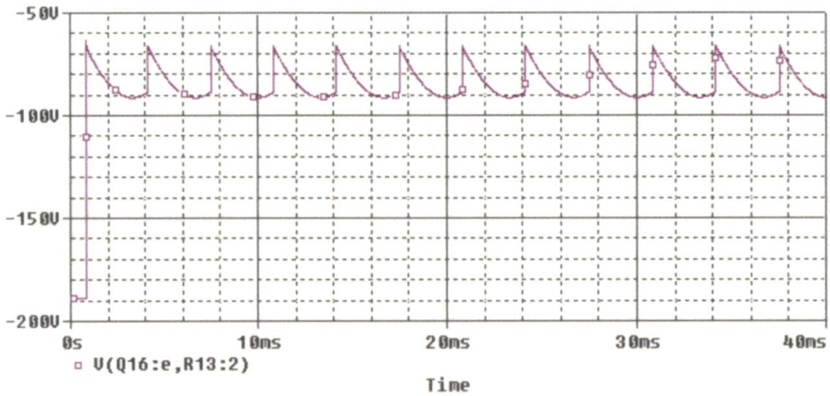

(f) α = 165^0

Fig. 7. DC output voltages at different α (Id=5A)

We make an analysis of the relation between firing angle and dc output voltage. Using the 6 pulse converter circuit in Figure 18, and varying the firing angle α in the range of $0^0 \sim 165^0$ (this range is taken after considered the commutation overlap), we measured the simulation results of dc output voltage. These simulation results are compared with mathematical calculation results. For mathematical calculation, the dc output current is given as,

$$I_d = \sqrt{\frac{3}{2}} I_m \left\{ \cos\left(\alpha + \frac{\pi}{2} - \phi\right) - \cos\left(\alpha + \mu + \frac{\pi}{2} - \phi\right) \right\} \tag{2}$$

rearrange it,

$$\cos\left(\alpha + \frac{\pi}{2} - \phi\right) - \cos\left(\alpha + \mu + \frac{\pi}{2} - \phi\right) = \frac{2I_d}{\sqrt{3}I_m} \tag{3}$$

and dc voltage is given as,

$$E_{dc} = \frac{3\sqrt{3}}{2\pi} E_m (\cos\alpha + \cos(\alpha + \mu)) \tag{4}$$

where, I_m : maximum ac current, E_m : maximum ac voltage, α : phase control angle, μ : overlap angle

From equation (10), if we change to the form of $\cos(\alpha + \mu)$, it will become as,

$$\cos(\alpha + \mu) = \cos\left\{ \phi - \frac{\pi}{2} + \cos^{-1}\left(\cos\left(\alpha + \frac{\pi}{2} - \phi\right) - \frac{2I_d}{\sqrt{3}I_m} \right) \right\} \tag{5}$$

adding $I_m = \dfrac{E_m}{\sqrt{R^2 + (\varpi L)^2}}$ into equation (13) and times ($\cos^{-1}$) both right and left, we will get,

$$\alpha + \mu = \phi - \frac{\pi}{2} + \cos^{-1}\left(\cos\left(\alpha + \frac{\pi}{2} - \phi\right) - \frac{2I_d\sqrt{R^2 + (\varpi L)^2}}{\sqrt{3}E_m} \right) \tag{6}$$

where, I_d : dc current, $\phi = \tan^{-1}\dfrac{\varpi L}{R}$

Insert all parameters given in Table 6 into equation (14) will become as follow,

$$\alpha + \mu = -0.1520^0 + \cos^{-1}\left(\cos\left(\alpha + 0.1520^0\right) - 0.0009I_d \right) \tag{7}$$

The result of mathematical calculation is determined by the equation (1), equation (4) and equation (7). Figure 8, Figure 9 and Figure 10 show the dc output voltage vs. firing angle at dc output current of 1A, 5A and 10A respectively. From these figures, we know that the curves of simulation results and mathematical calculation results are almost same. The values of dc output voltages are not too much different in each firing angle except in the range of 0^0 ~ 75^0, where the values of the simulation results are little bit smaller than the mathematical calculation results. It is may be happened due to some reason such as voltage drop during the turn-on and turn-off operation of the GTO thyristors, power losses due to commutation overlap and measurement error in maintaining the same level of dc output current during the simulation. From Figure 8, Figure 9 and Figure 10, we know that power transfer can be controlled by varying the firing angle, and power transmission direction can be feed either to the dc side or to the ac side. So, the 6 pulse converter circuit can be functioned either as a rectifier or an inverter.

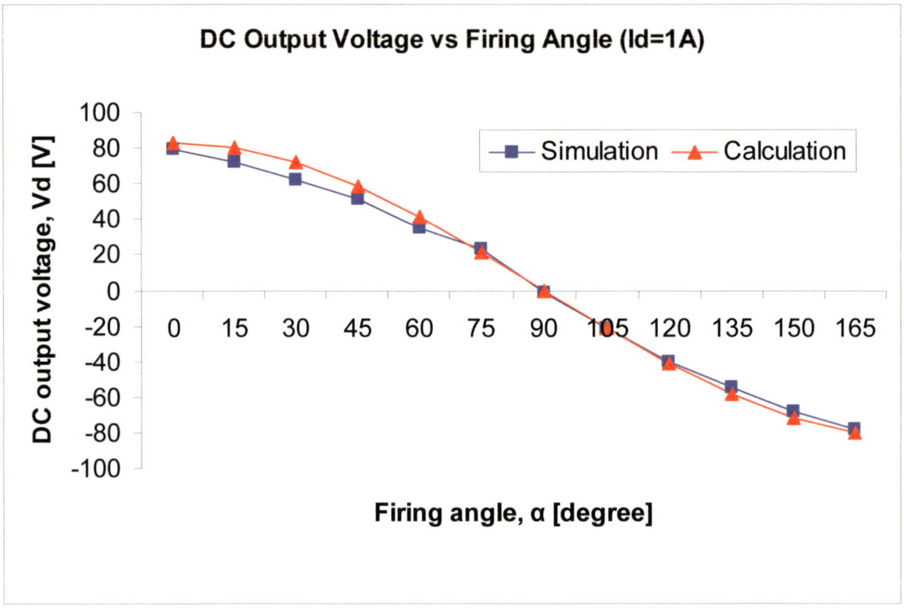

Fig. 8. DC output voltage vs. firing angle (Id=1A)

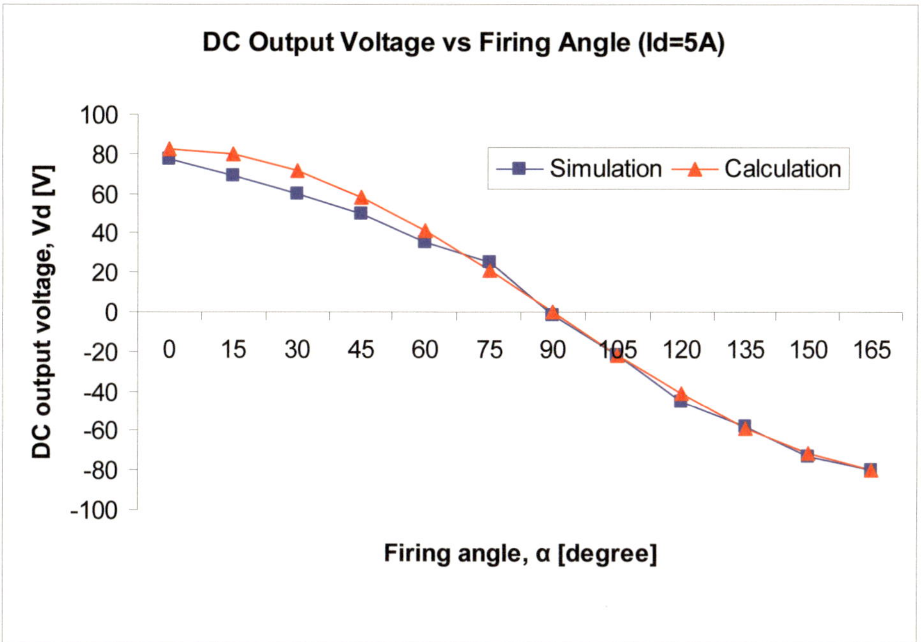

Fig. 9. DC output voltage vs. firing angle (Id=5A)

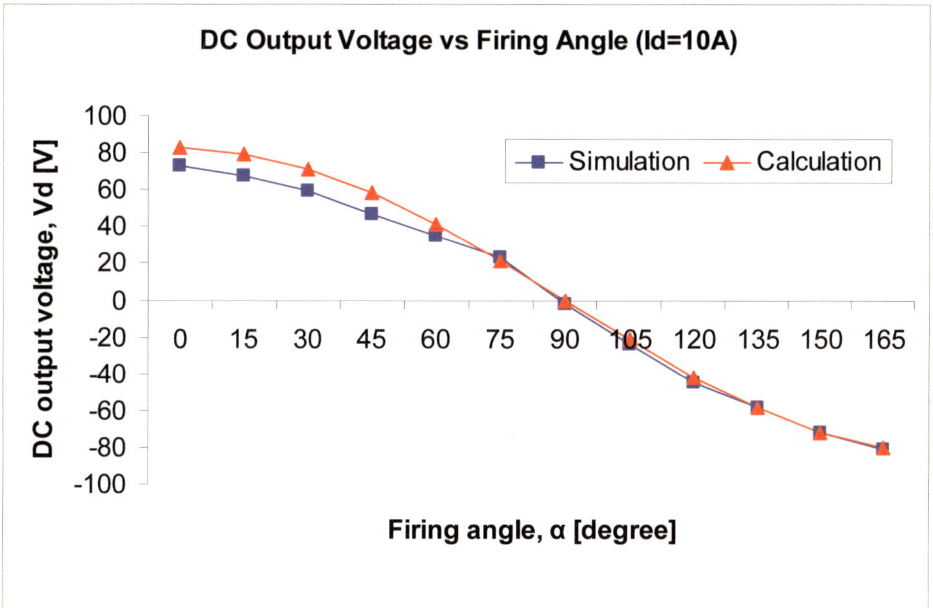

Fig. 10. DC output voltage vs. firing angle (Id=10A)

4. Conclusion

Using PSPICE simulator we create GTO thyristor model with its gate circuit and obtained the switching characteristics. We know that GTO thyristor can be turned on and turned off in the range current of 5A ~ 20A with a small turn-off time. This GTO thyristor model is being implemented in the 6 pulse converter circuit with controlled gate circuits. The characteristics curves of firing angle vs. dc output voltage show almost the similar characteristics except in the range of firing angle 0^0 ~ 75^0, where the simulation results are little bit smaller compared to the mathematical calculation results. We also know that power transfer can be controlled either as a rectifier or an inverter.

5. References

T. Wildi (2006). *Electrical Machine, Drives and power systems,* Prentice Hall, 0131969188 , USA.

Kaz Furmanczyk & Mark Stefanich (2004). Demonstration of Very High Airbone AC to DC Converter, *Crane Aerospace and Electronics Conference,* pp. 3210-3215, 2004-01-3210, November 2004, USA.

F. Schettler; H. Huang & N. Christl (2000). HVDC Transmission System using Voltage Sourced Converters - Design and Applications, *Power Engineering Society Summer Meeting,* pp. 715-720, 078036420, 16-20 July 2000, IEEE

Thadiappan Krishnan & Bellamkonda Ramaswami (1974). A Fast Response DC Motor Speed Control System, *IEEE Transaction on Industry Applications,* pp. 643-651, 349214, September/October 1974, IEEE.

Z. Zabar & A. Alexandrovitz (1970). Guidelines on Adaption of Thyristorized Switch for DC Motor Speed Control, *IEEE Transaction on Industrial Instrumentation,* pp. 10-13, 229594, February 1970, IEEE.

19

The Measurement of Bandwidth: A Simulation Study

Martin J. Tunnicliffe
Kingston University
UK

1. Introduction

Bandwidth dictates the potential speed at which a channel carries information and hence the services it can support. Speech telephony for example requires only 4kHz bandwidth, while high quality sound requires 15kHz and video 6MHz (Glover & Grant, 2004). When several services share a common channel it is crucial to know the accessible bandwidth such that it can be divided efficiently between customers. Furthermore senders may even have to modify their behaviour in order to make best use of their bandwidth share (Yu et al., 2003). In an IP network bandwidths can be measured directly using the SNMP protocol to interrogate link components for their capacities and traffic loads: However since administrative access is not typically available to customers, numerous "end-to-end" measurement techniques have appeared whereby network traffic and infrastructure can be inferred from "probe" transmissions (Prasad et al., 2003). However, these techniques are only as good as their underlying assumptions and a plethora of misunderstandings and ambiguities have arisen (Jain & Dovrolis, 2004). Some of these problems are technological; wireless components introduce complications not experienced in wired networks (Johnsson et al., 2005) and traffic-shaping mechanisms can make the instantaneous bandwidth different from that experienced by sustained transmissions (Lakshminarayanan et al., 2004). However difficulties still arise under the simplest technological assumptions due to the complex behaviour of packet-streams within bottleneck links.

This chapter develops a simulation framework geared specifically towards bandwidth quantisation and measurement. The simulator does not represent any specific technology, but supports the networking of generic FIFO nodes on which the major probing philosophies (together with their various strengths and pitfalls) can be demonstrated. The reader is encouraged to experiment with the C++ source-code which is available online (http://staffnet.kingston.ac.uk/~ku12881/probesim1.0/).

The chapter is not fully comprehensive and several tools and techniques have not been covered. For more in-depth information the reader is directed to the references at the end of the chapter.

2. The Definition of Bandwidth

The exact meaning of "bandwidth" depends on the context in which it is used: In the analogue world it specifies the frequency range (in Hz) over which channel gain is principally effective; typically the difference between the upper and lower half-power points (though the definition used for noise calculations is slightly different). Bandwidth also has a separate digital definition: The maximum rate at which a channel can process data in bits per second.

Analogue and digital bandwidths are linked by the Shannon-Hartley equation which expresses the maximum error-free transmission rate R_{max} (bits/s) in terms of the analogue bandwidth B (Hz) and the signal-to-noise ratio S/N (simple ratio, not decibels):

$$R_{max} = B \cdot \log_2(1 + S/N) \text{ bits per second.} \tag{1}$$

R_{max} is directly proportional to B but falls to zero as $S/N \to 0$, indicating that a noisy channel has smaller capacity than a noiseless channel of the same bandwidth. By boosting the signal relative to the noise R_{max} can be increased indefinitely, though the logarithmic function introduces a law of diminishing returns. R_{max} represents the maximum *potential* digital bandwidth, though of course binary-coded data cannot necessarily be carried at this rate. In practical terms digital bandwidth may refer to a number of throughput-related concepts:

- *Link Capacity*. The maximum rate at which a specific link can operate.
- *End-To-End Bandwidth*. The bandwidth effective across a series of links.
- *Available Bandwidth*. The unused portion of link capacity accessible to new connections.

Figure 1 shows a hypothetical network path connecting source-node A to sink-node B. The path consists of four "hops" and passes through intermediate nodes C, D and E. Each link has a capacity of 100Mbit/s with the exception of DE which has only 50Mbit/s; this is the "narrow-link" which dictates the end-to-end capacity of the path. However, two cross-traffic flows are also present: A 70Mbit/s flow in the link CD and a 10Mbit/s flow in the DE. Thus the *available* bandwidths of CD and DE are 100-70=30Mbit/s and 50-10=40Mbit/s respectively, making CD the "tight-link" (the smallest available bandwidth) which dictates the end-to-end available bandwidth of the path. Note that the tight- and narrow-links are not necessarily the same.

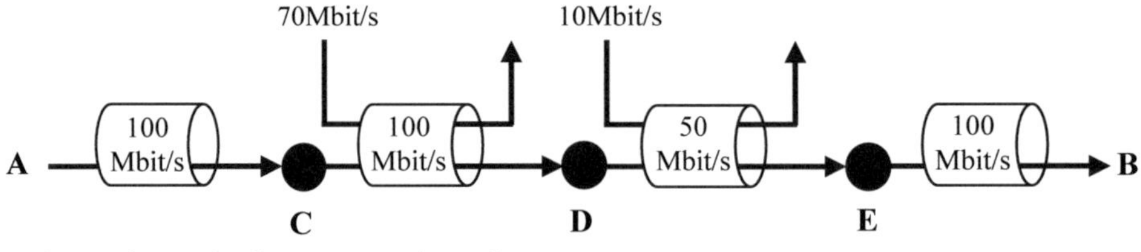

Fig. 1. A hypothetical 4-hop network path.

Often the best way to investigate a potential measurement algorithm is by computer simulation: The measurement can be compared directly with the "truth" (specified in the simulation parameters) and the investigator's "omniscience" provides information not otherwise accessible. It is easy for example to see the relative benefits of pairs and streams of probe-packets, the limitations of techniques based on the server idle-rate, the effects of multiple hidden infrastructural nodes and cost of bandwidth measurement in terms of increased utilisation and reduced quality-of-service.

3. The Simulation Software

All the simulations reported in this chapter were performed using a software system devised by the author. Readers are free to download this software, repeat the experiments using different parameters and modify the source code for their own purposes. The tool is not a program *per se* but a collection of classes which allow the user to write bespoke simulations in C++. Results are generated as text files which users can analyse using their preferred spreadsheet software. All the `.h` and `.cpp` files must be downloaded from http://staffnet.kingston.ac.uk/~ku12881/probesim1.0/ and added to the project, and the files `node.h`, `network.h`, `traffic.h`, `user.h`, `probe.h`, `connection.h`, `channel.h`, `simulation.h` and `constants.h` must be linked to any user-written code. There are eight classes in all: `network`, `node`, `channel`, `connection`, `user`, `probe`, `simulation` and `packet`. (The `packet` class is only ever used internally and will not be discussed here.) Since pseudorandom numbers are used, random seeding is required to ensure statistically independent repetitions. (Use `srand((unsigned)time(NULL))`.)

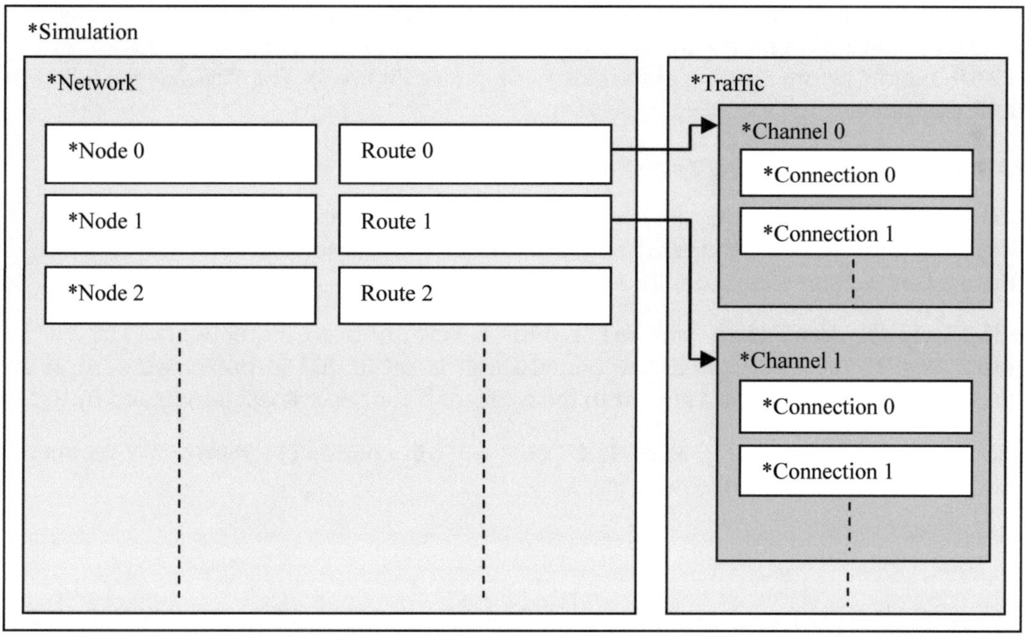

Fig. 2. Simulation architecture

3.1 The Simulation Class

Figure 2 shows the arrangements of objects within the `simulation` class, all of which are referenced by pointers. The class has two main attributes: A `network` object defining the network infrastructure and a `traffic` object defining the network traffic. It also has three public methods:

`simulation()` creates an empty unconfigured simulation object. The new object can perform no simulation function until its `configure` method has been called and returned `true`.

`bool configure(network *n, traffic *t)` gives the simulation network infrastructure `*n` and traffic `*t` and sets the virtual clock to zero. It returns `true` only if `*n` and `*t` are consistent with each other. Once it has been successfully called, the `advance` method (see below) may be used to make the simulation run.

`double advance(double duration)` advances the simulation's clock for a period of `duration` seconds, during which the behaviour of the network is simulated. Since a whole number of events must always be processed, the simulation time may overshoot the specified value, in which case the "actual" new time is returned. If the simulation fails (because it is not correctly configured) the returned time is identical to the time at which the method was called.

3.2 The Network Class

An object of the `network` class consists of nodes and routes. Nodes are objects of the `node` class (see below), and are identified by integers 0,1,2… which indicate the order in which they were added to the network. Routes (which represent allowed paths through the network) are strings of nodes' integer-identifiers. For example, `{0,1,2,-1}` passes through nodes 0, 1 and 2 before arriving at the sink node -1 (see Figure 3). The class has the following public methods:

`network()` creates an empty network with no nodes and no routes.

`bool insert_node(node *n)` adds a new node (identified by its pointer) to the network. It returns false if too many nodes are added (limit is set at 200 in `constants.h`) or if the method is parameterised with a NULL pointer.

`bool insert_route(int route[])` adds a new route to the network. The method returns false if too many routes are added (limit is set at 200 in `constants.h`), if any nonexistent or repeated nodes appear in the route, or if the array is not terminated by a -1.

`int get_no_of_nodes()` and **`int get_no_of_routes()`** return the number of nodes and routes added to the network.

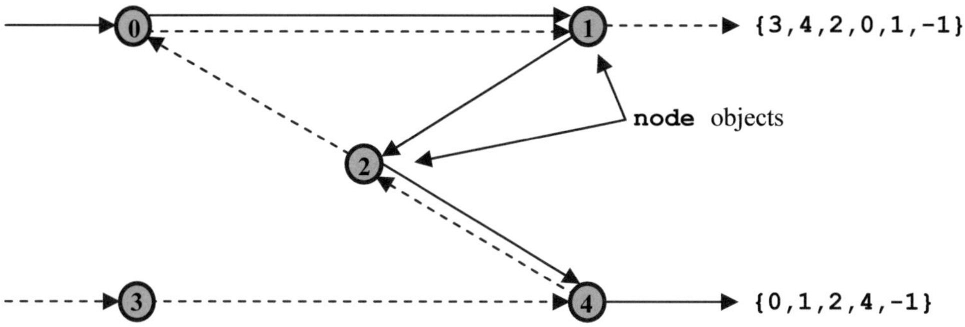

Fig. 3. Example topology specified by a `network` object.

3.3 The Node Class

An object of the `node` class is basically a FIFO (first in first out) queuing system which mimics the behaviour of a drop-tail router or store-and-forward switch. Its methods are as follows:

`node(int maxsize,double setspeed,double fixlatency)` creates a node which forwards data at `setspeed` bits/s, and adds an additional fixed delay `fixlatency` seconds to each packet. `maxsize` specifies the maximum amount of data (in bytes) that the node can hold before packets are dropped.

`double getidletime()` returns the time (in seconds) that the server has been idle since the start of the simulation, or the last time `resetidletime()` was called. This is useful for determining the server's average utilisation and idle-rate.

`void resetidletime()` sets the idle time to zero. This is useful for detecting changes in utilisation over time.

3.4 The Traffic Class

An object of the traffic class specifies the traffic applied to the network during the simulation. It consists of a collection of `channel` objects identified by integers 0,1,2..., indicating the order in which they were added. When loaded into a `simulation` object along with a network object, the channels in the traffic object correspond to the routes in the network object (channel 0 follows route 0, channel 1 follows route 1 etc, as shown in Fig.2). The class has the following public methods:

`traffic()` creates an empty traffic object with no channels.

`bool insert_channel(channel *new_channel)` inserts a channel object into the traffic.

3.5 The Channel Class
Channels specify the traffic applied to each route within the network: They are container-objects for connections, which specify actual traffic processes or transmissions. The channel class has two public methods:

channel() creates a new empty channel with no connections.

bool insert_connection(connection *c) places a new connection object within the channel.

3.6 The Connection Class
Objects of this class contain one of two attributes: A `user` object which specifies a user-related traffic process, or a `probe` object which measures the bandwidth of the path. It has three public methods of interest:

connection() creates a new empty connection object, containing neither a `user` nor a `probe`.

bool insert_user(user *u) and **bool insert_probe(probe *p)** insert a user or probe object into the connection, thereby deleting any existing user or probe object.

3.7 The User Class
An object of the `user` class represents an application which generates packets. Every `user` object is associated with a `connection` object (see above). In its default mode it generates a single packet of specified size, a specified number of seconds after the start of the simulation. However it can also be configured to generate a continuous stream of packets. Its public methods are as follows:

user(int size,double start,bool trace) creates a new `user` process which transmits one packet of `size` bytes, `start` seconds into the simulation. If the `trace` flag is set `true`, the progress of the packet through the network is tracked by a series of messages to the console window.

bool set_stream(double r,bool p,char *d,char *t ,double startrec) tells the user process to produce a continuous stream of packets at a rate `r` bits/s. If the flag `p` is set true then the stream will be governed by a Poisson (random memoryless) process; otherwise the packet interarrival times will be constant. The parameters `*d` and `*t` specify the filename/paths under which the packet delay and transmission times are to be stored. (If this data is *not* to be recorded, these pointers are set to `NULL`.) The parameter `startrec` specifies the time (from the beginning of the simulation) after which this recording is to commence.

bool set_limits(double t1,double t2) tells the user to generate packets only during the interval (`t1`, `t2`) seconds.

bool pareto_modulation(double mean_on,double min_on,double mean_off) switches the packet arrival mechanism to a Pareto ON-OFF process (Pitts & Schormans, 2000). the ON periods follow a Pareto distribution while the OFF periods are exponentially distributed. The parameters specify the mean and minimum ON times as well as the mean OFF time.

double get_packets_sent(), **double get_packets_carried()** and **double get_packets_dropped()** are the accessor methods for the number of packets transmitted, carried and lost since the simulation began.

double get_latency(), **double get_latency_stdv()** and **double get_jitter()** are the accessor methods for the mean packet latency (delay), latency standard deviation and jitter in seconds. (Jitter is defined as the absolute difference between successive packet latencies.)

bool closefiles() closes the files whose names are specified in `set_stream`.

3.8 The Probe Class

Probe objects are used to measure the bandwidths of the connections into which they are inserted. The class has a number of methods, but these will be described later in conjunction with the bandwidth measurement algorithms to which they apply.

3.9 Some Typical Results

Figure 4 shows a three-hop network scenario, with link bandwidths of 5, 1 and 2 Mbit/s respectively. The 1Mbit/s link is clearly the narrow-link, though the 2Mbit/s is the tight-link due to its 1.5Mbit/s cross-traffic stream. Figure 5 shows the program listing which generates this infrastructure as a `network` object: Each network node has a maximum capacity of 100,000 bytes, and introduces zero additional delay per packet. The end-to-end route AB is represented by the route `rt0`.)

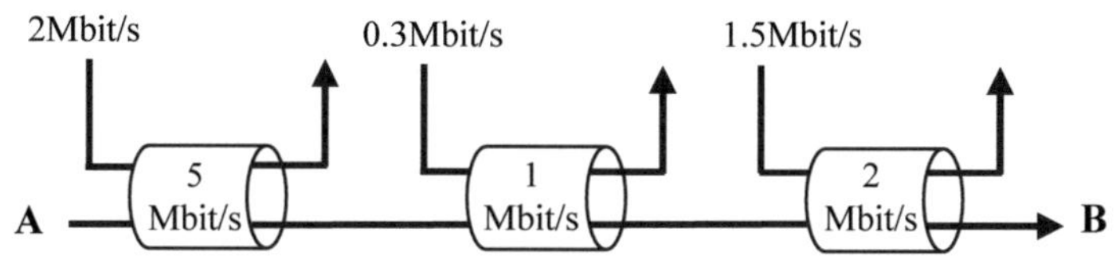

Fig. 4. Three hop network path

```
network *net=new network();

net->insert_node(new node(100000,5e6,0));
net->insert_node(new node(100000,1e6,0));
net->insert_node(new node(100000,2e6,0));

int rt0[]={0,1,2,-1},rt1[]={0,-1},rt2[]={1,-1},rt3[]={2,-1};

net->insert_route(rt0);
net->insert_route(rt1);
net->insert_route(rt2);
net->insert_route(rt3);
```

Fig. 5. Code to establish network infrastructure (routes and nodes).

```
//Set cross-traffic granularity
int Sc[]={60,148,500,1500};
double alpha[]={0.0477,0.0218,0.0950,0.8292};

//Establish cross-traffic processes
user *crosstraffic1[4],*crosstraffic2[4],*crosstraffic3[4];
for (int i=0;i<4;i++) {
    crosstraffic1[i]=new user(Sc[i],0,false);
    crosstraffic1[i]->set_stream(alpha[i]*2e6,true,NULL,NULL,0);
    crosstraffic2[i]=new user(Sc[i],0,false);
    crosstraffic2[i]->set_stream(alpha[i]*0.3e6,true,NULL,NULL,0);
    crosstraffic3[i]=new user(Sc[i],0,false);
    crosstraffic3[i]->set_stream(alpha[i]*1.5e6,true,NULL,NULL,0);
}

//Establish monitored process
user *thisuser=new user(500,0,false);
thisuser->set_stream(1e3,false,"d:\\delay.txt","d:\\time.txt",0);
```

Fig. 6. Code to establish traffic.

Fig.6 shows the code for generating the traffic processes. The process under observation is `thisuser` which sends 500 byte packets at 100kbit/s at equally spaced intervals (the `p` flag in `set_stream` is set to false) and record the packet launch-times and latencies to two `.txt` files on the d: root directory. The cross traffic is composed of four different packet-sizes: 60, 148, 500 and 1500 bytes, which constitute 4.77, 2.81, 9.5 and 82.92% of the total traffic respectively. (This profile was used by (Johnsson et al., 2005) and based on real observations.) Note that traffic of each packet size is generated by a separate Poisson `user` process. Figures 7 and 8 show the code to create the `traffic` object, and configure and run the simulation for 100 seconds.

```
//Establish cross-traffic connections
connection *crossconnect1[4],*crossconnect2[4],*crossconnect3[4];
for (i=0;i<4;i++){
    crossconnect1[i]=new connection();
    crossconnect2[i]=new connection();
    crossconnect3[i]=new connection();
}

//Associate cross-traffic processes with connections
for (i=0;i<4;i++){
    crossconnect1[i]->insert_user(crosstraffic1[i]);
    crossconnect2[i]->insert_user(crosstraffic2[i]);
    crossconnect3[i]->insert_user(crosstraffic3[i]);
}

channel *ch[4]; for (i=0;i<4;i++) ch[i]=new channel();
for (i=0;i<4;i++){
    ch[1]->insert_connection(crossconnect1[i]);
    ch[2]->insert_connection(crossconnect2[i]);
    ch[3]->insert_connection(crossconnect3[i]);
}

//Associate monitored process channel 0
connection *thisconnect=new connection();
thisconnect->insert_user(thisuser);
ch[0]->insert_connection(thisconnect);

//Establish traffic object
traffic *traff=new traffic();
for (i=0;i<4;i++) traff->insert_channel(ch[i]);
```

Fig. 7. Code to create connections and channels and create `traffic` object.

```
//Establish simulation
simulation *sim=new simulation();
sim->configure(net,traff);

//Run simulation
double endtime=sim->advance(100);
thisuser->closefiles();
```

Fig. 8. Code to create and run the simulation.

Figure 9 shows the latencies of `thisuser` packets, both as time-profiles and histogram distributions. (The `histogram.h` utility is available for producing these distributions.) Notice that the performance deteriorates as the transmission rate approaches 500kbit/s, the end-to-end available bandwidth of the path. Close to and exceeding this rate the buffer begins to overflow and packets are dropped at the tight-link buffer. This illustrates that the tight-link is the most important bottleneck under any specific loading conditions, though the narrow-link capacity represents the "best case" scenario when cross traffic is at a minimum.

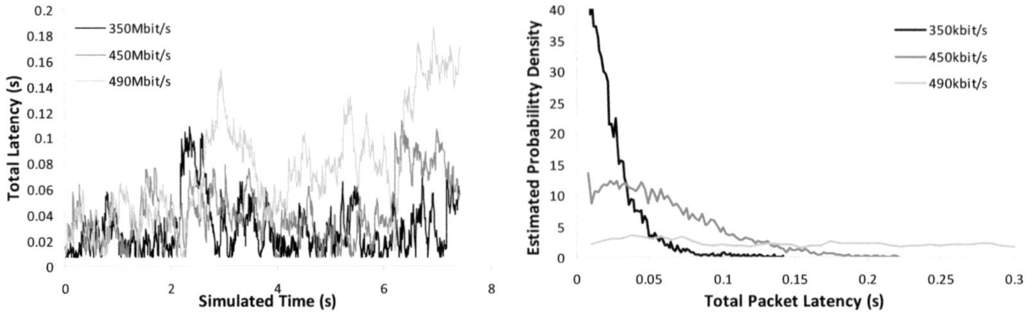

Fig. 9. Simulated packet delay profile and distribution for the three-hop network of Fig. 4.

4. Taxonomy of Bandwidth Measurement Algorithms

It will be recalled that bandwidth estimates may refer to the total link capacities or available bandwidth of individual hops or of end-to-end paths. There are many specific *tools* available for bandwidth measurement such as *pathload* (Jain et al. 2002) and *pathchirp* (Ribeiro et al., 2003) these are based on a limited number of fundamental approaches. Here we examine four such approaches: Idle-Rate, Packet Pair/Train Dispersion (PPTD), Self-Loading Periodic Streams (SLoPS) and Trains of Packet Pairs (TOPP). (A fifth approach Variable Packet Size (VPS) probing is also worth discussing but its reliance on IP technology puts it somewhat outside the scope of this chapter.) The approaches may be classified according to the quantities they aim to measure (see Table 1).

	Link Capacity	Available Bandwidth
Per Link	Iterative TOPP/VPS	Iterative TOPP, Idle Rate
End-To-End	PPTD	SloPS/TOPP

Table 1. Classification of Bandwidth Measurement Algorithms

5. Narrow-Link Measurement: PPTD

The Packet Pair/Train Dispersion (PPTD) technique measures the end-to-end capacity of a path using the "bottleneck spacing effect". It has been studied for some years; one of the earliest and most thorough investigations was published as early as ten years ago (Lai & Baker, 1999). Multiple pairs (or trains) of probe packets are sent back-to-back along the monitored route and their dispersion (the time difference between the last bit of each packet) is measured. First consider a single network link *without* cross-traffic: If the input and output dispersions are Δ_{in} and Δ_{out} seconds then

$$\Delta_{out} = \max(\Delta_{in}, L/C) \text{ seconds} \quad (2)$$

where L is the packet size in bits and C is the link capacity (bits/s). We shall refer to the condition $\Delta_{out} = \Delta_{in}$ as "sub-congestion" and $\Delta_{out} = L/C$ "congestion"; it is under the latter that the link capacity can be calculated as L/Δ_{out} bits per second. Figure 10 illustrates this for the simple case of a packet pair.

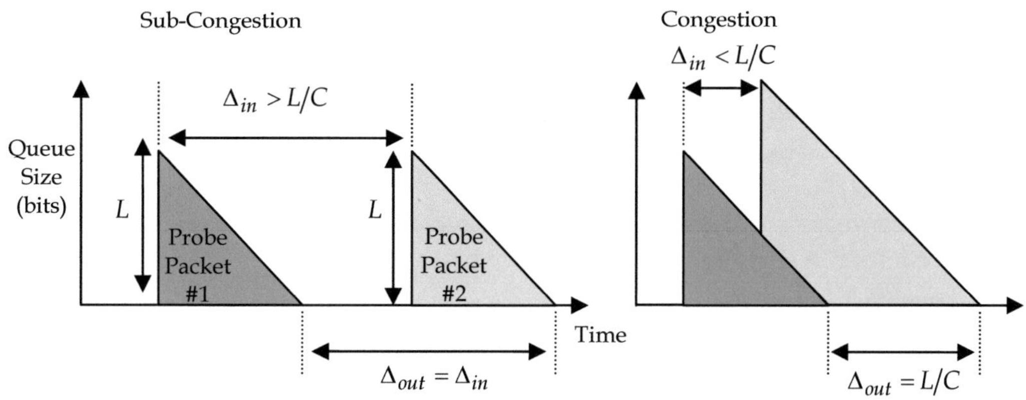

Fig. 10. Packet pair without cross-traffic.

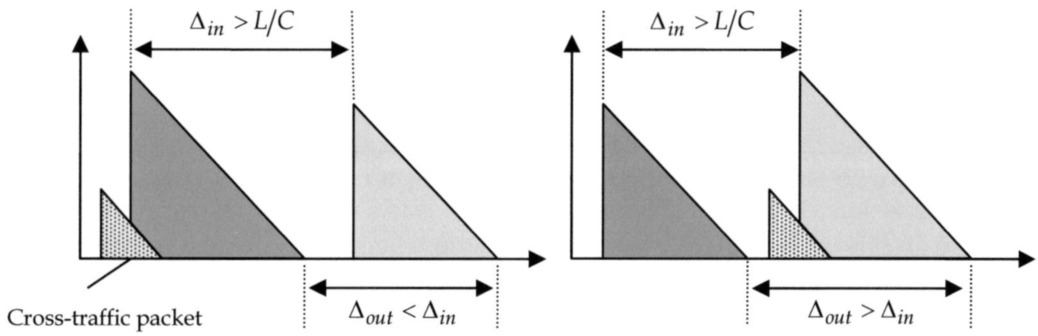

Fig. 11. Cross-traffic in a sub-congested link: Output dispersion may be pushed below or above Δ_{in}.

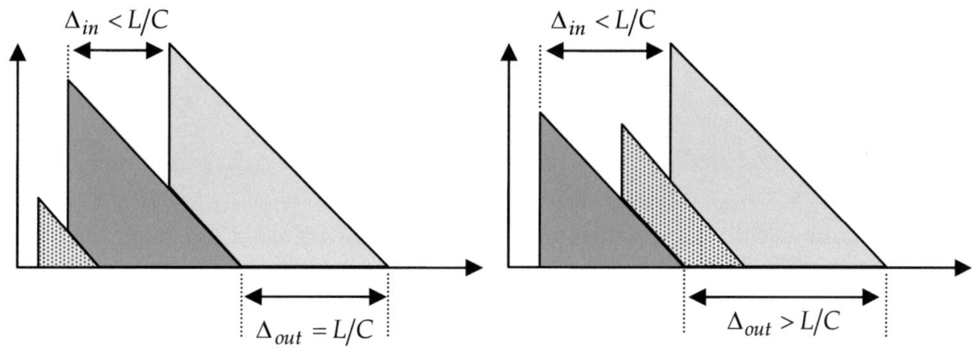

Fig. 12. Cross-traffic in a congested link: Dispersion may only be forced *above* L/C.

Figures 11 and 12 illustrate (with some simplification) how cross-traffic interferes with dispersion: In sub-congestion the output dispersion can be increased ("dialated") or decreased ("compressed") relative to the value given by Eqn.2, depending on which of the two packets is delayed the more. However, under congestion the output dispersion can only be dialated by the presence of cross-traffic. Now let C_{min} be the capacity of the narrow link in the path: As Δ_{in} is decreased gradually from a large value, the effective probing rate $R = L/\Delta_{in}$ increases until it exceeds C_{min} at which point it pushes the narrow-link into congestion. Now since the nodes upstream of the narrow-link are sub-congested, R may be above or below L/Δ_{in} when the probe-pair reaches the narrow-link. However, the node immediately downstream of the narrow-link experiences a *minimum* input dispersion of L/C_{min} which (as it is also sub-congested) it may cause to increase or decrease. The overall process is shown in Figure 13.

To simulate a PPTD, a `probe` object is created using the following methods of the probe class:

`probe(double separation,int measurements,bool trace)` creates a new probe. The parameters `measurements` and `separation` specify the number of probing measurements and the time separation between them. If the `trace` flag is set true, the progress of each probe packet is traced through the network by a series of messages to the console window.

`bool set_PPTD(int L,double din,char *dout,char *b,char *d1,char *d2)` configures the probe for PPTD measurement using pairs of probe packets `L` bytes long with an input dispersion `din` seconds. The remaining parameters specify filenames for recording the output dispersion Δ_{out} (`dout`), the bandwidth estimation L/Δ_{out} (b) and the end-to-end latencies for the first (`d1`) and second (`d2`) packet of each packet pair.

`bool set_streamsize(int stream_size)` tells the probe to use streams of `stream_size` packets. (The default stream-size is 2.)

Figure 14 shows the code modification (relative to Figures 7 and 8) required to probe the three-node network path with 1,000 pairs of spaced 0.1 seconds apart. (The methods **`openfiles()`** and **`closefiles()`** merely open and close the files **`odisp.txt`**, **`bw.txt`**, **`del1.txt`** and **`del2.txt`** where the probe-packet data are stored.)

Figure 15 shows the distributions of bandwidth estimations for three different packet sizes for a probing rate $> C_{min}$ (R was held constant at 1.6Mbit/s). C_{min} =1Mbit/s appears as a local maximum within each distribution: The maxima below C_{min} may be caused by dispersion "dialation" at nodes upstream or downstream of the narrow-link, but the modes *above* C_{min} must be caused by dispersion "compression" in downstream nodes. The "true" bandwidth can be identified since it maintains its position as the packet size is changed (Pasztor & Veitch, 2002). Notice that when the packet size is small, the distribution modes (both true and spurious) are much crisper and better defined than when the packet size becomes larger, and the true result ceases even to be the dominant mode of the distribution.

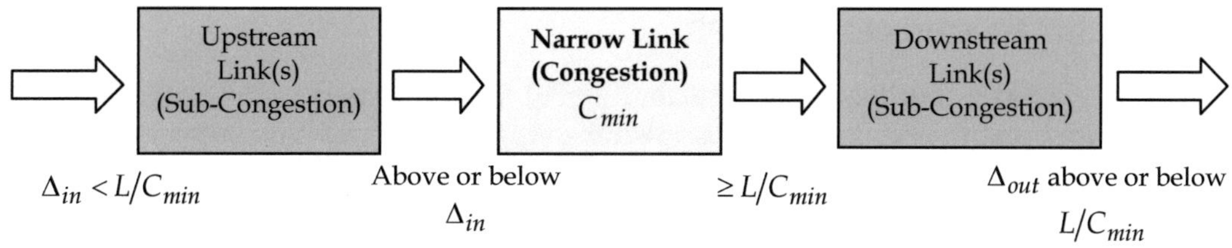

Fig. 13. Variation of packet dispersion across path where only the narrow-link is in congestion.

```
probe *thisprobe=new probe(0.1,1000,false);
thisprobe->set_PPTD(100,0.5e-4,"d:\\odisp.txt","d:\\bw.txt",
                              "d:\\del1.txt","d:\\del2.txt");
connection *thisconnect=new connection();
thisconnect->insert_probe(thisprobe);
ch[0]->insert_connection(thisconnect);
traff->insert_channel(ch[0]);
simulation *sim=new simulation();
sim->configure(net,traff);

thisprobe->openfiles();
double endtime=sim->advance(100);
thisprobe->closefiles();
```

Fig. 14. Code to to create and run PPTD probing experiment.

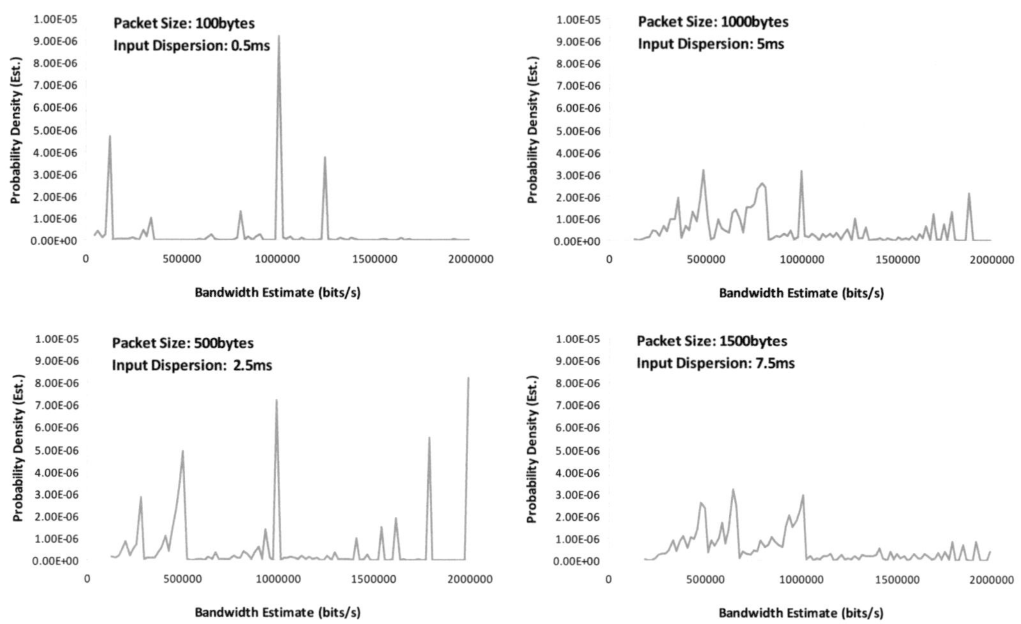

Fig. 15. Estimated bandwidth distributions for three-node path (Fig. 4) using 1.6Mbit/s probing rate.

6. Tight-Link Measurement: SLoPS

Like PPSD, the Self Loading Packet Stream (SLoPS) technique uses probe-packet streams, but measures end-to-end available bandwidth A_{min} instead of link capacity (Jain & Dovrolis, 2003). If a short-lived stream of equal-sized packets is sent at R bits/s, variations in one-way delays give an indication of congestion buildup. When R is greater than A_{min} short-term overload causes the one-way delay to increase steadily with time. If $R < A_{min}$ this is not the case and (once equilibrium is reached) the average delay remains approximately constant. The sender usually uses a binary search algorithm to probe the path at different rates, while the receiver reports the resulting delay-trends. Though the `probe` class has (as yet) no dedicated methods devoted to SloPS, individual packet delay files produced by the `user` object may be used to investigate certain features of SloPS.

Figure 16 shows the code used to generate streams of 63 packets over a mid-simulation interval of 0.1 seconds and measure the end-to-end latency of each packet. Figure 17 shows the delay trends (averaged for 5 independent simulations) for three different probing rates. An unambiguously increasing trend is only seen when $R > A_{min}$.

One drawback of SloPS is that it requires accurate end-to-end delay measurement, which in turn demands the accurate synchronised end-point clocks. PPTD does not suffer from this difficulty as it uses relative inter-packet times rather than absolute end-to-end times.

```
user *thisuser=new user(100,0,false);
thisuser->set_stream(500e3,false,"d:\\delay.txt","d:\\time.txt",0);
thisuser->set_limits(50,50.1);

connection *thisconnect=new connection();
thisconnect->insert_user(thisuser);
ch[0]->insert_connection(thisconnect);
traff->insert_channel(ch[0]);

simulation *sim=new simulation();
sim->configure(net,traff);

double endtime=sim->advance(100);
thisuser->closefiles();
```

Fig. 16. Code for SloPS demonstration. (Packet size 100bytes, stream rate 500kbit/s.)

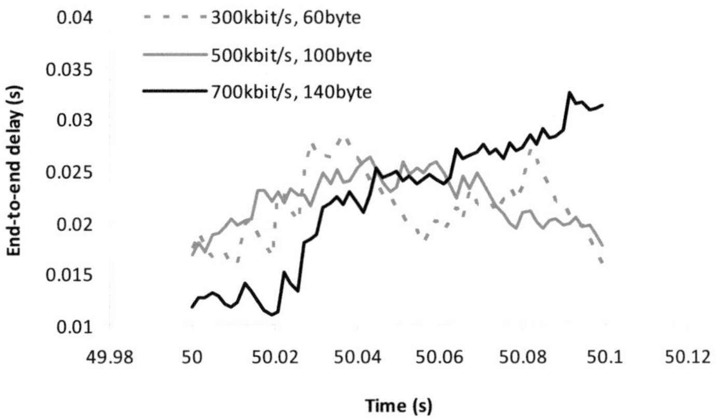

Fig. 17. Packet delay trends for three-node path (Fig. 4.) loaded with 300, 500 and 700kbit/s streams over a 100ms time-slice. Only the 700kbit/s stream shows a consistently increasing delay-trend. (Available bandwidth is 500kbit/s.)

7. Tight-Link Measurement: Idle Rate

This technique was proposed specifically for broadband access networks where the effects of self-induced packet congestion can yield misleading results (Lakshminarayanan et al., 2004). For a single link in isolation, the available bandwidth A is related to tight-link capacity C and server utilisation ρ by the formula

$$A = C \cdot (1-\rho) \text{ bits per second.} \tag{3}$$

where $(1-\rho)$ is the "idle rate", i.e. the ratio of time during which the link is inactive. If C is known then A can be calculated simply by multiplying by the idle rate, which can (in principle) be inferred from the delays of periodically-transmitted probe-packets. If these are plotted as a cumulative frequency distribution then the idle-rate should be visible as a "knee" in the graph where the latency begins to increase.

This works quite well for isolated links: Figure 1(a) has link capacity of 1Mbit/s and an available bandwidth of 500kbit/s. The cumulative plot in Figure 18(c) shows a knee (idle rate) at 0.5 and A =0.5×1Mbit/s=500kbit/s. However, the technique is not always so successful: Figure 18(b) shows the same path with a 2Mbit/s upstream link added: The corresponding cumulative frequency curve suggests a tight-link idle-rate of 0.25, giving an available bandwidth estimate of 0.25×1Mbit/s =250kbit/s; half its true value.

Aside from the obvious disadvantage that it requires prior knowledge of link capacity, the idle-rate method is clearly not always usable when there are moderately utilised links other than the tight-link. Also like SloPS it relies upon a capacity for end-to-end delay measurement.

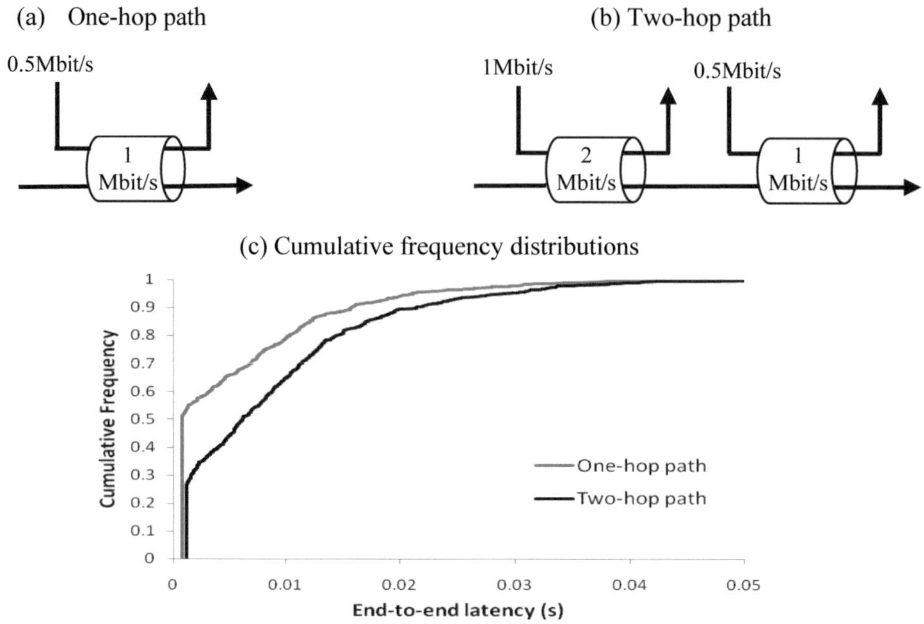

Fig. 18. (a) One node and (b) two node network paths each with 500kbit/s available bandwidth, (c) Cumulative frequency plots for end-to-end delays.

8. Tight-Link Measurement: TOPP

Like SloPS, the Train Of Packet Pairs algorithm (TOPP) measures end-to-end available bandwidth. Many packet pairs (or streams) are sent with a gradually decreasing dispersion: If Δ_{in} is the input dispersion and L the packet-size (bits) then the *offered rate* $R = (n-1)L/\Delta_{in}$. If this exceeds the end-to-end available bandwidth A then momentary congestion causes each packet to be be delayed (on average) longer than its predecessor. This increases the output dispersion Δ_{out} and decreases the *measured rate* $M = (n-1)L/\Delta_{out}$ (see Figure 19). On the other hand if $R < A$ then the average offered and measured rates should remain approximately equal ($R/M \approx 1$).

If only one bottleneck is visible then the governing equation can be shown to be (Melander et al., 2000).

$$\frac{R}{M} = \frac{\Delta_{out}}{\Delta_{in}} = \min\left(1, \frac{1}{C} \cdot R + \left[1 - \frac{A}{C}\right]\right). \tag{4}$$

Rearrangement of Eqn.(4) allows the link capacity and available bandwidth to be estimated from the slope and intercept of a regression lines fitted to the graph-segment $R > A$:

$$C = \frac{1}{SLOPE} \qquad A = \frac{1 - INTERCEPT}{SLOPE}$$

One difference between TOPP and SloPS is that the former increases the offered rate linearly while the latter uses a binary search algorithm. Another important difference is that TOPP can estimate the *capacity* of the tight link as well as the effective bandwidth.

To simulate TOPP, a further method of the `probe` class is called:

`bool set_TOPP(int L,double r1,double r2,double dr,char *r,char *m,char *v)`
configures the probe for TOPP measurement using pairs of probe packets `L` bytes long with an input rate starting at `r1` bits/s and increasing to `r2` bits/s in intervals of `dr` bits/s. The remaining parameters specify filenames for recording the probing rate (`r`), the mean output dispersion ratio $\Delta_{out}/\Delta_{in} = R/M$ (`m`), and the variance of the latter (`v`).

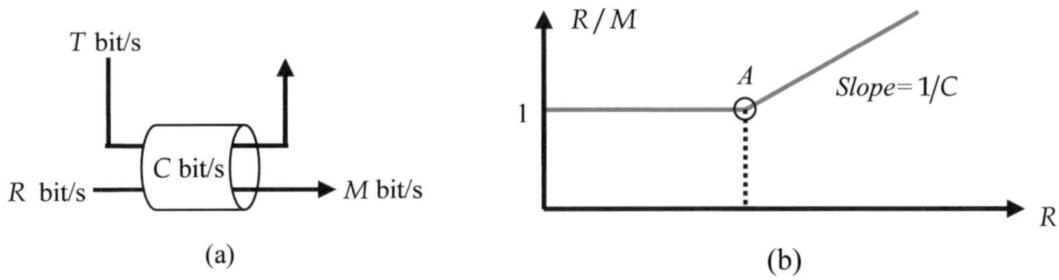

Fig. 19. The TOPP algorithm. (a) The available bandwidth is the link capacity C minus the cross traffic T. (b) A linearly increasing R/M with increasing R indicates that $R > A$.

Figure 20 shows the code for a simple TOPP experiment, and Figure 21 some results for a single hop path. The graphs roughly resemble Figure 19(b), though there is no abrupt transition between the two linear domains. This is due to the finite granularity of the cross-traffic (Park et al., 2006) which also affects the measured slopes of the graphs. Regression lines were used to obtain the estimates for C and A listed in Table 2, which show a tendency to overestimate C and underestimate A - particularly when the stream-size is small. This effect is is well documented and is commonly referred to as the "probing bias" (Liu et al., 2004).

```
probe *thisprobe=new probe(0.5,100,false);
thisprobe->set_TOPP(500,0.01e6,2e6,0.01e6,"d:\\rate.txt",
                        "d:\\mean.txt","d:\\var.txt");
thisprobe->set_streamsize(10);

connection *thisconnect=new connection();
thisconnect->insert_probe(thisprobe);
ch[0]->insert_connection(thisconnect);
traff->insert_channel(ch[0]);

simulation *sim=new simulation();
sim->configure(net,traff);

thisprobe->openfiles();
double endtime=sim->advance(50000);
thisprobe->closefiles();
```

Fig. 20. Code to to create and run TOPP probing experiment.

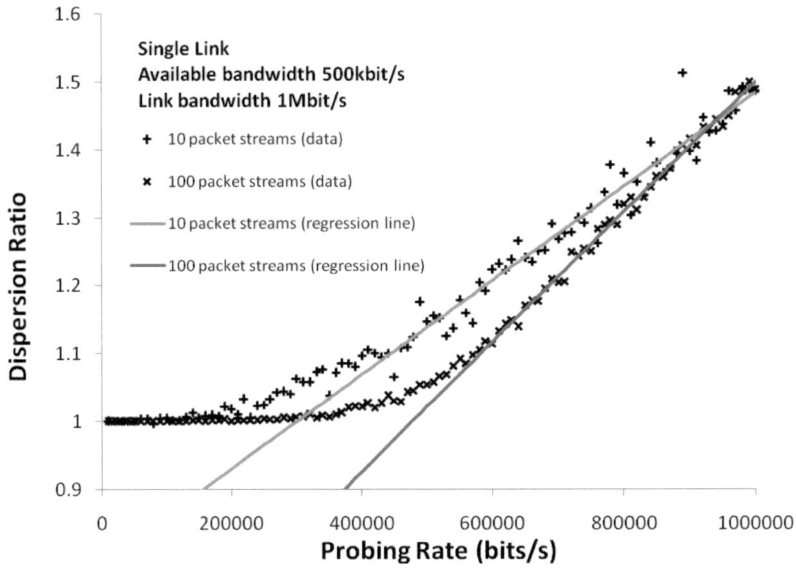

Fig. 21. Results TOPP results obtained by probing a single link with a total bandwidth of 1Mbit/s and an available bandwidth of 500kbit/s. Probe packets were 500 bytes each.

When applied to a multiple-hop network path, the graph displays multiple slope-changes (Figure 22). An iterative approach has been explored (Melander et al., 2002) whereby the available bandwidths of multiple bottlenecks can be inferred, using positive spikes in the second derivative $\partial^2(R/M)/\partial R^2$ to indicate the slope-changes. However this technique relies on prior assumptions about the order in which the bottlenecks appear and a policy of Shortest Surplus First (the smallest available bandwidth is assumed to be the furthest upstream) has been adopted as a worst-case scenario.

Stream Size (Packets)	Link Capacity (Mbit/s)	Available Bandwidth (Mbit/s)
10	1.440	0.300
100	1.040	0.477
True Value:	1.000	0.500

Table 2. TOPP bandwidth estimates for different sized streams of 500 byte packets.

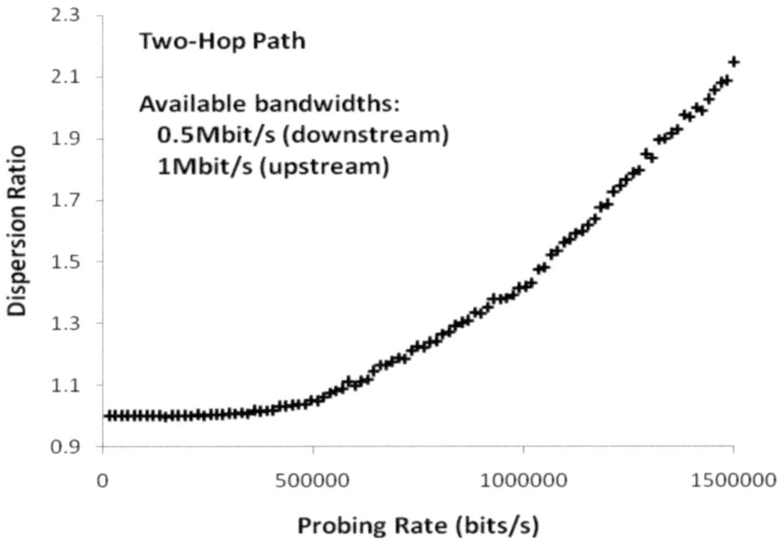

Fig. 22. Results TOPP results obtained by probing a double-hop network path with 100-byte packet streams. Slope changes at 0.5 and 1Mbit/s indicate the available bandwidths of the two bottlenecks.

9. Conclusions

This chapter presents a simulation framework for studying bandwidth quantisation and measurement. It does not represent any specific technology but rather an interconnection of generic FIFO queuing nodes which can approximate the behaviour of real networks. The reader is invited to experiment with the C++ source-code which is available online. The four algorithms investigated were PPTD, SLoPS, Idle Rate and TOPP. A fifth approach is Variable Packet Size (VPS) probing: This measures round-trip-times for a series of probe packets to each intermediate node (Prasad et al, 2003) using ICMP messages to signal back to the sender. By varying the packet size L, the serializdation delay L/C can be separated from the independent propagation-time and the effects of queuing delay minimised by taking the minimum of several measurements. Though this can provide quite detailed information, it assumes Layer 3 functionality in all congestible links. The technique has therefore not been included in this study.

The aim of this chapter is not to present any particularly significant new insights, nor to reproduce the full complexity of past research (which would require an entire book). We aim rather to show how a relatively simple tool can be used to demonstrate the principles and provide a starting-point for the reader's own investigations.

10. References

Glover, I.A. & Grant,P.M. (2004), *Digital Communications* (2nd Ed.), Pearson Prentice Hall, p.3.

Jain, M.; Dovrolis, C. & Mah, B. (2002). Pathload: An Available Bandwidth Estimation Tool, *Proceedings of Passive and Active Measurement Conference.*

Jain, M. & Dovrolis, C. (2003). End-to-End Available Bandwidth Measurement Methodology, Dynamics and Relation with TCP Throughput, *IEEE/ACMA Transactions on Networking*, Vol. 11, No. 4, pp. 537-49.

Jain, M. & Dovrolis, C. (2004). Ten Fallacies and Pitfalls on End-to-End Available Bandwidth Estimation, *Proceedings of 4th. ACM SIGCOMM*, pp.272-7, Taormina, Sicily.

Johnsson, A.; Melander, B. & Björkman, M. (2005) Bandwidth Measurement in Wireless Networks, *Proceedings of Mediterranean Ad Hoc Networking Workshop*, Porquerolles, France, June 2005.

Lai, K. & Baker, M. (1999). Measuring Bandwidth, *Proceedings of IEEE INFOCOM 1999*, pp. 905-14.

Lakshminarayanan, K; Padmanabhan, V.N. & Padhye, J, Bandwidth Estimation in Broadband Access Networks, *Proceedings of 4th ACM SIGCOMM Internet Measurement Conference* (IMC'04), Taormina, Italy, October 2004, pp. 314-21.

Liu, X.; Ravindran, K.; Liu, B.; Loguinov, D. (2004). Single-Hop Probing Asymptotics in Available Bandwidth Estimation: Sample Path Analysis, *Proceedings of ACM Internet Measurement Conference 2004.*

Melander, B.; Björkman, M. & Gunningberg, P. (2000). A New End-to-End Probing and Analysis Method for Estimating Bandwidth Bottlenecks, *Proceedings of IEEE Glogecom'00*, San Francisco, CA, USA, Nov. 2000.

Melander, B.; Björkman, M. & Gunningberg, P. (2002). Regression-Based Available Bandwidth Measurements, *Proceedings of 2002 International Symposium on Performance Evaluation of Computer and Telecommunication Systems.*

Park, K.J.; Lim, H. & Choi, C-H. (2006). Stochastic Analysis of Packet-Pair Probing for Network Bandwidth Estimation, *Computer Networks*, Vol. 50, pp. 1901-15.

Pasztor, A. & Veitch, D. (2002b). The Packet Size Dependence of Packet Pair Like Methods, *Proceedings of IEEE/IFIP International Workshop on Quality of Service (IWQoS)*, 2002.

Pitts, J.M. & Schormans,J.A. (2000). IP and ATM Design and Performance, Wiley, pp. 287-98.

Prasad, R.S.; Murray, M; Dovrolis, C. & Claffy, K. (2003). Bandwidth Estimation: Metrics, Measurement Techniques and Tools, *IEEE Network*, Vol.17, No.6, pp.27-35.

Ribeiro, V.J.; Riedi, R.G.; Baraniuk, J.; Navratil, L. & Cottrel, L. (2003). Pathchirp: Efficient Available Bandwidth Estimation for Network Paths, *Proceedings of Passive and Active Measurement Workshop*, 2003.

Yu, Y.; Cheng, I. & Basu, A. (2003). Optimal Adaptive Bandwidth Monitoring for QoS Based Retrieval, IEEE Transactions on Multimedia, Vol. 5, No. 3, pp. 466-73.